THE NEXT
ONE HUNDRED
YEARS

Books by Jonathan Weiner

PLANET EARTH
THE NEXT ONE HUNDRED YEARS

THE NEXT
ONE HUNDRED
YEARS

Shaping the Fate of Our Living Earth

JONATHAN WEINER

BANTAM BOOKS
NEW YORK · TORONTO · LONDON · SYDNEY · AUCKLAND

For Aaron and Benjamin

THE NEXT ONE HUNDRED YEARS
A Bantam Book / March 1990

*Grateful acknowledgment for permission to reprint excerpts from "Easter
1916" by William Butler Yeats, reprinted with permission of Macmillan
Publishing Company, from* The Collected Poems of W. B. Yeats,
*copyright 1924 by Macmillan Publishing Company, renewed 1952 by
Bertha Georgie Yeats; and excerpts from "Little Gidding" by T. S. Eliot,
reprinted by permission of Harcourt Brace Jovanovich, Inc., and
Faber & Faber, Ltd., from* Four Quartets, *copyright 1943 by T. S. Eliot
and renewed 1971 by Esme Valerie Eliot.*

Portions of the book appeared (in different form) in Smithsonian and
The Sciences.

Library of Congress Cataloging-in-Publication Data

Weiner, Jonathan.
  The next one hundred years: shaping the fate of our living earth
Jonathan Weiner.
     p.   cm.
ISBN 0-553-05744-8
1. Ecology. 2. Man—Influence on nature. 3. Biosphere.
I. Title.
QH541.W37 1990
333.9516—dc20   89-28108
                                                            CIP

Design and production supervised by M 'N O Production Services, Inc.

Published simultaneously in the United States and Canada

PRINTED IN THE UNITED STATES OF AMERICA

0 9 8 7 6 5 4 3 2 1

For the matter at hand is no mere felicity of speculation, but the real business and fortunes of the human race . . .

Francis Bacon
The New Organon

CONTENTS

▨ CHAPTER 1

THE
QUESTION

And God blessed them, and God said unto them,
Be fruitful and multiply, and replenish the earth,
and subdue it: and have dominion over the fish of
the sea, and over the fowl of the air, and over
every living thing that moveth upon the earth.

Genesis

Engineering and Research Associates is based in Tucson, Arizona. It is
housed in a nondescript one-story building on North Tucson Boulevard,
next to a vacant lot surrounded by a chain link fence.

In the front rooms, engineers work on the company's line of hospital
equipment—a blood shaker, a blood bag, a blood-weight monitor, a
"SafeTee" needle guard, and other tools of modern phlebotomy, or
bloodletting.

In the back rooms, a husband and wife work on an otherworldly
product. There, Daniel and Michel Harmony make crystal balls.

The Harmonys begin with a glass globe about the size of a for-
tuneteller's, or a Civil War cannonball, with a small hole in the top.
They pour in a few cups of salt water. With a pipette, they drop in
miniature red shrimp, each with ten legs and long tentative feelers and
a tendency to turn pale when startled. With a tweezer, they insert a
green frond of seaweed. One pass of a glassblower's torch and the
mouth of the globe is sealed.

The shrimp browse on the seaweed as if they have always lived in a
crystal ball. They swim to the North Pole and look up; they swim to
the South Pole and look down; they act in every way like owners of a
small planet. If they are aware of the Harmonys, they show no sign of

1

alarm—though human faces must be distorted by the walls of the fish-bowl into apparitions as gigantic as the Four Horsemen of the Apocalypse.

Only when the fingers of the packers stretch across their glass skies do the creatures turn pale. Then each sphere is immersed in darkness.

The Harmonys turn out these live crystal balls in batches of fifty or one hundred. They pack the globes individually in well-insulated cartons and ship them out to customers around the country and the greater globe. Most end up on coffee tables or executive desktops. They sell for $250 apiece, under the brand name of EcoSpheres.

These crystal balls are spin-offs of the space program. The founder of Engineering and Research Associates, Inc., bought the recipe from the U.S. National Aeronautics and Space Administration. NASA's aim was the design of space colonies. If astronauts ever travel far from Earth, they will have to go in chambers as tightly sealed as Eco-Spheres. Their lives will depend upon what amounts to a bubble in space, a bubble in which—unlike a closet or an elevator—the air will stay healthy and breathable day after day, month after month, absolutely guaranteed, all the way to Mars and back, despite the team of men and women who are breathing, eating, working, playing, sleeping, defecating, and perhaps even multiplying (or at least going through the motions) inside it.

The EcoSphere is one small step by a NASA engineer in these celestial directions. The red shrimp represent astronauts; the plants represent a system of living things that might restore air and support the astronauts.

The EcoSphere is also a working model of life on our planet. It is a world in miniature. Unlike an ordinary goldfish bowl or aquarium, it is sealed shut and thus absolutely self-contained, except for the requirement of sunlight. You can't sprinkle in fish food. You can't add oxygen to the water by bubbling gas through it—gas can't pass through glass. You can never change the gravel, clean the inside walls, clear the air, or replace any casualties. You can set the sphere in a warm place, with the right amount of light. Beyond this, the animals and plants are on their own in there.

Our own sphere is just as self-contained. When astronauts and cosmonauts in orbit look homeward, they see seven seas, seven continents, and two patches of ice, all enclosed in a glassy ball of gases. Snapshots from space say, "That's all there is." Here is the grand sum of all the water we have, all the air and rock. This is what we have to live on—or more precisely, live within, since the blue dome of gases is over our heads.

From a space engineer's point of view, an EcoSphere has five working parts:

1) **Earth:** There is a thimbleful of sand and gravel at the bottom of the sphere.
2) **Water:** The sphere is about two-thirds full.
3) **Air:** fills the rest of the sphere.
4) **Fire:** Sunlight streams in each day. Without this energy there could be no life.
5) **Life:** the seaweed, shrimp, and microbes that float and swim in the water.

Of course there is also the hollow glass ball itself. To keep the list short we may include the ball under the heading 1) Earth, since silicate glass is made from melted sand. The globe holds the system together, so it looks like the single most important working part, but in fact (as in any well-made thing) the parts are all equally important. Dan and Michel have found that the shrimp will not survive in an EcoSphere if any of the five parts is left out—even the gravel at the bottom.

Planet Earth, too, is a system of a few basic working parts. There are seven of them, and they can be thought of (not only figuratively but also, to a surprising extent, literally) as seven spheres.

1) **Earth:** a round mass of minerals and metals, spinning, more or less solid. This comprises the vast bulk of the planet. Its outermost layers are sometimes called the lithosphere: *lithos* for stone, and *sphere* because these layers are a great shell enclosing the core, like the skin of an orange. More than 4 billion years old.
2) **Water:** From a cosmic point of view, the planet's supply of water also forms a great round shell, or sphere, enclosing much of the lithosphere. It is sometimes called the hydrosphere, and it covers two-thirds of the planet's surface. We live on a blue planet.

   Most of Earth's water spewed as steam from the volcanoes of the lithosphere in the first years of the planet. It condensed in pools and rivers and seas when the crust had cooled enough for rain to fall. The cooling took hundreds of millions of years.

3) **Air:** A third sphere, hollow. This is the only one of Earth's working parts that we recognize as a sphere in everyday speech: the atmosphere. Like the hydrosphere, the atmosphere spewed from volcanoes as hot gases after the crust formed. Ever since, the planet has been wrapped in a thin loose shell of gases—though the mix of gases has changed greatly over time.

4) **Fire:** All planets are bathed in the light of the star they orbit. Our Sun formed in space more than 4.5 billion years ago, and our planet is one of nine that coalesced on the Sun's periphery. The Sun is a great sphere of fire and it heats Earth's atmosphere and the hydrosphere, stirring up powerful currents in both. These currents are bent and twisted by the spinning of the lithosphere into all the whorls of weather.

5) **Life:** Standing or sitting in the middle of life, it takes an act of imagination to perceive that in shape, the whole of life is much like the lithosphere, hydrosphere, and atmosphere: one of the concentric shells that are wrapped around the bull's-eye of the planet's core. The sphere of life is an incredibly thin veneer, like the green patina on a bronze cannonball in the park.

One of the first scientists to think of life in the round was the Swiss geologist Eduard Suess, who coined the term "biosphere" in the nineteenth century near the end of a monograph about the Alps. The pioneering Russian geochemist Vladimir Vernadsky revived and established the term in the 1920s.

The biosphere could not exist without the lithosphere, the hydrosphere, the atmosphere, and the sphere of fire. Thus it is, necessarily, younger than the other spheres. But not by much: life seems to have arisen soon after the other spheres had fallen into place. The biosphere is more than 3.5 billion years old.

In the EcoSphere, life, water, and air are inside the ball. But in the planet, life, water, and air are wrapped *around* the ball, in three very thin concentric shells.

Besides earth, water, air, fire, and life, our world has at least two working parts that cannot be included in a desk-top EcoSphere:

6) **Ice:** The planet at present has two big caps of ice, one at each pole. Some of the taller mountains are ice-capped, too. This ice forms yet another thin concentric shell, the cryosphere (*cryo* from the Greek for cold or frost). Of course, most of the globe is too warm for ice; but all of the scattered patches of ice on Earth do lie in the shape of a sphere.

This sphere is much younger than the other five; the early Earth was much too warm for significant amounts of ice. Indeed the first traces of extensive ice cover appear in the geological record only in the Late Precambrian Era, more than 2 billion years ago.

Chemically speaking, ice is water in solid form: ice is just water going through a phase. In this sense it might be considered a part of the hydrosphere. But the cryosphere's behavior is so distinctive and so influential (as in Ice Ages) that scientists who are trying to understand how Earth works as a system find it useful to think of it as a separate working part, a sixth sphere.

7) **Mind:** By far the youngest entrant on the list. Its point of origin is a small tribe of foragers in the African savannah, a species called *Homo habilis,* which arose roughly 2 million years ago. This was a transitional species, as the evolutionary biologists E.O. Wilson and Charles J. Lumsden note: "We can describe *Homo habilis,* without serious distortion, as the head of an intelligent ape riding on the body of a man." The brain of *Homo habilis* (Latin for "Handyman") was significantly larger than that of other primates, and as the species evolved the brain grew at a steady rate, until our kind—*Homo sapiens sapiens,* Man the Doubly Wise—appeared about 50,000 years ago.

Physically, our species is unremarkable. It is not as strong as a gorilla, not as fast as an antelope or a big cat. But thanks to the power of mind, more particularly the power that results from our ability to communicate mind to mind, to share knowledge from individual to individual and across generations, *Homo sapiens* has become far more powerful than the animals with which we once competed on the savannah—so powerful that we are now driving many of them to extinction.

Indeed, thanks to the power of mind, and meetings of minds, and actions governed by mind, we are now strong enough to have a distinct influence upon the spheres of water, air, and life.

Because this seventh sphere in the Earth system, this invisible quality we call mind, has so much influence on the planet, Vernadsky, who established the term "biosphere," also introduced the term "noosphere," the sphere of mind. Unlike the other six, it is only figuratively a sphere. Strictly speaking it is not even physical, although it has the power to change the face of the Earth. "The noosphere is a new geological phenomenon on our planet," Vernadsky wrote in 1943, at the end of his life. "In it for the first time man becomes a *large-scale geological force.*"

Whatever we choose to call it—noosphere, anthroposphere,

technosphere, human sphere—we are talking about a phenomenon that is at once part of the biosphere and apart from it, rather as ice is a part of the hydrosphere and apart from it. Our species is closely related to the chimpanzee and indeed we share our spiral DNA with every other species in the biosphere. But with the creation of mind, the slow forces of evolution have led—using the same molecular materials as always—to a new phase of life on Earth.

"This view can be made clearer with a geological metaphor," write Wilson and Lumsden. "The origin of mind was like the radical transformation of the highest peak of a tropical mountain range. In its history and composition the eminence does not differ in any fundamental way from the foothills and peaks around it. But because it was located in just the position where the forces of crustal uplift pushed it a little bit higher, it acquired snow and ice and unique forms of alpine life. A threshold was waiting; a small quantitative change then resulted in the abrupt creation of a new world."

It would be easy to extend this list; but when scientists try to study Earth as a system, these seven spheres are usually enough, sometimes more than enough. For the parts are all in motion and they are hooked together in odd ways, attached with amazing strength, so that a change in one sphere can affect many of the others. Sometimes a seemingly trivial event can reverberate in ways that are unexpected, even astonishing—in the jargon of science, "counterintuitive."

Most Earth scientists believe that because of the influence of the seventh sphere, the sphere of mind, four of the other spheres—the hydrosphere, atmosphere, cryosphere, and biosphere—are now on the brink of drastic changes. We may see these changes in our lifetimes and our children's. We may be seeing their onset right now. It is true that the system has withstood large shocks in the past; that some of the subtle changes we worry about today loom large only because our instruments are supersubtle. Still, according to this view, we are in for a rough ride in the next one hundred years. We can expect a crescendo of environmental alarms and emergencies. The worst storms we will face in the next century are of our own making, and we will need luck to weather them.

In the darkest view, we are looking at a crisis in the history not only of our species, but of the whole biosphere. In this view the next one hundred years will be one of the most dangerous periods since the origin of life.

*   *   *

In the late 1950s, scientists began putting together a new picture of this planet. The lithosphere is cracked like an eggshell and the pieces drift, creak, and groan out loud. The hydrosphere is agitated by storms that reach from the surface all the way down to the bottom. The atmosphere (viewed from outside for the first time in the early 1960s) is as full of swirls as the irridescent colors in the surface of a soap bubble. So much turbulence was discovered in each of the seven spheres that the period is often described as a scientific revolution. In the space of a few decades, Earth scientists replaced our old globe—a static, dusty, rather dull globe—with a home world full of restless change.

Those who were born in the second half of the twentieth century take this view for granted; but many of the revolutionaries, the pioneers who discovered the turbulence, have not even reached retirement age. For them the New World is so different from the old that they sometimes feel like strangers in a strange land. It is as if they had turned their telescopes inward and discovered a new planet.

Today, many Earth scientists feel that the study of the planet is on the verge of a second revolution. The first was characterized by the discovery of turbulence; this revolution is marked by the discovery of connections. Earth scientists are finding more and more intricate links among the seven spheres. These studies are revealing how tightly each sphere is joined to the others. This new vision is raising questions both beautiful and disturbing.

If the rock beneath our feet, the sea around us, the air above our heads, and the very face of the Sun, are all in motion, then how does the agitation of one affect the others? How do the links among the spheres affect our lives? Most urgently: if our species' power and sophistication are growing daily, if our breath is tainting the atmosphere, if our population is fast increasing from five billion toward ten, how then do our lives and works affect rock, sea, air, ice, life, and fire?

How does it all fit together? Are we looking at a planetary chaos? at a finely tuned mechanism, like a clock? at a kind of living being on a scale beyond imagining?

"It's curious," the oceanographer Arnold Gordon mused recently. "We look at the world as separate spheres—earth, air, fire, water, life. . . . But what's most interesting about the planet is the connections among the spheres."

Making connections is difficult because it requires workers in all

■
7

sorts of scattered disciplines to get together. Each of the seven spheres has its specialists, subspecialists, sub-sub-specialists. Each has its own journals and jargon. This discourages cross talk. Still, in big, cooperative programs, scientists are beginning to seek out connections between life and all the other spheres. They are trying to band together and watch all the spheres at once from as many angles as possible, and see how the system works—how it all fits together.

To ask how it all fits together is also to wonder where it is going. Earth scientists are now striving toward a global forecast. They hope to learn enough to be able to project the trends of global change some distance into the next one hundred years.

All forecasts are notoriously risky. Nevertheless, on five points most experts would agree at the outset.

First, elements of the Earth are changing faster than they have in at least ten thousand years—since the end of the last Ice Age. Infants born today may experience more change in their lifetimes than the planet has undergone since the birth of civilization.

Second, the elements that appear likely to change the fastest are the ones that concern all of us most urgently and deeply: the biosphere and the atmosphere—which, through weather and climate, affect every living thing in the biosphere.

Third, our species does not know its own strength. We are putting a new spin on the planet. Some of our effects are visible and familiar to the naked eye: cities; burning forests; plowed fields; artificial molehills like the Fresh Kills landfill on Staten Island, New York, the biggest garbage dump in the world. (When it is completed in 2005 it will be the tallest peak on the East Coast between Florida and Maine.) Other effects, though wide-scale enough to affect air, soil, water, and the biosphere itself, are so subtle that scientists are only just beginning to discover them.

Fourth, it is often hard to determine whether a particular planetary change is natural or artificial; for, as the earlier revolution in Earth science has demonstrated, Earth is naturally turbulent. With our present state of knowledge, no one is sure just how the world would be changing right now if our species weren't here.

Fifth, and last, global change is progressing much faster than we are learning to understand it.

*　　*　　*

The Harmonys offer a life insurance policy with each crystal ball:

> WHEREAS, one year shall be defined as twelve (12) months from the date of issue of this policy,

> The Company hereby agrees to replace this EcoSphere at no cost to the Owner at any time within one (1) year should fewer than three (3) shrimp remain alive.

This policy comforts customers, because no one can guarantee the survival of any particular globe.

There is no life policy for the planet Earth. The fate of our home planet is a subject of such bewilderment and anxiety that it is painful to think about it. Yet the question hangs above our heads. It is already several decades now since we first became widely concerned about atmospheric pollution, water pollution, wastes, pesticides, overpopulation, erosion. In the United States under the presidency of Ronald Reagan the mood of the country turned away from such problems. However, the question did not fade away in West Germany, Switzerland, Mexico, and other countries, where alarm only increased. Even in America the question was still there, like the Moon on a bright afternoon.

Then the year 1988 brought a record drought, record flooding, the hurricane of the century, grotesque pollution in the waters off the eastern seaboard of the United States. Global change became an issue in the American elections. People around the world wondered if Earth was striking back.

There have always been *local* pollution crises, of course. The air in London and Pittsburgh was much fouler once than it is today. In fact, in most thickly settled places in the Northern Hemisphere air was worse in the days of wood burning and coal burning. In the U.S. the rash of legislation since the 1970s made much local progress.

But today the problems we fear most are global and potentially irreversible. These include the build-up of greenhouse gases, the thinning of the ozone layer above the South Pole (first reported in 1985), the destruction of rain forests, the accelerating extinctions of other species in the biosphere. These changes are hard—some would say impossible—to stop. The world's economy is built into them. Because they are so long-lasting and ominous and have so much momentum, these global changes are forcing scientists to try to make hundred-year predictions; and events are forcing their predictions more and more often onto the world's front pages.

All these concerns, new and old, shape themselves into a single great curling question mark that rises today from every landscape we look at. We live with that ghostly question mark floating above the world, out of place. And sometimes we find ourselves looking at a tree or a hill or a sunset as at a loved one in mortal danger, so that our admiration for a leaf feels something like a prayer.

The question troubles even those who try to ignore the headlines, and worry only about whether the old garage is sagging or the roof is leaking or the mortgage is due. Whether we look up at the sky or not, the question mark curls above our roofs and makes a mockery of our hopes. If your Earth is falling apart, there go your plans for summer vacation. As Henry David Thoreau said, "What good is a house if you don't have a decent planet to put it on?"

A few years ago, as I was turning out the light in an apartment in Manhattan, I saw a great orange flash of light in the sky in the direction of the East River. I sat straight up in bed. A pillar of fire lit the sky over Staten Island. Without even thinking, I waited to see if this pillar would be joined by another and another—if it was the first light of the nuclear holocaust.

Within minutes radio announcers were explaining that the pillar of light came from an explosion in a chemical plant in New Jersey. It was a big explosion, but not the end of the world. Afterward, I was more disturbed by my first reaction than by the fire itself. Though the thought is seldom at the surface, it is seldom far below. We all live braced for the sight of that mushroom cloud.

So it is with the thought of environmental apocalypse, although here our anticipations are more confused. Here most of us do not know of any single threat to brace for; we do not fear a mushroom cloud, but rather a fusion of a thousand threats. With each headline about a planetary fever, poisoned seas, tainted air, radioactive soil, lost soil, spilled oil, the Ozone Hole over the South Pole, we sometimes wonder, "Is this it?"

The Harmonys know how hard it is to control the machinery of nature, even on the smallest scale. They have looked into the crystal ball, and they have seen how much can go wrong.

In the factory in Tucson, on any given day, dozens of new Eco-Spheres are queued up on the shelves, awaiting shipment. Some will survive for years. Some will fail inside their cartons in a United Parcel Service truck. Sometimes a whole batch will go bad. The Harmonys can't predict the fate of the EcoSpheres they make, and by now they don't even try.

Once, the producer of a television documentary about the science of global ecology brought his production team to the factory. The TV crew set up lights and cameras and smashed one crystal ball after another, trying to film a dramatic illustration of the fragility of the biosphere. Dan Harmony does not like to say how many spheres were sacrificed before the team got the shot it wanted. "That was something a little unusual for us," he says.

Another batch of EcoSpheres died at the offices of the Center for Environmental Education, in Washington, D.C. The director of the center kept one EcoSphere on his desk, and gave one to each member of his staff. He kept the office lights burning twenty or twenty-four hours a day while he and his team wrote briefs and lobbied on Capitol Hill, trying to shape a concerned international eco-policy. EcoSpheres require twelve hours of darkness. The director's sphere burned out, and soon after that, so did his staffs', and soon after that, so did he. He quit environmental activism, and is now the Director of Conventions and Tourism at the Washington D.C. Chamber of Commerce.

Often the shrimp die, but the algae live. Sometimes the algae die, too, and the water grows as crystal clear as a dead lake. On the other hand, Dan Harmony once got a call from Sister Leone, of St. Elizabeth's Clinic, in Tucson. Sister Leone told him that one of her elderly roommates, Sister Louise, was dusting in a corner of the living room when she cried out, "One of the shrimp is getting black!"

That day, Sister Leone read up on shrimp in an encyclopedia. She learned that shrimp carry their eggs externally, holding them against the full length of their bodies by their tentacles as they swim. "We took a magnifying glass and watched," Sister Leone told Harmony. "One day we noticed the eggs were gone. 'What's happening?' we said. Then the next morning we looked in and saw a little baby shrimp! We have a baby!"

"Oh, we've never had any reproduce," Harmony said, over the phone. "It must be bacteria or algae or something. Could you check if the glass is cracked?"

"Dan, I'm a nurse. I know a baby when I see one." So Sister Leone brought her crystal ball straight to the offices on North Tucson Boulevard. She and Harmony met beside what Harmony calls his Evolution

Rack, a floor-to-ceiling rack-on-wheels with rows and rows of flasks. He had tinkered with the original recipe from NASA. He liked the fact that the shrimp never multiplied; that was just as well, given the space they had. But he kept playing with mosses and fungi, looking for the most stable arrangements of animals and plants. The fruits of Harmony's experiments had given the Evolution Rack the look of a Dr. Seuss fantasy. There were red ones, blue ones, brown ones, green ones, pink ones. Most were labelled only with a birthdate: "8/15/82," "8/17/82," "9/10/82." One flask was labelled "Milky Way Productions." The old flasks on top were dusty and primitive. Progressive refinements filled the middle shelves. The lowest shelves held the latest batch of spheres.

"Mine has more than it started with," Sister Leone said.

"That's impossible." Harmony held her EcoSphere up to the light and cocked his head to one side. There were six, twelve, sixteen, twenty live baby shrimp, swimming around in the globe with their parents.

"Sure enough!" he said. Now it was Dan's turn to get excited. "This is a first! This is the first one in history!"

"Well, I don't know why you're so surprised," said Sister Leone, walking around the Evolution Rack. "Look at that one. That one. And that one . . ." Three more spheres had given birth.

Harmony hurried Sister Leone down the hall to show her crystal ball to his boss, Loren Acker. Acker glanced at the sphere sitting on his own desk. Lo and behold, the shrimp inside that one had been multiplying unnoticed. And that day, when Acker visited the Valley National Bank, in Tucson, he looked at the EcoSphere on his banker's desk. The population in there was booming, too.

My own EcoSphere was delivered several years ago. I lived in Brooklyn then. Soon after I moved to a hill in Pennsylvania. And soon after that a few brown spots appeared on the inner walls of the glass. The spots grew into blotches. Then shrimp began to die one after another and fall to the gravel at the bottom.

I called Dan Harmony, described the sphere over the phone, and asked him what was going wrong. Harmony said the spots sounded like fungi. There was nothing anyone could do.

Too many changes, Harmony said, are dangerous to an EcoSphere. Just shifting the sphere from one side of a shelf to the other can sometimes precipitate a crisis. The community in the sphere seems to seek a new equilibrium each time it is moved. Jostle it after it has settled down and it is forced to seek equilibrium a second time. Move it a third time and it may collapse. Like each of us it has thresholds of stress.

My EcoSphere crossed many thresholds, beginning with the delivery man. I remember listening to his spiral stomping up the stairs in Brooklyn. On the landing he jerked the box this way and that to remove a mailing label.

"Was this treated as fragile?" I asked him.

"I don't know." He looked at the top of the box, stamped "Rush. Perishable. RUSH. LIVE MATERIAL. OPEN AT ONCE. Keep from heat and frost."

"It isn't marked fragile," he said.

I pointed at the word FRAGILE on the side of the box.

"Then it *is* fragile," he said.

Later I myself delivered it to a class of second graders for a day. (Walking through the elementary school hallway with the thing gurgling audibly in its cardboard box, I felt like Elliot entrusted with the care of E.T. the Extraterrestrial.) Then I carted it from the city to the country. Then I moved it around in my new office, from shelf to desk and back to shelf. I also kept changing the thermostat. My study is detached from the rest of the house and at the end of every evening I turned the heat down a little more, to keep carbon dioxide and my fuel bill from rising.

Now the blotched EcoSphere sits on my desk as a sort of memento mori, like the skulls that medieval scholars kept upon their writing tables. "Alas, poor Yorick!" The last shrimp has disappeared. The frond of seaweed is turning brown. The green tint of algae is gone. Bacteria and fungi do survive in there, but they are small consolation for a human being. If the glass should ever fall off the edge of my desk there would be an apocalyptic stink. My crystal ball died.

I hesitated to ask Harmony for a new EcoSphere. My study still gets cold during the night. It gets hot during the early afternoon, when the sun streams in through the branches of the trees outside the picture window. Who could say the next EcoSphere would fare better? While I hesitated the life policy expired, and any grace period the Harmonys might have granted me expired, too.

Apparently the state of this sphere is my fault. Every living thing has thresholds and I was careless about crossing them.

But I must say those thresholds were easily crossed.

 **CHAPTER 2**

MINUTE PARTICULARS

He who would do good to another must do it in
minute particulars . . .
For art and science cannot exist but in minutely
organized particulars.

William Blake
"Jerusalem"

My crystal ball holds about a half a cup of air and two cups of water. In this miniature atmosphere and ocean there is a small amount of carbon dioxide gas. And this trace of carbon dioxide, measured in parts per million, is absolutely essential for the survival of the last few green plants (such as they are) that float in the water.

Each morning, when sunlight reaches the EcoSphere, the plants begin to inhale carbon dioxide (among other things) from the air and water. Molecule by molecule, the plants break apart the carbon dioxide. They hold on to the carbon but throw out oxygen. As a result, the amount of carbon dioxide in the water and air goes down, while the amount of oxygen goes up.

At sundown, or whenever I turn off the lights in my study, the plants in the EcoSphere stop inhaling carbon dioxide. Slowly, the living things in there return the carbon they have borrowed. In a long slow exhalation, the plants release carbon to the air and water. All night, in the darkness, the amount of carbon dioxide goes up, while the amount of oxygen in the sphere goes down.

Air and water are full of invisible cycles like this. Besides carbon and oxygen, the most important elements of life on Earth are hydrogen, nitrogen, phosphorus, and sulfur. Each of these elements circulates in perpetual motion through the crystal ball. Each cycle is linked to the others, as carbon is linked to oxygen. These cycles proceed not only within the curving walls of the EcoSphere but all around us, day and night. Being invisible they seem remote but they are as intimate as our own breathing.

The study of these invisible cycles is called geochemistry. Geo-chemists study all of the seven spheres, earth, water, air, fire, life, ice, and mind, along with all of the matter and energy that pass at every moment from one sphere to another. They study lava, mud, fire, star-light; leaf mulch, cow dung, sapphires, termite breath. Geochemists also watch the way these substances interact with others. They see visions of an intricate, invisible web of chemistry that binds all things, chemicals arising from every sphere at every point of the compass, transporting vapors and currents from earth to sea to sky, each min-gling with each. There are hints of secret societies of elements, of vast, interlocking systems, of a planetary physiology.

Geochemists also ask hard-edged questions about the health of the planet. Is life on Earth near a threshold of stress? How do the seven spheres work together to keep the planet habitable? What is the human prospect in the next one hundred years?

If the questions have urgency, it is due in part to the holdfast career of Charles David Keeling. He began his life's work as a young man with a simple study of air trapped in hollow glass balls. That first look led to a view that changed the world. He has spent the rest of his career repeating the same measurement in the same way using the same in-struments. Today this ever-lengthening record, Keeling's curve, pro-vides a sort of time-lapse X-ray movie of the workings of the spheres, a surprising inside view of our planet's metabolism.

In 1954, Keeling graduated from Northwestern University, in Evans-ton, Illinois, with a Ph.D. in chemistry. He was twenty-six. Nine out of ten of his classmates were taking work in the chemical industry, where they would be paid, in Keeling's words, to "make breakfast cereals crisper, gasoline more powerful, plastics cheaper, and antibiotics more expensive."

Keeling had discovered camping and backpacking in college. He de-cided that he wanted to work outdoors, where the horizon is wider than the meniscus in a test tube. Although his degree was in chemis-try, he wrote brash letters to the deans of ten geology departments

("all west of the Continental Divide," he says, "on account of the scenery.")

As luck would have it, the geology department at the California Institute of Technology, in Pasadena, had just set up a geochemistry program. This was something new—the chemistry of the Earth was not a subject normally treated separately. Keeling was hired by the leader of the new program, Harrison Brown.

Soon after Keeling arrived at Caltech, he heard Brown make an offhand remark. Brown was in the middle of shoptalk with a small court of his geochemists. He was describing the natural acidity of lakes and rivers. He was building an argument about bicarbonate in water, and his hypothesis—Keeling noticed—assumed that the carbon dioxide gas that is dissolved in the water is always in balance with the carbon dioxide in the air above the water.

Keeling challenged that. He told Brown that the amount of gas in the water and the air might be out of balance. Actually Keeling had never given the subject much thought (he says now), but it had the merit of being impossible to pursue indoors. "So I said to Harrison Brown, 'I'd like to make an experiment to see whether you're correct.'"

With his boss's blessing, Keeling set out to check. He planned a simple experiment. He would measure the amount of carbon dioxide in a stream, and in the air above the stream, and he would see if the gas pressures were the same in both. To do that he would need a device for measuring carbon dioxide in air or water, in small quantities, in parts per million. There was no such instrument on the market, and Keeling could find no instructions in the scientific literature to suggest how to build one. After a search he did find an old article (circa 1916) describing a manometer—an instrument for measuring small quantities of gases—that might suit his purposes, with some work.

The first man to make a measurement of carbon dioxide was also the first man to discover that the air we breathe is not one single substance but a mixture of substances. He was a Flemish alchemist and physician named Johann Baptista van Helmont. In a manuscript published after his death in 1644, van Helmont argued from direct and indirect evidence that an invisible "spirit" curled from every one of the bubbling flasks in his alchemical laboratory, and from each of the red coals in his furnaces. "I call this Spirit, unknown hitherto, by the new name of

Gas," he wrote—coining the word from the Flemish pronunciation of the Greek word *chaos.*

Van Helmont was particularly interested in carbon dioxide. He called it *gas sylvestris,* spirit of wood, because it arose from burning logs and charcoal. Although he was an alchemist, working in a long tradition of medieval magic, he was just post-medieval enough to appreciate the value of careful measurements—one of the tricks that was about to transform the practice of black magic into modern science. Among other things, van Helmont tried to measure how much gas he added to the air by burning coals in a furnace. When he burned "sixty-two pounds of Oaken coal" and weighed what was left there was just one pound of ashes. "Therefore, the sixty-one remaining pounds," he wrote, "are the *wild spirit.*"

One century later a medical student was looking for a cure for kidney stones. The most popular remedy for "the Stone" included lime, a whitish substance that can be made by heating chalk, limestone, or eggshells. Dissolved in water, lime makes a mild, clear drink.

Joseph Black experimented with limewater and a few other substances and on January 3, 1754, at the age of twenty-six, he wrote an excited letter to his professor at the University of Edinburgh. It begins with a dashed-off apology:

> I fully intended to have wrote last post, but really I happened to be intent upon something else at the proper time, and forgot it. It was, indeed, an experiment I was trying that amused me . . .

The night before (Black wrote), he had dropped some chalk in the bottom of a tall glass and poured acid over it. The chalk fizzed madly. Then the candle beside the glass was snuffed out as if by the hand of a ghost.

Black, who had read van Helmont's memoirs, wondered if a gas from the fizzing chalk had put out the candle. He took a piece of paper, set one corner of it on fire, and cautiously dipped it into the mouth of the glass. The flame went out "as effectually as if it had been dipped in water."

Black had rediscovered carbon dioxide. He soon found that limewater makes a good carbon-dioxide detector (if not a cure for kidney stones). When he exposed a glass of limewater to a strong source of carbon dioxide gas, such as fizzing chalk, or logs burning in a fireplace,

17

the lime that was dissolved in the water began to settle to the bottom like snow. The more gas, the more snow.

Using this detector Black found carbon dioxide gas almost everywhere. It bubbles up from mineral waters, such as the celebrated springs of Perrier. It spills from vats of fermenting yeast. It seeps from the walls of mines. It rises copiously from almost anything that burns—not only wood but also paper, coal, oil, even cremated corpses.

One day Black put a straw in a jar of limewater and blew bubbles. Then he sat back and watched the blizzard he had started. Human breath is loaded with carbon dioxide.

Carbon dioxide became a hot topic in science—especially after Priestley, Lavoisier, and others established that the gas is exhaled by all animals and inhaled by all green plants. It seemed to have a virtually infinite number of sources, yet there was only a trace of it in the atmosphere. Among those who tried to measure it were the German naturalist and explorer Alexander von Humboldt, the French chemist Joseph Louis Gay-Lussac, and the father-and-son geologists Horace and Theodore de Saussure. Gay-Lussac took a jar of limewater in the first high-altitude ascent in a hot air balloon. De Saussure (the elder), who is often called the father of mountaineering, took a jar of limewater with him on his first ascent of Mont Blanc.

The exact amount of carbon dioxide gas in the atmosphere proved to be hard to measure. The amount was not only small but also varied from sample to sample. The average was about $3/100$ths of 1 percent.

In the late nineteenth century, one of the many scientists who became fascinated with carbon dioxide was Jean Reiset. He mounted a water barrel in a horsedrawn carriage and rode it day and night, summer and winter, through the streets of Paris, and down the country lanes of Ecorcheboeuf, on the northwest coast of France. To take an air sample he would stop the horses and unplug the barrel. Six hundred gallons of water spilled out and the same number of gallons of air were drawn in. On its way into the apparatus, the air was sucked through more chambers than a cow has stomachs, and in each chamber it set off little blizzards of precipitate.

Reiset found that there was much more carbon dioxide in Paris than in the country, a fact he attributed (rightly) to the smoking chimneys of the city's houses and the smokestacks of its factories ("The chimneys," he wrote, "emit torrents of carbon dioxide, day and night."). Late nineteenth-century numbers showed a large amount of variation, but again they averaged about $^3/_{100}$ths of 1 percent, or 300 parts per million.

Twenty years after Reiset, measuring carbon dioxide went out of fashion. In the first half of the twentieth century, one of the few who tried to do it was a Swede named Kurt Buch. He reported that the amount of gas in the air varies wildly from breeze to breeze, from place to place, and from latitude to latitude. He got a low of 150 parts per million and a high of about 350. The average was still about $^3/_{100}$ths of 1 percent.

Keeling had arrived at Caltech in the fall of 1953. He spent all that winter and spring redesigning the manometer and devising methods to extract carbon dioxide from air and water so that he could put the appropriate samples into the manometer. He was on his own. Brown was away most of the time, as Keeling remembers it: he was in Jamaica, writing a book, *The Challenge of Man's Future*. In any case, Brown liked to let people do what they wanted. In Brown's absence, an older hand in the geochemistry group advised Keeling to carry out his project using tools they already had in the lab—there was really no need for Keeling to build a manometer. But Keeling has a stubborn streak and it is concentrated at more than a few hundred parts per million. "For no particularly good reason," he says, "I decided to make it as accurate as possible." In fact, he says, he made the thing "about ten times more precise than made any sense." He was still puttering when Brown strolled into his laboratory and presented him with an author's copy of *The Challenge of Man's Future*. Keeling keeps that book in his office today. Not long ago, at my request, he took it down from the shelf, put on his silver-framed reading glasses, and opened it to the title page. It is inscribed,

> To Dave Keeling (who knows what he is doing).
> With all best wishes for the future.
>
> > Sincerely,
> > *Harrison Brown*
> > April, 1954

"Hmm," Keeling said, "April, 1954. Now, that's *before* I knew what I was doing! What he really meant was that I was too stubborn to take suggestions." He threw back his head and laughed.

Brown left town and Keeling went back to puttering. But Brown's deputies were growing uneasy. Keeling's appointment was for only one year, though it was renewable for up to a three-year appointment. "They wanted some evidence that I was doing something," Keeling says, "and there was darn little to show for it in September of 1954, when my first year was up."

However, Keeling had meanwhile gotten married. The year had been productive in at least one way. Brown's deputies decided, "Well, we can't really throw this guy out. He's got a pregnant wife and no job." They let him stay.

By spring of 1955, working feverishly now, Keeling finished his manometer. He had now spent twelve months on preliminaries. With his supervisors drumming their fingers and his first child due in two weeks, he might have been expected to drive straight out to the nearest field and stream and get cracking. Once again Keeling overdid things.

On a fine morning in March he walked out of his penthouse laboratory in Mudd Hall and emerged on the rooftop bearing a hollow glass sphere about one foot in diameter. He had pumped the air out of it in the lab. He opened the flask's stopcock, holding his breath and backing away so that the fresh air that rushed into the globe would not be contaminated with his own carbon dioxide. Then he darted back, closed the stopcock, and went into the lab with his glass flask. It looked empty as ever, of course.

Keeling isolated the carbon dioxide in the flask, using liquid nitrogen. Then he put the carbon dioxide into one of the chambers of his new manometer and compressed the gas with a tall, gleaming column of mercury. The air in the flask held 310 parts per million carbon dioxide.

Something drove Keeling to do it over—not just once, but every four hours for a twenty-four hour stretch, hitting the roof all through one day and one night, sometimes sleeping on a cot in the lab, sometimes going home and coming back once or twice a night. He recorded the results of each of these measurements in a little green notebook. Then he started a second round-the-clock sequence.

He was in the middle of yet another twenty-four hour test when his wife went into labor. He got her to Altadena Hospital, paced around the waiting room, and watched the clock. Every four hours he ran back to the laboratory roof. ("After all," he says, a little defensively, "there is absolutely nothing a husband can do.") At the moment their son Drew was born, he was at the lab.

("Well, Millikan," Keeling adds, still defensive. "Not to compare myself with Robert Millikan in any other respect. But he was late to his wedding, because he was doing the Oil Drop Experiment. He was trying to find out the charge on the electron, and it was so fascinating that somebody had to get him and take him away and get him dressed up.")

For weeks, while Louise nursed their newborn son, Keeling rose for air in the middle of the night and his wife rose for Drew. Then the two of them packed the baby and a box of glass flasks and went camping. From May 18 to May 19, 1955, they camped by the Big Sur River, surrounded by coastal redwoods, and filled nine flasks with air. From June 2 to 3, they filled flasks at a stream in Yosemite National Park. In July, they were in the Inyo Mountains. In August, the Cascade Mountains. In September, Olympic National Park.

At Yosemite, to get away from other campers' fires, Keeling asked permission from the Forest Service to camp below the Tioga Pass before it was open to the public. He and Louise washed some clothes and spread them on bushes to dry in the sun. The snow had not melted in the pass, and the deer up there were half-starved for grass, flowers, buds, and the tourist trade. A big mule deer came along and snatched some of their things from the bushes.

That night when Louise nursed Drew, his mouth was ice cold. Keeling trudged off between snowdrifts at 8:00 P.M. to fill a flask, and once again at midnight, and curled up in the sleeping bag to doze until the next flask or the next feeding, whichever came first. At some nameless hour, he heard a rustle. "I rummaged around, grabbed my flashlight, looked out, and the flashlight was just like a policeman's apprehending a suspect. Two big eyes, looking right at me! It was that darn mule deer (or another one just like it) and he had my research notebook between his teeth. And as soon as I got him started he ran off into the woods with the notebook."

He had just lost every measurement he had made since the first one on the roof of Mudd Hall. He stumbled out after the deer, sweeping the ground with a flashlight. There was a black bear around that night, but Keeling did not know enough about bears to worry. At last he found what was left of his notebook. The pages were indented by a big set of teeth. The deer had ripped off the binding. It had not eaten the data.

*   *   *

Back at his penthouse laboratory, Keeling measured the carbon dioxide in his samples and pored over the taped-up notebook. He saw a pattern. The carbon dioxide concentration always dropped as the sun rose in the sky and increased as the sun went down. It stayed high all night. It bottomed out in the afternoon, and began climbing again after sundown. He plotted this rise and fall on graph paper. At Yosemite the pattern looked something like this:

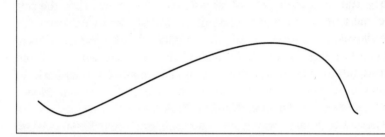

This line is a sort of executive summary of a day in the life of the biosphere. Each day, as the sun rises, every green thing, from redwoods to skunk cabbage to club moss, begins inhaling carbon dioxide for use in photosynthesis, and the amount of gas in the air begins to drop. Photosynthesis means literally "building with light," and the construction process is basically the same in a forest or within the curving walls of an EcoSphere. It all happens inside plant cells within organelles called chloroplasts, which look under the microscope like emerald green EcoSpheres.

Inside each chloroplast, plants break apart molecules of carbon dioxide into carbon and oxygen. They also break water molecules into hydrogen and oxygen. Then they put most of these atoms back together in new combinations to build simple sugars like sucrose (throwing out some of the oxygen as trash). The work requires steady supplies of sunlight for energy, and steady supplies of carbon dioxide and water for raw materials.

Photosynthesis in a forest wouldn't work without the carbon from carbon dioxide in the air. All sugars—indeed every molecule in the biosphere, including the spiral staircase of DNA—are held together by carbon. Carbon atoms hook together into long chains and rings to which other elements can be attached. They are like the little wooden hubs in the Tinkertoy set. With them you can build almost anything, even a spiral staircase; without them the staircase would collapse in an instant.

By afternoon plants have taken a lot of carbon dioxide out of circulation. At the same time, however, plants are busily eating the sugars they have made for themselves. This is the metabolic process of respiration. Respiration means literally "to breathe back, to blow back" and it is a form of combustion, a very slow burn. It consumes oxygen and produces carbon dioxide, as surely as logs burning in a fireplace.

Here are two of the most fundamental processes of life on Earth, and they run in opposite directions. Photosynthesis takes in carbon dioxide and releases oxygen; respiration takes in oxygen and releases carbon dioxide. The two processes also run on different timetables, which is a fact that opens up a world to geochemists.

Photosynthesis works a day shift, because the process requires sunlight, and most plants take in carbon dioxide only while the sun shines. The gas enters through a myriad of microscopic pores, stomata, on the undersides of each green leaf. These doors open at sunrise and close at sundown.

Respiration works a day shift and a night shift. At four o'clock in the morning, while the stomata are closed, and green leaves are taking in virtually no carbon dioxide, the leaves are still respiring, blowing back carbon dioxide to the air.

Only by the end of the night do the books balance, more or less. That is, at the close of each twenty-four hour period, most plants have borrowed and returned about the same amount of carbon dioxide to the atmosphere.

While Keeling had hiked through the woods with the crates of glass flasks, panting once or twice a second, the trees had been breathing, too, at a rate of once a day. (Animals don't count for much in this daily cycle. They have no chloroplasts, the green agents of photosynthesis. Until a genetic engineer designs a green cow or a green-haired boy, animals will go on getting all their energy and raw materials by eating plants, and by eating animals that have eaten plants, and by inhaling the oxygen released by plants. Animals' role in the grand scheme is peripheral.)

For geochemists, all this makes the atmosphere a window on the biosphere. If photosynthesis and respiration ran on the same schedule, then the level of gas in a forest or a crystal ball would always be dead flat, boring, a straight line—not much information. Because these two processes are out of synch, so that the amount of carbon dioxide in

Earth's atmosphere goes up and down, the atmosphere is always loaded with information about the biosphere.

The view from the air is Olympian. Up here the evidence of a deer and a man in pursuit and a roaring campfire and a sleeping mother and infant disappear. Trees disappear. Streams disappear. A cacophony of contradictory processes like photosynthesis and respiration all resolve into a single rolling line, the average or ensemble of everything that is growing, breathing, and dying in the forest. From this cosmic point of view what matters is not the individual but the biosphere as a whole.

What puzzled Keeling was the value he got for midafternoon air. It always bottomed out at about 315 parts per million. Whether in Yosemite, or Big Sur, or the Cascade Mountains, the concentration of carbon dioxide always came down to that amount by two or three o'clock in the afternoon.

According to the textbooks, carbon dioxide was supposed to wobble from breeze to breeze, from place to place, from much more than 315 to much less. But Keeling's mid-afternoon value, the low for each day, was always roughly 315. No one had ever reported this. Why should carbon dioxide in a forest always dwindle to 315?

That winter, on a hunch, Keeling packed a big crate of glass flasks and drove back into the Inyo Mountains of eastern California. He camped at a remote high-altitude field station, across from Mount Whitney, at 12,000 feet during a winter gale. Once every four hours, day and night, he pushed out into the storm, staggering into the wind a few steps on the hard, crunchy snow to fill a flask. The wind howled for five days, and he filled thirty flasks with Essence of Pacific Mountain Storm. Then he went home to his manometer.

"And here was a carbon dioxide concentration—" Keeling says now, leaning forward across his desk in his old swivel chair, excited yet. "Not only was it nearly constant, but it was right smack in the middle of that range of lower numbers. It sat there at 315 parts per million."

Now Keeling thought he understood the number 315. The storm in his bottles had swept across thousands of miles of the Pacific Ocean before brushing the Inyo Mountains. This was air beyond local influences. It was a wind so well-travelled, so cosmopolitan, that it might represent something like the average of all the air on Earth.

People had been looking in the wrong places. They had tried in the streets of Paris, orchards, forests. What if the trick was to go to the most remote, godforsaken, lifeless spots on Earth, spend a night on a bald mountain in a winter storm? Go where the air is pure and all the hubbub of photosynthesis and respiration, campfires and smokestacks, has been smoothed, mixed, and blended? What if the wind in the storm holds something like the average of all the carbon dioxide on the planet? What if the amount of carbon dioxide in Earth's atmosphere as a whole was about 315 parts per million?

That would explain why his numbers always approached 315 at mid-afternoon. A forest is a tangle of local influences. But by noon the Sun has warmed the ground and made the air rise—the way the draft from a campfire lofts its smoke. As the ground-warmed air rises, cooler air from high in the sky sinks to take its place. Masses of air turn over and over gently above the whole landscape. The ladle of noon stirs so well that even in the middle of a thick forest on an apparently windless day, the air holds a hint of the carbon dioxide level of the atmosphere of the entire planet.

"So!" Keeling says. He opens a file drawer, digs out his first published paper on the subject, whips on his reading glasses again, and points to that magic number 315. "Completely contrary to what was gospel at the time, see?" he says. "And based on a *few* measurements, and based on the whimsical desire for an accurate manometer. *No* attempt to copy the procedures that Buch used in Scandinavia. I wasn't paying *any* attention to *anything*, was I?"

■ CHAPTER 3

KEELING'S
CURVE

So it cometh often to pass, that mean and small things discover great, better than great can discover the small: and therefore Aristotle noteth well, "that the nature of every thing is best seen in its smallest portions."

Francis Bacon
The New Organon

Back then, the mid-1950s, almost nobody was worried about the greenhouse effect. But geochemists did know about it, and had known for a long time. The basic theory of the greenhouse effect was first stated by a mathematician who served under Napoleon in Egypt. Jean-Baptiste-Joseph Fourier did well in Egypt—so well that a few years later, when he made his most important scientific breakthrough, the theory of the conduction of heat, Napoleon used the occasion to make Fourier a baron.

Fourier was the first man to realize that the atmosphere keeps us warm. Outer space is a very cold place, and if it were not for the layers of gases that wrap the planet, we would all freeze. Without air, Earth would not be the blue planet: it would be white. From the Moon the face of the whole globe would look like the nether view from the South Pole.

In 1827, Fourier compared this fortunate influence of Earth's atmosphere to a hothouse. He said Earth's gases are like the greenhouse's glass walls. In other words, air has a greenhouse effect.

A few decades after Fourier's death, a British physicist, John Tyndall, analyzed the gases of the atmosphere one by one to see which of them have the most powerful greenhouse effect. In the late 1850s, he discovered that nitrogen and oxygen do not have what it takes. That means ninety-nine percent of the atmosphere has almost no greenhouse effect at all. Three gases that do have what it takes are water vapor, carbon dioxide, and ozone.

It surprises some people that water vapor should be considered an atmospheric gas. Maybe the surprise comes because "domestic" water vapor, like water itself, is an everyday part of our lives, from humid air to steaming kettles to venting dryers. Other gases seem more esoteric, more remote, though we know we are enclosed by all of them and breathe them in and out.

Water when it evaporates forms an invisible gas, as wood does when it burns. There is a lot of water on the surface of our planet so there is always a lot of water vapor in the atmosphere. In fact water is the single most common greenhouse gas on Earth. It is much more common than carbon dioxide, which in turn is much more common than ozone.

These three gases have one thing that molecules of nitrogen and oxygen do not. They have a third atom. Nitrogen is N-N, and oxygen is O-O: doublets. The three most common greenhouse gases are triplets: water is H-H-O (H_2O), and ozone is O-O-O (O_3), an aberrant and highly unstable form of oxygen, a ménage à trois. Carbon dioxide of course is O-C-O (CO_2). The actual arrangement in space is a flying bird:

Having three atoms instead of two ("little triads," Tyndall called them) gives these gases a special property. Like nitrogen and oxygen they are almost perfectly transparent to the sunlight that streams to Earth from the Sun. Unlike these other gases, however, they are partially opaque to the heat radiation that rises from the sun-baked ground. This heat radiation is infrared (literally, below red). It is below red in the rainbow spectrum, placing it just outside the range of colors to which human eyes are tuned. A few animals, including ticks and pit vipers, do sense their targets in infrared; and we can feel it on our hands and faces near a campfire or a hot stove. Infrared is earthlight. The planet shines mildly in the infrared by day and night.

When infrared radiation strikes molecules with three atoms it sets them shaking and trembling. Carbon dioxide molecules flap their bonds like birds:

and as they flap and shake, they give off energy in the form of more dark rays, more infrared. Every carbon dioxide molecule in the atmosphere is like a dark star shining in all directions, up, down, and sideways.

In this way, invisible rays of energy get passed back and forth many times between the atmosphere and the spheres below—the lithosphere, biosphere, hydrosphere, and cryosphere—before the energy finally migrates to the top of the atmosphere and escapes to the relative calm and vacuum of outer space, where there are few flapping birds.

And that is the greenhouse effect. The dark rays bounce around inside the atmosphere many times before they finally manage to leak out into space. Water vapor, carbon dioxide, and ozone, rare though they are, turn the world's air into a giant heat trap. And for billions of years, life on Earth has depended on this peculiar property of these three gases (and a few others that are even rarer) to keep the planet liveable.

The British physicist Tyndall was quick to appreciate the terrific punch that carbon dioxide, in particular, can pack by being both powerful and rare. He realized that plants are constantly breathing carbon dioxide in and out, and that the gas fluctuates naturally for a hundred other reasons as well. If the amount of carbon dioxide in the air ever dropped even a little bit too much, the change could chill the planet. Tyndall even suggested that this might be the explanation for ice ages.

Oddly enough Tyndall never made much of the other side of the coin—in retrospect so obvious. He was not dull. He was a polymath who made important discoveries in chemistry, physics, bacteriology, and the theory of the origin of life. He even explained why the sky is blue. He was also a great mountaineer and a brave controversialist and he would not have flinched from the implications of the dark side of the greenhouse effect.*

Perhaps he would have come to it in time. But in his early fifties his health began to fail and he retired to a villa on the heath to write his autobiography. His young wife Louise looked after him, giving him a big dose of magnesia every morning for his indigestion and a small dose of chloral every night for his insomnia. One wintry morning in 1893 she got the two bottles mixed up and gave him a giant dose of chloral. He swallowed it and said it tasted sweet.

"John, I have given you chloral!"

"Yes, my poor darling," he said, "you have killed your John." He was dead before sundown.

Three years after Tyndall's death a Swedish chemist, Svante Arrhenius, finally turned the coin. Arrhenius, who won one of the first Nobel prizes in chemistry, put together a few simple facts: Every year people were burning a lot of coal, oil, and firewood, each year more than the year before. Burning these fuels injects millions of tons of carbon dioxide into the atmosphere. Carbon dioxide is a greenhouse gas.

Arrhenius explained it in the *London, Edinburgh, and Dublin Philosophical Magazine* of April, 1896. "We are evaporating our coal mines into the air," he wrote. Adding so much carbon dioxide gas to the air must be causing "a change in the transparency of the atmosphere." With each passing year, air must be trapping more and more dark rays, more and more earthlight. Eventually this change might very well heat the planet to heights outside all human experience.

The pages of the *London, Edinburgh, and Dublin Philosophical Magazine* are so old and acid-damaged now that they fall apart as one turns them, like the sensational instructions that are supposed to be burned as soon as read: *"Mission Impossible.* This message will self-destruct." But there it is: published during the reign of Queen Victoria.

In the first half of the twentieth century this idea was neglected. Earth scientists did not doubt that carbon dioxide has a greenhouse effect. But (among other things) they doubted that the gas was accumulating in the air. There were reasons to think it was accumulating only very, very slowly, if at all. Carbon pollution from coal and oil might

---

*"It is as fatal as it is cowardly to blink facts because they are not to our taste," wrote Tyndall in "Science and Man."

be falling out of the air just as fast as smokestacks and chimneys put more of it up there. For instance the gas might be absorbed by the ocean. In a sense the ocean is like a big jar of limewater. It holds billions of tons of lime dissolved within it in the form of calcium carbonate. Geochemists assumed that as human beings injected carbon dioxide into the air, the extra gas would react with the lime, and rain safely down to the bottom of the sea. The more gas, the more snow. The more snow, the less gas. The world's climate was safe.

During a series of unusually warm years in Europe in the 1930s, a British coal engineer named George Callendar took the trouble to compile the previous hundred years' worth of carbon dioxide measurements and check them over. By throwing out what looked to him like unreliable measurements, and accepting what looked like the best, Callendar found hints of a gas build-up. This finding was neglected, too.

Not even Keeling realized at the start of his project that the amount of carbon dioxide in the atmosphere was about to become a subject of grave and even morbid planetary interest. Keeling just wanted to make the measurements. Gas for gas's sake. He wasn't worried about carbon dioxide in the least. The Polynesians have a saying, "Standing on a whale, fishing for minnows."

Meanwhile, however, an oceanographer, Roger Revelle, discovered that the ocean does *not* act like a jar of limewater. The chemistry of seawater is such that it strongly resists taking in more carbon dioxide than it already contains. Revelle was director of the Scripps Institution of Oceanography, in La Jolla, California, at the time. Then as now he was one of the most respected voices in science policy, a man with a gift for absorbing complicated pictures and finding simple truths. His explanation of seawater's resistance to the absorption of carbon dioxide is now known as the Revelle Effect. He published it in 1957, in a paper written with Hans Suess. They summed up the new situation on the planet in words that have been much quoted since: "Thus human beings are now carrying out a large scale geophysical experiment of a kind that could not have happened in the past nor be reproduced in the future."

When Keeling came down from the mountain with the magic number 315, things began to happen fast. A scientist at Caltech who had been following Keeling's progress gave him a telephone number to call in Washington. Investigators from around the world were planning an ambitious study of the planet: eighteen concentrated months of global observations of earth, air, water, fire, and ice, with participants from seventy countries and from every discipline of Earth science. This International Geophysical Year (I.G.Y.) had been in the works for years and it was just about to begin. The unworldly post-doc had not heard much about it. But Roger Revelle was one of the planners of the I.G.Y. Having proved that carbon dioxide *might* be rising, Revelle wanted to know if it really *was* rising.

Two weeks after he got down from the storm on the mountain, Keeling found himself on a plane to Washington. There, he was ushered into the center of planning in the United States for meteorological research for the I.G.Y.

The interview began promptly at 8:00 A.M., and ran at a staccato pace. The head of the Weather Bureau's Office of Meteorological Research, Harry Wexler, quizzed Keeling about his number 315. What would Keeling do if he were planning to measure carbon dioxide in the I.G.Y.?

Keeling said that he would monitor the gas all around the world. Moreover, he would find a way to make the measurements not just by spot checks, by filling a few flasks a day, but *continuously*.

Wexler didn't blink at this proposal. If Keeling could measure the level of carbon dioxide in the atmosphere of the whole planet, Wexler wanted him in the I.G.Y. He knew of remote weather and research stations around the world from which carbon dioxide could be monitored. In particular, Wexler said, the U.S. Weather Service had just built a station on the Hawaiian volcano Mauna Loa. There was a concrete hut up there where people could eat, sleep, and tend the instruments. He thought Mauna Loa would do.

So Roger Revelle invited Keeling to Scripps, where Keeling proceeded to drive Revelle crazy. At the time, Revelle was not only the director of the Scripps Institution of Oceanography and a planner of the I.G.Y. He had also served as the Navy's oceanographer, and he had been leading scientists, teams of scientists, and major oceanographic expeditions for years. Yet he had never run into anyone like Keeling.

"His outstanding characteristic," Revelle says today, "is that he has an overwhelming desire to measure carbon dioxide. He wants to measure it in his *belly*. Measure it in all its manifestations, atmospheric and oceanic. And he's done this all his *life*," Revelle says, somewhat incredulously. "Very single-minded, and very, I suppose, narrow in his views, thinking only about this one problem. His overwhelming focus makes him rather difficult to deal with, as you can imagine."

"How unusual is this degree of obsession in a scientist?" I asked Revelle.

"Well, he's more single-minded than anybody I've ever known."

"You've known a number of scientists."

"I should imagine."

When Keeling arrived at Scripps, he told Revelle that he wanted to try out a new kind of gas analyzer. It worked by passing an infrared beam through the air sample, and measuring how much of the beam got through. The more carbon dioxide in a sample, the more it blocked the beam. Each gas analyzer would cost $10,000, and every air-sampling station in Keeling's global air-sampling network was going to need one.

Next, with the deadline for the start of the I.G.Y. upon them, Keeling also told Revelle that he intended to build a new and better manometer, with more chambers. Keeling wanted to increase its accuracy by another factor of ten. Instead of measuring the gas to about a half a part per million, he told Revelle, he would try to measure it to five-hundredths of a part per million.

For a while it looked to Revelle as if the I.G.Y. would be over before Keeling had finished building any of this new equipment. Revelle kept looking in on him and nothing much was happening, except that Keeling's plans for the new manometer were getting more and more elaborate. Meanwhile the first analyzer was supposed to go to Little America, an Antarctic ice shelf that had been explored by Admiral Byrd. The last ship bound for Antarctica that season was scheduled to sail on the day after Christmas of 1956. Keeling began crating it on Christmas Eve.

"So my marriage was stressed considerably," Keeling says. "My wife was just about to have our second child on the second of January, and I spent Christmas Eve loading the ship . . . I had one graduate student at Scripps, helping me screw boxes together on Christmas Eve! There was a party at Scripps, and we had to break away from the party and load this damn thing and take it over to San Diego harbor, the two of us."

When the numbers came back from the analyzer in Little America, Keeling looked them over. Gibberish. The analyzer's pumps were leaking.

Keeling screwed together the parts for a second analyzer, bound for Mauna Loa. By now his new manometer, still struggling to be born, had filled his lab to overflowing. He had to build the Mauna Loa analyzer in the corridor outside his lab. Colleagues had to step around him.

Keeling thought he knew what the gas analyzer would say if it worked. The air at Mauna Loa, on the island of Hawaii, way out in the middle of the Pacific, is about as clean as it gets. Hawaii is the most isolated island archipelago on Earth. The trade winds that blow to it should represent something like the average of the air in the whole of the planet (or at least the Northern Hemisphere, since air does not mix well across the equator). The air that blew up the sides of the volcano from the Pacific was the same air that Keeling had sampled in the storm in the Inyo Mountains, only with still less taint of land. Keeling predicted that if his analyzer worked, the concentration would be about 315 parts per million.

A man from the Weather Bureau installed the gas analyzer on the slopes of the volcano in March, 1958. The first day he got it working, he looked at the graph the machine was tracing. It read 314. It was measuring the amount of carbon dioxide in the atmosphere of the Northern Hemisphere.

The second month's reports from the analyzer on the volcano did not agree with the first. That month, carbon dioxide went up by one part per million. The next month, it went up again. Then the observatory's power blacked out, and the analyzer was shut down for a few weeks.

By the time the observatory was running again in July, the concentration of gas had fallen *below* what it had been in March. "I became anxious that the concentration was going to be hopelessly erratic," Keeling recalls, "especially when the computed concentration fell again in late August." Then there were more power shut-downs.

Were Keeling's measurements as erratic as Buch's? Or was there after all no rhyme or reason to the ups and downs of carbon dioxide?

The forecasters and technicians on the volcano remember long, anxious phone calls from La Jolla. "Here was a very special type of program in which he had the most *intense* personal as well as scientific interest," one forecaster remembers. "And yet Keeling had practically no hands-on experience. It was all happening thousands of miles and thousands of feet vertically from where he was."

Late that autumn, the concentration started climbing again. Harry Wexler, of the U.S. Weather Service, dug deep into his pockets to buy large electric generators for the observatory. There were no more power failures. Keeling watched the concentration rise throughout the winter, to a high of 318, then sink once again the next spring. The first year's data from Mauna Loa, from March to March, made a rolling line like this:

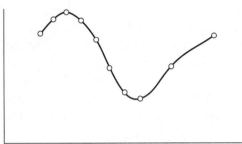

By then Keeling thought he had figured out what was going on. He had discovered another invisible cycle, this one on the scale of the whole planet.

To understand it, he had to re-imagine the whole pageantry of the seasons, the annual passage of foliage from green to red and yellow to brown and black, in terms of invisible effects. Plants take up carbon dioxide mainly in the spring and summer, their green and busy season. They drop their leaves in the fall. The leaves wither and decay, and the carbon that the plants had borrowed from the air that summer returns to the air.

Here again, photosynthesis and respiration march to different drummers. Photosynthesis is mostly a thing of summer. It begins in April, peaks in June, and drops near zero in October, when there is too little sunlight. In other words it runs hard during the light part of the year and all but quits during the dark part of the year.

Respiration peaks in June, too, but unlike photosynthesis it never stops*—it keeps on going throughout the winter and all year round. The life forms that decompose the fallen leaves include a host of fungi, Bacteria, worms, termites, slugs, leaf molds like penicillium, soil microbes, the dark underbelly of the biosphere. They compete to eat the dead leaves, to rot the fallen branches, and together they return most of life's borrowed carbon to the air.

Every year when green things inhale carbon to put out buds, shoots, leaves, and stems, the biosphere inhales. When the leaves fall and

---

*Except where the ground is frozen.

molder on the ground, the biosphere exhales. Keeling had discovered one of the most beautiful, regular, and global of all cycles in nature. A year or two before, he had watched the breathing of a forest; now he saw the breathing of the planet. A forest takes one breath a day. The planet takes one breath a year.

What is more, the biosphere breathes so smoothly and regularly that even the slightest change stands out. During the second spring, Keeling, reading the numbers from Mauna Loa, saw that there was slightly more carbon dioxide in the atmosphere than there had been the previous spring. The gas had gone up by about one part in a million.

There it was—just one year after the I.G.Y. Carbon dioxide was rising. It was really happening. The change in the air was measurable, and he had measured it.

He said years later, only half joking, that he felt as if he had become personally responsible for the rise in carbon dioxide.

After that, most men would have looked around for other peaks to conquer. But Keeling went right on pacing the same laboratory at Scripps, year after year. He kept his original gas analyzers running— by now they look like Model T's—and also the manometer that he built during the I.G.Y. For a decade, he watched carbon dioxide go up around the world by about one part per million each year. Then the concentration started going up even faster, one and a half parts per million per year.

He still watches from the slopes of Mauna Loa, and a station near the South Pole, and as much of a global network as he can hold together. The hallway between his office and his labs is almost always stacked with wooden crates full of glass flasks: samples of fresh air from Alaska; from Samoa; from Christmas Island; from New Zealand. Dozens of other monitoring stations are maintained around the planet by the U.S. National Oceanic and Atmospheric Administration, and by countries belonging to the World Meteorological Organization. They do about 6,000 flasks of air a year. "It's a cottage industry now," says Revelle. Because the numbers have gone up for each of the past decades the now-famous graph looks like the holdings of a successful company with a seasonal trade. Each fall, there is a rise in the record. Each summer, there is a dip in the record. So the slope of the line wriggles like a snake. Nevertheless, each winter, the high is higher than the winter before. In mathematics, straight lines, spirals, and the silhouette of a flight of steps are all called curves. This is the Keeling curve:

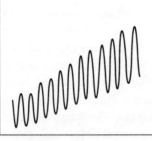

By the thirtieth anniversary of the I.G.Y., 1988, the amount of gas in the atmosphere was approaching 350 parts per million. Keeling's curve had become almost an icon among Earth scientists: the key image of the greenhouse effect, and the central symbol of global change.

When Keeling began this record the idea of monitoring the planet seemed new and unconventional. Today this close watch is universally accepted as a necessity for our survival in the next hundred years. More big changes appear every year. Recently an analysis of Keeling's curve turned up another revelation.

The breath of life is changing. Since the mid-1970s, the breathing of the biosphere is no longer quite steady. Earth's inhalations and exhalations seem to be getting bigger and bigger.

Geochemists are struggling to figure out what this means. What makes the world breathe at all? A forest has no lungs, only green leaves, bogs and swamps, fresh-water lakes, standing pools. And the biosphere has no lungs, either, only the green-mantled continents, with their forests, plains, steppes, farms, tundra; and the plankton-bearing seas. If the breathing of the biosphere changes, it cannot mean the same thing as a change in the breathing of a forest or a dog or a fern or a human being. Temperature, rainfall, high carbon dioxide levels—these are the sorts of things that would matter to the breathing of the world.

An ecologist once picked up a copepod with an eyedropper, placed it under a Cartesian diving bell, and measured its breathing rate. A copepod is a crustacean, a distant cousin of the red shrimp in an Eco-Sphere. This particular copepod was native to the cavernous spaces between grains of sand in forest riverbanks. There it contributed a modest amount to the respiration side of the breathing of the world. (As the Aborigines say, "Nothing is nothing.")

In the tiny diving bell, for the first time in its life, the copepod found itself without sand around it. The creature flailed about in the water and its respiration rate began to climb higher and higher.

Experimentally the investigator threw in a few grains of sand from the animal's home in the riverbank. The copepod caught one grain and curled around it with its whole length. Slowly its respiration rate steadied again.

The ecologist tried this with other specimens and every copepod reacted by breathing faster, hugging the grain of sand, breathing quietly again.

With the breathing of the biosphere, the cause of the change, the nature of the change, and the implications of the change for the future are all beyond reach of such a simple and repeatable experiment. We know that the amount of carbon dioxide in the air is rising. The temperature of the planet may also be rising. These two changes in the atmosphere are presumed to have triggered the change in life's breathing; although the biosphere has weathered a thousand other shocks in these same years, including sharp increases in acid rain and snow, in the expansion of deserts, in the burning of tropical forests. Whole ecosystems have been swallowed or irreparably altered, from the dessication of the Aral Sea in the U.S.S.R. to the loss of the sagebrush of the American West. Global cycles not only of carbon and oxygen but of nitrogen, phosphorus, sulfur, and trace metals like lead and zinc have been perturbed, in many cases more severely than the cycles of carbon and oxygen.

It makes sense that these changes should show up first in the breathing of the world, the grand sum of all the action of life on Earth. The effects of global change would be expected to appear on the largest scale before they would become noticeable in our own backyards, as one global ecologist, Richard Houghton, has noted: "The integrated effect of many environmental changes may in fact be more readily observed for the whole Earth than for individual ecosystems."

Every year geochemists discover more vast changes in the workings of the seven spheres and try to figure out what it all means. Without disentangling cause and effect they cannot all agree that the changes are alarming. With the breathing of the world, these are a few of the possibilities:

GROWTH: The green plants of the biosphere *like* the extra carbon dioxide we are putting into the air. It gives them more raw material for photosynthesis. Each year the biosphere gets bigger. Because it is bigger it takes in more carbon dioxide. It inhales more and more deeply.

DECAY: The biosphere is decaying faster than before. There is more and more respiration each winter. Each year it exhales a little more. More and more of the stuff of life is unravelling and returning to the air.

GROWTH AND DECAY: Both may be accelerating. A bigger biosphere would be expected to inhale and exhale more deeply. Each summer there are more plants to inhale more gas; each winter there may be more plants and animals to devour and decompose the summer's fruits.

TIMING: Some say the change can't be explained with either growth or decay. The breathing of the world is changing too fast for that. Something else is going on. Houghton suggests that the build-up of carbon dioxide in the atmosphere may be altering the timing of either photosynthesis or respiration or both. If their work schedules are changing positions on the calendar that would also change the breathing of the world.

This change makes a sort of global Rorschach Test. Technological optimists tend to feel that Earth is breathing more deeply. The biosphere *likes* the extra carbon dioxide. Life on Earth is flourishing.

Technological pessimists tend to feel that life's breath is labored—each year more labored than the year before. The biosphere is getting out of breath. Earth is gasping.

Of course, for the occupants of an EcoSphere, any change this big should be cause for concern. And this is not the biggest change to be expected from the build-up of carbon dioxide. It is only among the first.

■ CHAPTER 4

ATROPOS

We have constructed a fate, an *Atropos,* that never turns aside. (Let that be the name of your engine.)

Henry David Thoreau
Walden

From near the summit of Mauna Loa, we can see that carbon dioxide is being released into the atmosphere in one long, titanic sigh. But we cannot see just where the gas is coming from. Which of the seven spheres is exhaling it? Surely not the Sun. Not ice. But is the gas rising from the lithosphere, the sphere of stone? The hydrosphere, the sphere of water? The biosphere, the sphere of life? Or the sphere of human affairs?

After Keeling had watched his curve rise for about ten years he did the logical thing. He went to the library and inspected the reports of the United Nations Statistical Office, which keeps track of the progress of all the member nations' economies. There, Keeling found detailed production reports of crude oil, natural gas, coal, lignite, coke, wood, and peat, compiled year by year for every country on Earth, from Afghanistan to the island then called Zanzibar.

Roger Revelle and others had studied the Statistical Office reports before Keeling, but no one had ever spent quite as much time and energy in what Keeling calls "morosing over the data." He figured out how much carbon there is per ton of each type of fuel. (Coal is about 70 percent carbon by weight, while methane—natural gas—is less than 50 percent.) He figured out how much of this carbon enters the air as carbon dioxide when the fuel is burned. He calculated what fraction of the fuel produced each year is burned in that year (most of it), and what fraction ends up as asphalt and lubricants that are not burned, and how much as waxes, paint solvents, and dry-cleaning fluids that are only burned occasionally. He included the tons of carbon dioxide that are released when cars are driven, when planes are flown, when lime is heated in the manufacture of cement.

Keeling also cross-checked and double-checked the accuracy of the numbers that had been reported to the United Nations in the first place. He discovered that some countries and some administrations make better reporters than others. With statistics from the People's Republic of China, for instance, data from 1958 to 1960 were associated with the Great Leap Forward, while those for 1967 to 1970 were associated with the Cultural Revolution. Keeling noticed that leaders of the Great Leap Forward were so committed to great leaps forward that they reported the production of whole mountains of coal that almost certainly did not exist.

Having sorted all this out, Keeling added up his figures for the year 1958, when he first began keeping track of the gas increases. In that single year, he calculated, the nations of the world had released approximately 2,294,000,000 metric tons of carbon into the atmosphere. In the next year, the world had released a few percent more carbon, and the year after, a few percent more again. In fact in every year from 1959 through the year of Keeling's report, 1972, the world released more carbon than the year before, an average rate of increase of 4 percent per year. (This extraordinary pace faltered during the oil crisis of the 1970s and early 1980s; but by the end of the 1980s, the rate of burning was on the increase again. Human beings are now releasing more than 5 billion tons of carbon into the air each year.)

Keeling also considered the 1860s, the days of his great-grandparents. That was the decade of the first practical internal-combustion engine, the first machine-driven refrigerator, the first open-hearth steel furnace. Those years saw the first Gatling gun, the cross-Atlantic cable, pasteurization, oil pipelines, dynamite, torpedoes, celluloid, bicycle races, the birth of the National Academy of Sciences, the Massachusetts Institute of Technology, and an infant named Henry Ford. Economic data for the 1860s are not as extensive as for modern times; on the other hand there is much less industry to keep track of. In 1860 the Industrial Revolution released about 93,000,000 tons of carbon into the air. Between 1860 and 1958, industry burned fossil fuels at a rate that doubled every two decades or so, injecting a total of more than 76 billion tons of carbon into the air.

To visualize all this, Keeling drew up a long scroll showing the rise of the gas injection rate since 1850. This mural now hangs in the corridor outside his office (the hallway where he assembled the gas analyzer bound for Mauna Loa). It is a panoramic time-line of the march of progress, as recorded in the most basic by-product of progress, carbon dioxide gas. The record shows an exponentially rising curve, in lock step with the rising curve of the human population. In one hundred years there had been only three hesitations in either rise. These hesitations occurred around the years 1915, 1930, and 1940: one world depression and two world wars. During the depression, millions of people were out of work; during the wars, millions of people died. The momentum of the rising lines is so great that these events appear only as three small dips. This is history without leaders or followers, saints or assassins, a completely unsentimental view of the twentieth century. Here our species is simply one planetary sphere influencing another, in a progress that would be visible to astronomers on Mars.

All this amounts to an astonishing geological event. We talk about the Industrial Revolution; this is an Industrial Eruption. The lithosphere's single biggest eruption in modern times was Mount Tambora in the Java Sea in 1815. One-third of a mountain 13,000 feet tall blasted into the air; stones "fell very thick" at Saugar, a town about twenty-five miles away, 100,000 people were killed, and the whole planet was so thickly shrouded in a debris of sulfuric droplets that Yankee farmers on the other side of the world suffered through "a Year without a Summer."

The volcanologist Haraldur Sigurdsson estimates that Tambora released somewhat less than one-tenth of a billion tons of carbon into the air. Each year, by burning fossil fuels, the human sphere is putting about as much carbon into the air as one hundred Tamboras. Indeed, human beings are injecting at least one hundred times more carbon dioxide gas each year than all the volcanoes of the world, on land or at the bottom of the sea.

The grand totals for fossil fuels: almost 80 billion tons of carbon went into the air between 1860 and 1960. Since 1960, another 80 billion tons, and counting. That is another one of the strange facts to emerge from these morose tabulations. It took one hundred years to release the first half of the fossil carbon.* It took less than thirty years to release as much again. Such is the power of an exponential rate of

---

*Actually, the first fossil fuels were burned long before that. The Chinese were mining and burning coal about two thousand years ago. The Burmese were drilling oil wells about one thousand years ago. Five hundred years ago the poor used to beg outside the doors of Scottish churches for lumps of coal for their stoves. (For that matter, human beings have been burning wood in caves and camps for more

increase, doubling over and over again. Though Keeling began watching from Mauna Loa only in 1959, almost two centuries after the start of the Industrial Revolution, he saw the gas from more than half the fossil fuel ever burned in all of human history. Put another way, anyone born in the years just after World War II—the Baby Boom—has witnessed more than one-half of the Industrial Eruption.

In a way it all started with the medical student Joseph Black back in 1754. His rediscovery of carbon dioxide brought Black celebrity, professorships, and assistants. One of his first assistants was a young man from Greenock named James Watt. Watt, after absorbing Black's ideas about gases and heat, developed into a master engineer (which originally meant engine-builder). He built engines that could burn coal to boil water to make steam to do work. These were not the world's first steam engines (the very first was a toy in ancient Greece) but Watt patented the first engine that could recycle the steam; then a double-acting engine; then a centrifugal "governor" with which an engine could regulate itself; and finally a steam engine locomotive.

Watt's engines were the genies of the Industrial Revolution. They helped to throw the human sphere into high gear. People began burning more coal and charcoal to fuel the engines and to smelt steel to make more engines. They kilned clamshells and limestone to make lime for concrete for more and more factories, cities, roads between cities. They built better engines that did more work and they fed them more coal, oil, and natural gas, in a crescendo of carbon dioxide that is still building today.

In effect, every human being on the planet is now shovelling one ton of carbon into the air each year. Americans are doing more than their share of the work: each American shovels about five tons of carbon each year, or five times the global average. The Swiss burn one quarter of that. The comparison is not quite fair because the United States' national average includes coal burned for purposes other than heating. The United States burns a large share of its coal to make steel, for example, whereas Swiss industry is mostly light—watches and pharmaceuticals. However, Americans living in Europe soon discover that one can get along on a quarter of the fuel they burn back home in the United States. It is not easy in Europe to find a hundred-

---

than one million years. As Loren Eiseley says, "Man is himself a flame.")

Nevertheless, the rate of burning of fossil fuels remained insignificant by modern standards, and it did not become a force for global environmental change until around 1860.

watt light bulb for a house, and one can find quite a few fifteen-watt bulbs.* Americans learning about wine are surprised to learn that when serving a red at room temperature, room temperature means about 50° F. (9° C.)—European room temperature. When Keeling visited Stockholm in 1961 to work with the operators of a Scandinavian carbon dioxide network, he asked for a space heater for his office. The next day the Norsemen laughed outside the doorway to see Keeling at work in his shirtsleeves, jacket draped over the back of a chair, with the heater on. "Look at that Yankee!"

The differences are even more striking between the Northern and Southern Hemispheres. About 90 percent of all fossil fuel is burned in the north. Because it takes a year or so for the air of the two hemispheres to exchange across the equator, the composition of air in the Northern Hemisphere is always laden with more carbon dioxide than the Southern. The air above the North Pole contains a few parts per million more carbon dioxide than the air above the South Pole.

The numbers from the United Nations and the numbers from Mauna Loa are evidence that dovetails. Enough carbon dioxide gas is coming from the human sphere to account for the change in our atmosphere.† World economy has infiltrated world ecology so intimately that we can gauge global industrial output equally well in the United Nations library in the middle of Manhattan, or in an observatory on the top of a volcano in the middle of the Pacific.

Without this shove from the human sphere, the pattern in Keeling's curve would be, on average, level. The breathing of Earth, the pulse of the planet, would trace a zig-zag pattern rather like the one in an electrocardiogram, oscillating up and down around a baseline of zero.

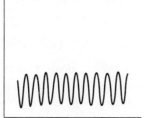

---

*A watt is a unit of power named in honor of James.

† In fact, more than enough—about twice as much gas as we need to explain the rise in the record. Scientists assume that the rest is being taken up by seas and forests, and they debate how much of the gas goes to each.

But we are steadily injecting extra carbon dioxide into the system. So we see a long slow rise superimposed upon the zig-zag, pushing it up and up, as in the Mauna Loa chart.

Not long ago a poet addressed the publishers of the world at a book fair in Turin, Italy. More than 50,000 books are published each year; and the poet Joseph Brodsky, winner of the 1987 Nobel Prize in Literature, waved his hand with European world-weariness at the long rows of book-lined stalls. "Since we are all moribund," he said, "and since reading books is time-consuming, we must devise a system that allows us a semblance of economy." He spoke of our need for "concision, condensation, fusion—for the works that bring the human predicament, in all its diversity, into the sharpest possible focus; in other words, the need for a shortcut." As a shortcut, the poet recommended the reading of poetry.*

The Mauna Loa record is a cosmic shortcut. The first line shows the balance of nature. The second line shows our species in the act of unbalancing nature. It also shows what has been called—until recently, without irony—the march of progress. Here, the sum of life on Earth; there, the sum of our impact upon life on Earth. These two lines bring the human predicament, in all its diversity, into the sharpest possible focus.

It gets worse. In the 1970s, while climate experts were worrying about carbon dioxide, a few investigators took a sharp look at other gases in the atmosphere. They realized that even rarer gases, measured in some cases in parts per *trillion,* can have powerful greenhouse effects. Now these gases, too, are monitored by the stations of the carbon-

---

*This trend, too, has been marching a long time. "As writers become more numerous, it is natural for readers to become more indolent," observed another poet, Oliver Goldsmith . . . in 1759.

dioxide networks. Their rise is being watched closely from the far north to the far south: from Point Barrow, Alaska; to Mauna Loa, Hawaii; to the South Pole.

The most notorious of these trace gases are the chlorofluorocarbons (CFCs). Unlike carbon dioxide, these are artificial compounds, which chemists make by linking chlorine and fluorine atoms together with atoms of carbon. The very names of these compounds suggest a certain amount of cobbling-together in the laboratory. The two most important chlorofluorocarbons are CFC-11 (trichlorofluoromethane) and CFC-12 (dichlorodifluoromethane). One of the world's biggest manufacturers, the E.I. du Pont de Nemours & Company, markets them under the name of Freons. They make extremely effective refrigerants, spray-can propellants, and foam-blowing agents. They also linger in the air a long time: for about 75 and 110 years, respectively.

CFCs 11 and 12 were developed in 1930 by Thomas Midgley, Jr., of the General Motors Research Laboratories. Midgley was one of the great chemical inventors of the twentieth century. He was the son of a prolific inventor (many patents on automobile tires) and a grandson of James Emerson, inventor of the inserted-tooth saw. When he was 33, Midgley (a bubbly man, known to friends as Midge) created the anti-knock agent tetraethyl lead, which vastly improved the performance of gasoline engines. That made him a golden boy at G.M., and the chief engineer in the Frigidaire Division asked him to find a new refrigerant, something nontoxic and nonflammable. Frigidaires used sulfur dioxide, which was dangerous. The competition was using ammonia, but an ammonia spill had just killed some people in a hospital in Cleveland.

Midgley immersed himself—as he wrote later—in "slide rules and log paper, eraser dirt and pencil shavings, all the rest of the paraphernalia that take the place of tea leaves and crystal spheres in the life of the scientific clairvoyant." Soon he was standing on a platform before "a distinguished and dignified audience" with a bell jar full of a brand-new gas, and a candle. Filling his lungs with the gas, he blew out a candle, thus demonstrating to the world with a single breath the perfect safety of Freons.

Midgley's compounds were so immediately useful that the air-conditioning business in the United States grew by sixteen times from 1930 to 1935. The chlorofluorocarbon industry just kept growing. In the 1960s production rates were increasing at a rate of about 20 percent a year.

A few chemists became alarmed about chlorofluorocarbons in the early 1970s. CFCs are nontoxic and nonflammable because they are so extremely stable, very reluctant to react with anything under the Sun, and this paradoxically is what proved dangerous. They stay in the air. Virtually nothing breaks them down but ultraviolet radiation, and there is not much ultraviolet radiation down here on the ground because it is blocked by the stratosphere (fortunately for the biosphere, whose compounds are also broken down by ultraviolet rays).

Over the decades these near immortal gases drift up from the troposphere and accumulate in the stratosphere. There, ultraviolet radiation from the Sun does strike them and breaks them apart into fragments. Intact the molecules are inert, but fragmented they are highly reactive. In a series of chemical reactions, the fragments attack and deplete the ozone in the stratosphere. The thinner the ozone layer gets the more ultraviolet radiation reaches the ground.

Despite a few chemists' warnings, the global manufacture of chlorofluorocarbons kept growing; and by the end of the 1980s, the early warnings had proven correct. Indeed even the doomsayers had underestimated the power of the chlorofluorocarbon fragments to eat ozone. An ozone hole the size of a continent appeared in the stratosphere above the South Pole. The inventory of ozone around the whole globe grew measurably thinner.

Notorious environmental crises, which are often reported separately in the newspapers, are in reality linked as tightly as the seven spheres. The ozone hole and the greenhouse effect are two faces of a single crisis. For chlorofluorocarbons are not only ozone-eaters but greenhouse gases. Even at concentrations of less than a part per billion, they capture a significant amount of heat and hold it in.

In fact, because of a quirk of nature, they have extraordinary power as greenhouse gases. The first atmospheric chemist to realize this fact was Veerabhadran Ramanathan, of the University of Chicago. The infrared rays that rise from sunbaked ground come in a range of wavelengths, and carbon dioxide molecules absorb most, but not all, of these wavelengths. There is a small window, as Ramanathan calls it, through which infrared rays can still escape.

In our atmosphere's present state of disturbance this tiny window has assumed as much importance as the last chink in the wall of a prison cell. For as it happens, CFCs absorb just those wavelengths. They are slowly closing the window.

Midgley's two inventions, CFC-11 and CFC-12, stood at only 220 and 380 parts per trillion in 1985. But because of this appalling ability to close the window, adding a single molecule of CFC-11 to the atmosphere today traps 17,500 times more heat than adding yet another molecule of carbon dioxide. A molecule of CFC-12 traps 20,000 times more heat than a molecule of carbon dioxide.

In September, 1987, at an historic international convention in Montreal, negotiators from most of the world's major industrial nations signed a treaty to slow down global chlorofluorocarbon production. However, more of the compounds are still being made. One year after the signing of the treaty, CFC-11 and CFC-12 were still accumulating at a rate of about 5 percent a year. CFC-113, which is the best solvent for cleaning computer microchips, was increasing at 11 percent a year. They were by far the fastest increasing of greenhouse gases (carbon dioxide is increasing at a little less than half a percent per year). And nothing can be done to remove the millions of tons already released into the atmosphere since 1930, including the Freon in the breath with which Midgley triumphantly blew out the candle. These chemicals will continue to drift into the stratosphere. They will go on eating ozone and magnifying the greenhouse effect for more than a century.

By 1989, the hundredth anniversary of his birth, Midgley's invention had stirred more than 16 million tons of CFCs into the atmosphere. His other great invention, tetraethyl lead (the antiknock agent) had raised the level of lead in the atmosphere so high that it was more than 200 times above normal in snows in the central icecaps of Antarctica and Greenland. But Midgley himself was spared any glimpse of the true nature of his legacy. He caught polio in young middle age. His legs were paralyzed, and he devised a clever harness with pulleys to get himself out of bed in the morning. Early in November of 1944 he got tangled in the harness and strangled to death. He died of his genius for benign invention.

At the funeral the minister read from the Bible, "We brought nothing into this world, and it is certain that we can carry nothing out." Driving home from the cemetery, Midgley's boss and mentor, Charles Kettering, remarked, "It struck me then that in Midge's case it would have been so appropriate to have added, 'but we can leave a lot behind for the good of the world.'"

Methane is also a greenhouse gas, and is also helping to dirty the all-important window. Adding one molecule of methane increases the greenhouse effect of Earth's atmosphere as much as adding twenty more molecules of carbon dioxide. If the atmosphere contained as much methane as it does carbon dioxide, the planet would be uninhabitable. Methane is sometimes called swamp gas, or marsh gas, because it is a by-product of decay. It is also called natural gas, because it seeps from the walls of coal mines, where it can be mined as a fossil fuel in its own right.

Methane's concentration is now growing at a rate of about 1 percent per year—twice as fast as carbon dioxide. Its concentration is now about 1.7 parts per million, which is already more than double the preindustrial level.

When methane drifts into the stratosphere it is broken down into carbon and hydrogen. The carbon atoms link up with oxygen to form carbon dioxide. The hydrogen links up with oxygen to form water vapor—which is normally extremely scarce in the stratosphere. Two more greenhouse gases.

What is worse, in the coldest parts of the stratosphere this water vapor tends to form tiny ice crystals. The ice crystals as they drift through the stratosphere collect the stray atoms of chlorine from the shattered chlorofluocarbons. Many chemical reactions are strongly promoted by the presence of solid surfaces, and a chlorine atom on the surface of this ice can eat many thousands of times more ozone than a chlorine atom adrift.

Methane watts up into the atmosphere at a rate of more than 500 million tons per year; and until modern times it was eliminated from the atmosphere just as quickly, so that the amount there stayed level. No one knows why it is rising so fast now. The gas seems to be erupting from the very top and the very bottom of the food chain. It is released by human beings at the top and by anaerobic bacteria at the bottom. We release it chiefly by mining pockets of natural gas and by burning petroleum; the bacteria release it by breaking down the decaying leaves and other organic litter and debris in swamps, marshes, and rice paddies.

These bacteria need water as shelter from the oxygen in the atmosphere, a deadly poison to them. Ralph Cicerone, chair of the Geosciences Department at the University of California, Irvine, has led a special study of rice paddies—which are expanding in step with the expanding human population. Cicerone says a rice plant is essentially a hollow tube sticking up out of soggy ground, and like a smokestack each tube sends invisible billows of methane gas rising into the air.

Anaerobic bacteria also hide out from oxygen inside animals. There are vast populations of them within the rumen of cattle, sheep, and goats, and in the guts of termites. There they digest cellulose—which the animals cannot do by themselves—and release methane as a waste product.

Cows belch about twice a minute, and put a few pounds of methane into the air every week. Thus, clearing a rain forest to make a cow pasture releases methane twice over. First the gas rises from the explosion of termites that eat the wood, then from the gassy herds that eat the grass.

Until recently the living arrangements of cows and their bacteria, one of the classic examples of symbiosis in nature, seemed completely harmless. Now with each passing year more people on the planet means more and more herds a-grazing and more and more methane.

Methane's rise is so inexplicably rapid (it is increasing by about 50 million tons a year) that there may well be other sources still undiscovered. Part of the problem may be that we are not only adding to the sources of methane but also taking away the sinks—the places where methane is destroyed. Since so much methane is produced each year, it would take only a small drop in the rate it is cleared from the air to cause the rise of the gas. Some invisible check or balance among the seven spheres may now be unchecked and out of balance.

Part of the problem may be carbon monoxide. This gas, too, has doubled since preindustrial times, and it is increasing at a rate of roughly 1 percent per year, on a global average. More than half the carbon monoxide in the air comes from human beings: from exhaust pipes and factory smokestacks in the Northern Hemisphere, and from the smoky fires in the damp forests of the tropics.

At high concentrations, carbon monoxide is poisonous, and it is a common choice for suicide in the twentieth century—automobile exhaust is loaded with carbon monoxide. A recent study in New York City found that men who work under the Hudson River inside the Holland Tunnel for ten years or more have been almost 90 percent more likely to die from heart disease than men in the general population, presumably because of carbon monoxide exposure.

The metabolism of the planet may be even more sensitive to this gas than the metabolism of a human being. Carbon monoxide prevents air from cleansing itself, and in doing so it may be clogging a pathway of exquisite importance to the stability of atmospheric chemistry.

Not all of the Sun's ultraviolet radiation is blocked by the ozone layer in the stratosphere. Some of it filters through, striking molecules of water vapor and methane and splitting them apart. One of the fragments is a highly reactive combination of atoms called hydroxyl, composed of a hydrogen atom and an oxygen atom. Hydroxyl is to the atmosphere what antibodies are to the immune system. It does not attack the major, stable components of the atmosphere, such as nitrogen, oxygen, and carbon dioxide. But it does attack methane and carbon monoxide. Hydroxyl helps to break down these trace gases into such stable compounds as carbon dioxide and water. Without hydroxyl the atmosphere would be poisonous with methane and carbon monoxide within a few millennia. Hydroxyl clears the air.

By putting more and more carbon monoxide into the air, we are overwhelming the atmosphere's immune system, exhausting the antibodies of the atmosphere. More and more hydroxyl is being used up in attacking and dismantling carbon monoxide. Because there is only so much hydroxyl to go around, methane is free to increase. The more methane there is in the air, the less hydroxyl—so carbon monoxide can increase faster, too. All this was worked out on paper by atmospheric chemists more than a decade ago, but it was dismissed as a paper tiger, according to Cicerone. "At the time," he says, "no one knew that methane was increasing, and we did not dream that it could increase as fast as it is now."

Here again, the lives of gases in the atmosphere are intertwined. Carbon monoxide has no direct greenhouse effect (it has only two atoms, and a greenhouse gas needs at least three). With carbon monoxide, the greenhouse effect is a side-effect.

Nitrous oxide, popularly known as laughing gas, is accumulating in the atmosphere, too. The concentration of this gas has now risen above 300 parts per billion, increasing by 2 percent per decade. "This rate may sound small," says Cicerone, "but it actually signals a large global perturbation, and one that has been sustained and growing since at least the early 1960s." It represents 5 million tons of extra nitrous oxide per year, about a quarter of the amount produced naturally by the biosphere.

Nitrogen molecules make up most of every breath we take and they are highly stable. It takes a lot of energy to break them apart and use them in living molecules—work that our lungs are not equipped to do. For this reason plants and animals are often starved or stunted for the lack of nitrogen—one of those cases of "water water everywhere but not a drop to drink." Only a few specialized soil bacteria are capable of pulling nitrogen out of the air. All plants get their nitrogen from these species of symbiotic bacteria, and all animals, including the human animal, get their nitrogen from the plants. Eventually still other species of bacteria, the decay experts, return the borrowed nitrogen to the air.

It is rare that a link between the spheres is so small and specific. Here is an element that fills the bulk of the atmosphere and is needed desperately by the entire biosphere, and virtually the only connection between the two spheres is the microscopic bacterium.

Human beings are now improving the nitrogen cycle with a broad brush, making global adjustments at least as dramatic as in the carbon cycle. In 1950, for instance, about 3 million tons of artificial nitrogen fertilizers were being produced each year and spread on farmers' fields. Now the annual total is more than 50 million tons. This and other abrupt agricultural advances are changing the nitrogen cycle in ways no one has begun to understand.

In addition, burning fossil fuels produces not only carbon monoxide and carbon dioxide but also compounds of nitrogen and oxygen. Nitric oxide (NO) has one atom of nitrogen, one of oxygen; nitrous oxide (N_2O) has two atoms of nitrogen, one of oxygen.

Nitric oxide is implicated in a host of environmental problems, including smog, acid rain, and water pollution. Nitrous oxide (with three atoms) has a greenhouse effect. One molecule of this gas is equal to about 250 molecules of carbon dioxide. (This gas also lasts and lasts. The average molecule of nitrous oxide lingers in the atmosphere for about 125 years.)

It is amazing that chemicals measured in parts per million, billion, or trillion, should matter to a planet. Yet, together with carbon dioxide, all these trace gases will shape Earth's next one hundred years and beyond. We are turning up the planet's thermostat a little more each year, committing the planet to a higher and higher temperature. And this year, nearly half of the twist we give to the thermostat will come from gases other than carbon dioxide.

It gets worse yet. Our contributions to the greenhouse effect are built on top of an earlier contribution at least as massive and spectacular. "Building castles in the air." It is as if we are stacking a new city upon the ruins of a previous city, whose existence we have forgotten.

Europe's population doubled between 1750 and 1850, thanks to advances in medicine, industry, intensive large-scale scientific farming, sanitation, and the end of great plagues. By the first half of the nineteenth century, the population increase had produced enormous pressures, political and economic. Historians debate the various pushes and pulls within the various European powers, but in the global view the population of the continent simply exploded across the face of the Earth. In the first three-quarters of the nineteenth century, colonial powers claimed new territories at a rate of more than 80,000 square miles per year. During the last two decades of the nineteenth century and the first two of the twentieth, they claimed almost 250,000 square miles a year. By 1914, according to *Encyclopaedia Britannica,* "the colonial powers, their colonies and their former colonies extended over approximately 85 percent of the Earth's surface."

Tens of millions of people poured out of Europe: English farmers and house-painters, potters and convicts, Welsh tinplaters, Scottish miners, Italian quarrymen and street acrobats, Irish laborers, Bavarian spinners, Prussian glassworkers, Russian Jewish tailors. Whole villages transplanted themselves over the ocean, hopping in the course of a few generations from the Scottish Highlands to Upper Canada, from the Rhineland to Wisconsin, from Calabria to São Paolo, from Kristiania to Montana.

They settled not only in North and South America but also in Australia, New Zealand, the Indus Valley, Siberia, Inner Mongolia, and Manchukuo. Thirty-three million of them arrived in the U.S. between 1821 and 1924.

Most of the emigrants were young and they not only started families but also brought with them the advances in medicine, industry, intensive farming, and sanitation that had made possible the European population explosions. So they set off more explosions wherever they went—explosions that are still in progress today, though population growth has meanwhile leveled off in Europe itself. The human population of the globe has tripled since 1850, notes Roger Revelle, who has made himself an expert on population growth as well as carbon-dioxide growth; and this rise was "probably accompanied by a roughly equivalent increase in the areas of agricultural land, in part at the expense of forested areas."

In other words the explosion of Europe levelled forests around the world. By 1820 there were more than a thousand ships engaged full time in carrying timber from North America to the British Isles. By 1840 there were more than two thousand ships. (These shipowners did their share to spur the wave of emigration because they wanted cargo in their empty ships on the way back. Human cargo filled them.) Europe needed timber for firewood, charcoal, and mine props; for houses, limekilns, and smelters; for the masts, spars, and beams of more ships. Woodsmen marched west from New York in 1850, to Michigan in 1870, to Wisconsin in 1880, and Minnesota in 1890. Often they cleared as much as 90 percent of the trees in a forest, white pine, yellow birch, hemlock, maple, oak. Great fires broke out in the slash, leaving the vast desolate "barrens" of Michigan and Wisconsin.

They cut down trees to make ties for the rails for the steam engines, and to make farms for the families who crossed the continents pulled by the steam engines. In 1845, Henry David Thoreau doubted that there was a spot in Massachusetts where one could not hear a train whistle. He bought the boards for his cabin from an Irish railroad man on the Fitchburg line. The Fitchburg trains passed Walden Pond about a hundred rods south of his cabin.

Railroads carried waves and waves of immigrants westward and advertised for more. The historian Maldwyn Allen Jones reports that in the railroads' heyday, the 1870s and 1880s, the Northern Pacific, Burlington and Missouri, Santa Fe, and Southern Pacific each had its own land and immigration departments. Some railroad companies offered to teach settlers how to farm the plains. Some offered free "land-exploring" tickets. Others offered to build churches and schools for new towns. In 1872 the U.S. had 61,000 miles of railroads, and about 15,000 acres of prime woodland were cut down in that year alone for more railroad ties.

"Here goes lumber from the Maine woods," Thoreau wrote; ". . . pine, spruce, cedar,—first, second, third, and fourth qualities, so lately all of one quality, to wave over the bear, and moose, and caribou." It was on its way into houses, fences, barns, and outhouses. In *The Earth as Modified by Human Action,* in 1874, George Marsh—the first American conservationist—reported that more than 100,000 young evergreen trees were sold at Christmas in New York City in 1869, "besides 20,000 yards of small branches twisted into festoons." Tracts of pine forest "hundreds and even thousands of acres in extent" were felled to supply clear knotless wood for "lucifer matches."

> If we add to all this the supply of wood for telegraph-posts, wooden pavements, wooden wall tapestry-paper, shoepegs, and even wooden nails, which have lately come into use—not to speak of numerous other recent applications of this material which American ingenuity has devised—we have an amount of consumption, for entirely new purposes, which is really appalling.

Even in those days Americans were out-burning Europeans:

> For instance, in rural Switzerland, as cold as is the winter climate, the whole supply of wood for domestic fires, dairies, breweries, distilleries, brick and limekilns, fences, furniture, tools, and even house-building and small smitheries . . . does not exceed *two hundred and thirty cubic feet*, or less than two cords a year, per household. . . .
>
> The report of the Commissioners on the Forests of Wisconsin, 1867, allows three cords of wood to each person for household fires alone. Taking families at an average of five persons, we have eight times the amount consumed by an equal number of persons in Switzerland for this and all other purposes to which this material is ordinarily applicable. I do not think the consumption in the Northeastern States is at all less than the calculation for Wisconsin.

All this burning changed the face of the biosphere. According to the botanist John T. Curtis, the American pioneers took vast tracts of "an essentially continuous forest cover" with scattered meadows, and converted them into an essentially continuous grassland with scattered trees. This was the end of the line for many natives, including Indian tribes and indigenous plants and animals. It was not good for the soil exposed by the razing of the woods, which often became "unstable and frequently devoid of plant cover as a result of regular plowing" (in the nineteenth century)—or as a result of the asphalt of city streets and parking lots (in the twentieth century).

The burning also changed the atmosphere, because in every ecosystem, trees represent carbon that the biosphere has borrowed from the atmosphere and is holding on to—an old oak has held on to much of its carbon for more than one hundred years. Whenever human beings thin out the biosphere, replacing an ecosystem that is dense with carbon with an ecosystem that is lighter in carbon, they put a bald spot in the biosphere and put carbon dioxide into the air.

In an unbroken forest, plants hold an average of anywhere between four and twenty-five kilograms of carbon in *each square meter*—a plot the size of a coffee table. In an interrupted forest, one that has been infiltrated by roads and houses, plants hold three to six kilograms of carbon. In land that is cropped, residential, or commercial, plants hold even less: for instance a forest contains ten to twenty times more carbon per square meter than a field of wheat. Forest floors also contain a great deal of carbon in leaf and pine-needle litter and in what the ecologist Aldo Leopold called "the accumulated wisdom of the duff."

Much of this carbon rises into the air after the forest is cleared or disturbed.

When a tree falls in the forest it may or may not make a sound, but it does make a contribution to the greenhouse effect.* Indeed the fall of each tree contributes a small legacy to the greenhouse effect year after year in perpetuity, because the tree no longer draws down more carbon dioxide each spring and summer as part of the breathing of the world.

So the pilgrims' progress of the nineteenth century had a greenhouse effect. Alex T. Wilson, a New Zealand geochemist, calls this episode in the life of the planet "the pioneer explosion," because the change was "almost synchronous all over the world," and led to the release into the atmosphere of enormous quantities of carbon dioxide. Wilson and others can see all this carbon dioxide indirectly in the rings of trees one and two hundred years old. The extra carbon dioxide injected into the air around the world produced measurable changes in the ratios of the carbon isotopes of the nineteenth century atmosphere. This change in the air has left a progressive "signature" of the pioneer explosion in the isotopes in old tree rings.

Wilson calls the pioneer explosion "the first and perhaps the most significant of mankind's assaults on our environment at the global level." By 1850, it may have been dumping about half a billion tons of carbon into the atmosphere each year. Cumulatively, it may have yielded more carbon than the grand total from the burning of fossil fuels.

The troposphere is the lowest layer of air, the one that lies in contact with the ground; the layer we breathe, the layer of all our weather and climate. The name comes from the Greek *tropos,* turning; and, true to its name, the troposphere takes a million twists and turns. All that carbon began putting a new spin on the troposphere some decades before Arrhenius first dreamed of the greenhouse effect. We were already on a collision course with the weather and climate of the world.

Today the Pioneer Explosion has entered its second phase. There

---

*Of course some of the timber that was cleared in the great pioneer rush was used in church steeples, ship's masts, and Swiss chalet shingles that have lasted to this day. But not the Christmas trees or the lucifer matches or even most houses. As Keeling says, "There's got to be darn little lumber that lasts 50 years before it's turned back into CO_2."

are population explosions in the last forested areas of the world—the hot tropical forests that were until now too forbidding for much development. Brazil, Indonesia, Colombia, the Ivory Coast, Thailand, Laos, Nigeria, the Philippines, Burma, Malaysia, Peru, and Vietnam are experiencing explosive deforestation. In Brazil the story of the United States' pioneer days is being played out to the last detail, complete with unequal fights with Indian tribes, gold rushes, murders, ruinous land-clearing leading to soil erosion and badlands, and the threat of new Dust Bowls. The citizens of São Paolo read Bang-Bangs, pulp westerns about pioneers and Indians in the Amazon. Once again, Indian tribal leaders are travelling to big cities—São Paolo, New York—in company of explorers who have befriended them, to plead for their land. Again great economic powers are busily importing fresh timber. The world's biggest importer is Japan, and recently the Japanese opened negotiations with politicians about another remote corner of the Amazon.

Like the first pioneer explosion this one straddles the turn of a century—the last decades of the twentieth and the first decades of the twenty-first. It may run until all but a few last stands of rain forest are gone. Each year it contributes to the atmosphere about 2 billion tons of carbon. In terms of carbon, what is happening in the tropics today is about twice as big as the first Pioneer Explosion.

When Thoreau watched the Fitchburg steam engine roll by Walden Pond "with its train of cars moving off with planetary motion," he was reminded of the three sister Fates of the ancient Greeks. The first Fate spun the thread of life; the second cast the lots that set each mortal's destiny. The third sister was Atropos, whose name means "not to be turned." Atropos held the shears that cut the thread of life.

Thoreau knew that a new force of nature was at work. He wrote, "We have constructed a fate, an *Atropos,* that never turns aside. (Let that be the name of your engine.)"

■ CHAPTER 5

A
SLOW EUREKA

Omens were as nothing to him, and he was unable
to discover the message of prophecy till the fulfillment had brought it home to his very door.

Joseph Conrad
Typhoon

It is astonishing to go back and reread what people thought about the
greenhouse effect in the beginning. In his popular book *Worlds in the
Making,* in 1906, the Swedish chemist Arrhenius actually welcomed
the heat. "By the influence of the increasing percentage of carbonic
acid [carbon dioxide] in the atmosphere," he wrote, "we may hope to
enjoy ages with more equable and better climates, especially as regards the colder regions of the Earth. . . ."

In a paper, in 1938 (once obscure, now often-cited), the British engineer George Callendar announced that Earth's temperature was already rising. Almost nobody ever cites Callendar's conclusion: he
declared that the carbon dioxide we were putting into the air would not
only improve the world's climate but would fertilize every farmer's
crops. "In any case," noted Callendar, "the return of the deadly
glaciers should be delayed indefinitely."

In 1957, Revelle and Suess published the famous lines from which I
have already quoted. "Human beings are now carrying out a large-scale
geophysical experiment of a kind that could not have happened in the
past, nor be repeated in the future," wrote Revelle and Suess. "This
experiment," they added, "if adequately documented, may yield a far-
reaching insight into the processes determining weather and climate."

Today these are commonly cited as words of warning. One writer characterized them recently as "morbid understatement." Knowing what we do now, it is hard for us to read them any other way. But the words on the page are neutral at best, and Revelle himself acknowledges that when he wrote them he was not really worried about the greenhouse. He thought of it mainly in a spirit of scientific enthusiasm. He and Suess were pleased to have this experiment in progress in their lifetimes. They thought it would be very interesting to watch.

As for Keeling, in the 1960s, people walking down the hall at Scripps used to look into his office and see him laboriously wrapping glass globes. "What are you doing that for?" they would ask.

"To collect air at the South Pole."

"Why?"

"You mean, what does it mean for the man on the street?" Keeling would reply, irritably. In other words, the subject meant absolutely nothing for the man on the street.

We have known about this thing a very long time, but we have understood it a very short time. From Arrhenius on, people simply did not know what they were looking at. Nor was there any single moment when everyone cried "Eureka!" There was only what one student of the greenhouse calls "the evolution of an awareness."

In the 1960s, for example, new tools allowed scientists to begin to test Arrhenius's hypothesis. The first electronic computer was built during World War II. By the early 1960s, computers were sophisticated and reliable enough to help climate experts analyze the immensely complicated mechanisms that determine the world's weather.

Arrhenius had estimated how much warming the planet could expect from the greenhouse effect, latitude by latitude. He had included this table of predictions in the *Philosophical Magazine* of April, 1896. It was a remarkable forecast, considering that it was the first one, and took the whole song from the top. Arrhenius began by estimating the concentration of water vapor and carbon dioxide in the atmosphere.* He explained step by step the physical mechanism by which these gases warm the air.

---

*He based these estimates on an American astronomer's observations of moonrise. Samuel Langley had measured the infrared radiation from the full moon as it rose above Lone Pine, Colorado. Using Langley's tables, Arrhenius was able to estimate how much infrared radiation the Earth's atmosphere absorbs, and therefore how much greenhouse gas was in the air. (Already the greenhouse was interdisciplinary and international.)

He even tried to take into account what we now call feedback. He observed that as the planet warms up, a great deal of ice and snow near the poles will probably start to melt. That will expose dark tundra and dark seas. That will warm things up—like painting a white roof black. The darker the terrain gets, the warmer those parts of the world will get. More snow will melt there, making the terrain even hotter . . . and so on.

All these explanations fill more than thirty pages of rather small print in the *Philosophical Magazine,* and every one of the calculations had to be solved by hand. At last comes Arrhenius's table of predictions. According to Arrhenius, if the concentration of carbon dioxide in the atmosphere doubles, the average temperature of the planet Earth will rise between 5° and 6° C. (between 9° and 11° F.)

In the 1960s, climate experts began reworking this forecast using computers. One of the first serious analyses was published by Syukuro Manabe and Richard Wetherald, of the Geophysical Fluid Dynamics Laboratory, in Princeton, New Jersey, in 1967. As more and more scientists grew computer-literate, and as many of them grew interested in the greenhouse effect, this work ultimately became one of the hottest subspecialties in science. The use of computers helped investigators to think things through at a level of detail that Arrhenius would have found fantastic.

To make a greenhouse forecast, experts now build what amounts to a working scale model of the Earth inside a supercomputer. They start with a blank globe, divided into a grid like the grid of latitude and longitude. Typically each box in the grid covers several hundred miles on a side. These boxes are stacked from the surface of the planet high into the atmosphere—a dozen layers of giant boxes of air.

On the surface of this blank globe the modelers draw a map of the world, including the world's greatest lakes, rivers, and mountain ranges. Then they tell the computer the physical rules that govern the motions of air masses: hot air rises; cold air sinks; for every action there is an equal and opposite reaction . . . and so forth. (Most of the rules are simple—a mathematician can write them on the back of an envelope.) Then the investigators program a computer to employ these rules to calculate the weather within each box of the grid, from the bottom to the top of the atmosphere, always taking into account how the weather in each box will affect that of its neighbors.

The four most sophisticated of these global circulation models, or G.C.M.s, are housed at the British Meteorological Office headquarters at Bracknell, outside London; the National Center for Atmospheric Research, in Boulder, Colorado; the Goddard Institute for Space Studies, in New York; and the Geophysical Fluid Dynamics Laboratory, in Princeton, New Jersey.

When you turn on one of their model Earths, and let it spin, somewhere within the silicon circuits of the supercomputer a shining Sun begins to rise and set. Winds rise and die. Jet streams wriggle west at 30,000 feet. If you run the model long enough, summer turns to fall, the Sun arcs lower in the sky, ice films the Arctic Ocean, blizzards fall in Kamchatka and Ontario. From a few simple rules in a digital code of 0's and 1's the computer evolves something like the weather on the planet Earth.

National weather forecasters use models like these. Meteorologists collect masses of data from weather stations and weather satellites. Then they let their model Earth spin the weather one day ahead. The world's fastest supercomputers can make a billion calculations per second, but weather is so complicated that even at that blinding speed the calculation of tomorrow's weather takes the supercomputer about half an hour in real time. During that half an hour, cold fronts and warm fronts migrate across the face of the model globe—in jerky, old-home-movie steps—to the positions that they *may* occupy tomorrow.

Climate is a different problem, in some ways easier. Climate is *average* weather. More precisely, climate is the average weather that a given spot on the planet can expect to receive during a typical spring, summer, fall, and winter. Weather is a surprise downpour in Allentown, Pennsylvania on Wednesday at 12:08 P.M.; but climate is the number of inches in the Lehigh Valley in the average April. Weather is the path of a single storm; climate is the storm track that has been beaten across a corner of a continent by a million storms, like the path that generations of students' feet wear in the corner of a college green.

The life of an individual is unpredictable, but the life of a million individuals is statistically quite predictable. That is why physicists can foretell the behavior of gases made up of swarms of individually unpredictable molecules; and why insurance companies have the money to build monumental offices in the world's major cities.

For climate studies, modelers simplify their twin Earth and then let it spin for the equivalent of decades, centuries, even millennia, taking seasonal averages for each spot on Earth. The results are a fair approximation of the climate of the real world. The models reproduce the broad-brush features of each continent in all four seasons. They are not yet able to discriminate details like counties or congressional districts: anything much smaller than a continent has to be considered a detail.

Prediction comes from the Latin for "telling ahead." *Prophecy* comes from the Greek for "ahead of fate." In Japanese the word is *ura* or *uranai,* "that which is behind, and hence invisible." Sometimes (but not always) computer models can help us to tell ahead, get ahead of fate, see the invisible. Over and over again, in Bracknell, Boulder, Princeton, and New York, modelers have been running the same experiment with their toy worlds that the human race is now performing with the planet. The modelers inject an extra 300 parts per million of carbon dioxide into the atmosphere, crank up the model, let it run, and watch what happens. And in each of these Earths, after the injection of carbon dioxide, the surface temperature of the planet begins to climb, slowly at first, then faster and faster.

Of course, as one modeler says, these are only "dirty crystal balls." The actual rate at which temperatures will climb is uncertain. The height the mercury will reach at each spot on Earth is uncertain. The height the global temperature will ultimately reach is considered to be certain only plus or minus 50 percent.

Nevertheless, the *average* temperature of the surface of the planet rises between 2° and 6° C. (between 3.5 and 11° F.), which is about what Arrhenius predicted in 1896.

In the 1960s, while climate experts were making their first computer simulations, astronomers discovered that the night sky holds two real-life demonstrations of the power of the greenhouse effect. One is Venus, and the other is Mars.

These planets formed at about the same time as Earth did, about four and a half billion years ago. They hold roughly the same constituent elements as Earth. They orbit at similar distances from the Sun— neither very far out, like Pluto, nor very far in, like Mercury. Venus and Earth are about the same size; Mars is somewhat smaller.

Yet despite these strong family resemblances, the three worlds have travelled parting roads. Astronomers found that out in the 1960s and 1970s, through a series of microwave observations they made from Earth, and through a series of space probes that visited the planets.

The surface of Venus is as hot as a self-cleaning oven, about 450° C.

(840° F.), day and night, all year round, from the equator to the poles. Any water that may have existed at one time on Venus has long since boiled away.

Mars, on the other hand, is colder than Antarctica year round, from the poles to the equator. Any water there is locked below the surface in permafrost.

One cannot explain these extreme differences in temperature in terms of distance from the Sun. It is true that Venus is the closest, at 67 million miles (108 million kilometers); then Earth, 93 million miles (150 million kilometers); then Mars, 173 million miles (228 million kilometers). Distance alone would indeed act to make Venus warmer, Earth milder, Mars colder, like three campers sitting ten, fifteen, and twenty feet from a big fire. But the effect of distance on temperature can be calculated with precision, and it is not nearly strong enough by itself to make Venus a hothouse or Mars an icehouse. This is sometimes called the Goldilocks problem: Why is Venus too hot, Mars too cold, and Earth just right?

The significant point is what the three worlds have done with their carbon. They are all endowed with roughly the same amount. But most of the carbon on Earth is locked up in sediments and rocks. It is stowed safely beneath our feet, where it has no greenhouse effect. On Venus, most of the carbon somehow got out. It escaped. The Venusian atmosphere holds 350,000 times as much carbon as Earth's. That is so much carbon that it makes Venus unliveable by its weight alone. Carbon dioxide bears down upon the planet's surface with one hundred times the pressure of Earth's entire atmosphere. At that pressure, the air is so thick and soupy that even the mildest breeze has the force of a hurricane. Soviet engineers had to make their Venera robot explorers as sturdy as submarines, because landing on Venus is the equivalent of submerging more than half a mile beneath the sea on Earth.

Venus is cloud-wrapped, and very little sunlight penetrates to the surface. The ground is in such deep shadow that its temperature should be below freezing. Yet Venus's massive supply of carbon dioxide keeps the surface temperature not only above the freezing point but above the boiling point—hot enough to melt lead.* From Earth, with

---

*The greenhouse effect on Venus not only prevents the evolution of life. It even stifles the evolution of the lithosphere, the planet's solid crust.

On Earth, big broken pieces of lithosphere, called plates, are forever sliding down into the depths of the planet in some places and rising out of the depths in others. Their motion is part of a pattern of convection resembling the churning of a

the naked eye, the Evening Star looks cool and beautiful (hence the name Venus). Up close it is an inferno.

Mars is the negative of Venus. Its atmosphere is a hundred times thinner than Earth's, and it is ten thousand times thinner than Venus's. Virtually all its carbon is locked away in sediments. For lack of a strong greenhouse effect, the Martian surface is frozen stiff.

Once Mars was probably livelier. There are carvings in its frozen terrain that look very much like dry riverbeds. There are also numerous extinct volcanoes. When they were still alive and fuming, they may have released enough carbon dioxide to build up an atmosphere one hundred times thicker than the one it has now—as thick as Earth's. Thus Mars may once have had a stronger greenhouse effect and a climate as temperate as ours, complete with rain and running water (and perhaps primitive life).

The planet's color is red and fiery (hence the name Mars) but it is so cold that water cannot melt, not even in summer, not even at the equator. Winters are so bitter that some of the Martian atmosphere freezes to the ground.*

These contrasts are so striking that space scientists make an allegory of the three planets, much as ancient astronomers used to do. They speak of Venus and Mars as warnings, object lessons for the human race. Venus: four hundred times our greenhouse warming; an oven. Mars: less than half our greenhouse warming; a freezer. If Earth had as much carbon in the air as Venus does, our oceans would boil away. If Earth had as little carbon in the air as Mars does, our oceans would be a solid mass of ice. Clearly for planetary good housekeeping we should watch where we put our carbon.

Generations of children have made a wish upon the first star they saw in the night sky—more often than not the Evening Star, Venus.

---

pot of boiling water (and it is driven by the same forces: hot stone rises and cold stone sinks). The churning of the planet is measured in the tens of millions of years. One superficial consequence is the drifting of continents across the surface. The phenomenon is known as plate tectonics.

On Venus, by contrast, the surface is too hot to sink. "From Venus," writes the geophysicist Don Anderson of Caltech, "we have learned that a thick atmosphere and greenhouse heating can heat the surface to the point where it remains buoyant, preventing the foundering and sinking of the crust."

If Earth had a greenhouse effect that powerful, our planet would be dead. There would be no biosphere, no hydrosphere, no cryosphere, and no noosphere; and in the lithosphere, the very continents would stop drifting.

*It forms dry ice: frozen carbon dioxide.

All these generations, working toward their wishes, are making this world a little more like Venus.

These space studies not only supported the greenhouse theory. They showed that in extreme cases the greenhouse effect can be a matter of life and death. The climate experts William Kellogg and James Hansen and the astronomer Carl Sagan were among the first scientists to look into the Venusian inferno. Each of them later became outspoken about the greenhouse effect on Earth. In part they were radicalized by Venus.

In the 1980s another evidence was uncovered in Earth's icecaps, after a long search that began in the I.G.Y. During that great year of exploration a team of American ice experts drilled more than a thousand feet down into an ice sheet in northwestern Greenland. The team managed to extract the ice from the hole. They cut it up into short, gleaming cylinders, which they called ice-cores (the ice from the core of the hole).

The drilling team shipped some ice to laboratories for analysis. There, geochemists immediately discovered that an ice sheet is arranged in geological layers, rather like the mud on the floor of a lake, or the silt and stone at the bottom of the sea. The layers are very young near the surface and grow progressively older in the depths. Many of the annual layers are quite distinct (although the demarcations are usually chemical rather than visible to the eye). Using chemical and isotopic markers it is possible to count backward through the years, as with tree rings.

The layers turned out to go a long way back. Near the bottom of the ice sheets in Greenland and Antarctica, thousands of feet down, there is ice that first fell as snow approximately half a million years ago.

At first, the ice-drillers were just trying to find out more about ice. However, the seven spheres of the Earth are so interlinked that examining any one of them can lead to revelations about all seven. On careful analysis, the icecaps turned out to hold traces of everything from the sudden brightening and dimming of the Sun to the prehistoric eruptions of volcanoes. Traces of a strong volcanic eruption show up in the ice around the year 1645 B.C. At about that time, the volcano Thera, or Santorini, exploding in the Aegean Sea, may have wiped out Minoan civilization and started the legend of Atlantis.

The ice also showed how much the human presence is changing the atmosphere. Consider, for instance, the amount of lead in the air we breathe. Not very long ago there were experts who argued that most of this lead is natural and comes from volcanoes, sea spray, and soil dust. Then Claude F. Boutron, an ice expert in Grenoble, and Clair C. Patterson, an American geochemist at Caltech, looked back through the past 27,000 years of ice layers. They found that the amount of lead in snow in Antarctica and Greenland is 200 times what it was in prehistoric times. "Our results," write Boutron and Patterson, "establish that more than 99 percent of the lead now in the troposphere of the Northern Hemisphere originates from human activities."

Ice also showed how fast the acidity of precipitation is increasing. A team lead by Paul Mayewski of the University of New Hampshire and Willi Dansgaard of Copenhagen analyzed an ice-core from south Greenland, covering the years 1869 to 1984. They found that the sulfate concentration has tripled since around 1900. The nitrate concentration has doubled since around 1955.

These changes are attributable to human activities, as is the radioactivity of the youngest layers of the cores. Those layers are marked clearly by the radioactivity that fell out from the nuclear test explosions that were conducted in the open air in the 1950s.

But the most dramatic story in the ice is about carbon dioxide. The ice holds an abundance of bubbles the size of seltzer fizz, and each bubble holds a sample of Earth's atmosphere that has been hermetically sealed and preserved for decades, centuries, or millennia. (In fact, about 10 percent of the volume of every glacier is trapped air.) Anthropologists have bones; geologists have rocks and fossils; archaeologists have pots, pyramids, and papyruses. As early as the 1960s, ice drillers realized that they had uncovered a mother lode of comparable value for climate experts. They had found fossil air. If they could crack open the tiny bubbles and analyze the gases trapped inside they could find out what Earth's atmosphere was like in prehistoric times.

Among other things, that would settle a nagging question. Thanks to Keeling, people knew that carbon dioxide gas was accumulating in the air *now*. But without a sample of fossil air, no one really knew how much carbon dioxide was in the atmosphere before the Industrial Revolution. No one even knew for sure what was in the air before Keeling started his global network. This uncertainty clouded the whole subject.

Throughout the 1960s and 1970s, competing teams run by Hans

Oeschger, of the University of Bern; Claude Lorius, in Grenoble; and others, perforated the ice sheets of Greenland, Antarctica, and the Alps. They published dozens of technical papers and they amassed a collection of ice-cores more than six miles long. Most of this ice is now stored in the ten-story freezer plant of the Buffalo Refrigerating Company in Buffalo, New York. (Scientists rent space on the company's best floor, the second, where the lobsters are stored.)

By the early 1980s the Bern group had found a reliable technique for analyzing the air in the bubbles. First they would cut an ice-core into samples about the size of gaming dice. In the laboratory, they would pick up a cube with tongs, drop it into a vacuum chamber known as "the cracker," seal the chamber, and pump out all the air. At the flick of a switch, steel needles would press through a grid in the chamber like a diabolical trap in *Raiders of the Lost Ark*. The ice cube was instantaneously crushed to bits. Air escaped in a single rush and was sucked into a tube. There a laser shot a beam of infrared light through the sample, measuring how much carbon dioxide they had in the chamber. The scientists repeated the process a few times and took an average reading.

Only one-tenth of the volume of each ice cube is air. Of this air, only about one three-thousandth is carbon dioxide. To compare the amount of carbon dioxide in this old air with the amount of carbon dioxide in modern air, the scientists must measure this pinch of a pinch of colorless, odorless, tasteless gas with an accuracy of a few parts per million. "So you have to be rather sensitive," says a physicist in the Swiss group.

While they were perfecting this elaborate laboratory technique, a team of American and Swiss air hunters drilled a core at Siple Station in West Antarctica, where the snow layers of the past several centuries are unusually regular and distinct. Analyzing the air in the ice with the help of the cracker and the laser, ice-core experts could sketch the story of the gas for the last 250 years.

In the early 1700s, the gas level stood at about 280 parts per million. It began rising in the mid-1700s, soon after Watt built his first steam engine. It was pushed up in the 1800s by all the burning forests and felled timber of the Pioneer Explosion. By 1958, it had risen to about 315 parts per million. The story of the gas from 1734 to 1958 looks like this:

The year 1958 in this record in the ice is like the golden spike that connects two railway lines built toward each other from opposite coasts. For the number the drillers found in the ice for that year matches Keeling's number for that year. The two lines of evidence link up. Adding Keeling's record, the story of the last 250 years looks like this:

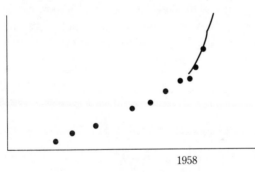

1958

A much older ice-core was drilled by Russian scientists and technicians at Vostok Station, in East Antarctica, the coldest place on Earth. In the 1980s, the Grenoble group began analyzing this core, which is more than one mile long. It goes back all the way through the Holocene, the warm period in which we live today, to the most recent ice age. It goes all the way through that ice age to the warm period before. It goes through that to the penultimate ice age, 160,000 years ago. In the mid-1980s the French group published a record of the carbon dioxide concentration in the atmosphere for the whole length of this core: probably the single most important piece of greenhouse evidence besides Keeling's curve.

It would have meant a great deal to Arrhenius to have seen those results. To him, the prospect of global warming seemed so benign and remote that he found it necessary to apologize to his readers for going on about it in the pages of the *Philosophical Magazine.* "I should certainly not have undertaken these tedious calculations if an extraordinary interest had not been connected with them," Arrhenius wrote. And what was this extraordinary interest?

> In the Physical Society of Stockholm, there have been occasionally very lively discussions on the probable cause of the Ice Age; and these discussions have, in my opinion, led to the conclusion that there exists as yet no satisfactory hypothesis. . . .

That is what excited Arrhenius, and the British physicist Tyndall, and the American geologist Thomas Chamberlin. As I have mentioned, they suspected that a drop in carbon dioxide levels some tens of thousands of years ago might have caused the last ice age.

The ice-core from Vostok proves that the amount of carbon dioxide in the air plummets with each ice age, and shoots up as the ice age begins to break up. In warm times on the planet there are between 260 and 280 parts per million. In cold times, there are between 190 and 200. It is a millennial roller coaster:

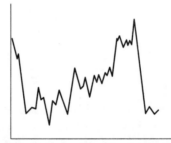

No one knows what drove carbon dioxide up and down before human beings got into the act. Here, cause and effect are still shrouded in mystery. Sometimes the gas seems to have changed first, and sometimes the world's temperature changed first. Does the ice react to the change in the gas, or does the gas react to the change in the ice? Either way, the Vostok core is direct evidence for Arrhenius's hypothesis. It is clear that in the past, swings in carbon dioxide have been coupled with some of the biggest and fastest climate changes that our planet has ever experienced—ice ages.

The ice from Vostok has also been analyzed to produce a record of global average temperatures.* The rise and fall of Earth's temperature in the last 160,000 years looks like this:

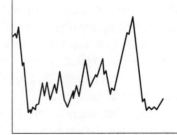

In the mid-1980s, the Swiss physicist and ice expert Hans Oeschger spread out these two charts, temperature and carbon dioxide, in his office in Bern and shook his head. Most of the peaks and valleys in the temperature record match the peaks and valleys of the carbon dioxide record. They might be two views of the same roller coaster, or a profile of the same Alps. "Too nice," Oeschger pronounced. Meaning, too close to be a coincidence. Carbon dioxide seems to be some kind of master switch in the climate of this planet. And we have already pushed the switch up as far as the last ice age pushed it down.

In Princeton, New Jersey, the computer modeler Syukuro Manabe studied the data from the icecap and decided to plug it into his G.C.M. He reduced the carbon dioxide level of his model Earth to 200 parts per million. The temperature of the Earth plummeted into an Ice Age. He raised the gas to 300 parts per million. His Earth rose up out of the Ice Age. In principle, Manabe could tweak the carbon dioxide level up and down in the model, just as the level has gone up and down in the real world in the last 160,000 years. Turn after turn, global temperatures would follow, in tandem with carbon dioxide, riding up and down just the way they did during the last 160,000 years.

"This convinced me all over again," says Oeschger, in Bern. "You know, I am now involved with this so many years that I am personally convinced of the Warming. But then as a scientist one must remain skeptical. One has always to start from scratch—do you know what I mean? When I read what Manabe did, this made me actually . . ."

He shivered.

---

*This is done indirectly, by analyzing oxygen isotopes in the ice. See "The Climate Puzzle" in my book *Planet Earth.*

*   *   *

While all this hard evidence was accumulating, Earth scientists' world view was changing. They were becoming more and more aware of the turbulence of the seven spheres, and the spheres' bewildering inter-linkages. They were realizing how much can go wrong. One turning point was a book that an American biologist began writing in the spring of 1958—coincidentally, the same months that Keeling began measuring global carbon dioxide from Mauna Loa.

Rachel Carson had worked for years at the U.S. Fish and Wildlife Service, and she had written two lyrical best sellers, *The Sea Around Us* and *The Edge of the Sea*. For what was to be her last book, she began collecting information about insecticides. She was reluctant to leave the lyrical mode for the polemical. But she felt the evidence left her no choice.

At the time, most people thought the wholesale spraying of insecticides was a marvelous way to fight gypsy moths, mosquitoes, house-flies, and ticks. The industrial chemists who had invented DDT (dichloro-diphenyl-trichloroethane) and other pest-killers took the same pride in their work that Thomas Midgley had taken in his CFCs.

In *Silent Spring,* published in 1962, Carson explained that the in-tended targets of DDT often develop an immunity to it, while birds, bees, fish, sheep, cows, and human beings are poisoned as the chemical migrates through the ecosystem. She catalogued the millions of tons of pesticides that were being sprayed and some of the horror stories that were resulting. "Can anyone believe it is possible to lay down such a barrage of poisons on the surface of the Earth without making it unfit for all life?" she asked. "They should not be called 'in-secticides,' but 'biocides.'"

The book's working title was *Control of Nature,* and although the biologist focused on insecticides she argued that our species' attempts at controlling nature by brute force will often backfire as badly as DDT. She cited the fallout from the testing of nuclear weapons in the open air and the fouling of streams, rivers, and lakes with detergents, all part of a general "contamination of air, earth, rivers, and sea with dangerous and even lethal materials." (She did not mention the most general con-taminant of all. Carbon dioxide was still decades away from notoriety.)

For many people it came as a shock in 1962 to think that a trium-phant technology could backfire; that chemicals measured in parts per million, billion, or trillion could hurt them; that our kind might inadvertently silence the groves of spring. *Silent Spring* helped to launch the environmental movement of the 1960s and 1970s.

Before the environmental movement, scientists had found it easy to assume that the build-up of carbon dioxide was benign. After all, the gas is the most fundamental by-product of material progress, besides people themselves, and scientists tended to take a professional pride in the advance of the human population and material progress. Callendar, for instance, was an engineer—he identifies himself in that now-famous paper in 1938 as "Steam technologist to the British Electrical and Allied Industries Research Association." He served the industrial engine that Watt helped to start. It was natural for him to describe the build-up of waste carbon in the air as a lucky side-effect of the engine. "Today it keeps our homes warm; tomorrow the world"—that was the tone of his appreciation in 1938.

Soon after Rachel Carson's book came out scientists began to fear that the fundamental by-product of progress might be negative: to see carbon dioxide as pollution, and to speak of it with some of the same feeling of sin that attached to the word pollution in the Old Testament, or miasma in Greek tragedy.

This was more than just a change in intellectual fashion. The results of the explosion of world industry after World War II (clearly visible in the record from Mauna Loa and in the ice sheets of Greenland and Antarctica) were making themselves felt around the planet. In those two decades, people were learning about the control of nature on many fronts at once, not only with DDT and fallout but with litter, eutrophied lakes, lead in the air, oil spills, ozone, species extinctions, overpopulation, Love Canal, acid rain, the meltdown at Three Mile Island.

One decade after *Silent Spring,* the American ecologist Barry Commoner published *The Closing Circle.* Commoner stated as a general law of ecology "that any major man-made change in a natural system is likely to be *detrimental* to that system."

Suppose you were to open the back of your watch, close your eyes, and poke a pencil into the exposed works. The almost certain result would be damage to the watch. . . . [T]his result is not *absolutely* certain. There is some finite possibility that the watch was out of adjustment and that the random thrust of the pencil happened to make the precise change needed to improve it. However, this outcome is exceedingly improbable. . . . One might say, as a law of watches, that "the watchmaker knows best."

In the 1960s, 1970s, and 1980s, some Earth scientists began to look at the seven spheres as a whole the way ecologists like Commoner were looking at the biosphere. As they did so, they realized that what human beings are doing with carbon is the equivalent of jabbing a pencil point into the single most important chemical cycle in nature.

Understanding of the greenhouse effect will continue to evolve, of course. But no one on this planet is ever likely to write about it as exuberantly as Arrhenius did in *Worlds in the Making* in 1906. This is Arrhenius's last word on the greenhouse effect, quoted in its entirety:

> We often hear lamentations that the coal stored up in the earth is wasted by the present generation without any thought of the future, and we are terrified by the awful destruction of life and property which has followed the volcanic eruptions of our days. We may find a kind of consolation in the consideration that here, as in every other case, there is good mixed with the evil. By the influence of the increasing percentage of carbonic acid [carbon dioxide] in the atmosphere, we may hope to enjoy ages with more equable and better climates, especially as regards the colder regions of the Earth, ages when the Earth will bring forth much more abundant crops than at present, for the benefit of rapidly propagating humankind.

Yet despite the gathering evidence and despite the environmentalist movement, a whim of nature still retarded the Eureka. Back in 1938, when Callendar announced that global temperatures were rising, the record of Earth's temperature for the previous fifty years had looked like this:

1938

After Callendar's paper appeared, however, the globe's average temperature began to fall and it fell for a quarter of a century:

72

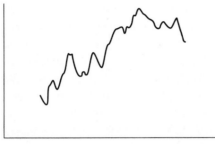

1968

Almost anything could have done that. Earth's temperature is always jiggling up and down from decade to decade, pushed and pulled by a thousand gremlins besides the greenhouse effect. There may have been a shortfall in the quantity of sunlight that was reaching the Earth in those years. The dimming of the light may have been caused by changes in the Sun itself, for the Sun is a mildly variable star. Or the change may have been caused by dust in the air, which, like a dirty skylight, may have made the Sun seem dim. The load of dust could have come from volcanoes, or smokestacks and exhaust pipes, or the clearing of new fields by farmers. Because scientists weren't watching the Earth as closely in those years as they are now, these explanations are all possible, and we may never know.

For poor Callendar, though, it was as if a trapdoor had opened beneath his soapbox. He went on talking about the power of the greenhouse effect for the rest of his life but almost no one stopped to listen. "As long as the world was cooler year after year," Revelle says now, with a sardonic smile, "it was very hard to see that there could be much of an effect."

After Keeling's network detected the rise of carbon dioxide, in the early 1960s, world temperatures started dropping even faster. By 1975, there was talk of an impending ice age. This talk never reached the stage of consensus among the world's climate experts. However, the U.S. Central Intelligence Agency prepared an alarming report about it, predicting major disruptions in the world's food supplies. There were "instant books," too, with titles like *The Cooling*, and *The Weather Conspiracy: The Coming of the New Ice Age.*

The cooling kept the greenhouse effect unfashionable. Every kind of evidence was piling up except the kind that mattered most. "Politically," one observer lamented, "carbon dioxide is like chalk on a white wall—or rather, like some additional darkness in the night."

In the early 1980s, researchers at the University of East Anglia, in Britain, reviewed all the temperature records they could get from around the world. The team, led by Thomas Wigley, director of the university's Climatic Research Unit, gathered more than a century of thermometer readings that had been made over the years by weather stations on land and sea from the late nineteenth century through to the present. Wigley's team pooled these hundreds of millions of numbers.

Analyzing the results, they saw that Earth's temperature had now risen higher than it was in 1938. The globe was warmer than it had been in a hundred years. From 1860 to the decade of the 1980s, Earth had warmed by about half a degree C., or 1° F.

Independently, a team led by James Hansen at NASA's Goddard Institute for Space Studies, in New York, performed the same study. (Hansen is one of the Venus veterans.) The Goddard team started more or less from scratch, collected all the global temperature data they could find, and analyzed it. They found approximately the same upward trend for both the Northern and Southern Hemispheres.

Both groups discovered that the year 1981 had been the warmest for the planet in at least one hundred years—that is, for as long as there are any reliable temperature records. The year 1983 was warmer than 1981. The year 1987 (the year after Wigley's first study was published) turned out to be even warmer than 1983. Each of these years broke the previous record: three world records in six years.

The trend was also accelerating. The rate of warming in the 1980s was much faster than the average rate for the twentieth century. In fact, temperatures rose as much in that one decade as they had between 1860 and 1950. No one had predicted a jump like that, and no one expected the jump to last much longer. If it did, said the climate expert J. Murray Mitchell, "that would bring us to the hothouse in ten, twenty years, never mind one hundred years."

Mitchell told me this news on a very muggy September afternoon in 1987, at his home outside Washington, D.C. It was the worst heat wave of that year, and the year was the hottest on record. Mitchell had spent a good part of his career as a respected advisor on climate affairs in several Washington administrations, in the World Meteorological Organization and the United Nations Environment Programme, sometimes in Congress and the Senate. His house has a 70-foot-antenna studded with weather instruments, some of them of his own design. As we sat in his study, these instruments' printouts were clacking away on walls, shelves, and tables, rat-tat-tat, like machine gun fire, recording the temperature, speed and direction of the air above the roof—the kind of data that help to feed the giant pools of numbers in the computers in East Anglia and Manhattan. The instruments went on chattering like monkeys throughout our conversation.

Mitchell had been one of the first students of the global temperature trend. It was his thesis project at M.I.T. in the late 1940s. Even then it was clear to him that the overall trend of the twentieth century planet might be a warming. But of course, not many people were interested in the greenhouse effect back then. In the perspective of the century, the cool spell looks brief, but it was a long time in a man's career. Mitchell had gone on to other things.

That afternoon Mitchell accepted the heat with the same calm humor with which he regarded the uncertainties in the prognosis of the planet, and in his own personal prognosis (he was ill, and had taken early retirement). He spread out Wigley's and Hansen's papers and preprints, and showed me how the temperature of the planet had risen, dipped and risen again, tracing the line with his pipe.

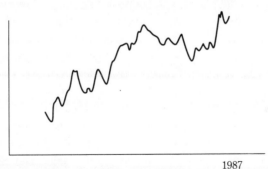

1987

A rise of about half a degree C., or 1° F., is about what the G.C.M.s had indicated for 1986. Given all the greenhouse gases that human beings had put into the air, it was a somewhat smaller temperature increase than the models predicted. But it was within their range of uncertainty.

Mitchell explained to me the way Wigley's and Hansen's teams had prepared their temperature data. He explained the ambiguities in the data, and why he believed that on the whole the trend could be trusted. "So it looks as though that's really happening," he said. "Onward and upward!"

In a few heads, the evidence began to snap together: the rise in temperatures, the rise in more and more greenhouse gases, the story in the ice-cores, the story on Mars and Venus, the confirmations in the computers. Climate experts began to realize that the long-term trend on Planet Earth would almost certainly be upward and unpleasant.

Scientists' interest in the greenhouse effect began skyrocketing. In 1986, the U.S. Department of Energy's Carbon Dioxide Information Center received 2,200 requests for information—up more than 150 percent from the year before.

Wigley's and Hansen's reports also set off waves of greenhouse stories in the press. After the hot year 1987, Wigley told a reporter from *The New York Times* that if the 1990s proved as warm as the 1980s, "it would be very hard to deny the greenhouse effect." He added, "It is very hard to deny now."

"There's little scientific uncertainty that it's going to happen," Richard Houghton, of the Woods Hole Research Center, told me. "The question is, how fast."

More and more scientists were realizing what Revelle had in mind in 1957: this is a great geophysical experiment. By artificially amplifying the greenhouse effect on Earth, our species has started a cascade of changes in the seven spheres. Specialists in the atmosphere, hydrosphere, cryosphere, and biosphere were now scanning their fields' horizons, searching for ways that the greenhouse effect might already be changing their spheres. Some were looking for early changes is the stratosphere. Among other things, adding greenhouse gases to the air should make the stratosphere dramatically colder.

That is one of the paradoxes of the greenhouse effect. Suppose you were walking through a snowstorm in a thin shirt. The snowflakes that landed on the tops of your shoulders would melt. But suppose you pulled on a few more layers. Your skin would be warmer and warmer; but the wool of your outermost sweater would grow so cold that the snow that landed there would last and last.

Earth is swinging through the chill of outer space, and the atmosphere is its only clothing. Adding greenhouse gases to the air is like pulling on more and more layers of wool. Down here, we should soon start to feel warmer and warmer; but fifteen or twenty miles up, the stratosphere, which is the equivalent of an outer layer of wool, is expected to grow cold enough for ice to form there.

In the mid-1980s, a few teams of scientists collected and reviewed thousands of records of the temperature of the stratosphere (as measured by satellites, rockets, and balloons). Then a team led by Mark Schoeberl, of the Goddard Spaceflight Center in Greenbelt, Maryland, reviewed some of the reviews. Schoeberl's group found that the upper stratosphere cooled between 1.5° and 2° C. (2.7° and 3.6° F.) between 1979 and 1985. The lower stratosphere is cooling, too.

This did not prove that the cooling of the stratosphere is caused by the greenhouse effect. It could have been just a coincidence. But it was consistent with the predictions.

In 1986, there was also a change in the cryosphere. Great pieces of ice began falling from the icy coast of Antarctica, a process that glaciologists describe picturesquely as "calving." All of a sudden the White Continent began giving birth to some monster-sized calves. The Larsen Ice Shelf calved an iceberg with an area of at least 8,000 kilometers. That is more than twice the size of the state of Rhode Island, and represents more ice than normally breaks off from the White Continent in a single year. In the same year, the northern edge of the Filchner Ice Shelf calved several icebergs whose combined area totalled at least 11,500 kilometers. The next year, for the first time in at least three-quarters of a century, there was a "major calving episode" on the Ross Ice Shelf. An iceberg of more than 6,000 square kilometers drifted away. The map of Antarctica had to be redrawn.

By then there was enough interest in the greenhouse effect that after each big iceberg calved off the coast, glaciologists' phones rang off the wall. In all of Earth science, glaciologists tend to be the most cool and conservative. "If the greenhouse warming has arrived, it is probably *not* what we are seeing here," Stanley Jacobs, of the Lamont-Doherty Geological Observatory, in Palisades, New York, told reporters from small-town newspapers, hosts of radio talk shows, and specialists in other spheres of Earth science. "This is a natural process that would probably have happened anyway." *Ring.* "This is *not* a response to trends of the last few years." *Ring.*

Meanwhile there were changes in the biosphere, too. Like the change in the breathing of the world, first detected by Keeling in the late 1970s, these discoveries were invisible and made no headlines. However, they were tied unequivocally to the rise in carbon dioxide.

In 1987, for example, a botanist at Cambridge University, in England, took a close look at the old pressed leaves of trees and plants in the university's herbarium. F. Ian Woodward noticed that the most antique leaves—those that were collected in 1750, just before the start of the Industrial Revolution—are anatomically different from modern leaves of the same species. The old leaves have more pores.

The botanist looked at leaves of half a dozen plants that grow in

Great Britain: a sycamore, a lime tree, two species of oak, and a bil-berry plant. Some of these species' leaves had more pores than others, but in every case, the leaves of these plants have had fewer and fewer pores since the Industrial Revolution began. An oak leaf today has an average of 40 percent fewer pores—stomata—than its ancestor in the reign of King George III.

A pore in a leaf is a delicate compromise. The leaf must take in carbon dioxide, so it must be open to the air. But the more air that circulates through it, the more water it loses to evaporation. So the cells around each pore open and close in a fascinating optimization of sunlight, humidity, temperature, and carbon dioxide, following strat-egies that botanists are learning to study as if they were part of sophis-ticated game theory.

Woodward had found a new move in the game from generation to generation of trees. With more carbon dioxide in the air, leaves need fewer pores to take in enough of the gas; and with fewer pores, trees are more efficient in the use of water and therefore hardier in droughts.

The botanist tried growing some of these plants in small green-houses. As he added carbon dioxide to the air, as many as two-thirds of the pores in the leaves shut down. Pores are little things—micro-scopic—but through them, apparently, trees all around the world are quietly adapting to the changes in the air. If we are in for droughts and stormy weather, modern plants are better prepared than their an-cestors. The trees outside our windows are detecting and adapting to the change in the air much faster than we are.

Taken by itself this is good news, at least for trees; but unfor-tunately Woodward's latest findings are not so encouraging. Biologists distinguish between two kinds of adaptation. Genetic change is caused by natural selection—the survival and propagation of the fittest. Plastic change is caused by the adaption of the individual to its circumstances.

The change in the plants is plastic. Oak leaves are adapting as they bud, unfold, and meet the modern atmosphere. The genes in the acorn, bud, and leaf remain the same as always. "Which implies," says Woodward, "that so far the stress has not been so great that it has caused natural selection.

"But we're at the limits of this plastic behavior," he says. Leaves cannot adapt any further to the changing atmosphere without a change in the genes themselves. "That raises a host of interesting questions.

Will there now be selection *for* the change? What will the plant do if it can't *make* the change?"

"Much more complicated to understand what will happen next than what has already happened," says Woodward.

By the second half of the 1980s, many experts were frantic to persuade the world of what they thought was about to happen. Yet they could not afford to sound frantic, or they would lose credibility. They were placed in a curious position as human beings. They were so worried about the changes they saw coming, and the difficulty of persuading the world that the changes were coming, that they sometimes caught themselves rooting for the changes to appear. In fact it was hard to know how to feel. One hot summer afternoon at the Ecosystems Center of the Marine Biological Laboratory in Woods Hole, Massachusetts, Thomas Stone dashed into the office of Richard Houghton with a preprint from the U.S. Geological Survey. The report said geophysicists at U.S.G.S. had measured temperatures in the boreholes of oil wells in Alaska. They found that Alaskan permafrost has warmed by 2° to 4° C. over the last few decades, or perhaps over the last century. This suggested to the geophysicists that Arctic air had been warming strongly—a fact for which it is hard to get data directly. The Arctic is one of the places on Earth that should be warming the most, and the lack of any sign of warming there had worried and embarrassed greenhouse experts.

The oil wells were scattered among the foothills and lakes of the Alaskan coastal plain, between the Brooks Range and the Arctic Ocean. Stone and Houghton knew that part of Alaska very well. Most of the Center staff camped in the shadow of the Brooks Range every summer, studying the ecology of the tundra. Tundra represents vast stores of carbon, because the remains of millions of years of vegetation are packed into the soil. The ecologists suspected that if the warming ever reached Alaska, the tundra could begin to release billions of tons of extra carbon. An added nightmare for the greenhouse effect: Will this carbon get back into the air?

Two to four degrees is in the range of the predictions. Stone ran in beaming, waving the paper aloft like a broadside, or as if he and Houghton had won the lottery. "We're out of the fire now!" Stone said.

Houghton looked at him.

"And into the frying pan," Stone added, self-consciously.

*　　*　　*

From the cosmic point of view, what is happening is catastrophically abrupt. In geological perspective, the collective exhalations of human industry will look like a single eruption, a sharp spike in the air. The petroleum geologist M. King Hubbert was the first to chart the modern age in this way, and the spike is sometimes referred to as the Hubbert blip:

But from the point of view of mortal scientists, and the man and woman on the street, standing somewhere on the rising side of the Hubbert blip, everything to do with the greenhouse effect has seemed to be happening in extreme slow-motion. That may be the ultimate reason that it has taken us all so long to begin to worry about it. Even those who believed it was happening thought it was happening slowly. People lived in its shadow as comfortably as they live in the city of Hilo, under the volcano Mauna Loa.

We don't respond to processes. We respond to events. It takes an eruption or an earthquake or a weird belch from a poisonous lake in Cameroon or the collapse of an ice sheet to rivet our attention. I once read of a teacher who illustrated this point with a frog. First the teacher dropped the frog into a beaker of hot water. The frog jumped right out. Then the teacher put the frog in a beaker of cool water, and turned on a Bunsen burner. The frog kept swimming in the beaker and it boiled to death.

For one hundred years the build-up of the gas and the rise in global temperatures have been too gradual to catch our attention. Its pace affected even the manner of Keeling's discovery, the one real Eureka in this century. Our image of the way a scientific discovery should take place dates from ancient Syracuse. Archimedes, the Greek mathematician, discovered a law of physics while musing in his bathtub. According to legend, Archimedes ran naked through the streets shouting, *"Eureka! I have found it!"*

In Victorian England a banknote engraver named George Smith spent years searching the cuneiform tablets in the British Museum, looking for confirmation of the Biblical story of Noah and the Ark. One day Smith was handed a freshly cleaned tablet. The cuneiform inscription was a fragment of a Babylonian narrative of a World Flood. "Setting the tablet on the table," a colleague records, "he jumped up and rushed about the room in a great state of excitement, and, to the astonishment of those present, began to undress himself!"

Archimedes' echo.

I have asked many people who were close to Keeling's project in the early days about the Eureka moment. I talked to the Swiss ice-expert Oeschger in Bern. Oeschger had worked at Scripps when Keeling was just getting started. "I knew Keeling very well in '58," Oeschger told me. "We played together. He plays piano and I the violin. I think he was very early aware that he did something important." Although they had stayed in touch ever since, and although Keeling recently had spent a year in Oeschger's lab, Oeschger told me he knew of no Eureka moment.

John Chin is a technician at the Mauna Loa Observatory. He and the other technicians on the volcano kept Keeling's gas analyzers running. They changed the graph paper, and each week they sent the tracings to Keeling. Sometimes the technicians used an ordinary ruler to line up the charts and look for a rise or fall in the tracings. "I was here in '60. In '60, we already saw the increase," Chin says. ". . . Maybe Keeling got very excited. But we just went, 'More work.' We got to measure more often."

In his office at the University of California at San Diego, I asked Revelle about the Eureka moment.

"I don't remember that. It's an interesting point," Revelle said. "But I really don't think it was a sudden flash of insight. Just an accumulation of evidence. That's the nature of the monitoring process. You've got to monitor it for long enough so that you get above the noise level. And the noise level here had been quite high . . . Anyhow it wasn't a problem that many people thought about. . . ."

At Scripps, in an office on the same hall where Keeling put together his first gas analyzers, I asked him if he remembered the moment when he first realized that his global carbon-dioxide network was picking up a rise in the gas. "I can tell you that," Keeling said, promisingly, and he rummaged around in his files. There was a long silence. "I don't know why it's not there, but it's not there." At last he produced a paper. "*Tellus*, June, 1960," Keeling pronounced, and read aloud: "Where the data extend beyond one year, averages for the second year are higher than for the first year."

"But when did it hit you?" I asked him. "What was the atmosphere like in this laboratory when you knew?"

Keeling remembered no particular moment of joy, dismay, or reflection. "I didn't have *time*. I was just up to my ears trying to keep this experimental program going. It was all kinds of logistics, and communicating, repairing. . . . It was such an enormous effort to keep that program going. I almost decided to quit measurements at the end of '63."

I visited Saul Price at his office in the U.S. National Weather Service in Honolulu. Unlike Chin, Price is trained as a research meteorologist. And unlike Keeling and Revelle, Price spent many nights on the volcano in the early days. He watched the gas analyzers trace out what became some of the first points on the Keeling curve. "Earth-watchers generally don't get to shout Eureka," said Price. "Generally what happens is that somebody writes a paper *as soon as he dares,* and says, look, this is how things are. Then you can say *Eureka!*—but not too loudly. Because how do you know that after two dots, or three dots, or four dots, the thing isn't going to turn around again? What constitutes a trend? You might say two dots, for two years, at least. Only after quite a while—maybe ten years—you're sure you're dealing with something real and authentic now. In spite of tremendous variability in the sources and sinks all over the world, in the atmosphere, the biosphere, the hydrosphere, the net effect is still showing up year by year by year. Finally you say to yourself, 'My goodness.'"

The road to the Mauna Loa Observatory climbs first between two giants, Mauna Loa and Mauna Kea, the Long Mountain and the White Mountain and then, at the twenty-seven mile marker, turns south to ascend Mauna Loa. These volcanoes are so young and their slopes so gradual that the convicts from Kulani Prison Camp who built the road had little need for switchbacks. According to local legend, they bulldozed through the rubble straight toward the summit, and when the money ran out, there they built the Mauna Loa Observatory. Because the mountain is so smooth, one does not have to change gears to drive higher than the summits of some Alps. The grade of the road is like the grade of the global warming—you hardly know you are climbing until you are almost there. Suddenly you feel as though you have left Hawaii. You are 3,400 meters above sea level. The Sun is harsh, the air is thin and cold, the sky a dark and astronomical blue, and the view, wider than from the Jungfrau, is an endless wasteland of black frozen lava, like a giant heap of cinders, receding on all sides nearly as far as the eye can see. (Far, far below you can see the rain forests of Hilo and the palm beaches of Kona.)

Some visitors to the Mauna Loa Observatory need oxygen. Many feel nauseous. It impresses us at such moments of need how thin the atmosphere really is. You can drive almost halfway out of it in an hour in a jeep. You can fly all of the way out in a few minutes in a rocket. On his first flight in outer space an East German astronaut looked out the window and for the first time in his life he saw the curving line of the planet's horizon. "It was accentuated by a thin seam of dark blue light—our atmosphere," Ulf Merbold wrote afterward. "Obviously this was not the ocean of air I had been told it was so many times in my life. I was terrified by its fragile appearance."

The road ends at the Mauna Loa Observatory's main building, a small plain box of cinderblock with a roof of corrugated aluminum. Around it, bulbous white plastic shapes sprout from the basalt like a Martian flora and fauna—instruments to measure ozone and to watch the Sun. There are also nephelometers, hygrometers, maximum-minimum thermometers. Instruments to measure dust particles, water vapor, extremes of temperature. Most of the scientists who watch the planet through these robot instruments live many thousands of miles away and many thousands of feet below. The observatory's staff scientists and technicians tend the robot garden from day to day.

On my visit, John Chin (who has now spent a quarter of a century on the volcano) led me across the black rubble on bare wood-plank walkways. I asked him if he ever worries now about the trend in Keeling's curve. He told me that he sleeps well at night. "Sometimes I look at it and I say, 'Well . . .'" He enjoyed explaining the purpose of the new monitors around the observatory, each of them the best of its kind. Each year another dangerous gas is added to the watch: methane, CFCs, sulfur dioxide, carbon monoxide. A final exam question at York University once asked: "List six unknown substances that will be found to harm the ozone layer." When those six substances are discovered, sensors will be invented for them and Chin will help to install these in the black rubble on Mauna Loa.

One squat, unpainted wooden platform near the main building holds particle-monitors belonging to the atmospheric chemist William Zoller.

The pumps suck in air greedily—fifty liters a minute. Each year, Zoller can tell when plowing starts in China. In Japan they call it "Yellow Dust." Zoller calls it "Gobi Dust."

Standing among these prodigies of environmental sensitivity are an outhouse and a green tank. The tank holds 1,000 gallons of extra water for the technicians who run the observatory. "We won't drink it—we don't know what's in the bottom," Chin said, without irony. "We use it to wash our hands."

And rising above the rest is the tower. It is by far the tallest structure on Mauna Loa, erected by the National Oceanic and Atmospheric Administration: an open-frame vertical Jungle-Gym of aluminum pipes with flights of aluminum steps zig-zagging into the sky. The purest air in the world is sucked down through an aluminum straw at the top of the tower, 120 feet above the observatory, and drawn down to the carbon-dioxide detectors that are housed below in the main building, including the ancient black-box detector that Keeling purchased during the I.G.Y. and has never allowed anyone to replace.

"He's a very careful man," Chin said. "Very particular in his research. It's got to be *so-so*. Don't just change anything—even an intake line—without a lot of intercomparisons."

Lately there had been dozens of phone calls about the new tower. Keeling wanted Chin to flush each new intake line with lots of fresh air before hooking it up to his gas analyzers. "I am flushing and flushing day and night—until I pick up the phone and say, 'Is it OK to change tubes?' I think people call him a super-careful man. He was born with it."

Keeling had just given Chin permission to connect a piece of aluminum tubing from the new tower to the carbon-dioxide detectors. Now Keeling wanted to know exactly how long it took a sample of air entering the valves to reach the main building, and to be recorded there on the scrolls of computer paper. Chin proposed an experiment.

The sun was getting lower in the sky by the time I started climbing the steps of the tower, but it still stung the back of my neck. (According to the UV radiometer, the ultraviolet light is much stronger at the top of the volcano than at the bottom—there is so much less atmosphere to block it.) I started out too fast and ran out of breath about ten feet up. On the neighbor volcano, Mauna Kea, astronomers often drive up to the observatories for a few nights' work and then faint on the floor of the telescope room. "I lose ten percent of my mental circuitry up here," a technician had told me when we were driving up the road to the observatory. "You'll be surprised. You won't remember much of your visit here. And you won't be able to read your notes."

I sat down for a moment on the steps of the tower and scribbled in my notebook until I caught my breath. That page is an accidental imitation of free verse.

> Strenuous to walk—
> > breath comes loud—
> hear it loud in
> ears as if I were
> a diver—
> long slow pants—

The first intake valve was thirty feet up, mounted outside the railing. To reach it, I had to straddle the aluminum banister and lean way out over the volcano. I puffed into the valve as if testing a microphone. Since the average human breath contains thousands of parts per million of carbon dioxide, even a puff a few inches away from the valve should make a big impression down in the main building. I climbed to the valve at sixty feet, and puffed into that one. Then eighty feet.

The air was so clean and transparent that from the top of the tower the observatory below looked like a tinkertoy affair—a model train set without many pieces. The road rolled down the slope of the volcano with no perceptible diminution of clarity. The eye of an eagle might have counted a thousand utility poles running down the Mauna Loa Road through the spilled desert of lava. Away across the valley the white astronomical domes on Mauna Kea were lit pink at the summit in alpenglow. From one of those white observatory domes an astronomer recently sighted the farthest known galaxy in the universe.

"Hey!" yelled John Chin. "Do one more time!"

"OK! When I lower my arm I've done it!"

"OK!" Chin stood in the shade of the aluminum shed, watching me and his stopwatch. I exhaled into the intake pipe, leaning out over the aluminum rail to give it a good blast, and lowered my left arm. Chin darted back into the main building.

It was strange being alone up there. All around there was almost nothing but lithosphere, black newborn lithosphere, as far as the eye could see. Overhead was the blue pennant, the old blue friend, and on the horizon was less than half of the sphere of fire. It was one of the most abstract landscapes I had ever seen. It felt like Mars. Several spheres were missing from the scene, and I was, for the moment, the sole representative of my species and of the biosphere. In a sort of schematic diagram of our situation on the planet, molecules of carbon dioxide, which did not care if they arose from the lithosphere, the atmosphere, the biosphere, or the human sphere, kept flying down the aluminum hole whether I intended them to or not. I scribbled some wild notes—"I am part of the experiment"—that I can decipher but won't print.

In the main building, Chin clicked his stopwatch. A breath had taken one minute and 50 seconds to travel down 300 feet of new aluminum tubing and make Keeling's old gadget jump. "Not bad—that's good!" Chin cried out.

Then Chin whooped. "Dr. Keeling will be mad! Dr. Keeling will say, not too much horsing around!"

Future generations may wonder how we lived so long under the volcano without doing anything. The fact is that we did not know what the volcano meant. Scientists were slow to warn us and we were slow to hear them. At the time I climbed the tower I had been writing about Earth science for several years. I had been gathering material for this book for one year. I had spent one week in Keeling's laboratories, and many weeks in many others. Strange to confess: but the subject of global change was still just so much hearsay and doomsday until I climbed the tower. At that moment it all came together for me: that carbon dioxide is building up, and that each of us is responsible. At that moment it finally dawned on me that the greenhouse effect might be real.

A few weeks later an envelope from Chin arrived in my mailbox. It contained a page of printout. The Mauna Loa record; one piece of it.

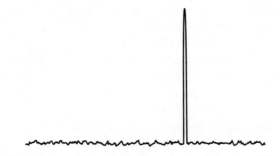

"Aloha!" Chin wrote. "Your breath—about 378 ppm CO_2."

For me, it was that experience. For most people, it was the Summer of '88.

CHAPTER 6

THE FIRST SUMMER OF THE THIRD MILLENNIUM

> There is no law of history that says a new century
> must start ten or twenty years beforehand, but . . .
> it has worked out that way.
>
> Tom Wolfe
> *A Eulogy for the*
> *Twentieth Century*

On Sunday, July 10, 1988, at the weather station in the Castle in Central Park, the high for the day was 99° F. The relative humidity was 93 percent at one o'clock in the morning. It had been one of the hottest weeks in living memory. Cabdrivers could actually feel their tires sinking into the asphalt in the middle of Fifth Avenue. Air conditioners were breaking down all over town and Ira Parker, the air-conditioner salesman at Uncle Steve's electronics store, would soon be laughing in customers' faces: "I've sold demos," he said. "I've sold displays. I've even sold the pictures."

No relief at the beach. The shores of Long Island and New Jersey were fouled by a backwash of New York City's raw sewage and trash. Children playing along the tideline found used hospital blood-bags, latex gloves, and syringes contaminated with the AIDS virus.

For city police and criminologists the number of consecutive 90-plus days is a predictor of urban violent crime. That week Wednesday had been 92° F., Thursday 93, Friday 97, Saturday 88. And that weekend in the five boroughs more than three dozen people were shot, stabbed, beaten, or strangled to death.

In the South the heat was stunting the cotton. In the Midwest, drought was killing wheat, corn, sorghum, soybeans, and it was clear that the summer would be the worst since the Dust Bowl. Some small towns in Iowa folded in the summer of '88.

In the West and across the country more than 6 million acres burned: the worst forest fires in recorded history. They were battled by 30,000 firefighters, including convicts who were flown in under guard from California jails.

All but 5 percent of the big rivers in the U.S. were running low. The Mississippi dropped so low that it stranded thousands of barges and exposed old shipwrecks: paddle-wheelers from the Gilded Age, and (on one tributary of the Big Muddy) the skeletons of three Civil War ships, the *Dot*, the *Charm*, and the *Paul Jones*, scuttled during the Confederate retreat from Vicksburg in 1863.

Wheat died in Canada and the Soviet Union, and rice died in the People's Republic of China. China (where 1988 was the Year of the Dragon) lost more than 10,000 people and 500,000 houses in droughts, floods, typhoons, and freak hailstorms. Shanghai in July was even worse than New York City; more than 1,000,000 people took sick from the heat.

In the Yucatán Peninsula, whole villages and beaches were swept into the sea by Hurricane Gilbert, the most powerful storm of the century. There were torrential rains and flash floods in India, Nigeria, The Gambia, Mali, Burkina Faso, and the Sudan. In Bangladesh, floods put more than three-quarters of the country underwater. By September the executive director of the United Nations' World Food Program called for donations of 300,000 tons of food to meet the unprecedented series of ecological emergencies.

The drought was particularly bad in North America. It was the worst since the 1930s. Once more, as in Dust Bowl Days, in Montana, Nebraska, North Dakota, Kansas, Texas, farmers stared at the dark clouds on the horizon: their rich black topsoil blowing away. The Agriculture Department Soil Conservation Service estimated that almost twelve million acres had been damaged by wind erosion—as of June 1. Prize heifers and pregnant cows had to be sold for slaughter because there was too little grass to feed them (there was hardly enough for the grasshoppers, farmers said). By the first week in July the Midwest was so hot and dry that when a few drops fell in Kansas City, Missouri, during the ninth inning of a close game, with the Kansas City Royals trailing the Chicago White Sox, the 23,000 fans in the stadium did not boo the rain. They stood up and cheered.*

The drought of the thirties had sent the Okies rolling toward California, inspiring John Steinbeck's *Grapes of Wrath* and perhaps T.S. Eliot in "Little Gidding":

> Dust in the air suspended
> Marks the place where a story ended.
> Dust inbreathed was a house—
> The wall, the wainscot and the mouse.
> The death of hope and despair,
> This is the death of air.

In July, President Ronald Reagan was photographed in an Illinois cornfield in the middle of the Big Dry. The corn, which should have been over his head, was waist-high. Near Vicksburg, Mississippi, and the dwindling Mississippi River, a farmer and his sons searched the Confederate wrecks for gold. Scrambling beneath the willow trees by the banks of Big Black River, on the border of their farm, they cleared piles of broken branches from the mud. They found only a few engine pipes and a glass medicine bottle labelled "fever & ague antidote."

People knew they were participating in a historic misery. In Custer County, Montana, John L. Moore took his two young children to a hilltop and pointed to three range fires spilling black smoke from the badlands south of Miles City. "Remember this day," Moore told them. "This is something you will someday tell your children about."

But August was the cruelest month in the summer of '88. The National Weather Service's Monthly Summary in Minneapolis:

Excessive heat continued. The high of 92 on the 3rd marked the 37th time this year the daily high reached 90 degrees or above, breaking 1936 record . . . warmest summer period ever recorded . . . new record high temperatures set in August: 101 on 1st . . . 99 on 2nd . . . 99 on 16th.

On the worst days of that August, Detroit factories shut down assembly lines. Harvard University canceled summer classes and closed

---

*The heat made even baseball more dangerous that summer. A study by psychologists at the University of Michigan shows that when the temperature in the stadium rises over 90° F., more pitchers bean more batters.

its doors on account of the heat for the first time in its 352-year history. In New York City (which had thirty-two days above 90° by the middle of August) 200 people were murdered, a 75 percent jump from the same month the year before, and yet another record. Americans spent an extra half-billion dollars in August running Freon-cooled air conditioners.

The Chubb Corporation was squabbling with farmers about "rain insurance" that month. The company had rejected thousands of new applications and premium checks that farmers had mailed in, and offered thousands of other customers $2,500 apiece to cancel their insurance.

Reagan signed a $3.9 billion farm relief bill, commending farmers' "indomitable spirit." The North American Seed division of Pioneer Hi-Bred International Inc., the biggest seed company in the world, was scrambling to plant new fields of seed corn—many in South America—to make up for the lost corn in time for next year's crop. At the Illinois State Fair in Springfield, Joe Beall, a 4-H judge, awarded blue ribbons to children's best tomatoes, cabbages, carrots, and eggplants. "In a normal year," he told a reporter, out of earshot of the children, "these would not have been brought in."

In Yellowstone that August, fires fanned by fifty-mile-an-hour gusts came within five miles of the Old Faithful geyser. The flames spared the Old Faithful Inn but two dozen other buildings in the park burned down. In all, nearly 1,000,000 acres of forest were burned or singed that summer in Yellowstone—nearly half the park, and more than 45 times more than had burned in the park in any year in recorded history.

In a sense, the fire in America's oldest national park began in the Pioneer Explosion one hundred years before. The logging slash of so many chopped trees was fueling unprecedented fires across North America by the turn of the century. One fire in the hot dry year 1894 drove the entire town of Hinkley, Minnesota into the river for their lives (". . . the skies turned red," wrote one eyewitness, "and all the earth looked as if it had been dipped in blood.")

So the Forest Service spent most of the twentieth century trying to prevent forest fires. Thanks to their success the woods were thrown off balance. Because there were no longer any quick small fires to clear the understory, fallen branches and leaf litter and humus piled up in national parks at a rate of as much as half a ton per acre per year. At last in the early 1970s the Forest Service decided that it had better reverse its policy and let fires burn away that litter, because they feared a conflagration. Which came, in 1988.

Smoke from the West blew East. In St. Louis the forecasts called for "smoky sunshine." In Chicago the smoke created millennial sunsets. Watching the nightly news it sometimes seemed as if the whole continent was on fire. Near Livengood, Alaska, a 323,000-acre fire came within seven miles of the trans-Alaska oil pipeline. In Montana a fire came within a mile of a nuclear missile silo before turning away.

It is often said that there will be winners and losers in a global warming. There were a few winners in the Summer of '88. It was a good summer for tobacco, which is a hardy weed. It was a profitable summer for the Accu-Weather forecasting company. It was a good summer for contributions to environmental groups. It was a great summer for American air-conditioning companies: they sold 4 million air conditioners and still could not keep up with the demand.

It was a busy summer for Robert Haack, an entomologist with the U.S. Forest Service's North Central Forest Experiment Station in East Lansing, Michigan. Haack is interested in the high-pitched sounds that trees make as they wither in a drought. The water tubes that normally suck water from the ground begin to snap, and the plants literally cry out for water. Haack thinks the sound may be detected by marauding bark beetles. He had many drought-stricken trees to tape-record in Michigan.

It was also a busy summer for the beetles. Bark beetles killed cedar, fir, and pine. Flatheaded borers killed oaks and birches. Caterpillars prospered among the dry leaves. The borers bored millions of those long mazy galleries that one finds carved beneath the bark on fallen logs in the woods, like illegible hieroglyphics. In short, says Haack, of the Forest Service, "forests throughout much of the country were being slowly nibbled to death."

Robert H. Mohlenbrock, a botanist at Southern Illinois University, had read about certain remarkable adaptations that prairie grasses displayed during the Dust Bowl in the 1930s. There is not much virgin prairie left in Illinois, but in the Summer of '88, Mohlenbrock drove out to Goose Lake Prairie, a virgin tract near Joliet, to see how the prairie grass was doing. He found that the leaves of some of the native grasses had folded up, or rolled inward. The pores, or stomata, were all on the side folded in, and the blades were reducing their water loss by as much as 95 percent. The prairie grass did fine in the Summer of '88. But then there is not much prairie grass left.

It was a good summer for spider mites, because the heat killed the mold that normally keeps them in check, and they had a field day in Iowa's soybeans.

The summer caused the sharpest one-year drop in world grain stocks in history, but it was a good summer for the farmers the weather spared. With world prices for grain soaring, the billionaire Olacyr de Moraes, of São Paolo, the world's biggest soybean farmer, made about 50 percent more in 1988 than the year before. Argentina's farmers did so well that national revenues on grain exports jumped more than 100 percent. In one spot in northwestern Iowa, there was enough rain. Farmers there got an extra dollar for every bushel of corn they trucked to the grain elevators in Ida, Cherokee, Buena Vista, Sac, Carroll, and Crawford counties.

And it was a good summer for black humor. Roger L. Welsch, a folklorist in Nebraska, dug up old jokes that were collected in the Dust Bowl by teams from the Federal Writers Project in the thirties. The editors of *Natural History* Magazine reprinted them:

I had a three-inch rain Tuesday. One drop every three inches.

It was so dry over in Sherman County that I saw two trees fighting over a dog.

Over at my place I accidentally dropped my best log chain down one of the cracks in the yard over by the barn. I went out the next morning to see if I could retrieve it, and by golly, that crack was so deep I could still hear the chain rattling on its way down.

Not only was it the hottest year on record for the planet. It was also the first year in which we all seriously wondered if we were feeling the greenhouse effect on our skins. If the models were correct, then we were experiencing a typical summer of the twenty-first century. If the models were correct, then people looking back might call '88 the first summer of the third millennium.

On June 23, the temperature was 101° F. in downtown Washington, D.C. An all-star panel of climate experts, including James Hansen, of NASA, Syukuro Manabe, of the Geophysical Fluid Dynamics Laboratory in Princeton, Michael Oppenheimer, senior scientist at the Environmental Defense Fund, and George Woodwell, director of the Woods Hole Research Center, had assembled in a well air-conditioned hall one block from the Capitol Dome.

The hall was packed with reporters. Three television cameras were rolling. A record of the proceedings has been published by the U.S. Government Printing Office:

HEARING

BEFORE THE

COMMITTEE ON

ENERGY AND NATURAL RESOURCES

UNITED STATES SENATE

ONE HUNDREDTH CONGRESS

FIRST SESSION

ON THE

GREENHOUSE EFFECT AND GLOBAL CLIMATE CHANGE

JUNE 23, 1988

The hearing was chaired by the Hon. J. Bennett Johnston, U.S. Senator from Louisiana.

THE CHAIRMAN: The hearing will come to order.

Last November, we had introductory hearings on the question of global warming and the greenhouse effect. We listened with mixtures of disbelief and concern as Dr. Manabe told us that the expected result of the greenhouse effect was going to be a drying of the southeast and midwest. Today . . . the words of Dr. Manabe and other witnesses . . . are becoming not just [a source of] concern, but alarm.

We have only one planet. If we screw it up, we have no place else to go.

Senator Kent Conrad, of North Dakota, said he had spent the weekend in his state, and "the pastures looked like a moonscape." Senator Dale Bumpers, of Arkansas, reminded the audience that the first witness would be James Hansen, one of the scientists who had recently shown that the planet has been warming for one hundred years. Bumpers told reporters that what Hansen had to say that day "ought to be cause for headlines in every newspaper in America tomorrow morning."

When it was Hansen's turn, he reviewed the evidence of a hundred years of global warming. Then he said it. "Altogether this evidence . . . represents a very strong case, in my opinion, that the greenhouse effect has been detected, and it is changing our climate *now.*"

Scientists had been saying that in private. This was the first time a responsible scientist said it for the public record. In that setting, and in that heat, it had the force of a global announcement. Senator Bumpers was right about the headlines. The front page of *The New York Times:* GLOBAL WARMING HAS BEGUN, EXPERT TELLS SENATE. The *Philadelphia Inquirer:* SCIENTIST: GREENHOUSE EFFECT AT WORK. The *Providence Journal:* THE GREENHOUSE EFFECT IS HERE.

Millions of people had been hearing about the greenhouse effect ever since the drought of '88 began. It was reported as a threat that loomed in the near future. "But 'destined,' 'future,' 'projected,' 'predicted,' 'forecast,' 'expected'—these are the words that land a topic on 'Nova,' not the Evening News," as the writer Bill McKibben noted that year ("Is the World Getting Hotter?", the *New York Review of Books*).

After Hansen's testimony, the greenhouse effect was explained and re-explained in every other edition of the papers and every other weather report. It ceased to be a fear for the future and became a concern for the present. Global change was a fact of life. What a world of difference between heat in the world to come and heat that we feel on our skins! It is not surprising that people on the street—with the streets at 101° F.—soon began to speak of "a sense of foreboding," "an impending sense of doom." The thought that we might have caused the hot weather made the heat much more oppressive. For if we had brought it on ourselves, the heat was a kind of punishment, which is what we have always imagined Hell would be like.

In the U.S., the heat came on top of the worst ozone smog in history, the filthiest beaches in recent memory, and even an alarming alert about indoor radon gas that was issued by the E.P.A. The summer turned everybody into environmentalists, at least for as long as the heat wave lasted. It was an election year and for the first time in that decade the environment became a hot political issue. Candidates for president of the United States made speeches about the greenhouse effect. George Bush said in Erie Metropark, Michigan, on August 31: "Those who think we're powerless to do anything about the 'greenhouse effect' are forgetting about the 'White House effect.' As President, I intend to do something about it."

Bush pledged to convene an international conference on the environment at the White House in his first year in office. "We will talk about global warming. We will talk about acid rain. We will talk about saving our oceans, and preventing the loss of tropical rain forests. And we will act." He said, "1988, in a sense, is the year the Earth spoke back."

Newsweek devoted two covers to the environment: one to the fouled beaches and one to the greenhouse effect. *Time,* instead of naming a "Man of the Year" at the end of 1988, named Earth "Planet of the Year." Fear of the greenhouse effect had helped to re-ignite the environmental movement in the United States. The previous movement, which had largely spent itself by 1980, had little to do with the greenhouse effect. This movement began with the greenhouse effect (and if predictions of global warming are correct the movement may build with the greenhouse effect for a long time). As Senator Max Baucus, from Montana, observed at the committee hearings that June, "I sense that we are experiencing a major shift. It's like a shift of tectonic plates."

Unfortunately, part of what was pushing those plates was a popular misconception about the greenhouse effect and the Summer of '88.

At the Senate hearing on June 23, Tim Wirth, of Colorado, author of a major bill to counter the greenhouse warming, wanted the most dramatic testimony he could get. In the question-and-answer session, he was looking for a ringing declaration that it was the greenhouse effect that was making everybody sweat outside.

SENATOR WIRTH: I think the question that everybody is asking today with all the heat and everything going on across the Middle West and the Southwest and so on is [whether] the current heat wave and drought [are] related to the greenhouse effect. And a subpart of that is how sure are you of your response. [Laughter.]

Now, Hansen had not said that the Summer of '88 was caused by the greenhouse effect. He was talking about the rise in temperatures of the twentieth century, and the very sharp rise over the previous three decades.

DR. HANSEN: Well, I mentioned in my testimony that you cannot blame a particular drought on the greenhouse effect. You can say—at least our climate model seems to be telling us—that the greenhouse effect impacts the probability of having a drought.

Wirth tried again.

SENATOR WIRTH: So, you would say that the heat wave and the drought are related to the greenhouse effect. Is that right?

DR. HANSEN: Yes. If you look over a time period of, say, 10 years, the number of droughts you get in that period, it appears that will be larger because of the greenhouse effect. But whether you get a drought in a particular year depends upon the weather patterns that exist at the beginning of the season, and that is a noisy phenomenon which is basically unpredictable. So, I can't tell you whether next year is going to have a drought or not. All that we are trying to say is that the probability is somewhat larger than it was a few decades ago.

Not good enough. The senator did not want "on the one hand, on the other hand." (They have a saying in Washington: "I'd like to meet a one-handed scientist.")

SENATOR WIRTH: Dr. Oppenheimer, do you want to take a shot? Any of the others of you want to answer the question? I think it is a perfectly logical question to ask, isn't it? I mean, the American public is out there. It is getting very, very warm. . . . Are we having the drought because of the greenhouse effect? And it seems to me we have to be in a position of saying yes, no.

DR. OPPENHEIMER: I think I would just sort of recapitulate and maybe restate what Jim and Suki have said which is that no one episode, no one drought, no one heat wave can be ascribed uniquely to the greenhouse warming so that that part of the question has to get a maybe.

Oppenheimer recapitulated: one hundred years of warming; four world records broken in the past eight years.

DR. OPPENHEIMER: . . . So, it is reasonable to assume that the greenhouse effect is here. It is happening. The warming has begun. It has started. But no one I don't think in their right mind is ever going to say this one climate event in particular is related.

SENATOR WIRTH: Do any of the others of you want to comment? Dr. Moomaw?

The next morning, of course, 50 million people stooped to pick up their newspapers. It was 7:30 A.M., already 80° F., and the headlines read GLOBAL WARMING HAS BEGUN. As people made their way to work—the temperature now 83°—this was all they could think: "They're saying it's the greenhouse effect." So the hearings caused just the kind of sensation the senators wanted.

Meanwhile the scientists' colleagues across the country picked up their newspapers and decided that Hansen had jumped the gun. Hansen had said, of the rise in temperatures in the previous three decades, "The probability of a chance warming of that magnitude is about 1 percent. So, with 99 percent confidence we can state that the warming during this time period is a real warming trend."

Somehow most U.S. climate experts got this wrong. They did not understand what Hansen had declared himself to be "99-percent confident" about. Like everyone else, they thought James Hansen was announcing that the greenhouse effect had caused the 100-year warming trend; or the 30-year warming trend; or the long hot summer of '88.

Now, the warming of the planet *may* be a purely random event—the possibility cannot yet be ruled out—and most climate experts feel that the probability of purely random warming events of this magnitude is a lot better than 1 percent. Thus, looking only at the temperature statistics, and admitting no other evidence whatever, the probability that the warming of the planet was due to the greenhouse effect must be less than 99 percent.

Most people in Hansen's field did agree with him that the warming had probably started. Almost everyone agreed that the warming is likely to accelerate. Almost everyone agreed that it was past time the world woke up.

Almost everyone was saying that—in private. So it may seem strange that they fastened upon that "99 percent." But scientists weigh probabilities the way Keeling weighs carbon dioxide. That is what they do. Hansen's "99 percent" became notorious. Lecturers on everything from Venusian lightning bolts to solar flares to South American earthquakes could get a laugh from their colleagues that awful summer by saying, "Of course, I'm not *99 percent* sure."

Still Hansen was glad he said it. After the hearing he told a reporter from *The New York Times,* "It is time to stop waffling so much and say that the evidence is pretty strong that the greenhouse effect is here."

Hansen, Stephen Schneider, and others often use the metaphor of dice. Roll a pair of dice: low numbers are cool summers, and high numbers are hot summers. In the old days, we might have had an equal chance of rolling two ones, snake eyes, for a very cool summer, or two sixes, boxcars, for a very hot summer. But putting greenhouse gases into the air is like loading the dice. We can still roll a low number sometimes. We are more likely to roll two sixes, for a long hot summer.

Each year we load the dice a little more. Each human being on the planet loads the dice with more than one ton of carbon each year. In the United States, unless one is very poor, it is almost impossible not to help load the dice in a big way. The average American car contributes its weight in carbon dioxide to the atmosphere each year.

So we are likely to get boxcars boxcars boxcars; and the overall trend in temperature, in coming decades, will probably be upward, steeply upward.

Suppose we were *trying* to load a pair of dice. Never having done it before, how would we know when we had done it right? If we rolled experimentally eight times, and four out of eight rolls were boxcars, we would suspect that the dice were loaded properly. But those rolls *could* be a coincidence. A scrupulous statistician would say, let's roll them ten or twenty times more.

And that is how things stood in 1988. In the previous one-hundred-odd rolls, boxcars had been coming up slightly more frequently—enough to raise the average temperature of the planet by half a degree C. That is about what we would expect from the gradual loading of the dice. During the 1980s, four years in eight had been the hottest in recorded history. That too looked like loaded dice. But it could still have been chance. "To be absolutely sure scientifically," as Schneider said, "we need to have more warmer years."

The year 1988 did prove to be the hottest yet (in a photo finish with 1987). However, no one could say the greenhouse effect was at work on that particular summer—any more than one could say from a single roll that dice are loaded. After the hearings the editor of *Nature,* John Maddox, re-explained this point in an editorial in his journal. "What the Congress, and the rest of us, must understand is that it will never be possible to answer affirmatively the question, 'Is this the year the greenhouse effect began to bite?' The best that can be hoped for is that it will be possible retrospectively to note that this or that climatic effect is probably a consequence of this or that driving force."

*   *   *

Before the year was out, Kevin E. Trenberth, head of NCAR's Climate Analysis Section, began circulating preprints of a paper, "Origins of the 1988 North American Drought."

According to Trenberth's analysis, the drought was part of a dance between the atmosphere and the hydrosphere. Every five or six years, the interplay of winds and currents pushes a great mass of unusually warm water toward the Pacific shore of South America. This patch of warm water is called El Niño, the Boy Child, because it often arrives off the coast of Peru around Christmas. The warm water seems to touch a sort of pressure point in the global circulation system—perhaps because it sits right on the equator, where the winds of the Northern and Southern Hemispheres meet. In any case the Boy Child is often strong enough to convulse weather around the world.

El Niño also has a dark twin. A patch of abnormally *cold* water sometimes appears in about the same spot. In 1988 this discovery was still so new that no one was quite sure what to call the cold water—perhaps La Niña, the Girl Child. La Niña, too, can hit the pressure point, and she convulses the general global circulation in her own way.

In 1988, according to Trenberth, this is what happened: The patch of cold water off Peru displaced the normal meeting place of the two hemispheres' winds and pushed it northward. These winds met southeast of Hawaii—where weather is usually serene—and brought heavy thunderstorms. The storms were so heavy that they disrupted the trade winds. That pushed the Northern Hemisphere's jet stream farther north.

Normally this jet stream is the good shepherd that brings the continent of North America its spring and summer rains. But the jet stream shifted so far north that a hot, dry high-pressure cell crept up from father south and squatted right in the middle of the continent, blocking the rains for months.

Trenberth was careful to say that this scenario did not disprove the greenhouse effect. As he noted in his paper, the greenhouse effect "may tilt the balance such that conditions for droughts and heat waves are more likely." Trenberth was only trying to trace the long chain reaction in sea and air that had resulted in this particular drought.

All that summer, however, people had thought that the scientists were telling them, "It's the greenhouse effect." So when Trenberth's paper appeared in *Science* all the headlines and decks in the country rocked the other way. GREENHOUSE EFFECT CLEARED IN '88 DROUGHT.

SCIENTISTS LINK '88 DROUGHT TO NATURAL CYCLE IN TROPICAL PACIFIC. GREENHOUSE EFFECT WAS NOT THE CULPRIT THIS TIME, RESEARCHERS AGREE.

Anyone who understands the metaphor of the loaded dice will understand the error in those headlines.

To load a die, a cheater puts a small lead weight under the die-face that he likes—usually under the six. When he rolls that die, it lands at random on the table, its corners catch and tumble, and a thousand and one forces come into play—not just the weight in the die, but also the trajectory and momentum that he gave it in his throw, and the tiny imperfections in the gaming table, the grain of sand in its path, and even the smallest breeze or eddy in the room.

Suppose casino guards at Las Vegas filmed the roll of his dice in super-slo-mo with fifty movie cameras from fifty angles, and they landed on six and six. If the guards challenged his dice, he could protest that the lead weight had very little to do with the six—the grain of sand was much more important. And he would be right. On any single throw, the little weight he put in that die is never going to be the only reason, or even the chief reason, the die lands on the six. Other factors will always be more important. Again, only by rolling the dice over and over again and seeing sixes come up more often than anything else could the guards be sure the dice were loaded.

After all, the lead weight in the die doesn't *throw* the die. It is only because of the energy the gambler puts into each throw that the die comes up anything at all. Without all those other factors—the palm, the throw, the table—the die wouldn't be rolling. It would be sitting there on the table doing absolutely nothing.

So the gambler says he's innocent, but he is guilty as hell.

Likewise with the weather. The greenhouse effect doesn't roll the troposphere. The troposphere is rolling and spinning because of the heat of the Sun, the temperatures of the sea and land. The gases we are putting in the air merely *load* the troposphere, and according to theory they make it more likely to land one way than another.

Of course, that is a pretty long explanation for the evening news. We like our forecasts in black and white. (Dice are black and white, too, but they have six sides.) For as long as the heat of that summer had lasted in the United States, the Soviet Union, and China, the question of the hour had been, "Is this it?" And people thought the answer was *yes*. Now that the fall had arrived, and with it presumably the possibility of cool reflection, it became just as popular to say that the answer was *no*. That is what the new headlines suggested: "They're saying it *wasn't* the greenhouse effect."

At the 1988 fall meeting of the American Geophysical Union in San Francisco there was a special session on the Drought of '88. One of the speakers was Jerome Namias, a retired meteorologist who had been the director of the National Weather Service's extended-forecast division for thirty years. Namias had been telling people for most of his career that we could predict the world's weather if we spent more time and money watching patches of cold or warm water in the Pacific. At the meeting, Namias said that Trenberth's patch-of-cold-water chain reaction could "explain what went on quite adequately without the greenhouse effect." He called the drought "a classic example of air-sea interactions." He called the greenhouse effect "a very convenient scapegoat."

"There's going to be a greenhouse effect, but that doesn't say where or when it's going to happen," Namias declared. "I'm denying it's here now."

The mood in the hall was with Namias. The summer was past, heads were 99 percent cool. The experts at the meeting took turns criticizing the global temperature statistics and the global sea-level statistics. (No one ever criticizes the accuracy of Keeling's carbon-dioxide statistics.)

William Kellogg, a climate expert recently retired from NCAR, was also at the meeting. Like Hansen, Kellogg was a veteran of the study of the greenhouse effect on Venus. He had once served as *rapporteur* at an international meeting on climate change convened by the World Meteorological Organization in Moscow. The Soviet climate experts at that meeting argued that it is extremely likely that the greenhouse effect is here. They found the tendency of their American counterparts to deny the evidence rather puzzling. That was in 1982.

Kellogg looked at his colleagues' viewgraphs of patches of hot water, cold water, El Niño, and La Niña, and was reminded of the Hindu fable of the blind men and the elephant. He knew that the global warming is bound to make each heat wave worse, whether a particular heat wave is started by the Boy Child, the Girl Child, or anything else. This is precisely what makes the greenhouse effect dangerous.

It is the same case as with storm surges. When a storm surge comes at low tide it does little damage. When it comes at high tide it does a lot of damage. If sea levels rise, even the low-tide storm surge can hurt us, and the high-tide storm surge can be devastating.

Kellogg stood up and mentioned the Hindu parable. Perhaps they were all looking at different parts of the same thing, he said. "The temperature's going up; that's no secret," he said. "This year may be typical of the kind of year we will see in a global warming . . ."

There were protests. Kellogg defended himself. No one stood up in his support. The next day there were more stories in the newspapers. (EARTH NOT WARMING YET, SAY SCIENTISTS. *San Jose Mercury News.* GREENHOUSE NOT BLAMED FOR DROUGHT. The *Oregonian.*) So the patch of cold water in the Pacific ended up disturbing for a brief while the main current of world opinion.

I called Kellogg after the meeting. He was good-humored about it. "I don't know why we can't say it's a *combination* of things that made the summer what it was," he said. "It's always that way with weather."

As recently as 1986, most G.C.M.s were predicting a rise of only 2 or 3° C. (3.6 to 5.4° F.), rather than 4 or 5.* People tended to feel almost cheated by this forecast. "I've given that number out to people at lectures," one climate expert told me in 1986. "And they come up to me afterward and say, 'Three degrees? That's the difference between June and July, or between yesterday and today. What difference is *that* going to make?"

But even a two or three-degree change is not small if it involves the whole planet, and lasts for decades or centuries. Three degrees represents a change as big as the arrival of an Ice Age. For a *drop* of three degrees, if sustained, would start an Ice Age.

At the depth of the last Ice Age, 20,000 years ago, the average temperature of the planet was colder than it is today by only 5° C. That was enough to cover eastern Canada, New England, and much of the Midwest in a sheet of ice more than a mile thick. (On Manhattan Island in the Summer of 16,000 B.C. the ice was half a mile thick.) In western North America, the ice covered parts of Washington, Idaho, Montana, and all of Western Canada. In Europe it buried Scandinavia and Scotland, most of Great Britain, Denmark, France, Germany, much of Poland, much of the Soviet Union. In the Southern Hemisphere, there was ice in Australia, New Zealand, and Argentina. In Hawaii the ice

---

*Temperatures rose after modelers refined their treatment of water vapor and clouds. Clouds are still the climate expert's Achilles Heel. Until the modelers have gotten the clouds right, their predictions may rise or fall again, as scientists try to calibrate just how hot things can get.

even capped Mauna Loa. "In all," writes the climatologist John Imbrie, of Brown University, in *Ice Ages,* "the ice covered about 11 million square miles of land that is today free of ice." Sea levels fell by 350 feet.

All that from a drop of 5° C. And that was an especially *severe* Ice Age.

Thus what the computer models are suggesting is that children born today may see a climate change approximately the size of an Ice Age. The change, of course, is in the opposite direction, and it will create a climate that is outside the experience of our species. *Homo sapiens sapiens,* Man the Doubly Wise, evolved about 50,000 years ago. A rise of 1.5° C. (2.7° F.) would make Earth warmer than it has been in the last 100,000 years—since before the beginning of the last Ice Age. A rise of 5° C. (9° F.) would make Earth warmer than it has been in millions of years—since well before the beginning of the Pleistocene Epoch.

Syukuro Manabe, of the Geophysical Fluid Dynamics Laboratory, in Princeton, is a world grandmaster of greenhouse models. He has been testing and refining the forecasts since the 1960s. For a doubling of carbon dioxide* Manabe lists eight predictions on which his models seem reasonably firm. †

First, the temperature of the troposphere will rise, and the temperature of the stratosphere will drop.

Second, the warming at high latitudes will be two or three times larger than the warming at low latitudes (because of the kind of feedback that was foreseen by Arrhenius. Sea ice will retreat. The poles will be darker. Dark terrain soaks up more warmth from the Sun.). This does not mean the equator will escape unscathed. The broad hot band of tropical climates will grow about 2° C. hotter if the global mean rise is 3° C. That change would be very serious for India, for example. However, countries at middle latitudes, including much of Western Europe and the northern United States, will be 5° C. warmer than they are now. Above the latitude of Stockholm, Sweden, and Anchorage,

---

*The doubling of carbon dioxide (due some time in the twenty-first century) is only a benchmark. Major warming should begin before carbon dioxide doubles. And there is enough coal and oil in the ground to raise the level of carbon dioxide about ten times higher.

†Ironically enough, these eight predictions may be more accurate for the year 2070 than for the year 2001. Our crystal balls are not very helpful in predicting the transient: the transition period in which we are living now.

Alaska, in the Northern Hemisphere, the warming could be as much as 10° C. (18° F.).

Third, over the Arctic Ocean, the temperature increase will be at a maximum in winter and a minimum in summer. In other words, winters there will be much warmer, while summers will be only somewhat warmer. (The Arctic seems to be exceptional in this regard, Manabe notes; elsewhere on Earth, all seasons will grow warmer.)

Fourth, the global water cycle will grow hyperactive. At present, 500,000 cubic kilometers of water go around the cycle each year. With the warming, more water will rise and fall each day: a conservative estimate is 5 percent more, or 25,000 extra cubic kilometers of water. This extra tonnage will not rain down evenly over the surface of the planet. Some places will get much damper while other places will dry out.

Fifth, the white caps of sea ice at both poles will grow smaller and thinner. Manabe's latest models suggest that this will happen at surprisingly unequal rates, very soon in the north, and very late in the south—there, only after five centuries or so.

Sixth, on the continents, snows will melt earlier in the year.

Seventh, much more water will flow into the Arctic from the river basins of Siberia and Canada: as much as 30 percent more. No one knows what practical significance that may have, but it is a big change.

Eighth, because winter snows will melt earlier, and because spring rains will come and go earlier in the year, summers in many parts of the world will be dry. The interiors of the continents of the Northern Hemisphere will see more summer droughts. Not every year will be as bad as the Summer of '88. However, when the greenhouse warming is superimposed on top of natural fluctuations, the Great Plains of the United States will more often experience summers as hot and dry as they were that long hot summer, or in the 1930s, the time of the Dust Bowl.

This short list suggests the power of even three degrees C. The change in global weather patterns that Manabe is outlining is extensive. His model predicts much drier soils in summer over the mid-continental regions of North America, the Corn Belt, and the Grain Belt. The same kind of chronic summer drought is forecast for Western Europe.

Of course, some climates could improve for agriculture. "Canada and northern Siberia would have a longer growing season," as Roger Revelle has pointed out in an interview in *Omni*. "The wheat-belt climate will move north."

"The United States could become a grain importer and the U.S.S.R. could become a grain exporter," Walter Orr Roberts, former director of NCAR, has said. "At the very least, it would be a major economic, political, and social dislocation."

"But then," notes Revelle, "you'd have another problem, because the soils are much poorer farther north. The best soil in the world is in Iowa—lovely, thick, loamy soil. Whereas Canada has thin, acid soil."

An important point: because the warming will be greatest where the cooling of the Ice Age was also greatest—in high latitudes—both the icehouse and the hothouse will be centered around the poles. Yet the icehouse has left these places in poor shape to enjoy the benefits of the hothouse. Ice scraped away the soils that could profit from the heat, and ice age winds dumped them in places that may not be getting much rain in the next hundred years.

The weather patterns that Manabe sees in his model could lower water levels in the Western rivers of the U.S. by half or even by three-quarters in the summertime. "Snow will melt so much earlier in the year," he says, "that by the time summer comes, not much water trickles down from the mountains." In the hot weather, these streams will be half-spent before they ever reach a river. (Even before the hot decade of the 1980s, Revelle notes, 85 percent of the precipitation that falls in the upper basin of the Colorado used to evaporate and only 15 percent was carried by the river.) Virtually all Western rivers are seriously overdrawn already. Despite the pumping of underground aquifers, there are chronic water shortages, and the aquifers' water tables are sinking fast. If the greenhouse warming diverts some of the West's rainfall to higher latitudes, huge river diversion projects may be necessary to bring the water back down to the farmlands where rains fell before, and where there are soils and farmers ready to receive them. The American West has been called Cadillac Desert. The greenhouse warming may leave a lot of rusted Cadillacs.

Revelle has listed other major rivers that would dwindle in summer: the Hwang Ho in China, the Amu Dar'ya and Syr Dar'ya in the U.S.S.R., the Zambezi in Zimbabwe and Zambia, and the São Francisco in Brazil. The Tigris and Euphrates Rivers, cradle of western civilization, once home of the legendary Hanging Gardens of Babylon, and perhaps the Garden of Eden, will be dessicated. Meanwhile, so much more water would pour into the Mekong and the Brahmaputra rivers that they would bring terrible floods to Thailand, Laos, Kampuchea, Vietnam, India, and Bangladesh.

Climate expert Stephen Schneider believes the most pervasive impact of the global temperature change will be to increase the chances of certain kinds of extreme events. Not frosts, obviously—but heat waves, droughts. "We humans, as biological systems, do not feel climate shifts through slow changes," he explained to me in 1986. "What we feel is extreme events. What slow changes really mean to us is that they increase the probability of extreme events. That's how you'll notice them.

"People say, 'My God, what happened!' Not the one degree. It's the one degree that made these outlying, one-in-a-hundred-year events become one-in-twenty-year events, or the one-in-twenty-year events become one-in-five-year events."

For example, he and colleagues at NCAR have studied what the warming might mean to the Corn Belt of the United States. July is the month when corn grows its tassels. The health of the plant at that stage has a sharp threshold at 95° F., and higher temperatures can singe the corn. Runs of hot days are especially bad: a run of five days may be long enough to cover the entire silking stage and ruin that year's harvest. Schneider and his colleagues looked closely at the implications of the warming for Des Moines, Iowa; Fargo, North Dakota; Berne and Evansville, Indiana. They found that a rise of 3° F. in mean temperature makes heat waves there twice as likely—in some circumstances, six times as likely.

Hansen, of NASA, has calculated the likelihood of heat waves in Washington, D.C. Today, the capital gets an average of one day a year above 100° F. (So I picked just the right day to visit J. Murray Mitchell.) With a doubling of carbon dioxide, the city will get those temperatures twelve days a year. Ninety days out of each year will be hotter than 90° F.—compared to thirty days today. What we call a heat wave today will be where heat waves start.

When the atmosphere warms, so does the surface temperature of the sea. As the seas warm, the storms known variously around the world as hurricanes, typhoons, and tropical cyclones may increase in intensity. They owe much of their energy to warm sea surface temperatures. In fact, they often cut themselves short before reaching maturity, when the spinning, raging winds stir up cooler water from below the surface and kill the winds. Kerry A. Emanuel, of the Center for Meteorology and Physical Oceanography, at M.I.T., has calculated the implications of warmer sea surface temperatures for hurricanes. He believes the next one hundred years will be a century of tropical storms. There will be a general warming of the upper layers of the sea, with the biggest change coming—according to Emanuel's preliminary estimates—in partially enclosed ocean basins like the Gulf of Mexico and the Bay of Bengal. In such places, hurricanes could be more powerful by as much as 60 percent, even with only a very slight warming of global sea surface temperatures.

The Summer of '88 was a record summer for hurricanes. One of them caught up swarms of locusts in Africa and whirled them all the way across the Atlantic, where they rained down upon Puerto Rico, the Lesser Antilles, and Suriname.

Hurricanes, tornadoes, heavy winds, hailstorms, floods, blizzards, heat waves, droughts, untimely frosts, cold spells—these can strike one part of the country while others bask in mild sunshine, as anyone knows who watches national weather forecasts in the U.S. In 1983, for instance, weather damage cost citizens in the states of Utah, Mississippi, and Iowa about five hundred times as much money as in Rhode Island, Connecticut, Massachusetts, and Hawaii. This is a phenomenon that was noticed by the ancients, who sometimes had to migrate because of drought. Joseph's father moved—that's how the Jews got to Egypt.

With the warming, some parts of the country may become chronic hard-luck cases. Supercomputers paint the future with such a broad brush that they cannot tell which state or nation-state will be a winner or a loser. However, people who live along coastlines have special reasons for concern. Revelle estimates, conservatively, that we will probably see a one-and-a-half-foot rise in sea level in the next one hundred years. Part of this rise will come as glaciers on land melt faster and flow down to the sea. Part will come because as seawater warms it expands.

The sea level rise is a straightforward consequence of warmer global temperatures. Schneider: "If you just heat the oceans, it has to work, right? If you heat a tube, mercury rises in the tube, and you call it a thermometer. If you heat the ocean, it's a fluid, it goes up the tube, which is called the continental walls, and you call it a rise in sea level. And the level is about four inches higher now than it was a hundred years ago."

Sea-level rise is also a mechanism by which small global changes get

107

magnified into big local changes. "I can't understand it," Queen Juliana of the Netherlands once exclaimed, watching a computer demonstration in Amsterdam. "I can't even understand the people who understand it." Here is one prediction that does not require computer-literacy to understand. Where a shoreline is sheer cliff, a small rise in sea level may not make much difference. But where a shoreline is nearly flat, as in the Netherlands and Bangladesh, a rise in sea level of even one foot can make all the difference in the world.

Many countries around the world are already in the position of the Netherlands, with fingers in the dike. As sea levels rise, they are losing land. It has been estimated that a rise of one and a half feet would cost the state of Massachusetts 10,000 acres. It would cost Italy a fortune to save the city of Venice. It would cost Egypt a rich piece of the Nile delta.

Bangladesh alone is populated by more than 100 million people, packed at the extraordinary density of 2,000 people per square mile. At the rate their population is growing now, there will be 4,000 people per square mile some time early in the next century. Before sea level rises even two feet, millions will have to move.

Moreover a two-foot rise in sea level could have precisely the same effect on ocean waves that a 2° C. rise in temperature would have on heat waves. It would make the freak disaster commonplace. Today, when high winds come at high tide they sometimes push waves over the tops of dikes and seabreaks and cause the disasters we call storm surges. A two-foot rise in sea level gives a big lift to every storm surge in the next hundred years. "People say, 'Aah, two feet, that's nothing,'" Schneider says. "But it dramatically increases the probability of a transgression. So the hundred-year flood becomes a twenty-year flood, the twenty-year flood a five-year flood, and the insurance companies won't insure you anymore."

Meanwhile the western portion of the Antarctic ice sheet is unstable, because it extends out over the sea in a giant shelf. It is held there by small islands that lie below the ice and below sea level. It has been compared to a roof held up by a few pillars. Rising seas could break it up. About 2 million cubic feet of ice are up out of water on this shelf—a good part of the continent. If all of that ice falls into the sea, it will raise global sea level by as much as twenty feet, flooding New York and London and putting a vast acreage of farmland under salt water in Holland, Bangladesh, Thailand, Kampuchea, Vietnam, and China. Half the state of Florida would be wiped from the map.

Glaciologists familiar with the slow pace of change of the sphere of ice believe that the collapse of the West Antarctic ice sheet is still centuries away. If they are right, then the sea level rise in the next century is likely to be gradual. City buildings have an average half-life of between fifty and one hundred years. Thus their natural rate of decay and replacement is on a timescale that can respond comfortably to slow changes in sea level. Assuming the glaciologists are right, many coastal cities may retreat just as they expanded, haphazardly, from decade to decade, without really feeling the pinch of a disaster.

Of course, ice may surprise us. The long slow warming at the end of the last Ice Age led to some surprisingly fast action. One of the first things that happened was that about 15,000 years ago the Barents Ice Shelf, a vast piece of ice that sat north of Scandinavia, collapsed into the sea. It was so big and its fall was so swift that it may have helped to trigger the more widescale collapse of the cryosphere that concluded the Ice Age and ushered in the modern geological epoch, the Holocene.

In 1988, scientists at the Woods Hole Oceanographic Institution studied the death of the Barents ice indirectly through a close analysis of sediments taken in the Norwegian-Greenland Sea. The collapse of the Barents Ice Shelf appears to have been so rapid and at the same time so sustained that it may have raised sea level by more than ten feet per century for nearly five centuries.

If the greenhouse predictions are correct, then in the long run the world's sea level is *really* going to rise. One of the first scientists to try to look that far ahead was Keeling. He injected the Hubbert spike of greenhouse gases into the air and calculated how long it would all take to come down. If the gases had gone up into the atmosphere and fallen right down out of it again, then in the perspective of millennia the imprint of the modern age upon the air would have looked like this:

But in Keeling's model, the carbon dioxide we have put into the air takes so long to be absorbed by the sea that it lingers at least 10,000 years:

If so, we are living at the start of a new age on the planet, a greenhouse age, with a timespan comparable to the span of an ice age. The chlorofluorocarbons that we have put into the air will decay in a century or two, but the carbon dioxide will keep pushing Earth's climate for a longer period of time than any human empire or civilization has ever lasted; as far into the future as the Stone Age is in the past.

At the depth of the last Ice Age, 20,000 years ago, there was so much ice locked up on land, and sea levels fell so low, that the receding waters exposed an area of shoreland the size of Africa. The amount of ice that remains on this planet today is comparatively modest. However, if the new greenhouse age lasts 10,000 years, eventually it may put much of the ice back into the sea. We may redraw the face of the globe by *eliminating* an area of shoreland the size of, say, Europe. *Après nous le déluge.*

No Earth scientist doubts that the greenhouse effect is real. Scientists have known since the time of Napoleon that the atmosphere has a greenhouse effect. The effect is as inevitable as anything in physics. As Schneider says, it is as reliable a theory as gravity. It is not controversial.

And most Earth scientists believe that adding greenhouse gases to the air will warm the air some more. That is not controversial either.

Indeed, most climate experts believe that this artificial warming of the planet is probably happening right now. They fault Hansen's use of statistics, but his basic conclusion is not controversial. "It's perfectly responsible to say it's been detected," says Schneider. "Yes, it's been detected, in terms of a whole slew of evidence."

"I, too, believe that the greenhouse warming very likely is occurring," says Manabe. "That is perfectly reasonable to say."

We all speak of the greenhouse effect as controversial, but the shocking fact is this: the only important questions left are those that no human being can answer in this millennium.

How bad will it be? That has to be controversial. We are talking about an unprecedented experiment. There is a wide range of possibilities—although the Summer of '88 was one more illustration of the power of a few degrees. The difference between the Summer of '88 and a normal summer is about one and a half degrees F. In our lifetimes, if current theory is correct, the temperature of an average summer will rise 5 or 10° F. Numbers like these are dangerous to think about. They can make you want to pound your head against the wall.

And when will it get so hot that everyone knows it? That has to be controversial, too. The onset of the warming is so gradual that Schneider, Manabe, and others want to watch the next twenty rolls of the dice. At present that is the majority view in the United States.

Yet climate experts in the Soviet Union were sure in '82. The difference may be partly a matter of psychology. In the Soviet Union the stakes may seem lower, because the effect seems less threatening. Soviets can hope to come out winners (just think of what a warming would do for Siberia). And although their country is a major contributor to the greenhouse effect, at least it is not *the* major contributor.

In the United States, however, the stakes seem higher, for Americans stand to lose a great deal in a global warming. And between the burning forests of the nineteenth century and the smokestacks and exhaust pipes of the twentieth century, the United States has been the chief exporter of carbon dioxide on this planet for a very long time. Thus, for a responsible American scientist to declare, "It is really happening!" can be as hard as shouting "Stop the train!"

Late in the twenty-first century, only historians and schoolchildren will remember whether the date of the onset is finally fixed by convention at 1988, 1998, or 2008. By then, if current theory is correct, the new world will be here in force, its problems will be full-blown, and all that will really matter for the world's leaders will be how to cope with the planet's new terms and conditions. By then most people will be content simply to round off the date of the onset. They will say, "Ever since the turn of the century . . . In this millennium . . . For the past one hundred years . . ."

Right now, however, the date of the onset makes all the difference. As long as uncertainties linger, the world will go on loading the dice against itself with more than 5 billion tons of carbon a year. For this reason, those who understand how much is at stake, and how much is known, are exasperated by our national focus on what remains unknown. ("The right question isn't, Was '88 the start?" says Richard Houghton, of the Woods Hole Research Center. "The real question is, *"Did ya like '88?"*)

If the weather is cool when you read these words and people are saying, "Remember when we were all so worried about the greenhouse effect?", explain this to them. As Dante writes in Canto Twenty of the *Inferno:*

> Therefore, I charge you, should you ever hear
> Other accounts of this, to let no falsehood
> Confuse the truth which I have just made clear.

CHAPTER 7

THE
SEVEN SPHERES

If the Almighty had consulted me before embarking
on the Creation, I would have recommended something simpler.

Alfonso X of Castile

In the Planet Earth, almost everything is connected to everything else.
A *Gray's Anatomy* of our planet would have to cross-reference every
item on every page. When you look at all the bizarre things that can
happen in a system with so many working parts, the possibilities are
frightening.

In the past, climate scientists' models have focused on the atmosphere. Now many scientists are trying to look farther. With pens and
paper, pocket calculators and supercomputers, they are trying to take
into account all seven spheres.

They start by examining a single change in a single part of the system: in the sphere of ice, sea, life, air, fire, rock, or human affairs.
Then they try to follow this change as it may grow, propagate, meta-
morphose, multiply, or dissolve in the other spheres. Finally, the investigators try to estimate what all of these changes, taken together,
will do to the temperature of the planet in the next one hundred years.

This step-by-step approach is completely inadequate to the task.
But for the moment, step-by-step is the best we can do. And it is
becoming clear that we are taking more of a gamble with the planet
than we thought. In 1982, a panel of climate experts at the National
Academy of Sciences summed up a report: "Our calm assessment of
the CO_2 issue rests essentially on the 'foreseeable' consequences of
climatic change. . . . There may yet be surprises."

Today most climate experts would revise that. In a system of seven spheres, there are bound to be surprises. There will be chain reactions. We may be very surprised.

Ice. Until recently, when scientists tried to imagine the worst—what might snap as things warm up—they focused on the Antarctic icecap. As we have already seen, much of the ice on the western side of the continent projects way out into the ocean. There is almost no land to prop it up. The whole shelf of ice could someday fall into the sea.

However, the Antarctic is so cold and isolated and its icecap is so thick that it may not melt or break up for a very long time. Right now it is often too cold and dry down there to snow. If Earth warms up, the South Pole may simply get a lot more snow. The whole southern icecap may grow. In fact, so much snow may start falling in the middle of the White Continent that (if some of the most recent models are correct) global sea levels may even *drop* for a while.

We may have been worrying about the wrong pole.

From space, the planet Earth looks neatly symmetrical, one big white icecap on each pole. But the southern icecap is a continent, and the northern icecap is just a raft. Most of the northern icecap is simply floating on the Arctic Ocean.

There has been a northern icecap for a few million years—ever since the beginning of the Pleistocene. The area of the ice is formidably large. During the Arctic winter (which lasts from November to June) the ice expands from a summer minimum of 7 or 8 million square kilometers to a winter maximum of 15 million square kilometers (which makes it ten times the size of the state of Alaska).

The Soviet climatologist Mikhail Budyko was the first to realize that the whole Arctic icecap could completely disappear. He published his first notes on the subject as long ago as 1962. The possibility has taken a while to penetrate Western thinking, perhaps because Westerners are less conscious than Soviets of the importance of the Arctic Ocean.

Glaciologists who have watched the icecap's extraordinary growth during the winter, surveying it from planes and dogsleds and sometimes even diving underneath it in wet suits, know that the cap is often paper-thin. First the dark sub-zero waters are covered by a film of "frazil" ice, tiny crystals suspended in the water. Then the tiny crystals consolidate into a thin sheet that lies on the rolling sea and flexes with the swell like an oil slick: "nilas." When nilas has thickened a few inches it is called "young ice," and when it is a foot deep it is called "first-year ice."

In places, first-year ice is compressed into ridges as much as sixty feet thick. But it is still fragile. There are always tears and gaps, because the ice sheets are being pushed by the currents below. Long cracks, called leads, open up, from a few feet to a few miles wide. Mysterious holes open up, polynyas: large lakes that may be caused by warm upwellings, hot spots in the sea, or may have causes more exotic. The interplay of sea and ice often forms vast patterns that look from above like interlocking fingers, black fingers of water and white fingers of ice.

Ice and snow make excellent reflectors. A layer of fresh-fallen snow reflects as much as 98 percent of the sunlight that falls on it. Even rotten, bubble-ridden summer ice in the Arctic reflects four or five times more sunlight than the dark seawater around it. Sunlight bounces right off the ice and back out into space, without warming the surface. So the Arctic is much colder than it would be without the ice. In fact the icecap makes this pole a "heat sink" for the whole of the Northern Hemisphere. Just by being white, the ice in the Arctic Ocean helps to drive weather systems everywhere. The whole circulation of air currents and sea currents in this hemisphere, the circulation that brings each country in the hemisphere its endless pageants of weather, can be described from the cosmic point of view as a Sisyphean effort to warm the North Pole.*

The ice in the Arctic Ocean also drives a kind of vertical waterwheel in the sea beneath it. The doubling of the ice each winter expels a great deal of salt. This salt freights the water that has not frozen, and the heavy burden sends the water straight to the bottom. It is as if the salt were loading the buckets of a giant waterwheel; the buckets of water sink, sink, sink. This sends bottom water rising toward the top. As it rises it carries nutrients from the depths toward the surface and eventually it helps to feed most of the world's marine life.

---

*Ice also chills the North Pole another way. By lidding vast stretches of the Arctic Ocean, the ice keeps the water from touching the air. The water is warmer than the air (although not recommended for swimming). So the water would warm the air if the ice did not come between them. In fact, when cracks appear in the Arctic sea ice (in "leads" ten miles wide) thermal plumes rise from the open water. Some of these plumes of warm air are so powerful that they penetrate the stratosphere, like the plumes from major volcanic eruptions.

The northern icecap is less isolated from the rest of the planet than the southern, and because its ice is full of holes, it is a much warmer place. The average temperature of the air above the North Pole is hotter than the air above the South Pole by about 12° C., or more than 21° F. (the difference between Miami and New York City). A small global warming would stop the northern ice from expanding each winter; and a small further warming would make the summer ice, the permanent ice, start to retreat.

In the chain reaction that Arrhenius foresaw, carbon dioxide warms the air; warming the air melts ice at the poles; the melting ice exposes dark polar waters and dark tundra; dark water and tundra soak up more heat than the ice; and this change in the local color of the poles warms the poles still more. This series of events involves sun, air, ice, earth, water, life, and the sphere of human affairs: all seven spheres.

This chain reaction may not happen in the Southern Hemisphere for many millennia, because the Antarctic icecap is so stable. But in the Northern Hemisphere it may destroy the Arctic icecap within our lifetimes. We may live to see an Earth that has not existed for millions of years: lopsided, with one thick icecap at the southern end and nothing but dark water at the other. It wouldn't take long to get there from here. According to the climatologist Hermann Flohn, of the University of Bonn, "a unipolar glaciated Earth could occur after a short transition period (probably on the order of a few decades only)."

Meteorologists find the prospects of a world with just one icecap rather fantastic. They know how sensitive the global circulation is to changes in the Arctic ice that are microscopic in comparison. Ever since the eighteenth century, for example, weather watchers have noticed that when winters are colder than usual in Greenland, they tend to be warmer than usual in Northern Europe, and vice versa. This seesaw effect has been traced by modern meteorologists to subtle influences of the Greenland ice. Slight changes in the ice have the power to alter winter weather as far away as the Aleutian Islands, on the other side of the world.

What happens if there is no ice? The impact on the global circulation of air and sea would be immediate, extensive, and completely unpredictable. As the planet becomes aberrantly asymmetric, with a huge and growing icecap in the south and a vanishing chip in the north, even the Southern Hemisphere will feel the change.

What is more, the waterwheel in the sea might slow down if there is no longer the huge annual growth of sea ice to drive it. A large part of the marine biosphere might be starved for nitrogen and phosphorus.

Of course, if the Arctic ocean opens up, the Soviet Union would become, for the first time in its history, a country with a coastline, perhaps even a great maritime power. That is one reason that Budyko believes the Soviet Union will come out a strong winner in the global warming.

This is strong positive feedback. Warming the planet melts the Arctic ice, which robs the planet of a giant sun-reflector, which warms the planet some more.

Sea. A sudden global change like that would mean chains of new surprises. One of the messiest might come from the floor of the sea.

Under conditions of cold temperature and high pressure, methane gas turns into solid ice. At present, these conditions are found in many places on this planet: below the thick permafrost in the Arctic tundra, for example, and on the cold, muddy slopes of the continents from the Arctic Ocean to the Gulf of Mexico. These underwater shelves and slopes represent a huge area—about 5 percent of the surface of the Earth.

Methane is also thought to be locked in the sediments of two cold inland bodies of water, the Black and the Caspian Seas. The gas was accidentally discovered there in the 1970s by a team of geologists aboard the research ship *Challenger,* during the Deep Sea Drilling Project. The geologists used drill rigs to bore and pull up long cores of mud. When they pulled up the core liners and laid them out on the deck, mud began to splatter out of the tubes like pellets fired from an air rifle (to use the most polite of several images that come to mind). Chemical analysis showed that the gas that was propelling the mud out of the coring tubes was almost 100 percent methane.

On the sea bottom, the methane ice is bound with water ice in a remarkable chemical intertwining called clathrate. Each molecule of methane is locked up, like a goldfish in a goldfish bowl, by half a dozen water molecules. When the geologists pulled the mud up to the surface, the clathrate melted, the methane formed bubbles, and the bubbles boiled out of the mud. This is something like what happens when a deep-sea diver rises to the surface too quickly. Gases boil out of the blood, giving the diver a condition called "the bends," which can be fatal. The methane boiling out of the mud is what shot the mud out on the deck of the *Challenger.*

Methane clathrate is still an obscure subject for geologists and no one knows exactly how much of it there is. Published estimates range from 1,000 gigatons to 500,000 gigatons (a gigaton is 1 billion tons). Take, as a conservative estimate, 50,000 gigatons. There are about 5 gigatons in the atmosphere right now. So there is about 10,000 times more methane locked into methane ice than there is in the whole of the atmosphere.

As the temperature of the bottom waters on those continental slopes begins to warm, an awful lot of methane clathrate is going to start escaping from the mud. Of course the methane will still have to make its way through many fathoms of water to reach the air. But Roger Revelle, who has examined this matter closely, calculates that "close to 80 percent of the methane released from clathrate should escape from the mud in bubbles and should rise rapidly to the sea surface before it can be oxidized in the water."

Taking the middle-of-the-road prediction of a global warming of 3° C., Revelle has calculated that the total quantity of methane that will start rising from the bottom muds as the world warms up will amount to more than half a gigaton a year. In the course of a century, enough methane would be released (by this conservative prediction) to approximately double the amount of methane already present in the atmosphere today.

If the Arctic icecap disappears, then the bottom waters could warm fast enough in that ocean alone to release another twelve gigatons of methane.

Methane is already rising in the atmosphere at the rapid rate of about 1 gigaton per decade. As we have seen, the sheer volume of this increase is not only disturbing (since molecule for molecule, methane's greenhouse effect is twenty times more powerful than carbon dioxide's) but it is also unexplained. It is possible that the strange feedback effect is already underway and the rise in Earth's temperatures in the last hundred years has already sprung many gigatons of methane from their molecular prisons at the bottom of the sea.

Like the sudden disappearance of the Arctic icecap, this feedback effect from methane could make the planet warm up more and faster than is predicted. And of course, the two effects—the warming of the Arctic Ocean and the bubbling-up of methane—will speed each other on.

Fortunately, all of this methane will be broken down and oxidized in the atmosphere in a few hundred years. Unfortunately, it will break down into water and . . . carbon dioxide. As carbon dioxide, the great exhalation from the world's sea muds will last for many millennia, and may help unlock more billions of tons of methane from the Arctic permafrost and from the cold shores of Antarctica, when the thick southern icecap retreats at last.

Methane is already pouring in record amounts from the world's cows and goats, which release the gas from both ends. If the planet starts to release it from both ends, too, the conservative estimate of a 3° C. rise from carbon dioxide might be amplified by at least another 3° C., thanks to all that thawing methane. The gas has not assumed such cosmic-comic importance since one of Dante's devils, signalling his band to follow him through boiling, bubbling tar, turned his back and "made a trumpet of his ass."

Life. The biosphere's degree of control (or at least influence) in this global misadventure is fantastic. Think of the breathing of the world. The green plants on the continents inhale so much carbon in the course of photosynthesis that each year they take about 100 billion tons of carbon out of the atmosphere. At the same time, the animals and plants of this world *exhale* so much carbon dioxide in the course of respiration that together they put about 100 billion tons of carbon back *into* the atmosphere. Heavy breathing.

Since the entire atmosphere contains only about 700 billion tons of carbon, life's astonishing metabolic rate means that all of the carbon dioxide gas on the planet Earth must pass in and out of the biosphere every seven years (and life never takes a sabbatical).

As we have seen, Earth's breathing is already changing: each year it is deeper than the year before. If life should begin to inhale a little more than it exhales—if the rate of breathing were to go out of balance in this direction by even a few percent—that would be enough to take billions of tons of carbon out of the air, *each year.* The carbon would be locked up in the green world of woody stems, trunks, boles, leaves of grass, forest litter, toadstools, and sweet-smelling humus, none of which has a greenhouse effect.

On the other hand, if life should begin exhaling even a little more carbon than it inhales, then billions of tons of carbon would rise from the forests and their soft floors and become part of the blue sky each year. Life would throw some of its weight into warming the atmosphere.

In brief: if photosynthesis increases but respiration stays the same, then the biosphere will take carbon out of the air. If respiration increases but photosynthesis stays the same, then the biosphere will put carbon into the air.

It is easy to see why photosynthesis might increase. Carbon dioxide gas is a dandy fertilizer for green plants. Operators of commercial greenhouses routinely double or triple the amount of gas in the air because they know that carbon dioxide makes their tree seedlings, tomatoes, and orchids grow faster. Plants are greedy for it.

Is the extra gas we are putting into the air also fertilizing the great outdoors, in the Big Greenhouse? This is a tough thing to measure. For a conclusive test, an ecologist would have to grow several large forests of oaks and pines within several artificial atmospheres, and measure the results after fifty years. This test would require a very rich and very patient experimenter. Absent the experiment, Keeling, Revelle, and many other researchers think it is a safe bet that the gas really is fertilizing forests. They see this as a benefit of the global change that is now in progress. It enriches the biosphere and it helps to slow the rate of the rise of the gas, a welcome kind of feedback.

George Woodwell, director of the Woods Hole Research Center, is a world authority on the metabolism of forests. He is one of the few ecologists who have actually tried to measure forests' metabolism and see what is happening. He agrees that the gas is probably fertilizing the trees: but he thinks the scientists who focus upon that effect are missing something. Back in the 1960s, Woodwell, Richard Houghton, and others set up elaborate gas-monitoring equipment in a forest in Brookhaven, New York, to measure the amount of carbon dioxide the forest was inhaling and exhaling. This was the same sort of research that Keeling carried out by hand in Yosemite in the fifties with his crates of glass flasks; but in Brookhaven they carried out the monitoring continuously at sampling points throughout the forest, all year round.

The investigators noticed something ominous. The warmer the weather—in winter and in summer—the heavier were the forest's exhalations of carbon dioxide.

Physiologists have a term for the change in the rate of respiration that results from a 10° C. increase in temperature: the Q_{10}. If an oak tree has a Q_{10} of 2, that means raising the temperature by 10° C. will make the oak's rate of respiration proceed twice as fast.

Woodwell's team found that their forest had a Q_{10} of somewhere between 1.3 and 3. That means, as Woodwell explains, that raising the temperature by 1° C. could increase the rate of the forest's respiration by as much as 25 percent. A warming of 4° C. could increase the rate of respiration of the forest by as much as 100 percent.

When Woodwell reviewed all of his data on the forest he was genuinely horrified by the implications. "Photosynthesis isn't affected much by temperature," he says. "Photosynthesis is affected by light, the availability of nutrients, the availability of water. Way down on the list—maybe tenth or so—would be the concentration of carbon dioxide in the atmosphere.

"Respiration is affected by temperature, by temperature, and by temperature."

To Woodwell, this strongly suggests that the global warming will favor respiration over photosynthesis. It could more than double the respiration rate, while increasing the photosynthesis rate only very slightly. The breathing of the world will be thrown off balance, and the biosphere will dump carbon into the air in substantial quantities.

This may not happen. It is only one thread in the skein of possibilities. But Woodwell's scenario is alarming because of the quantity of carbon that is at stake. There is no question that the breathing of the world is changing; and the amount of carbon that is currently locked into the world's forests, and in the duff beneath the trees, represents about 1,500 gigatons. That is three times as much carbon as there is in the entire atmosphere today. And much of this carbon is highly mobile, as Woodwell points out: "Keeling's curve shows that the metabolism of forests has the ability to alter the atmosphere in a matter of weeks."

What makes Woodwell's scenario even more alarming is the very same feedback effect that also threatens to erase the Arctic icecap and to release billions of tons of methane from the mud beneath it. This is the kind of feedback that Arrhenius outlined in 1896 (before the invention of the word feedback). The warming of the planet will force snows to retreat from the upper latitudes of the Northern Hemisphere, exposing more and more dark soil and dark waters to the Sun's rays and causing temperatures in this part of the world to rise much faster and much higher than the global average. It will still be colder at the pole than the equator but it will not be as *much* colder—the temperature differential across the latitudes will be more and more reduced. Thus the northernmost quarter of the planet is the biggest hot spot in the greenhouse forecasts.

And where is the heaviest breathing in the world? In the hot spot. You can see that in Keeling's curve. Keeling's famous record is now one of many carbon-dioxide records that are compiled from detectors at many latitudes. Each detector picks up the breathing curve of the biosphere in its latitude. The University of Alaska's carbon-dioxide detectors at Point Barrow pick up an extraordinary amplitude of twenty parts per million:

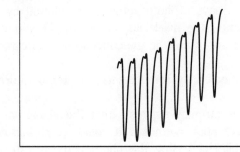

His detectors on Mauna Loa, which is more than halfway to the equator, pick up an amplitude of only five or six parts per million:

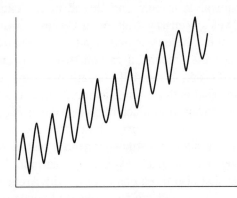

And his instruments at the South Pole pick up an amplitude of only one part per million, very shallow breathing:

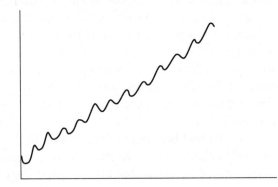

What this implies is that the enormous expanses of tundra and ever-green forest that stretch across Canada and Siberia, and the thick de-ciduous forests of North America, Europe, and temperate Asia, are doing the really heavy breathing on this planet. And those plants are in for a bigger rise of temperature than any other part of the biosphere. Already, in the last hundred years, the globe as a whole has warmed about one half a degree C., and the temperature of the hot spot is thought to have risen one *full* degree C.*

If Woodwell is right about the Q_{10} of the biosphere, the global warm-ing of the past century has already accelerated the respiration of the tundra and forests enough to push the respiration of the entire bio-sphere a few percent above normal. If so, the biosphere is now shed-ding a few gigatons of carbon into the atmosphere each year—each time the world breathes. In Woodwell's opinion, that explains the change in the breathing of the world.

It is Woodwell's nightmare that the warming will feed on the warm-ing. The faster the planet warms, the worse it is for the trees, and the more their carbon rises into the air, the faster the planet will warm. He believes we are now witnessing the start of the unravelling of a large part of the biosphere. "When respiration outstrips photosynthesis," he writes, "plants and other organisms cease growth and ultimately die." In the long run, other trees will grow up among their fallen trunks and take their place. The cone-bearing evergreens of the far north will die, and eventually deciduous trees from the south will catch up with the new climate and replace them. But in the short run of decades, vast stretches of the hot spot will be nothing but a wasteland: "a wave of biotic impoverishment as profound as any change imposed by the glaciation."

Woodwell writes, "The sudden destruction of forests by air pollu-tion, now being experienced in northern and central Europe and in the

*Warming the tropics may be dangerous, too, even though the tropics do not register in Keeling's curve as doing any "heavy breathing." Keeling's curve is a picture of the biosphere's response to the alternation of winter and summer. In the tropics there is so little difference between winter and summer that the rain for-ests' output of carbon dioxide stays about the same all year round. Every day from January to December the trees take carbon from the air and return carbon to the air.

Because the amount of carbon they borrow and return is always in balance, the rain forests make little impression on Keeling's curve. Nevertheless, if warming the planet changes the balance between photosynthesis and respiration in the rain forests, they could begin to inject many gigatons of carbon into the air each year (on top of the gigatons of carbon they give up as we cut, slash, and burn them).

eastern mountains of North America, is but a sample of the destruction that appears to be in store."

Air. There will be feedback effects in the atmosphere itself. Clouds, for example, may turn out to provide some of the most powerful feedback in the seven spheres. They cover about half the planet at any given moment, and they bounce away a great deal of sunlight before it ever has a chance to warm the planet's surface. So they cool the Earth.

On the other hand, the bulk of every cloud is water vapor, and water vapor is a greenhouse gas. So clouds also warm the Earth. Anyone who has ever felt a cloud pass overhead on a sunny day has felt their cooling effect. Anyone who has camped out on a cloudy night has felt their warming effect.

The greenhouse effect may make Earth cloudier, because the warming will heat the upper skin of the oceans (sea surface temperatures rose sharply in the decade of the 1980s, as measured by satellites). That warming is going to cause more water to evaporate, and should load the atmosphere with more water vapor, perhaps making more clouds.

On balance, will the new clouds tend to cool the planet or warm it? If they cool the world, then we have the makings of a global thermostat, which would work something like this: Air warms up. Sea surface warms up. Evaporation rate picks up. Sky clouds up. Temperatures go down. That would provide at least one strong check on the terrible possibilities that scientists are predicting in the years to come.

But what if the new clouds warm the planet? Then we may face a very different kind of feedback: Air warms up. Sea surface warms up. Evaporation rate picks up. Sky clouds up. Air and sea warm up even more . . . another nightmare. The new clouds would work in the same direction as the positive feedbacks of melting polar ice, rising bubble-streams of methane, and dying trees.

Details like the height of each new cloud are going to make a big difference. According to present theory, a cloud's character is just the opposite of what one might expect from looking at it. Very high clouds have a net greenhouse effect. In the next ten years, if we see more mare's tail cirrus, which looks for all the world like the wisps of ice crystals on a frozen windowpane, that may mean that clouds are going to overheat the planet.

Low clouds have a net cooling effect. If we see a lot more of the thick layers of stratus clouds that look like a down comforter sagging just over our heads, that may mean that clouds are going to help to cool the planet.

Supercomputer models can't yet predict which type of clouds we will be seeing more of. Since the planet has already warmed about half a degree C. (one degree F.), our skies may already have begun to change, but nobody knows about that either, because until recently, nobody has been watching clouds closely enough.

In the 1980s, intensive satellite programs were launched to monitor the clouds. One of the most ambitious of these programs is now watching Earth's cloud banks simultaneously from three satellites, launched between 1984 and 1986.

This program is called ERBE, for Earth Radiation Budget Experiment. Together the three satellites survey virtually all of the atmosphere, from pole to pole. They measure the sunlight coming in at each spot on Earth, the sunlight reflected off the cloudtops, and the energy reflected back up from the ground. By comparing incoming and outgoing radiation, researchers can begin to monitor the role that clouds are playing in the planet's energy budget.

The researchers published their first planetary budget report in January of 1989. The report covers only one month, April of 1985. However, from a preliminary inspection of a few other months' worth of data, the investigators decided that this report might prove to be typical. That April, there were extensive cirrus cloud decks above the tropical Pacific and Indian Oceans. Likewise above the rain forests of South America, and above the storm tracks in the Atlantic and Pacific. All these clouds had a strong greenhouse effect.

Meanwhile there were low, cool cloud decks in the Atlantic and North Pacific, and in the mid-latitude Southern Hemisphere, which is known for its infamous cyclones—the "Roaring '40s." These clouds had a strong cooling effect.

On a global average, clouds seem to have done more to cool the Earth that April than to warm it. The planet would have been much hotter without the clouds. In fact, that month's clouds appear to have cooled the planet much more than a doubling of the world's carbon dioxide would warm it.

In the next decade, the ERBE satellites and others may tell us more about the nature of the feedback we can expect from clouds. It may become possible to tell whether there are new clouds in the sky, and whether they are making matters better or worse for us.

Meanwhile climate experts recently ran a trial of a dozen different climate models of the planet Earth. Each model Earth was run with and without clouds. Without clouds, the models' predictions of global warming agreed almost perfectly. But *with* clouds, the models' predictions varied by a factor of three.

Ramanathan, the leader of the ERBE team, cautions that it would be a mistake to assume that clouds will save us. They may help. If they help a great deal, they may prevent the polar icecap from vanishing and the sea's methane from melting and the biosphere's carbon from unravelling, since all of those nightmares are predicated on global warming. But clouds may not turn out to be a thermostat at all. Clearly they are not infallible. The thick wrap of clouds on Venus, which blocks 95 percent of the sunlight from reaching the Venusian surface, does not prevent the Venusian greenhouse effect from heating that planet's surface to the melting point of lead.

"The effect of cloudiness is perhaps the major uncertainty, the major unknown, in the greenhouse," says Richard Somerville, of Scripps. "It is the main reason we can't predict how much warming we can expect from the greenhouse effect within our own lifetimes."

The Sun. Meanwhile the Sun beats down. Most predictions of the global warming assume (for lack of better information) that the Sun will be exactly as bright in the twenty-first century as it was in the twentieth. The computer models hold the Sun constant.

Solar astronomers know better. Seven generations of patient astronomers have watched the Sun to find out if the star is steady or variable. During the nineteenth and twentieth centuries, observers on lonely mountaintops compiled so many measurements and such prodigious lists of numbers that they were sometimes moved to measure the lists themselves: one tabulation was said to be 15 inches wide and 200 feet long.

Finally an exceptionally accurate instrument was launched into outer space to meter the sunshine. It was sent up by NASA on St. Valentine's Day, 1980, aboard a satellite nicknamed Solar Max. Solar Max orbited almost 400 miles up, which is above virtually all of Earth's atmosphere. Its instruments provided earthbound astronomers with their first really clear view of the Sun.

Max's light meter revealed that the amount of sunlight that reaches Earth varies from hour to hour, day to day, week to week, month to month, and year to year. From day to day the variations that the instrument picked up were as large as 0.25 percent. There was also a general trend. In the years between 1980 and 1985 the Sun dimmed an average of 0.019 percent per year. This trend was confirmed by independent measurements from rockets, high-altitude balloons, and the weather satellite Nimbus-7.

It is known that even a small change in the Sun means a big change on Earth. If the Sun grew only two percent brighter in the next one hundred years, the extra sunshine would heat Earth's atmosphere by about the same amount as a doubling of carbon dioxide. Four percent more sunlight reaching the planet would heat it as much as raising the carbon dioxide level fivefold. Eight percent more sunlight would heat the Earth as much as raising carbon dioxide levels thirtyfold.

Even very small changes in the Sun may make a big difference. In some climate models, for certain unstable points in the climate regime, Earth can snap from Ice Age to ice-free when the modeler cranks up the Sun by only 0.0002 percent.

Some Earth scientists suspect that the Sun shone with considerably above-average brightness at least twice in our geological era: about 5,000 years and 1,000 years ago.

The earlier episode is called the Altithermal ("high heat"). The Altithermal may have helped to set the world's first great civilizations on their feet, including the Chinese, the Minoans, the Sumerians, and the Harrapans of the Indus Valley.

The later episode is called the Medieval Optimum. In the eleventh century A.D., global temperatures were 1 or 2° C. higher than they are today. For a while, there were thirty-eight vineyards operating in England, and the grapes of York and Herefordshire were considered to be as good as any in Bordeaux or Champagne. We may never know for sure what caused those long, warm spells. But if the Sun did it, and if greenhouse gases make the planet overheat in the next century, then another brightening like that would be disastrous in our next one hundred years. It would accelerate the nightmares.

On the other hand the Sun also may have *dimmed* about ten times in the last 10,000 years. Most of these Little Ice Ages, as they are called, lasted a couple of centuries, too. The last time, the Sun seems to have dimmed very suddenly. Barbara Tuchman describes the results in *A Distant Mirror:*

A physical chill settled on the 14th century at its very start, initiating the miseries to come. The Baltic Sea froze over twice, in 1303 and 1306–7;

years followed of unseasonable cold, storms, and rains, and a rise in the level of the Caspian Sea. Contemporaries could not know it was the onset of what has since been recognized as the Little Ice Age . . . Nor were they yet aware that, owing to the climatic change, communication with Greenland was gradually being lost, that the Norse settlements there were being extinguished, that cultivation of grain was disappearing from Iceland and being severely reduced in Scandinavia.

It was as if someone had turned down the Sun with a dimmer switch, and left it that way for centuries. Glaciers in the Northern Hemisphere advanced farther south than they had in 15,000 years. Peter Brueghel painted his famous snowy scenes and Hans Brinker won his silver skates on the frozen Dutch canals.

According to the instrument aboard Solar Max, in 1986, the Sun stopped its six-year decline and began brightening again. Perhaps that is unfortunate. If the Sun had gone on fading at that same slow rate for a century, it would have been enough to offset much of the global warming that the models are currently predicting. It would have done as much good for us as fresh thick decks of low stratus clouds. It would have short-circuited the nightmares.

No one knows what makes the Sun dim and brighten, and no one knows which way the Sun will go in the next one hundred years. Unlike most of the spheres it is completely beyond our influence. We must hope for the best. "If the Sun's output of energy should permanently diminish or increase by considerable amounts," noted one of the early solar astronomers, Charles Abbot, "the whole future of civilization would be destroyed." In the next hundred years, it would take a smaller change than ever to destroy civilization, if the change happens to be in the wrong direction.

Lithosphere. Another sphere that lies beyond our influence. Molten rock is always percolating toward the surface of Earth's crust. Some of this rising magma will find outlets around the planet in the next one hundred years, just as it did in the last hundred years. Every bulletin of the Smithsonian's Scientific Event Alert Network lists new volcanic events:

Lonquimay (Chile): Fissure eruption produces tephra clouds and lava flow

Colima (Mexico):	Bombs ejected; small ash clouds; new fumaroles
Kick'em-Jenny (West Indies):	Seismicity suggests submarine eruption
Kilauea (Hawaii):	Continued lava flow into sea; tube breakouts upslope. . . .

and on and on—the headline news of the lithosphere. Even the namesake of all volcanoes, Vulcano (an isle a few miles north of Sicily, which the Romans thought of as the forge of Vulcan, the Gods' blacksmith) may erupt again someday, although it is quiescent at present.

Through volcanoes, even the lithosphere has the power to make the planet hotter or colder in the next hundred years. We are sandwiched between two spheres that we can't control, the sphere of fire and the sphere of stone, and either of these two spheres can change the rate at which a global warming takes place.

The biggest volcanic eruption of the last 500 years (and perhaps the last *10,000* years) came in 1815, when Mount Tambora exploded on an island in Indonesia. The April sky was pitch-black for a radius of 200 miles. Charles Lyell mentioned those black volcanic skies in his famous *Principles of Geology:* "The darkness occasioned in the daytime by the ashes in Java was so profound, that nothing equal to it was ever witnessed in the darkest night."*

By June, temperatures had dropped several degrees C. below normal on the other side of the world. In Vermont, Hiram Harwood wrote in his diary that corn was "badly killed and was difficult to see." In Connecticut, Calvin Mansfield wrote, "Great frost—we must learn to be humble." In Manhattan, songbirds dropped dead of exposure on Wall Street. As far south as Virginia, the distinguished farmer Thomas Jefferson lost so much corn at Monticello that he had to apply to his

---

*Tambora was one hundred times bigger than the eruption of Mount St. Helens in 1980 and ten times bigger than the eruption of Krakatoa in 1883. It was also bigger than the ancient Mediterranean eruption of Thera, or Santorini, around 1470 B.C., which destroyed the Minoan civilization on Crete and gave rise to the legend of Atlantis.

Thera may have been recorded in Egypt as the ninth plague of Exodus. According to the Bible, there was about that time a "darkness over the land of Egypt, even darkness which may be felt." This sounds like the implacable darkness after Tambora.

agent for a $1000 loan. The year passed into Yankee folklore as "Eighteen Hundred and Froze to Death." (Memory rounded the date.)

The oceanographer Henry Stommel and his wife Elizabeth relate these events in their book *Volcano Weather: The Story of 1816, The Year Without a Summer.* That same year, frost blighted the potatoes in Ireland. Peasants rioted over sacks of grain in France. In Switzerland, corn, potatoes, and bread were so scarce that beggars in the streets of Zurich were reduced to eating cats.

It was a global disaster, and people were going through near-identical miseries on opposite sides of the planet. In the United States, more than 10,000 people fled south and west from Vermont and Maine, in an episode comparable to the Dust Bowl in Oklahoma. Meanwhile in China, the corner of land that is farthest north and east (and lies in the same latitude as Vermont and Maine) is the province of Shanxi. Shanxi was hit by frosts and famines, too. Chinese peasants too abandoned their fields and fled south and west.

What chilled the planet was not the black volcanic ash that Lyell wrote about. Ash settles out of the air too fast to change the weather. Rather, the agent of change is now believed to have been sulfurous gases, which are lighter than ash and can be caught up in the thermal updraft from an eruption so that they penetrate the stratosphere. There they can form glistening droplets of sulfuric acid.

These droplets can reflect so much sunlight out to space that it is as if the sun had dimmed by 2 percent. The volcano opens a sort of sun umbrella or acid parasol over the planet. From the ground it looks like a very thin, high cirrus overcast. The droplets stay up in the stratosphere for a year or two.

Investigators at Wigley's Climatic Research Unit in East Anglia have compiled a historical survey of volcanic eruptions. They find that a significant cooling has followed most major eruptions on record. A big eruption anywhere on Earth can lower global temperature by more than half a degree C. for a year.

Earth has not experienced an eruption that big for decades. Even so, the minor volcanic debris that hangs like a series of tattered veils in the stratosphere is cooling the planet right now by some 3° C. (more than 5° F.) If we had a series of Tamboras in the third millennium (well-timed, one or two per decade) they might cool the planet much more.

Of course, a dimming of the Sun would be more convenient. The original Tambora killed 100,000 people, and the sulfuric acid from volcanic eruptions helps to erode the ozone layer in the stratosphere; and eventually it falls as acid rain. A century of Tamboras is not a pleasant prospect, except for the air-conditioning.

Volcanoes may already have fought off the greenhouse effect for us once, according to Reid Bryson, director of the Institute for Environmental Studies at the University of Wisconsin, Madison. During the years 1945 to 1975, as we have seen, the planet cooled in spite of the build-up of greenhouse gases. In those same years, Bryson says, the annual number of volcanic eruptions was double the average: it shot up from less than twenty per year to almost forty per year. Bryson has reexamined measurements of the Solar Constant made from Mauna Loa and other mountaintops during those years. He thinks the opacity of the atmosphere doubled, too. The volcanoes were fighting the heat.

Most likely, volcanoes and the Sun will have a much smaller impact in the next century than will carbon dioxide. "People look for the outside chance that we'll luck out," says one greenhouse analyst. "But the preponderance of evidence suggests we're in deep trouble." Nevertheless, there is a wrestling match going on over our heads, and we may hope that the opponents are evenly matched. If the next hundred years bring volleys of volcanic eruptions, the planet may heat up less than currently predicted. But if the twenty-first century is poorer in volcanic eruptions than the twentieth, the planet may heat up more than currently predicted. The Stommels conclude in *Volcano Weather:*

> Within the next century the preservation of our climate—and indeed our survival—may depend upon a precarious balance of two poorly understood mechanisms, one tending to increase global temperature and the other to decrease it.

Mind. Albert Einstein used to play out the implications of his theories in terms of simple mental pictures: an observer on a falling elevator; a twin and a ticking clock on a rocket ship. These were his famous *gedanken* experiments, thought experiments: much more illuminating, and much safer, than riding falling elevators oneself.

We are testing the greenhouse theory of climate change with a real experiment. The experiment envelops the planet. It makes all of us, and our children, and their children, observers. How long will it continue before it becomes frightening enough to upset populations and governments? How long before a critical number of minds decide that we must curtail the experiment?

In the early 1980s, Keeling tried a little *gedanken* experiment. Suppose the greenhouse warming had started one hundred years ago; that is, suppose we had started loading the air with carbon dioxide a century earlier. Keeling drew up a chart in which the planet's temperature wobbled up and down along precisely the same path that it really did follow during the last one hundred years, but with a slowly rising trend in temperatures superimposed. How much time would have passed before the trend was obvious to almost everybody?

In the 1850s, in this scenario, we would already be looking for the rise, and when the five-year report came in, we'd say, By God, it looks as if the greenhouse effect is here, because temperatures have peaked, and they're pretty alarming.

"But then," says Keeling, "after the alarm settled down, we would watch the temperatures going in the other direction. And by the time we'd gone another twenty years, to the year 1870 or so, everybody would have just about forgotten there was any problem at all.

"However, in the *next* ten years, it reaches a point that's higher yet, and higher than that, and higher than that, and finally even higher than that. So we're going to have a groundswell of concern in the year 1900.

"But even in the year 1900 there are a lot of people who don't believe it. Now we have a wait-and-see attitude. Because for the next ten years, the temperature doesn't go down, but it doesn't go up. Finally, we get hit by the great warming of 1930. At that point there's sure to be even more concern than there was in the 1850s.

"Even so, while they're arguing about it, the temperature starts to fall again. They've been alarmed as hell, and then it drops off again. 'Oh, my God, we can't tell!'"

By the year 1980, there would be a fairly large number of concerned people. The number depends on some details: If Havana is drowning; if London is sinking . . . "But," Keeling goes on, "I would say that approximately this point is where two-thirds of the House of Representatives would meet in a conference with two-thirds of the Senate in a joint resolution, in which they would agree there was a greenhouse effect. It would take just about that kind of evidence before you could get two-thirds of Congress to agree. And you *still* might not get the White House to agree. But you'd be close, see?

"Now the paradox is that before you really reach that agreement, you've got the doubling!" Carbon dioxide levels would be double what they were before the Industrial Revolution. "And of course by that time, you can't stop the warming. It's really moving along, hardly anything can stop it from going up year after year after year."

This is a *gedanken* experiment, not a prediction. In reality temperatures may rise faster or more slowly. But to Keeling the experiment suggested the nature of the problem before us in our next one hundred years. "If you're going to be skeptical about climatic change," he told me several years ago, "you can stonewall for a heck of a long time before you have to be convinced. Talk to the president of a tobacco company about the dangers of cigarettes. If there are economic reasons not to believe in solid evidence, you won't. That's why two-thirds of Congress, I would predict, won't agree to do something about the greenhouse effect until we're practically into the doubling, in the middle of the next century."

Maybe human beings have better reflexes and better sense than Keeling's experiment suggests. Maybe it will take less time for us to move into action. On the other hand, maybe not. The next time the global temperature drops, won't our anxiety level drop as well?

No one can calculate all of the feedback loops. (Consider just ocean currents. Warmer air will mean warmer water and new winds and new currents. The new currents may cool the planet, or warm it. They may absorb more carbon dioxide or release it. They may make marine life bloom, or stifle it. And so on, and so on.) Earth scientists are trying to figure out how it all adds up. In 1983, Kellogg, of NCAR, examined five key feedback loops, including the risks of the polar icecap disappearing and methane rising from the sea bottom. Kellogg concluded that there is likely to be a net amplification. Carbon dioxide may very well build up in the atmosphere faster than predicted, and global temperatures may rise farther than predicted.

In 1989, Daniel A. Lashof, of the E.P.A., published a more extensive study. He attempted to trace one dozen feedback loops. He, too, concluded that feedback loops are more likely to enhance the global change than to diminish it.

In models that do not include these feedback loops, the planet is due to warm about 6° F. in the next century. If we include these feedbacks, however, Lashof says the planet may warm another 6° F. Indeed the uncertainties are so great that Lashof cannot rule out a global warming of as much as 14 to 18° F. (8 to 10° C.)

It was early in 1986 when Keeling made his pessimistic prediction about the rate at which human beings will respond. Only a few months later, an announcement was made by a monitoring station in Antarctica. This discovery soon changed the world's attitude and outlook almost as much as had the monitoring station at Mauna Loa.

■ CHAPTER 8

OZONE
HOLES

"There's a hole in the bucket,
dear Liza, dear Liza,
There's a hole in the bucket,
dear Liza my dear."

"Then fix it, dear Willy,
dear Willy, dear Willy,
Then fix it, dear Willy,
dear Willy, then fix it."

"But I can't, dear Liza . . ."

American Folksong

The annual *Miner's Circular* of 1939 was published by the United States Department of the Interior under Secretary Harold L. Ickes. On its first page, the pamphlet listed American mining disasters of the previous year. There had been fifty gas explosions and mine fires, causing two hundred deaths and one hundred injuries.

There had also been a "substantial number" of cases of fatal suffocation: from too much carbon dioxide, too little oxygen, or both. In one case, two miners suffocated. Then four miners who went down to rescue them suffocated, too. It was a remote place and there were no gas masks. "Oxygen breathing apparatus had to be sent to the mine by airplane before the bodies could be recovered."

The authors of the miner's circular urged that every mine establish its own rescue station. They listed the rescue equipment each station should have, beginning with:

> 10 complete sets of self-contained oxygen breathing apparatus
> 1 extra small oxygen bottle for each breathing apparatus

The list includes a 1,000-foot lifeline, a portable electric generator, flashlights, and "flame safety lamps," which, unlike torches or kerosene lanterns, would not spark a gas explosion. The list also includes one item that seems out of place amid all the trouble and coal dust:

> 2 canaries and a small portable cage

In those days, canaries probably saved more lives than gas masks. Photographs from the first half of this century often show the somber leaders of rescue teams holding up canaries in cages as if they were lanterns that pointed the way.

The miners needed canaries because most of the deadly gases in mines—carbon dioxide, carbon monoxide, methane, hydrogen—are odorless. Miners could pass out without warning, unless someone saw a worker sink to his knees farther down the shaft and had the presence of mind to shout the alarm: "Gas!" The only mine gas they could smell was hydrogen sulfide (they called it "stink damp") and even hydrogen sulfide was perverse. At very low concentrations it smelled like rotten eggs but at higher, fatal concentrations it was completely odorless.

Miners tried using mice, chickens, small dogs, pigeons, English sparrows, guinea pigs, rabbits. By trial and fatal error they settled on the canary: in the presence of carbon monoxide and stink damp, at least, the bird usually collapsed sooner than the miner holding the cage.

After World War II, more sophisticated gas detectors were invented and installed in mines. But even today, the blue cover of the Department of the Interior's latest safety manual on mine gases is decorated with a single yellow canary.

Among the gases building up in the atmosphere today are the same ones that are fatal in mines, including carbon dioxide, carbon monoxide, and methane. One reason for the build-up is mining itself. "We are evaporating our coal mines into the air," as Arrhenius said in 1896. We are turning the crust of the planet inside out, and billions of tons of carbon that were once safely underground are now, thanks in part to the dangerous labors of generations of miners, over our heads.

We can wire the planet like a coal seam, with gas detectors in Point

Barrow, Mauna Loa, the South Pole. We can keep track of the rise of the gases in parts per million, billion, and trillion. We can try to calculate the sensitivity of the seven spheres to the changes in the air.

But we will not know precisely how fast the seven spheres will react to this new burden of gases until the seven spheres actually do react— until Earth performs the experiment. We are changing the atmosphere in slow, steady, annual increments. If the planet responds in the same way, in slow, steady, annual increments, then human beings will have time to deal with it. In the first half of the 1980s this was the view among many Earth scientists. The changes "will not be events," Revelle predicted. "They will be slow, pervasive environmental shifts. They will be imperceptible to most people from year to year . . ." Elmer Robinson, director of the Mauna Loa Observatory, told me, "Global change will probably come along slowly enough for corrective measures. Whatever's going to happen isn't going to happen overnight."

However, it is also possible that the system is extremely sensitive, and that the reactions will come on essentially overnight. Then there would be no way for us to turn back, and perhaps no way to go forward either.

One half of one percent of carbon dioxide in a mine shaft causes shortness of breath within minutes. Ten percent causes collapse within minutes.

We need indicators of the sensitivity of the Earth system. One early-warning sign has appeared above our heads—the closest thing we may ever get to a canary in a coal mine.

The discovery of this sign in the sky recapitulates the story of the greenhouse effect—but in fast motion. Here again is the early prophecy; the period of doubt, during which the inhabitants of the planet lived half-innocently under the volcano; the lonely monitoring work and the lonely discovery; the sudden crisis; and the angry scientific debate. But these events were so compressed that they seem in retrospect almost to fit the unity that Aristotle demanded of Greek tragedy: all the action in a single day.

The prophecy. In 1971, the U.S. government initiated a $21 million study called the Climatic Impact Assessment Program (CIAP). Congress was debating whether to go ahead with proposals to build a global fleet of Supersonic Transports, or SSTs. The British and the French were also planning to build the Concorde SST, and the Soviet Union was planning the Tupolev-144 SST.

Congress had commissioned the scientists in CIAP to figure out what this new international fleet might do to the atmosphere. The concern was not the SST's high velocity but its altitude. An ordinary subsonic jet flies six or seven miles up. The Concorde and the Tu-144 were expected to fly at ten miles, and Boeing's SST at twelve miles. That would take them high above the troposphere and well into the stratosphere.*

At that height, the burnt nitrogen that spewed from the jets' engines (as nitrogen oxides) would linger in the stratosphere a long time, because the stratosphere is very dry and can't easily wash out pollutants. It is like an eye without tears. Scientists on the CIAP panel estimated that 500 SSTs on daily flights through the stratosphere would inject enough nitrogen oxides into the stratosphere to reduce the ozone there by 10 to 20 percent.

In a way it was odd to be worried about the loss of ozone. Ozone is a deep blue, acrid, poisonous gas. It has a distinct odor that is especially noticeable around electrical machinery and during and after lightning storms. Keeling's first carbon-dioxide lab was across the hall from the lab where pioneering ozone experiments were going on (in the days when ozone was still pure science). Everyone on that hall learned to know the gas's sharp scent very well. Keeling still has a nose for ozone.

Even though ozone is poisonous to breathe, in its proper place, the stratosphere, the gas is vital for our health. It blocks ultraviolet rays from the Sun that would otherwise damage the DNA molecules in birds, bees, green leaves, and human skin down here on the ground. It is like an invisible membrane between Earth and outer space. About 500 light-years from Earth, in the shoulder of the constellation of Orion, there is a red supergiant star called Betelgeuse, whose diameter is almost a thousand times that of our Sun. Astronomers believe that Betelgeuse is now nearing the end of its life and may be about to explode—perhaps some time in the next few thousands or tens of

---

*The troposphere bulges at the equator: that is, it is thicker above the equator than above the poles. At the equator a plane must fly about ten miles up to get out of the troposphere and reach the stratosphere. At mid-latitudes, such as the transatlantic route of the Concorde, it must fly about seven miles up; and at the North Pole, only about five miles up.

thousands of years. One astronomer has conjectured that if Betelgeuse explodes into a supernova, it will shower our region of space with such intense ultraviolet light and X-rays that it will strip off Earth's ozone layer. Then the ultraviolet light of our own Sun will fry the biosphere.

During the SST debate, Sherwood Rowland and Mario Molina, working at the University of California at Irvine, discovered that we did not need a fleet of SSTs to hurt the ozone layer. We could do that just as well from the ground by using underarm deodorant sprays, along with all the other products that used chlorofluorocarbons—the coolants in refrigerators and air conditioners, the foaming agents in polyurethane.

In effect, these chemicals are the plastics of the atmosphere. They are inert. Nothing hurts them. They last and last. Rowland and Molina realized that such sturdy molecules would diffuse through the atmosphere until they reached the stratosphere. There, ultraviolet radiation would do what nothing on the ground could do: break them apart. That would release the chlorine that is one of their common denominators.

Chlorine is a poison gas, too—an asphyxiant, like carbon monoxide and dioxide. It was first used in war by the Germans on the Western Front at the first battle of Vimy Ridge in the spring of 1915. British soldiers pissed on their puttees and wrapped them around their faces, but they collapsed one after the other. This news of poison gas aroused great indignation in Britain, and by the end of that summer British troops were firing chlorine canisters back at the Germans.

In the stratosphere, the chlorine gas* would attack ozone. Ozone is an unstable form of oxygen. As we have seen, ordinary oxygen molecules—the ones we breathe—are molecules with two atoms of oxygen joined together. In the upper atmosphere these oxygen molecules, like everything else, are bombarded by ultraviolet rays. The rays break the oxygen molecules and the two atoms split up and wander off. If one of them meets up with another, they reunite. But if a loose oxygen atom meets an oxygen molecule, it forms a triangle: the ozone molecule.

---

*The active ingredient in the stratosphere is atomic chlorine (Cl). The war gas is molecular chlorine (Cl_2).

If this lovers' triangle hits a chlorine atom it breaks up. At first, Rowland and Molina assumed that since we were injecting only a relatively small amount of chlorine into the stratosphere, the chlorine would break only a small amount of ozone. But Rowland and Molina soon realized that the chain of chemical reactions following the break-up of ozone would leave the chlorine atom free to wander off and break up another ozone molecule, and another, and another. This is known as a catalytic cycle—the chlorine acts as a catalyst of change and is free to go on causing change after change. The chlorine atom doesn't stop until it bumps into nitrogen.

The world was injecting chlorofluorocarbons into the air at a rate of almost a million tons a year in the early 1970s. At that rate we would eventually put about half a million tons of chlorine in the stratosphere. In short, we were chlorinating the stratosphere. Rowland and Molina's first calculations suggested that this chlorine would eat between 7 and 13 percent of the ozone layer. If we allowed emissions to rise exponentially, doubling every five years or so, then we would lose even more of the ozone layer. "There was no moment when I yelled 'Eureka!'" Rowland told a reporter some years later. "I just came home one night and told my wife, 'The work is going very well, but it looks like the end of the world.'"

Under the volcano. Rowland and Molina published their results in *Nature* in June of 1974. By then popular attitudes toward the planet were very different than they had been the century before, when Arrhenius published his first paper about the greenhouse effect. People had been through the shock of the pesticide scare and *Silent Spring.* They were familiar with the power of man-made chemicals to magnify their effects and disturb the arrangements of nature. The lunacy of this new threat soon captured the public imagination. It had the improbability of reality. Could the *pssst* of an underarm deodorant can in the bathroom hurt the stratosphere? Could chemicals be dangerous precisely because they were inert? The *What* Layer? The history of the controversy is told in entertaining detail in *The Ozone War,* by Lydia Dotto and Harold Schiff. In the end, Boeing never built its SST— for reasons that had more to do with economics than ecology—but spray cans became one of the celebrated environmental issues of the decade.

Ozone reports were a roller coaster in the 1970s. In the next one hundred years, the ozone layer would be devastated. Not quite devastated—cut by 13 percent. By 2 percent. The ozone layer would be *enhanced*. In 1976, the National Academy of Sciences issued a report so cautious that *The New York Times* ran the headline:

SCIENTISTS BACK NEW AEROSOL CURBS
TO PROTECT OZONE IN ATMOSPHERE

while the *Washington Post* ran the headline:

AEROSOL BAN OPPOSED BY SCIENCE UNIT

But the weight of both scientific evidence and of public opinion did grow stronger, and in 1978, two U.S. agencies, the E.P.A. and the Food and Drug Administration, banned the use of chlorofluorocarbons from spray cans. As Dotto and Schiff write, "Arrid Extra Dry came out with a new product that says 'safe for the ozone' right on the can." Canada and Sweden banned CFCs from aerosol cans, too. And almost everyone forgot about the ozone layer.

In the early 1980s, people reminisced about the ozone scare in the spirit of Henny Penny and Chicken Little. How silly! We thought the sky was falling! In her memoir *Are You Tough Enough?*, Anne Gorsuch Burford, who ran the Environmental Protection Agency for two of those years, wrote, "Remember a few years back when the big news was fluorocarbons that supposedly threatened the ozone layer?"

The spray-can ban had not really cleared the air, of course. The global production of CFCs never actually decreased very much. After the ban, the U.S. chemical industry simply diverted its production of CFCs from spray cans to coolants, foamers, and cleaners. Other countries went on putting CFCs in spray cans—and made more spray cans than ever. World production probably shrank a little in the late 1970s, but by the late 1980s it was rising again. The world manufactured more than a billion pounds of CFCs in 1988. By then there was six times more chlorine in the atmosphere than there had been at the turn of the century.

Rowland continued to predict a global disaster. According to his calculations it would be a *gradual* disaster. The steady injection of chlorine would cause a steady erosion of ozone. The ozone layer would not begin to thin dramatically until around the year 2050. To most people in the 1970s and 1980s that threat sounded as remote and hypothetical as the greenhouse effect had sounded in the reign of Queen Victoria. Lawyers for Du Pont, the world's largest manufacturer of chlorofluorocarbons, argued in Congressional hearings that it would be folly to kill their product on the basis of such far-off possibilities. Why act before the first early warning signs? If and when ozone levels began to drop a bit, the lawyers argued, there would always be plenty of time to reconsider Freons.*

The lonely watchman. Meanwhile, in 1981, a team of scientists in the British Antarctic Survey were watching the sky at a solitary outpost at Halley Bay, on the coast of Antarctica. The leader of the British team, Joseph Farman, had been studying ozone since the I.G.Y., when instruments called spectrometers were set up to measure ozone around the planet. ("In those days ozone was pure science," a veteran from the early days at the Mauna Loa Observatory once told me, "—like atoms before war and peace.") Farman had been posted on the ozone watch ever since.

In the winter of 1981, Farman noticed a falling-off of ozone in the stratosphere over Halley Bay. Looking back through his records, he realized that ozone had been dropping for several years, always in the spring months. The decline was irregular, with some backsteps; but as a rule, each spring there was less ozone overhead than there was the spring before. The ozone layer was so thin over Halley Bay compared to the rest of the stratosphere that it was as if a hole had opened in the sky.

The spring after he made this discovery, there was once again less ozone overhead, and the next year even less. Each year the ozone recovered to its normal level, but the pulldown kept getting deeper.

Nothing like this had ever been reported.

Farman wondered why no one else was seeing what he was seeing. Could the ozone layer be disappearing only over his station? Even so, other eyes should be detecting it, too. One of the instruments aboard NASA's weather satellite Nimbus-7 is a Total Ozone Mapping Spectrometer, TOMS. Looking down at the stratosphere from outer space, this instrument has a better view of the ozone layer than any human

---

*Of course, that wasn't true. Once the chemicals are in, they are in. There is no getting rid of them for one hundred years. They will be eating ozone for a very long time.

observer on the surface of the planet. It was able to map ozone over the whole globe on a daily basis. Yet the NASA scientists who ran Nimbus-7 were reporting nothing out of the ordinary in the ozone layer above Halley Bay or anywhere else.

We are such a social species that when one of us finds something no one else has found, sees something no one else has seen, the discovery can seem doubtful to the discoverer. It was the biggest monitoring scoop in a quarter of a century—since Keeling's in the I.G.Y.—but Farman did not trust it. Four centuries ago, a young Danish astronomer named Tycho Brahe looked up on an evening walk and saw a new star in the sky—the supernova of 1572, a star in the throes of death. In those days most people still subscribed to the classical world view in which the celestial spheres were beyond change. "Amazed, and as if astonished and stupefied, I stood still, gazing for a certain length of time with my eyes fixed intently upon it," Tycho wrote. ". . . I was led into such perplexity by the unbelievability of the thing that I began to doubt the faith of my own eyes." Tycho asked his servants if they saw what he was pointing at. They did—but that could have been a group delusion. Tycho began stopping peasants in the street to ask if they too saw the new light in the sky.

After the discovery in Halley Bay, Farman scanned journals and technical research reports month after month, looking for independent confirmation of the hole in the sky. No one else saw it—not even those artificial stars, the satellites. The Antarctic team was under enormous pressure. The loneliness of the discovery matched the loneliness of the place.

By the spring of 1984, the Ozone Hole had gotten so big that it extended nearly to the tip of Argentina. There a second British monitoring station detected it. At last Farman and his team wrote up a report and submitted it to *Nature*.

In that year, the National Academy of Sciences issued its fourth state-of-the-art report on ozone. Ironically, the experts on the panel were more optimistic about the future than any previous N.A.S. committee. They had done some new calculations. The ozone layer was likely to decline only slightly, perhaps 2 to 4 percent in one hundred years. The total ozone level in the atmosphere might even *rise* by 1 percent.*

---

*They even changed the title. In 1982, the report was "Stratospheric Ozone Reduction." In 1984, it was "Changes in Stratospheric Ozone," since they thought the ozone might grow.

This committee report and Farman's report crossed in the mail, as in a melodrama or a bad dream, and it was the committee report that made headlines. (In the retrospect of another few decades, our current star-crossed debates about the greenhouse effect may seem just as nightmarish.) After the N.A.S. report, *Science Digest* ran a story, "Ozone: The Crisis That Wasn't." "In November of 1985," Rowland says, "I spoke on the Antarctic Ozone Hole at the University of Maryland (first time in public, I think). The university's press release went to the *Washington Post,* the *Baltimore Sun,* et cetera, but none of them covered it—just the student newspaper." Indeed it took so long for the full implications of the Ozone Hole to reach scientists and the public that as late as February of 1986 *The New York Times* would run a brief note about ozone under the heading "Questions Without Answers":

QUESTION: "Have aerosol sprays really destroyed the ozone layer?"
ANSWER: ". . . There is no definitive answer."

Farman attracted so much less attention than N.A.S. because the British group was little-known and the ozone problem was supposed to have disappeared. Word did reach NASA, however. Scientists there reexamined the data from Nimbus-7, and they realized what had happened. They had fallen victim to their own automation. The satellite Nimbus-7 had been launched in 1978. Data from the satellite had been beamed down to Earth by radio, automatically, and analyzed by a computer, automatically. In espionage terms, the satellite was the spy, and the computer was the control.

The computer had been programmed to screen the ozone data and to throw out any gibberish that might creep in among the good numbers. How can one instruct a computer in advance to tell good numbers from bad? Simple. Even in the worst case, Rowland's doomsday scenario, ozone levels did not fall very fast. And ozone levels in the stratosphere were presumed to be more or less uniform around the globe. Thus if the satellite beamed down excessively low numbers as it passed over Antarctica or any other spot on the planet, the computer was programmed to throw those numbers out.

While Farman's team agonized in Antarctica, robot eyes in space had been recording the same hole growing over the South Pole. And a robot brain on the ground had been setting the numbers neatly to one side.

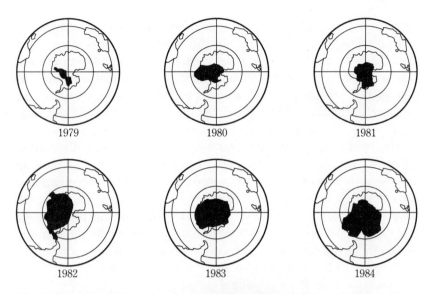

The Crisis: By 1985, scientists saw that they might be dealing with a planetary emergency, all the more alarming because in spite of early warnings, high-level committees, and satellite surveillance, it had taken the world by surprise, and appeared almost with the snap of the fingers. Many atmospheric chemists around the world dropped everything else to study it, and U.S. government agencies moved with unprecedented speed to mount a rush expedition to observe the Ozone Hole during the next austral winter. The National Science Foundation agreed to put up a special plane for the scientists. The U.S. Navy agreed to fly it to McMurdo Station, Antarctica, which does not get many tourists in the wintertime.

That first National Ozone Expedition (NOZE) was made up of four teams of specialists, led by Susan Solomon, of the National Oceanic and Atmospheric Administration. Solomon was born the year before the I.G.Y. She wrote an authoritative textbook on atmospheric chemistry at an age when many graduate students are still searching for a specialty. She won the prestigious McElwane Award of the American Geophysical Union at the age of twenty-nine. When Farman's news broke she was not quite thirty. In the next few years, when she lectured about the Ozone Hole, audiences around the world would express astonishment at her youth and she would reply, "Age gets to be less of a problem every year."

"This is outside anything we've ever seen anywhere on Earth," Solomon told me in her NOAA office in Boulder, Colorado, shortly before she left for McMurdo. "It's dropped out the bottom of the chart."

If this was just the beginning—if the trouble was likely to spread—then the Hole was the classic case of the canary in the coal mine, as a few scientists were already calling it. For Solomon that question was still open. "Any theory must attempt to explain: Why are things so different at the South Pole? Why only there? If we can't answer that, we can't say if this is a canary."

She reminded me that the Sun manufactures ozone in the stratosphere by smashing oxygen molecules, and the Sun never stops shining. So if there were no forces to oppose the Sun, it would long ago have smashed much of Earth's atmosphere into ozone, the air would have turned deep blue, and every plant and animal on this planet would have died of poison gas. Hence there have to be natural ozone-eaters, just as there is a natural ozone-maker. The destruction of ozone is just as essential to the well-being of life as its creation. Atmospheric chemists know of at least three natural ozone-eaters.

First, ozone is attacked and destroyed by other gases that are naturally present (in trace amounts) in the stratosphere: oxides of nitrogen* and oxides of hydrogen.

Second, ozone is attacked by natural traces of chlorine. Chlorine that is released by the sea can penetrate the stratosphere, and occasionally some more chlorine rises that far, during big volcanic eruptions, in the form of hydro*chloric* acid.

Third, oxygen atoms attack ozone.

There is a constant give and take among creators and destroyers, so the concentration of ozone in the stratosphere is always fluctuating. However, the evidence from the global ozone-monitoring network established during the I.G.Y. suggests that these ozone fluctuations tend to be small. Ozone seems to stay in rough balance, much as the creation and destruction of Earth's crust stays in balance (or else the planet would grow or shrink).

When the Ozone Hole was first reported, many scientists thought it was natural. In fact, some of the investigators who packed their bags for Antarctica, to gaze up into the Ozone Hole and do combat with global change—like knights on a dragon hunt or scientists in a grade B sci-fi horror movie—were *afraid* it might be natural, and therefore not a monster of any importance, nothing very interesting. *"That's the*

---

*These were the ozone-eaters that started the Ozone War in the first place: the hypothetical fleet of SSTs would have produced oxides of nitrogen.

scary part," one member of the expedition told me before leaving.

Which theory you picked depended in part on which sphere you studied. Some volcanists thought a volcano had punched the hole in the sky. They had a good candidate: the Mexican volcano El Chichón. El Chichón's eruption in 1982 had wrapped the whole planet in a broad band of not only sulfuric acid but also hydrochloric acid—again, first detected as it drifted over Mauna Loa. At one point, at El Chichón's latitude, the stratosphere held almost 50 percent more hydrochloric acid than normal. If El Chichón had caused the Ozone Hole then the hole would heal in a few years, as the droplets of acid drizzled down from the stratosphere.*

Some wind experts thought winds had poked the hole in the sky. A change in wind patterns might have carried ozone-poor air from the lower atmosphere into the stratosphere, diluting the ozone there. If so, then the Ozone Hole was a natural fluctuation and would heal eventually. The missing piece of sky at the South Pole would prove to be nothing more frightening than the blue holes that appear now and then in a mass of thick gray clouds, purely by chance.

Solar scientists blamed the hole on the creator of ozone. The Sun had been hyperactive in 1980 (the year of the launch of the Solar Maximum Mission, the satellite Solar Max). In fact that year had brought one of the largest solar maxima in centuries. Solar scientists theorized that this intense brightening of the Sun might have perturbed the chemistry of the upper atmosphere, creating an excess of oxides of nitrogen—much as the hypothetical fleet of SSTs would have done. These compounds might still be drifting down through the stratosphere, and might take a few more years to dissipate.

If the culprit was volcanoes, winds, or sunshine, then the hole in the sky was nothing to worry about. But if the culprit was chlorine from chlorofluorocarbons, as Rowland, Solomon, and others suspected, then we were in for it. The lower atmosphere is loaded with chlorofluorocarbons on a slow drift toward the stratosphere. In fact most of the chlorofluorocarbons ever made are still on their way to the stratosphere. The hole could go on growing for the next one hundred years.

Rival theories breed resentments when half the world is watching. (One early investigator described the Ozone War, with bitterness, as

---

*Of course, that would also mean that when human beings raised chlorine levels by 50 percent—in about thirty years—the hole would be back forever.

"science in a goldfish bowl.") Jerry Mahlman, director of the Geophysical Fluid Dynamics Laboratory, at Princeton, told one reporter that the chlorine partisans were suffering from a "Chicken Little syndrome: the ozone is dropping and the only thing they can think of that could do this is chlorine." Mahlman may have meant that lightly, but privately some of the scientists who thought the hole was natural were calling the scientists who thought it was man-made a bunch of panicky environmentalists.

Rowland found that ironic. Before he sounded the alarm about chlorofluorocarbons (which made him a panicky environmentalist) he was involved in a scare over the levels of mercury in swordfish and tuna. He had gone to museums and taken samples of fish that had been pickled in alcohol at the turn of the century. The levels of mercury were about the same in fresh fish and in the oldest specimens in museums. So Rowland reported that mercury in the sea was at natural levels. That had made him an industry apologist.

Politics aside, all of the theories were plausible. The only one that could be dismissed before the emergency expedition was the one on the cover of a supermarket tabloid: the hole was blasted with lasers by aliens in outer space.

Solomon's expedition* landed at McMurdo with a payload of 15,000 pounds, including oscilloscopes, sensors, tape drives, and tanks of liquid nitrogen: dozens of high-tech instruments that had never been tested in an Antarctic winter at 60° F. below zero, neatly packed away in styrofoam (which is made, of course, using chlorofluorocarbons).

---

*By coincidence, the first scientific expedition ever mounted by the United States in this direction—in fact, the first U.S. scientific expedition ever—began as a search for a hole at the South Pole.

It seems a hero of the war of 1812, John Cleves Symmes, Jr., a Newton from the backwoods state of Ohio, had convinced himself and many others that Earth is hollow, with holes in the poles. On April 10, 1818, Symmes sent a letter to all congressmen and the world's most eminent scientists:

To All the World:
I declare the Earth is hollow and habitable within; containing a number of solid concentric spheres, one within the other and that it is open at the poles twelve or sixteen degrees. I pledge my life in support of this truth and am ready to explore the hollow, if the World will support and aid me in the undertaking. . . .

J. C. Symmes

The scientists had been warned that in wintertime the pilot could not shut the motor off or he might not get back into the air. In the event of bad weather, the pilot would simply pause on the runway with his propellers whirling, while the scientists scrambled out and the crew opened the back of the plane. Then the pilot would rev off down the runway and the acceleration of the plane would dump out all of their gear.

But weather that day was with them. There they were, looking up into the Ozone Hole.

If the first Hole had appeared anywhere else on Earth, even in the most remote spot in the Arctic, Solomon and her colleagues would have had more clues to go on. There are so many scientists in the Northern Hemisphere that over the years, even with subjects as arcane as the composition of the Arctic stratosphere in winter, they have accumulated a tremendous wealth of data. "In the Antarctic," Solomon told me, "we really don't know very much at all."

In winter, Antarctica is the most isolated place on Earth. It is isolated from human visitors and in a sense it is even cut off from the rest of the atmosphere. The air in the stratosphere above the continent spins around and around in a giant vortex, like the swirl of water going down a drain. Winds on the fringe of this vortex travel at high speeds, but the air trapped inside the vortex just sits there all through the long, dark polar winter. Very little fresh air or sunlight ever gets in to intrude upon or dilute any exotic chemical reactions that may get started in there. And it may be (the point is still controversial) that not much of the air inside can get out—like the shades of the Greek dead who could not cross back over the River Styx. During the long polar night, temperatures in the stratosphere fall as low as −90° C. (−130° F.). It is a cauldron the size of a continent: the coldest, darkest, loneliest vat of air on Earth.

Solomon had mulled these facts before the expedition and had come up with a hybrid hypothesis—part chemistry and part temperature: "Now, I thought to myself, Antarctica is the only place in the world

To check this "Holes in the Poles Theory," President John Quincy Adams authorized a South Seas Exploring Expedition. The Exploring Expedition (or "Ex. Ex." as it was called in the newspapers) did not find a hole, but did bump into Antarctica. The Ex. Ex. lost credit for the discovery of a continent because the commander drew the coastline in the wrong place on his chart.

Today in key respects the geography of the seven spheres is as new, strange, and uncertain as in the early days of exploration. The real hole at the South Pole is bigger than the one envisioned by Symmes.

that is cold enough to get clouds in the stratosphere. Occasionally you get polar stratospheric clouds in the Arctic, too, but mostly in the Antarctic.* So maybe you need *surfaces* to catalyze the reactions. The surfaces of the ice."

The stratospheric clouds would also convert nitrogen oxides to nitric acid. And Solomon perceived that the formation of this acid could be damaging not only because it provides surfaces to catalyze the chlorine's attack on ozone, but also because it takes a great deal of nitrogen out of circulation, and nitrogen is the one element that stops chlorine from devouring ozone up there. Polar stratospheric clouds at the height where ozone is normally thickest could do incredible damage, Solomon reasoned. "If you have this combination in the lab, in a cloud chamber, it's hard to *prevent* these reactions from occurring."

These clouds might have been the factor that Rowland had omitted from his calculations—the factor that had allowed a big piece of the stratosphere to change not gradually but with a snap.

At McMurdo the NOZE team lofted instruments into the Hole aboard giant helium balloons, three times a day. (On the horizon they could see Robert Falcon Scott's hut from the first Discovery expedition.) They also scanned the atmosphere from the ground. For the visible spectrometer, holes had to be drilled in the roof of the base. There is a special can-do attitude in Antarctica. It is the last true frontier on this planet. The engineers at McMurdo cheerfully perforated the roof in three days. ("I have often thought," Solomon told audiences afterward, "that I really ought to try, just for fun, at my home institution, to ask to put some holes in the roof. And see how long it would take, you know. In weather sixty degrees *above*.")

The expedition found about one hundred times more chlorine than normal in the stratosphere above the base. That argued against winds—for if winds had fetched ozone-poor air from elsewhere the winds would not also have brought in that insanely high concentration of chlorine. The scientists also found evidence against the volcano El

---

*Clouds are rare in the stratosphere because the air there is so dry. Stratospheric clouds are one of the most beautiful sights in nature. Although they are common only in the Antarctic, they were observed in England at the turn of this century. "These clouds," wrote one observer, ". . . before dawn or after sunset were characterised by their brilliant prismatic colours. . . . The most luminous parts shone in beautiful colours like mother-of-pearl." They are spectacular.

Chichón: their measurements of volcanic particles floating in the Hole revealed little trace of the big eruption that had happened three years earlier. El Chichón's effects were long gone. The chemists also found low levels of nitrogen oxides—in fact, *record* low levels. That counted against the solar theory, since the solar theory required that the Sun had eaten the ozone by manufacturing extra nitrogen oxides.

To officials at NSF, the evidence seemed so strong that they called an emergency press conference beamed via satellite direct from McMurdo Station to Washington, D.C. Solomon said, "We suspect that a chemical process is fundamentally responsible for the formation of the hole."

This announcement infuriated scientists who thought the hole was natural. Linwood B. Callis, who held the solar theory, told a reporter from *Science News*, "Their suggestion that the solar cycle is not playing a role in this is wrong. And even if it is not wrong, it's certainly premature."

"The press conference was a circus," Mark Schoeberl, of NASA, told a reporter from *Discover* magazine. He favored a dynamic theory of the hole—that is, winds. "You send chemists to the South Pole," Schoeberl said, "and of course they denounce dynamics."

The Hole was bigger that year than ever before. But the chemistry of the stratosphere was so highly perturbed that no one could predict what the Ozone Hole was likely to do next.

When the Hole reappeared the next year, a second emergency expedition converged upon Punta Arenas, the world's southernmost city, near the tip of Patagonia. The travel writer Bruce Chatwin once dreamed that the grasslands of Patagonia might be the safest place on Earth to flee the trials and tribulations of civilization. Civilization had now reached Patagonia. There were rumors that local property values were already declining in Punta Arenas as outsiders decided against moving closer to the Ozone Hole.

The scientists at Punta Arenas flew right into the Hole aboard a gutted and revamped passenger plane, a DC-8: a flying laboratory that took them seven miles up. Solo pilots flew even higher and farther into the Hole aboard a converted U-2 spy plane. Together the planes logged more than 175,000 kilometers in six weeks. Again they found weird amounts of chlorine oxide: about one hundred times normal. At the altitude of the polar stratospheric clouds almost all the ozone was gone.

The view from the Nimbus-7 weather satellite (no longer censored by the computer) showed that the Ozone Hole had now grown bigger than the Antarctic Continent itself. It was about twice the size of the continental United States. As Rowland noted, the problem had become "something you could see from Mars."

The decisive experiment in Punta Arenas was conducted by a research group led by the atmospheric chemist Jim Anderson, of Harvard University. His group built the instrument with which the spy-plane sniffed for chlorine monoxide within the Hole. Wherever the ozone was thinnest, chlorine monoxide was thickest. As one chemist said, "Every wiggle in ozone is matched by a wiggle in chlorine monoxide."

Chicken Little, Rowland, Solomon, et al., were right. That year when asked if the problem could spread, Solomon said, "It is perhaps a question of by how much and exactly when, not a question of 'if.'"

But winds were playing a role, too, of course, not only maintaining the walls of the cauldron but stirring the witches' brew inside it. During one strange couple of days, scientists watched ozone levels drop suddenly by 10 percent over an area of 3 million square kilometers. That was too fast to be chemical. Apparently winds sometimes do lift ozone-poor air from below, just as the dynamicists originally argued. And when the polar vortex finally breaks up in the austral spring (during what is called, in a pregnant phrase, "the final warming") the cauldron spills into the stratosphere and winds carry gobs of ozone-poor air around the Southern Hemisphere. That year when the cauldron spilled, the city of Melbourne, Australia, experienced its thinnest ozone shield ever.

In the northern winter of 1987–1988, Solomon joined an expedition to Thule, Greenland. The scientists found chlorine levels ten times normal above the North Pole. That was not as heavy a load of chlorine as they had found at the South Pole, but the problem was definitely spreading.*

By this time the ozone question was moving faster than any other field in Earth science. Britain's Department of the Environment caused a scandal in 1987 when it issued a somewhat optimistic report on the ozone layer. The department was roundly criticized for relying upon data that were hopelessly out of date. The data were from 1985.

---

*By 1989, the chlorine oxide levels in the Arctic were just as high as in the Antarctic, according to the measurements of Jim Anderson, of Harvard University. And the return flight *across the U.S.* showed levels up about ten or twenty times above normal.

Using the latest information, an international panel of one hundred scientists made a retrospective analysis of ozone worldwide. They reviewed the evidence gathered from space and from the ground—the records from the Dobson network, the weather satellites, the polar expeditions. They concluded that the worst had happened. Earth's whole ozone shield eroded by 2.5 percent between 1978 and 1985. We were losing the shield not only at the poles but between the poles— over our heads.

We call the ozone layer a shield but it is really as flimsy as a sun umbrella. Only a millionth part of the stratosphere is ozone. If all the ozone in the atmosphere were spread out on the ground it would form a layer about as thin as a piece of canvas. Ripping this layer is like punching holes in the sun umbrella: some of the molecules that are next in line to absorb the Sun's ultraviolet rays are the proteins in our own skins.

There are two bands of ultraviolet radiation that matter to human health, UV-A and UV-B. Most UV-A is not absorbed by the atmosphere. It penetrates to the surface, and our hides are more or less used to it. UV-B is blocked only by ozone, however. According to Ralph Cicerone, of NCAR, a 10 percent decrease in ozone overhead can result in increases in UV penetration of 20 percent at one particular high-intensity UV wavelength, and as much as 250 and 500 percent penetration at others.

When this high-energy radiation strikes human skin, photons—packets of light energy—are absorbed by the chemical bonds in our DNA and in the rubbery ribbons of elastin that help to keep skin soft and supple. The impact of the photons can snap bonds or even cross-link them, leading to the kind of garbled messages that eventually produce cancer. While the cancer may not show up for years, the damage happens fast. A team of chemical physicists recently succeeded in timing how long it takes a chemical bond to break. When the compound cyanogen iodide absorbs a photon, the bond hangs together for one last fraction of a fraction of a second before it snaps. The speed of the whole reaction, from the impact to the break, is 205 femtoseconds, or 205/1,000,000,000,000,000ths of a second.

If photosynthesis is building with light, this is photolysis, splitting with light. It is a particular threat for climbers at high altitudes, where there is less air overhead to block the UV. I once spent a day on the

Grindelwald Glacier (an hour and a half from Bern) with a young Swiss climber and inventor. Among his inventions is an indicator dye for testing nylon ice-climbing ropes. These ropes are often strung all day in strong sunlight at high altitudes, getting a double dose of UV reflected off the ice. On climbers' and skiers' faces the result is visible as snowburn. But the rope can continue to look brand-new. The UV damage is invisible until one fine day, without warning, the rope snaps.

UV-B is blocked by ordinary window glass, also known as crown glass, so it is impossible to get a suntan sitting in a window. In wintertime—and sometimes even in summertime—Caucasians who are stuck indoors sometimes get artificial tans using the tanning lamps at beauty salons, health clubs, athletic clubs, drug stores. These lamps are mostly UV-A and they are advertised as safe. However several studies suggest that even UV-A can cause cancer and depress the human immune system. Apparently some people are willing to accept these risks, since the lamps already carry warning labels, like packs of cigarettes.

UV-B unquestionably causes several types of skin cancer, including basal cell carcinomas and squamous cell carcinomas, and it is strongly suspected as the cause of malignant melanomas. Carcinomas of the skin grow slowly and are rarely fatal—these are the cancers that Ronald Reagan had removed surgically many times during his two terms in the White House. Melanomas, which are rarer, grow rapidly and they often spread to other organs. Until recently, 40 percent of all diagnosed cases proved fatal. (This percentage seems to be dropping as medical awareness rises; the mortality rate is now about 20 percent.)

Ultraviolet light increases in intensity from the poles to the equator, and incidence of human skin cancer is greater the farther south in the United States one lives. There is 1 case in 1,000 per year in Des Moines, Iowa. There are 4 cases in 1,000 per year in Dallas, Texas. The highest incidence of skin cancer in the world today is in Queensland, Australia, where an unusually large number of fair-skinned people live near the equator.

Skin color, the biggest visible difference between the populations of human beings on this planet, around which so many bitter and divisive myths have been spun, is really nothing more than a schematic diagram of planetary levels of ultraviolet radiation. Black skin is protected because the dark pigments block the radiation. Caucasians lack the pigment because they are adapted to northern regions where levels of UV are low. If the deterioration of the ozone shield in the next one hundred years leads to more UV-B, Caucasians will be most at risk.

The incidence of malignant melanomas is already rising fast. Indeed malignant melanoma is increasing at a rate faster than any other form of cancer. The number of new cases in the United States per year roughly doubled between 1980 and 1989. According to the Skin Cancer Foundation, a child born in the 1930s faced a risk of 1 in 1,500 of developing malignant melanoma. In 1988, the risk was 1 in 135. If this trend continues through the year 2000 the risk will be 1 in 90.

The trend is thought to have been caused by fashions in this century—the appeal of suntans and of clothes that expose more of the body. A tan is a warning that ultraviolet radiation is strong enough to damage the skin. "Sun is good for the soul and bad for the skin," says James J. Leyden, a dermatologist at the Teaching Hospital of the University of Pennsylvania. Many dermatologists suspect that a single blistering sunburn in childhood can lead to malignant melanoma in adulthood.

The increase in skin cancer cannot be due to the ozone holes, since it started a little before the invention of CFCs and since little extra UV has penetrated to the ground as yet. When it does, however, it could make a bad trend worse. The E.P.A. estimates that every 1 percent depletion in ozone will cause something like a 2 or 3 percent increase in UV-B and a 5 percent increase in skin cancer, including a 1 percent increase in malignant melanomas. In our lifetimes, the thinning of the ozone shield may lead to a 60 percent rise in the incidence of skin cancers of all kinds in the United States.*

Ironically the ozone layer will be eroded more and more the farther one lives from the equator, in higher and higher latitudes. Although UV-B will pour down everywhere, it will increase by a greater and greater percentage at those higher and higher latitudes. The fair-skinned people who can take it least will get it most. W.H. Auden once

---

*UV-B can also cause cataracts, which are cloudy spots in the crystalline lens of the eye. Half a million cataracts are surgically removed in the U.S. each year and perhaps 10 percent of them were caused primarily by UV-B. As with skin cancer, incidence of cataracts increases closer to the equator and it also increases the more time one spends outdoors—cataracts are an occupational hazard for farmers, lifeguards, and construction workers. A recent study by Hugh R. Taylor, of the Johns Hopkins University School of Medicine, in Baltimore, suggests that for every 10 percent increase in UV-B we can expect a 6 percent increase in cataracts in the cortex of the eye's lenses. UV-B radiation poses the same threat whether eyes are black, brown, blue, green, or hazel.

remarked that after forty we are all responsible for our own faces. If the erosion of the ozone layer leads to the erosion of white faces, then Auden's epigram will take on a new dimension.

In the twenty-first century, tans will be as unfashionable as they were in the nineteenth. Already Caucasians are wearing more and more sunblock. They may even return to that antique ornament of high fashion, the parasol, in an effort to replace the now-tattered parasol that the atmosphere once provided us for free.

The extra ultraviolet light has another savagely ironic side-effect. As some of the Sun's harshest rays penetrate to the lower atmosphere, they will strike the oxygen molecules in the lower atmosphere and turn them into ozone, precisely as they do now in the stratosphere.

In the nineteenth century, sunlight was regarded as unhealthy. Ozone gas was regarded as healthy. Managers of resorts and health spas used to hire scientists to measure local ozone levels, and well-favored resorts proudly advertised themselves as "ozoniferous."*

We now know that ozone in the stratosphere is healthy for us but ozone down here in the troposphere is toxic. "Ozone leaves paint on a house, or rubber tires, or leaves on trees, dog-eared and tattered," says Robert Dickinson, of NCAR. It is the key ingredient in smog. The gas is so corrosive to living things that it is often bubbled through sewage to kill bacteria and viruses. Ozone also causes chest pains, pulmonary congestion, a burning sensation in the eyes and nose, and sore throats. In 1979, the E.P.A. set an ozone safety standard limiting ozone pollution to a maximum hourly dose of roughly a tenth of a part per million (0.12 ppm), not to be exceeded more than once a year. More than half the major metropolitan areas in the United States, including the crowded corridor between Boston and Washington—"Bosnywash"—regularly exceed this limit. About 115 million people (more than half the total U.S. population) are now breathing ozone levels that exceed the goals set by the EPA.

It now appears that even that limit is unsafe. Recent studies suggest that ozone concentrations of less than .1 parts per million attack the

---

*The city of Arosa, Switzerland, has been measuring ozone levels for a longer time than anyplace else on Earth. As Sherwood Rowland notes, the station there was started because in the 1920s almost all radiation was believed to be beneficial. Arosa, in the Swiss Alps, wanted to be able to advertise that they had very high levels of ultraviolet radiation.

In those days, the radiations from radioactivity were also believed to be beneficial. Spas advertised that they had uranium in their hot springs.

lungs and make healthy people lose their breath. In a study published in the journal *American Review of Respiratory Disesase*, researchers tested children playing outside at a YMCA camp in Fairview Lake, in northwestern New Jersey. Ozone levels never exceeded the federal standard during the tests. But the children's endurance dropped measurably in synch with relatively small rises in ozone, and their lungs sometimes took a week to recover. The cleaner the air during a test the more strongly the children blew into the researchers' test apparatus. Tests on laboratory rats suggest that ozone causes permanent damage, a premature stiffening or aging of the lungs. Indeed ozone may have similar effects inside the body as ultraviolet light has on the outside: snapping chemical bonds, leaving abnormal cross-links, and weakening the immune system.

It is almost as hard to regulate ozone levels as carbon dioxide levels because the chemical precursors of the gas come from a very wide variety of sources: fumes at gasoline stations and fumes from auto exhaust pipes; factories, paint shops, dry cleaning stores, aerosol deodorants, gas ovens. All of these are sources of compounds that UV can turn into ozone. Even the pollution in the stratosphere is causing more pollution here on the ground, since the chlorine up there is letting more UV down here. According to one E.P.A. study, each further 1 percent decrease in stratospheric ozone may cause a 2 percent increase in ozone on the ground.*

The troposphere already carries about double the ozone of one hundred years ago. The troposphere may be able to carry on the order of ten times more ozone than it does now, so this problem, too, has barely begun. The Summer of '88 brought record ozone levels in many parts of the United States. That June, monitoring stations in the Philadelphia area reported almost fifty incidents of unhealthy ozone levels— three times as many as in June of '87 and sixteen times as many as June of '86. In Washington, D.C., the peak ozone reading that summer was 22 percent higher than the previous record. In Chicago, 36 percent higher.

So we are losing the ozone where we need it and gaining it where we don't. We are clearing it where it prevents cancer and putting it where it causes cancer. People find this Jekyll and Hyde act confusing.

---

*UV can also cause dramatic increases in other undesirable compounds, including hydrogen peroxide, a key chemical precursor to acid rain. Again, pollution problems are as interlinked as the seven spheres.

Why are we worried about losing ozone in one place, and gaining it in another? Why is there good and bad ozone?

Again, ozone is like an umbrella. On a city sidewalk on a rainy day there are so many umbrellas that they form an umbrella layer. But if someone in the crowd carries his umbrella too low, the spokes can get in other people's faces. Umbrellas are helpful overhead but they are a nuisance, or even a menace, when they poke someone in the eye.

When the first news broke of the Ozone Hole, Donald Hodel, then Secretary of the Interior, considered recommending at most a national program of "personal protection." Industry could keep producing chlorofluorocarbons as before until a connection was really proven. Meanwhile Americans should wear big hats and stay in the shade. "People who don't stand out in the sun—it doesn't affect them," he said.

In reply, Representative Steven Scheuer, Democrat of New York, appeared on the floor of the House in a Chinese hat and dark glasses— and photographs of an owl, a lion, a tiger, a cat, a giraffe, and a goldfish, all wearing dark sunglasses and straw hats. He reminded his colleagues in the House that hats would not protect us from *breathing* ozone. And nothing would protect the rest of the biosphere from either the ozone gas or the harsh radiation.

In fact the change in the air and in sunlight in the next few decades may pose more danger to animals and plants than to human beings. Laboratory tests show that UV-B can damage fish, shrimp and crab larvae, copepods, krill, and the zooplankton and phytoplankton at the base of the food chains in the sea. Sayed El-Sayed, an oceanographer at Texas A & M University, has studied Antarctic phytoplankton, the grass of the sea, which live not only in the open waters but within the pack ice. Among the phytoplankton are diatoms, which bloom so heavily at times that they can cause "the surface of the ocean, from the locality of the ships, as far as eye could reach, to assume a pale brown color," as the botanist-surgeon J.D. Hooker wrote during the *Erebus* and *Terror* expedition of 1839–1843. Phytoplankton take solar energy and the minerals afloat in the water—including phosphates, nitrates, silicates—and convert them into a form that other creatures can use as food.

El-Sayed put phytoplankton in big plexiglass microcosms on the Antarctic shore outside Palmer Station and exposed them to various levels of ultraviolet light. He found that photosynthesis was severely impaired in the phytoplankton that received enhanced UV. A 10 percent increase in UV killed almost all of his specimens—few cells survived in that microcosm and those that did survive looked bleached. On the other hand, sparing the organisms from UV increased photosynthesis rates two to four times, he says: "the cells were bright gold and the total mass of cells was very great."

Because many of these organisms migrate up and down in the water column it is hard to estimate how much UV-B they are actually receiving in the Antarctic seas beneath the Ozone Hole. In some places seawater may shield all but the uppermost few feet of the surface from UV, but in other places, according to El-Sayed, UV can penetrate to a depth of sixty feet. Although the actual effects of increased UV in the wild will require further study, it is ominous that the plankton at the base of the food chain are so sensitive. Since the Ozone Hole is going to be with us for at least one hundred years, we could cause an evolutionary upheaval if thousands of species in the sea weaken and others more resistant to these rays take over. The billions of krill in Antarctic waters—which are shrimp-like crustaceans, cousins of the shrimp in an EcoSphere—depend on the phytoplankton. Baleen whales, sperm whales, squid, fur seals, the black-browed albatross, and the Emperor penguin are among the many creatures that depend on the krill. El-Sayed suspects that krill may be "among the first casualties" of the Ozone Hole. "If anything happens to the krill," he has said, "the whole ecosystem will absolutely collapse. We can say good-bye to the whales, to the seals, to the penguins, et cetera."

There is no question the extra ozone in the lower atmosphere is burning the biosphere, although ecologists have barely begun to assess the damage. According to the U.S. Agriculture Department's National Crop Loss Assessment Program, ozone is eating about $2 billion worth of American farmers' crops each year, including sweet corn, potatoes, peppers, cotton, soybeans, pasture grass, and alfalfa. Alan F. Teramura, a botanist at the University of Maryland, has grown soybeans beneath enough UV to simulate a 25 percent ozone-layer depletion. Crop losses were also 25 percent. Researchers at the Yale School of Forestry report that the growth of young poplars, cottonwoods, and black locusts is stunted by ozone levels that are well within the federal air-quality limit. In the Summer of '88, the ozone in the hot, humid, heavy air cut the wheat yields in experimental plots near Ithaca, New York by nearly one third.

Finally, ozone is a greenhouse gas, and when it descends to the troposphere, which is denser, its greenhouse effect becomes stronger. Already ozone's effect on the temperature of the planet has become about one-sixth as great as carbon dioxide.

There is one healthy side-effect of the ozone in the lower atmosphere. It may shield us from some of the extra UV that would otherwise penetrate all the way to the ground. Like that wayward low umbrella, it pokes people in the face but still helps keep us dry. We have not reduced the ozone shield very much yet; we have merely lowered it far enough to take it into our lungs.

As with the greenhouse effect, feedback may make matters worse. The dramatic loss of ozone in the hole not only lets ultraviolet radiation pour through, but also cools the hole (because the air in the hole is losing all that greenhouse gas). Already the air above the South Pole in October and November (springtime in Antarctica) is about 10° C. (18° F.) colder than it was in the 1970s. The less ozone there is in the hole, the colder it gets, and since more ice crystals form as it cools, the colder the hole the less ozone there will be. The hole is lasting longer and longer as it grows colder and deeper. The final warming, the break-up of the hole, is coming weeks later in the austral spring than it once did. That means the living creatures down below are being exposed to higher levels of UV for a longer period of time.

If predictions are correct, the greenhouse effect will chill the whole stratosphere by another ten degrees C. during the next fifty years, putting even more ice crystals up there. That could lead to bigger holes at the North and South Poles. Already the North Pole is loaded with chlorine compounds from CFCs—Robert Watson, of NASA, who oversees each Hole Expedition, says arctic stratospheric chemistry is in a state of "incredible perturbation."

The ozone crisis makes the rise of methane in the atmosphere much more alarming, because when methane breaks apart, one of the by-products is water vapor. Methane may already have raised the amount of water vapor in the stratosphere by nearly one-third since the 1940s (more water for more high-flying clouds) and according to Rowland's estimates, water vapor in the stratosphere could double above present levels in the next fifty years.

In the next few decades, thanks to all these intertwining effects, we may all be treated to sights of the once-rare mother-of-pearl, noctilucent clouds. We will see spectacular displays a few hours before dawn and a few hours after sunset—the foreglow and afterglow of each day on Earth. And we will receive an ultraviolet bath in the hours in between.

Of course, we did not make the pot—we merely poured a witches' brew into the pot. We will never erase the natural forces that have always been creating and destroying ozone. Even if we turn the troposphere and the stratosphere upside down, the Sun will always stir the pot. As the Sun brightens and dims in its more or less regular cycles from Solar Maximum to Solar Minimum, the ozone depletion crisis will worsen, improve, worsen; two steps forward and one step back. Each big Maximum, like the spectacular one of 1990, will appear to restore the ozone layer.

Volcanoes will continue to inject their own brands of aerosols into the stratosphere. Winds will act up, too: a year with strong stratospheric winds will sometimes disrupt the polar vortex, weaken the reactions inside it, warm the air, and spare some ozone. (That happened in 1988. The Ozone Hole at the South Pole was as deep as 1984, but not as bad as '85, '86, or '87.)

So the ozone crisis will not march upward on a straight line in the next one hundred years. Natural forces will continue to make it sometimes better and sometimes worse. Snapping-points and thresholds in the system will make it stall and lurch ahead. There may be more unsuspected feedback effects of the kind that threw off predictions in the 1970s—for who could imagine that a cauldron of air at the South Pole would combine with a high-altitude snow of nitric acid would combine with a chilling of the stratosphere from the greenhouse effect would combine with CFCs? The crisis will snake upward on a Keeling curve:

Chlorofluorocarbons are the products of a single branch of the chemical industry. It should be much easier to stop producing these chemicals than to stop burning coal and oil, or clearing rain forests. This should be a far more tractable problem than the greenhouse effect. Yet even now, after the discovery of the Ozone Hole, and after urgent international negotiations, the chemicals are still being manufactured at a great rate.

The world's foot-dragging brings many scientists to despair. It exasperates Sherwood Rowland, who sounded the first alarm back in the 1970s. "After all," Rowland has said, "what's the use of having developed a science well enough to make predictions, if in the end all we're willing to do is stand around and wait for them to come true?"

CHAPTER 9

LOVEJOY'S ISLANDS

It is possible to conceive an island that could contain a future time—something not quite in simultaneous relationship with the rest of the world. . . .

Loren Eiseley
The Accidental Universe

The world is too much with us; late and soon,
Getting and spending, we lay waste our powers:
Little we see in Nature that is ours . . .

Wordsworth's famous lament. By "the world," of course, he meant the human sphere, which even in 1806 already seemed to surround, enclose, and completely absorb its citizens. By "nature," he meant the rest of the planet.

After two centuries of getting and spending, we have a second lament: Little we see in nature is *not* ours. The world is too much with us, in ways that go beyond Wordsworth's meaning. At the North Pole, in the middle of the Pacific Ocean, and above the Antarctic icecap, the atmosphere is loaded with carbon, sulfur, nitrogen, phosphorus, chlorine—ours. There are holes in the sky now, and the sunlight that streams through them is not as benign as it was in Wordsworth's day. This hard new light is ours. The very weather threatens to change: and if it does, the new round of the four seasons will be ours.

Even the green biosphere is largely in our hands now, part of our world of getting and spending. Ecologists calculate that the green plants on the continents produce more than 100 billion tons of organic matter each year in the course of photosynthesis. They call this quantity "net terrestrial primary production," and they use it to make a global accounting. According to a study by the ecologist Peter Vitousek and his colleagues at Stanford University, human beings either eat, or feed their cattle, horses, sheep, goats, and pigs, or chop down for timber and firewood, about 4 billion tons of that primary production each year.

Four billion tons out of a hundred is 4 percent. That in itself would not be a shocking tithe for us to take, since we are the dominant species on the planet. However, if we include the amount of biomass that we burn when we clear the land, and throw away when we husk the corn and pluck the cotton, and forfeit in the fields that lie fallow, and so on, then we control 30 billion tons of the net primary production of the terrestrial biosphere, according to Vitousek and his colleagues. Thirty percent.

If we include the amount of organic matter or biomass that is foregone by the planet as we co-opt more territory each year for more and more fields and pastures, house lots, parking lots, town and city streets, then our share (adding together all of the carbon that we are taking, and all that we are preventing the biosphere from making) is now approaching 40 billion tons of the continents' net primary production each year. Forty percent.

Demographers project that the human population will double in the next one hundred years, from more than 5 billion today to more than 10 billion in 2100. As the ecologist Paul Ehrlich observes, "This implies a belief that our species can safely commandeer upwards of 80 percent."

The poet in us is horrified by these statistics. The businessman in us may wonder how to get the remaining 20 percent. But we should be completely horrified. Most of the changes we have made in nature's arrangements have occurred since Wordsworth's lament in 1806. From our point of view that is a long time; from the point of view of the rest of the planet it is nearly instantaneous. Most of the changes have also been cumulative, and whether they took place first in the air, in the sea, or on solid ground, they all alter the conditions of life on Earth.

Such sudden global changes do more than offend romantic sensibilities. They affect the bottom line, the ultimate bottom line, which is represented by the geological strata beneath our feet. These rock strata are full of the last fossil relics of species that died during short periods of stress. In the science of change this may be the one immutable law: all sudden global change leads to the extinction of species.

At the end of the last Ice Age, for example, when the great ice sheets collapsed and melted, sea levels rose several hundred feet.

Peninsulas around the world were drowned. Outlying hills were cut off from continents. Millions of animals and plants were marooned on brand-new islands.

Ecologists have made a study of these islands: Britain off the coast of Europe; Borneo and Java off Southeast Asia; Tasmania off Australia; Trinidad off South America; Fernando Po off the coast of Africa.

In the beginning each new island was like Noah's Ark. Its passenger list was a more or less complete inventory of the flora and fauna of its continent, as in God's instructions to Noah: "And of every living thing of all flesh, two of every sort shalt thou bring into the ark, to keep them alive with thee."

Then each island began to lose passengers, not just individuals but whole species. Salawati, cut off from Papua New Guinea, lost the red bird of paradise. Batanta, near Salawati, lost the king and twelve-wired birds of paradise, and also tree kangaroos and wallabies. On the very smallest islands, those of less than fifty square kilometers, local extinction rates ran so high that after 10,000 years virtually all of the isolated populations were gone.

A sudden change in the cryosphere and hydrosphere led to local extinctions in the biosphere. And that was a change we normally think of as benign: the end of an Ice Age.

Today the number of islands on this planet is increasing much faster than at the end of the Ice Age. The cause is not a change in sea level, for sea level is not rising that much, yet. The cause is the rising tide of human beings. All over the planet, the biosphere is tending more and more toward a checkerboard. Look out a plane window. There are exceptions, but as a rule the longer a place has been inhabited the more fragmented is the landscape. In the United States the checkerboard was drawn in first in the east and spread west.

Consider Cadiz Township, in Green County, Wisconsin. Four charts, made by the botanist John Curtis, show the area of woods in Cadiz in the years 1831, 1882, 1902, and 1950. At first, Green County really was all green. Then the Pioneer Explosion reached Wisconsin. In a single century, civilization created an archipelago of shrinking islands in a township six miles square.

The last pioneers in the United States are now busy in the last wilderness. The flight route from San Francisco to Seattle, Washington follows the Cascade Range, some of the most spectacular and lonely wilderness in North America. Even in those jagged mountains, which are really rows of young volcanoes—and even within a few miles of the

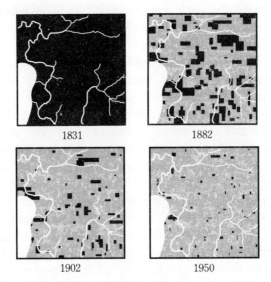

1831   1882

1902   1950

smoking crater of Mount St. Helens—one can see the outlines of the
universal checkerboard being sketched in. Valleys and ridges are
dotted with houses. Forests are bisected and trisected with roads. The
biosphere is being carved into thousands of odd-shaped fragments of
dark pelt.

These fragments are islands in the same sense that Hyde Park and
Central Park are islands. They are pieces of biosphere surrounded by
people. As the tide of human beings rises in the next century, and we
push toward a controlling interest of 80 percent, the biosphere can only
become more and more fragmented. Although human beings cluster
more and more in cities, and although we try to grow more and more
food per acre, we shatter the biosphere into a Milky Way of islands.

This trend alone, this single global change, puts the projections of
the demographers on a collision course with the projections of ecologists. It is such a bad business that it shadows the whole human project
with doubt. It is one of the key reasons why, as Ehrlich writes, a world
of 10 billion people is "a preposterous notion to ecologists who already
see the deadly impacts of today's level of human activities."

In the 1960s, two mathematically minded ecologists, E.O. Wilson
and Robert MacArthur, drew up formulas for predicting how many species can survive on any given island, based on its size and its distance
from the mainland. Their theory of island biogeography revolutionized
ecology. This was a theory of great generality. It applied to any island,
real or metaphorical. The slopes of coral reefs are islands underwater:

they are islands for the black hamlet, a fish that can live there and not in the open water that lies farther from the coral head. Mountaintops are islands in the sky. Lakes are islands for fish. The well in a glass microscope slide is an island for the amoeba, hydra, and paramecium beneath the cover slip. The hollow crystal ball, the EcoSphere, is an island for red shrimp (the ultimate island: no entrance and no exit).

Wilson and MacArthur's formulas apply to all of these islands because whenever a bit of biosphere is isolated, by rising tides or by any other catastrophe, natural or artificial,* the same thing happens. It is a simple matter of geography. On the mainland if the local population is wiped out—in a fire, or a drought—it can be replaced. Neighbors and immigrants will wander in sooner or later and take their place. But on an island, there are no neighbors and there are few immigrants. So the rate of extinction exceeds the rate of replacement.†

The smaller the island and the farther it lies from the mainland, the greater the disparity between the rate of extinction and the rate of replacement. The result is a decline in the number of species: an island effect.

After Wilson and MacArthur, it became clear that the fate of much of the biosphere in the next one hundred years now depends upon the island effect, just as the fate of much of Earth's climate depends upon the greenhouse effect. Ecologists sought to refine the theory of island biogeography with case histories. For this purpose old land-bridge islands like England and Ireland or Batanta and Salawati were less than ideal, since they were created so long ago. Ecologists needed a test case: a giant, brand-new archipelago that could be watched from the moment of its isolation.

A few days before Christmas, 1976, Thomas Lovejoy was brainstorming about this problem with a few other ecologists. For his Ph.D. thesis, Lovejoy had banded 20,000 birds in the Amazon. In his mind's eye he could see the Brazilian rain forest. The Pioneer Explosion had just reached the Amazon, and he could see the new farms and clearings

---

*A rocky peak projecting from an ice sheet is a kind of island—a *nunatak*. A green hill in a black sea of frozen lava is yet another kind of island—a *kipuka*. These outcrops, too, start out like Noah's Ark, overcrowded with survivors.

†Once in a century, an immigrant may wash up on a remote island aboard a drift log, but to make a difference she must be a *pregnant* immigrant.

along the new roads, the random patches of trees left standing in the muddy fields.

According to local law, a landowner in the rain forest could not clear his whole property. Half the forest had to be left standing. In practice, of course, this law was often honored in the breach. Each time the land was sold, whatever rain forest was left could be cut in half again. Two ranchers could pass a piece of rain forest back and forth between them until there was nothing left.

However, the Fifty-percent Rule, as it was called, had resulted in a patchwork landscape wherever farmers and settlers had moved into the Amazon. Driving down the new dirt roads one saw everywhere a sea of scrubby farmland in which bits of rain forest stood out here and there like tropical islands.

Lovejoy flew to Brazil and began negotiating. He is a gifted diplomat, fluent in Portuguese. In any case the grand project that he described had immediate value from the point of view of Brazilian officials. They had already resolved in principle to set aside parks and nature reserves in the Amazon. But it wasn't easy to decide where to draw the borders of the future parks. The carpet of the rain forest was still uncut, though it was fraying at the edges. There were no landmarks to draw a circle around—no Yosemites or Grand Canyons. For that matter, what size should the reserves be? How big a piece of rain forest would a jaguar require, for instance?

The Amazon is part of a green belt around the equator, from Africa to South America to Southeast Asia. It traces Earth's zone of strongest sunshine, where rates of evaporation and precipitation are greatest. This belt covers less than 10 percent of Earth's land area but it contains more than half its species of animals and plants.

Compared to the rain forest, the rest of the biosphere is impoverished. In the state of Pennsylvania, for instance, birdwatchers have compiled a list of 185 different species of birds that breed in one part of the countryside or another. In the state of Pará, Brazil, there is a city called Belém. It is on the very edge of the rain forest, near the mouth of the Amazon River. More than 425 different species of birds have been spotted within the city limits of Belém.

In northern New England—Vermont, New Hampshire, Maine—a hiker can pass through an entire forest and count only one or two species of evergreen. In a Pennsylvania forest there may be a dozen different trees. On the outskirts of Belém, in a single eleven-acre patch of the Mocambo forest, a botanist has counted 295 species of trees.

Kneeling on the floor of the rain forest, another botanist found the leaves of more than fifty different species of trees in a patch of ground just *half a meter square.*

These small samples suggest the size of the total, which no one knows. Knowledge, like Belém, is at the outer edge of the rain forest. Biologists believe there are more exotic lifeforms yet to be discovered there than all the species of animals and plants ever catalogued by scientists. Biologists have named about 1.5 million species so far. Those who study the exotic flora and fauna of the rain forests, particularly the profusion of strange beetles, moths, butterflies, and other insects that inhabit the canopies a hundred feet and more above the ground, believe the grand total in the rain forests may be more than 30 million species. Wilson says every biologist should go to the tropical rain forest at least once, if only on a pilgrimage. Lovejoy calls the world's rain forests "the greatest expression of life on the planet."

Rain forests are like carbon dioxide. They put into our hands a big lever that we would rather not have. With carbon dioxide, we can alter Earth's temperature drastically by changing a relatively small amount of gas. With the rain forest, we can alter the number of species on Earth drastically by clearing a relatively small amount of land.

Lovejoy's archipelago became the biggest planned experiment in the history of ecology. It is located just north of the Amazonian city of Manaus ("two hours and many thousands of potholes," as the project leaders say). Until recently, this was still virgin forest, home of jaguars, puma, tapirs, harpy eagles, and crested eagles. Today, flying overhead in a small plane, one can see thousands of acres where farmers have cut and burned away the forests to make way for cattle pasture. Here and there in the muddy fields there are remnant patches of trees, and some of these patches are neat squares and rectangles. These are Lovejoy's islands, and they stand out so sharply that a visiting naturalist once observed, on approaching one by plane, "It looks like a piece of shag carpet tossed down on a dirt floor." Today there are ten islands in the ecologist's archipelago, ranging in size from one hectare to one hundred hectares (a hectare is about two and a half acres). Someday there will be almost thirty islands, including a giant of ten thousand hectares.

Projeto Lovejoy, as the experiment is known in Brazil's popular press, is still just beginning. The archipelago would have to be monitored by hundreds of ecologists and volunteers for centuries before the full consequences of the island effect would appear. Nevertheless, as soon as the first of Lovejoy's islands were carved out of the rain forest in the early 1980s, there was a cascade of effects.

First, birds flocked in. Tropical ecologists can count birds by stringing invisibly fine nets—mist nets—across clearings in the forests before dawn. In newly isolated forests, the rate at which the ecologists caught birds in the mist nets *doubled*. This is a refugee effect. Birds have been displaced and they flock to the island in the middle of the new field as if alighting upon an ark.

Six months later, the population of refugees crashes. Trees at the edge of the forest begin to crash, too. They are not used to so much sunlight. Sun is stronger in tropics than anywhere else on Earth because it is directly overhead. But in the thick uncut rain forest there are so many layers of forest canopy that very little light gets through to the bottom ("to the frustration of those who try to use color film," says Lovejoy). Now trees from the dark heart of the forest had been placed on the edge of the forest. One tree in the family Bombacaceae (a relative of the balsa-wood tree) burst into flower six months out of season. Botanists had never seen that happen before. To their trained eyes the blooms were like the mad gaiety of Ophelia in the brook.

Monkeys were in trouble, too. The band of golden-handed tamarins fled across the new fields and were seen no more. Saki monkeys normally range in troops across hundreds of hectares. Two of them were marooned together on the little island. They ate almost all the fruits and seeds of the trees in their reserve. Then the saki monkeys disappeared.

One of the more bizarre changes involved army ants. Troops of army ants live on a month-long cycle. For part of each month each colony camps in a bivouac of half a million ants or more. But for a time during each cycle, they swarm. Each day the troop advances as a front across the floor of the rain forest, flowing under leaves and up over tree trunks like a stream of molten tar.

Insects on the forest floor normally sit still and try to be inconspicuous. But when the army ants are coming, they abandon their hiding places and flee for their lives. They leap into the air, or hop ahead, anywhere they can go. The march of the army ants is a sight to see, with thousands of multicolored butterflies, exotic grasshoppers and giant cockroaches bursting into the air in front of it.

Certain birds take advantage of this panic. They fly above the troops of army ants like air force above infantry. The birds swoop low and filch fleeing grasshoppers in mid-air before the ants can get them. Half a dozen species of birds in this part of the Amazon are professional ant-followers. They have pursued the trick for so long that it has become obligatory. Although there may be nearly 30 million species of insects hiding in the rain forest, these birds know only one way to find them. Without army ants to beat the bushes, the birds would starve to death.

A single army ant colony ranges across about thirty hectares of rain forest. So the troops of army ants on the new ten-hectare island soon disappeared. The guilds of ant-followers disappeared, too. A conspicuous portion of the fauna of the rain forest had vanished.

Associations still more peculiar began to fall apart. The ecologists monitoring the island had expected trouble for the ant-following birds. They had also expected that the islands would be too small for the great, pig-like peccaries. But they had not imagined that something as small as a frog would suffer. However, when the peccaries disappeared, their muddy wallows on the edge of the island began to dry up in the hot sun. Frogs had lived in the puddles in those peccary wallows. These frogs now fell silent.

On the windward side of the island, the number of wind-thrown and broken trees was striking. Lovejoy attributes their falls to the high winds that blew in from the open pasture—another edge effect. Each tree-fall opened up more of the forest within to sunlight, which meant weeds from the pasture could creep further into the forest. The edge crept inward.

Indeed the ten-hectare plot was really all edge. There was no core where the forest was untouched or unchanged—even in the very center of the reserve. Lovejoy says, "The number of standing dead trees jumped dramatically from nine in 1981 to sixty-five in 1982."

Volunteers who had explored and surveyed before the island's creation began to find the place unfamiliar. The dawn chorus of the birds and the midnight chorus of the frogs had been silenced. The familiar butterflies that had lived near the ground were nowhere to be seen. Instead there were strange butterflies, some of them from the topmost canopy, which fluttered near the ground as if the floor of the forest had begun to seem confusingly as bright as the top. The air was hot and dry, and each week there were fewer catches in the mist nets.

After only a year of isolation, the island had begun to resemble the nightmare fable that opens Rachel Carson's book *Silent Spring.* The groves had lost their voice, and life had fled from the trees. Here there had been no spraying of poison, only the innocent clearing of a field.

Lovejoy foresees slow, progressive losses for all his islands, large and small. Those of one hundred hectares or one thousand will not deteriorate as quickly as those of one or ten hectares. And it will be decades before the very largest preserve in the study, the ten-thousand-hectare plot, shows signs of trouble in its interior. But what has happened in the smallest islands will happen in the middle-sized ones next, and ultimately in the very largest.

Lovejoy calls this "ecosystem decay." Radioactive decay can be predicted with precision. A lump of uranium atoms decays very slowly and very predictably into a lump of lead. As a general principle, ecosystem decay is proving to be rather predictable, too.

Events like those that created Lovejoy's islands are being repeated at a rate of about one acre per second in rain forests around the world, and despite an infinity of local variations on the theme, everywhere there will be the same pattern of attrition. The only fundamental difference is that here the losses are being watched.

Outside the rain forests, where the pioneer explosions have been exploding longer, the islands are older. In many of them the last stages of ecosystem decay are now on display. Giant pandas, for instance, which once ranged across almost half of China, are now confined to a few small reserves in the wooded mountains of Sichuan province, on the eastern edge of the Tibetan plateau. In 1987, there were about thirty-five isolated populations in the wild, most of them of fewer than twenty pandas each.

When islands are that small, the island effect is at its most extreme. An entire generation can turn out all male or female, or the only breeding male in the group may die in a trap that a poacher set for musk deer. With each group cut off from the rest, no roving bachelor is likely to come along and discover the languishing harem. The stranger never comes to dinner—and that is the end of the line. Like many wild creatures, pandas do not breed well in captivity. Despite heroic international efforts to save them, pandas may be doomed by the island effect.

Panthers (also known as pumas or mountain lions) once ranged across the Eastern United States. In 1986, in Florida, there were only about two dozen left, all in a few hardwood swamps near the Everglades. A cross-state highway bisected their swamp. Each year a few panthers died on the highway, and the population of Florida panthers was reduced by another 5 or 6 percent.

Then state officials decided to add two lanes to the highway. To make it up to the black panthers they also built "panther crosswalks"— thirty-six underpasses. In theory, the panthers would scoot under the highway to get from one part of their shrinking island to the other. The state spent $10 million on the underpasses, but the island effect doomed the panthers.

The pronghorn antelope of Wyoming's Great Divide Basin escape the cold each winter by ranging south across the grasslands, as they have done since the depths of the last Ice Age. Cattlemen are putting up more and more barbed-wire fences, which cut the antelopes' range and block their escape routes south. At Oracle Junction, Arizona, near the Biosphere II project,* there is a little café decorated in Western kitsch: a red sombrero; a rack of antelope antlers; a steer skull with a cowboy and bucking bronco painted in black silhouette on its forehead. On one wall, the management has hung an impressive collection of old barbed wire, mounted on plaques and labelled in block letters, THE WIRE THAT FENCED THE WEST:

CURTIS '4 POINT'	1892
GLIDDEN 'OVAL TWIST'	1876
BAKER'S 'ODD BARB'	1883
SUNDERLAND 'KINK'	1884
WATKINS 'LAZYPLATE'	1876
DODGE AND WASHBURN	1882
ELLWOOD 'SPREAD'	1882

And so on. This assorted barbed wire has helped turn the West into a set of enclosures that are, for the antelope, almost as impermeable as the walls of Biosphere II. In a single fierce winter in 1983 more than half the pronghorn antelopes died.

That winter, wildlife biologist Bill Alldredge was following a radio-collared antelope he called Antelope E. "He was an impressive buck and we learned a lot from him," Alldredge told the writer Steve Yates. Alldredge and his son had watched Antelope E defend his territory against all comers for two years, courting, breeding, and shepherding a harem of females across the grasslands. During that third, hard winter,

---

*Biosphere II is a microcosm made of glass and steel by a private company called Space Biospheres Ventures. It encloses more than 2 acres of land and is designed to sustain 8 volunteers for years without opening a door or window or admitting any air, water, or food from outside. (The rest of us live in Biosphere I.)

the Alldredges radio-tracked Antelope E all the way down to Interstate 80, and along the highway for a hundred miles, and back toward Rawlins. Then Antelope E stopped moving.

They found him hanging by one hind leg in a barbed-wire fence. He had finally tried to jump the fence, which shows how desperate he must have been, says Alldredge. "We had seen him escape possibly twenty encounters with hunters over the years—and he ends up upside down in a stupid fence in a snowstorm."

When we try to save species like the antelope we generally do so by setting aside more islands, national parks. A recent study by the ecologist William D. Newmark found that in the United States, fourteen western national parks are too small to save all the mammals that once lived there. The smallest reserve in Newmark's study, Bryce Canyon, 144 square kilometers, has already lost more than a third of its mammal species. Yosemite, at 2083 square kilometers, had lost a quarter of its species even before the fires of the Summer of '88.

Parks this size are supposed to be arks. They are meant to carry the nation's wildlife, including grizzly bears and antelope, through the next millennium and beyond. But it is now clear that very few arks on Earth are really large enough for the purpose. In the American West, only the very largest assemblage of contiguous parks, a constellation of preserves that Newmark calls Kootenay-Banff-Jasper-Yoho, will do the job. Kootenay-Banff-Jasper-Yoho is 20,736 square kilometers, slightly larger than the state of New Jersey. According to Newmark, it has not lost any mammals, yet.

If the giant parks of the West are too small, what about the parks of the East, or the vest-pocket parks in Europe? Creatures that depend upon those arks may not last the next century, much less the next millennium. "We thought we could put a wall around nature and preserve it," says one ecologist. "But we were wrong."

One might suppose that migrating birds, at least, would be safe from the island effect, since many of them can fly more than a thousand miles in a single day. Unfortunately, these birds are in particular danger, because their future depends upon the preservation of a good portion of the face of the Earth. They spend half of each year in the middle of the old pioneer explosion and half in the new. Nearly half of the 700 species of birds found in the United States spend their winters in the tropics, including some of the country's most popular songbirds: thrushes, flycatchers, vireos, warblers, tanagers. If a relatively small amount of land is cleared in Mexico, Costa Rica, and the Caribbean Islands, many of these birds will vanish in North America, too.

Already many species of songbirds are growing rarer in the United States. Some ornithologists say the American woods are getting noticeably quieter. The dawn chorus is fainter and less melodious. A study at one nature preserve, the Greenbrook Sanctuary in Alpine, New Jersey, shows that thirty species of birds became significantly rarer there between the years 1957 and 1983. Hooded warblers, American redstarts, and a few other songbirds all but disappeared.

These birds have the misfortune to be endangered both by the expanding farms of South America and the expanding suburbs of North America. Some ornithologists think suburbia is hurting the birds more than tropical deforestation, because the island effect is so much more advanced in the North. All across America there are small towns like Cadiz, Wisconsin, with less and less unbroken forest and more and more edge.

There *are* birds who like edges, of course. For jays and crows the island effect is a bonanza. These are the kind of opportunists that are always favored by upheavals in the biosphere—they are the avian equivalents of rats and mice. They eat the eggs of vireos, warblers, thrushes, tanagers, orioles, hummingbirds, and flycatchers. Each new edge that a town permits in its remaining woods invites edge-lovers, egg-eaters, and nest parasites, and disinvites the migrant songbirds that love dark forest interiors. They lose habitat if even a single road is cut through their forest in the North or the South.*

Monarch butterflies migrate, too. Each fall, the Monarchs on the east and west coasts of North America fly south. In the east, as many as 100 million of them make it to the southwest slopes of a few volcanic mountains near Mexico City. The spectacular orange-and-black butterflies spend the winter roosting in dense forest stands of oyamel fir. Then in the spring they erupt from their fir trees and fly all the way back north.

All migration is a miracle, but the Monarch's is among the most astonishing. As many as five generations live and die between the flight

---

*Populations of jays and crows are now exploding in the United States, while vireos, warblers, thrushes, and the rest are headed for extinction in many parts of the country, including the most chopped-up parts of Illinois, and the Coastal Plain and Piedmont of Maryland.

north in the spring and the flight south in the fall. Yet the Monarchs always find their way back to a few stands of mountain firs, which they themselves have never seen—groves that have not been visited by a single Monarch since the time of their great-great-great-grandparents. Biologists do not know how the butterflies do it, but they know that a little logging in the wrong place would be the end of it.

Local Mexican farmers often cut down these oyamel firs for firewood and building poles. The Monarchs' islands in the mountains have been getting a little smaller each year. The International Union for the Conservation of Nature (which publishes the Red Data Books, lists of threatened species) has created a special category for Monarch migration: a "threatened phenomenon."

In 1986, the Mexican government declared the Monarchs' forests an ecological preserve. All logging and farming is now prohibited among the Monarchs' firs and is controlled in an 11,000-hectare buffer zone around them. The eastern population of Monarchs is safer than it was, if the government can enforce the law.

The western population of Monarchs has not been so lucky. Western Monarchs spend winters in a few select spots along the California coast, many of them near expanding cities. Hundreds of thousands of western Monarchs, winging back to the site of their ancestral groves, have found nothing but new condominiums.

For all of these migrants, we are burning the candle at both ends. In the next decades there may be a new bitterness between the U.S. and many tropical countries. Disputes will flare up like those between the U.S. and Canada over acid rain. Which country is killing the birds? The butterflies? Whose chain saw silenced our woods?

Some time after Lovejoy had begun his artificial archipelago, something prompted him to call on Stephen Schneider at the National Center for Atmospheric Research. Over lunch in Boulder, Colorado, the ecologist talked about the island effect and the climatologist talked about the greenhouse effect.

At length Schneider asked, "Tom, is this just a social call?"

"No, I don't think so," Lovejoy said. "Something's on my mind, and I don't know whether it's important or not. What's the connection between us?"

He meant the connection between their two effects. The question surprised Schneider, because like most of us he is used to thinking of the greenhouse effect purely in terms of what it will do to one species—ours. His supercomputer models are designed to predict the impact of climate change on cities and beaches, fields of wheat, rice, and sorghum. He often calls carbon dioxide a problem in redistributive justice. It's not the end of agriculture, he says, it's a shift of agriculture. Moving the corn belt one hundred kilometers north might be rough from the point of view of Iowa, and nice from the point of view of Minnesota.

The moment he heard Lovejoy's question, Schneider saw how important it was. It had never occurred to him to ask his supercomputer to predict the fate of one of Lovejoy's islands. "It almost struck me like a Eureka!" Schneider says now.

As we keep forgetting (and as the planet keeps reminding us) no global change proceeds in isolation. The greenhouse effect combined with the island effect would stress the biosphere far more powerfully than either effect alone.

Carbon dioxide gas would magnify the problem even *without* its greenhouse effect. The more the gas piles up in the air, the more it changes the terms of the struggle for existence in every patch of greenery on the planet. As we have seen, the gas is like fertilizer for plants. Putting more in the air gives a competitive edge to those species that can utilize carbon dioxide in photosynthesis most efficiently. Many of those plants are opportunists, too: weeds.

Boyd Strain, of Duke University, and other botanists are now growing assortments of crops and weeds in the richly carbonated atmospheres of experimental greenhouses, air that is 600, 700, 800 parts per million carbon dioxide. Like Lovejoy's islands, these greenhouses might be said, in Loren Eiseley's phrase, to contain a future time. They are "something not quite in simultaneous relationship with the rest of the world." Strain says it is clear from what is going on in there that the third millennium is going to be a very good time to be a weed.

Most habitats are defined not only by their climate but by their plants, and the future of much of the world's flora and fauna, trapped on shrinking islands, requires particular plants to stay just as they are. The diet of the giant panda, for instance, consists almost entirely of bamboo. If carbon dioxide gas favors some other grass over bamboo, the pandas may starve. The fertilization effect will unsettle every fragment of woods, marshes, and tundra on Earth. For millions of plants

177

and animals already living on the edge, the gas we are putting into the air may tip the balance.*

So we would be stressing the biosphere with carbon dioxide even if the gas did not have a greenhouse effect. However, if the greenhouse effect warms the planet, that will be a worse shock. The Soviet climate expert Budyko calls temperature and rainfall the two "master variables" of life on Earth. Together they draw the boundaries of Earth's climatic zones. A warming would redraw those boundaries, shifting the tropics into what is now the temperate zone and shifting the temperate zone toward the poles. The greater the warming the more the zones will shift; the faster the warming, the faster the boundaries will shift. A 1° C. change in temperature is equivalent to a latitude change of more than 100 kilometers, and in mid- to high latitudes the planet may soon be warming that much *per decade*.

The biologist Robert L. Peters and the ecologist Joan D.S. Darling began some years ago to think about the problems these shifts could pose for the biosphere. The last time the continent of North America was two or three degrees C. warmer than today was during the interglacials between some of the last few Ice Ages. The world was a very different garden then, write Peters and Darling. "Osage oranges and pawpaws grew near Toronto, several hundred kilometers north of their present distribution; manatees swam in New Jersey; tapirs and peccaries foraged in Pennsylvania; and Cape Cod had a forest like that of present-day North Carolina."

If we are heading toward a climate like that, then animals and plants that are adapted to cooler climates are going to have to move. They will either chase their shifting climate zones, or they will die. (No air conditioners on Lovejoy's islands.) They will have two general lines of retreat: uphill or toward the poles. Climbing 500 meters up a mountainside is like moving 250 kilometers north. Indeed, there are mountains

---

*One of the first studies of this important problem was published in 1989. Biologists at Harvard University's Museum of Comparative Zoology wanted to know what a double dose of carbon dioxide will do to the relationship between the plantain, which is one of the world's most common weeds, and the buck-eye butterfly, which eats a lot of plantains in California, parts of Mexico, and the Southeastern U.S.

The investigators found that the chemistry of the plantain's leaves is significantly altered by the extra carbon dioxide. These changes hurt the buck-eye during one early larval stage, or *instar*—but then a later instar flourishes. No one can tell whether the plantain or its predator will come out ahead in the end in the next one hundred years. But it is clear that life in the third millennium will be different even for common weeds and butterflies.

in South America where tree lines have migrated upslope as much as 1500 meters to beat the heat after an Ice Age.

As the world warms up, consider what happens to a population on the slope of a mountain. The peak is smaller than the base, so as the climate gets warmer and the species shifts upward, it is forced into a smaller and smaller space. Soon the population is cut off from those of neighboring peaks; where once it was joined to others at the base of the mountain, it now lives on an island. As the climate gets warmer and warmer it is confined to a smaller and smaller island.

"Climb to the top of a mountain. Now climb higher," runs an old Zen koan. The koan is supposed to jar the mind into a new state of insight. Today the saying jars the mind to see the predicament of life in the next one hundred years. If the temperature keeps warming, thousands of species of animals and plants will converge toward summits around the planet. And if the temperature climbs higher, where do they go from there?

Fleeing toward the poles will be dangerous, too. All forced marches are dangerous. Before the Ice Ages of the Pleistocene Epoch, there were sweet gum, tulip trees, moonseed, hemlock, and white cedar in Europe and North America. Their fates on the two continents are instructive. In North America they survived the Ice Ages, in part because the biggest obstacles, the Rockies and the Appalachians, run north to south. The mountains did not block their forced march across the latitudes.

In Europe, however, all these species went extinct. There the biggest obstacles are the Pyrenees, the Alps, and the Mediterranean Sea, which all happen to run east to west. For millions of animals and plants in Europe the path of retreat may have been blocked. Like pronghorn antelope in flight from a blizzard, they piled up at the fences and froze to death.

Today most nature reserves and national parks are hemmed in by cities, roads, and farms the way the hemlocks of Europe were blocked by mountains. They are man-locked islands. If the temperature and rainfall regime changes by 100 kilometers, there may be no place for them to go. As one ecologist has put it, "Few animals can cross L.A. on the way to the promised land."

Even where the path of retreat is still free and clear, the march could still be fatal. Everything depends on the rate of the warming. If it comes on slowly, then most species will survive. If predictions are correct, however, the world will warm ten to forty times faster in the next one hundred years than it did after the last Ice Age. The paleo-ecologist Margaret Davis, of the University of Minnesota, has calculated what that will mean for North American trees (and by extension, for much of North American wildlife).

Spruce 12,000 years ago   6,000 years ago   Now

Trees travel by dispersing their seeds. That is a very slow means of transportation. As the saying goes, the acorn does not fall far from the oak. Engelmann spruce seeds are light enough to be borne on the wind, and a spruce seed sometimes falls as far as 200 meters away from the parent spruce. At that rate, a forest of Engelmann spruce can migrate twenty kilometers in a century. Since the climate zone of the spruce is expected to shift by at least 200 kilometers in the next century, the spruce is too slow.

According to Davis, the ranges of yellow birch, sugar maple, hemlock, and beech may shift northward between 500 and 1,000 kilometers. These trees move more slowly than spruce.

Macbeth thought Birnam Wood could never come to Dunsinane. In the last act of the tragedy a messenger runs to warn him:

> As I did stand my watch upon the hill,
> I look'd toward Birnam, and anon, methought,
> The wood began to move.

An army had massed beneath the castle and was carrying the wood up, tree by tree, for camouflage. That is what the world is coming to. In the next century, if we want to preserve thousands of habitats in the temperate zones, we may have to move whole forests ourselves.

The prospect for life on many of Lovejoy's islands in the twenty-first century is desolating to think about. The climate that has shaped them will leave them behind. (Yellowstone's climate is expected to end up somewhere over the border in Canada, for instance.) And the new climate will bring new invaders with it. Hot weather can bring pests like locusts, aphids, moths, and bark beetles—as in the Summer of '88. Hot weather can also bring drought and fire—as in the Summer of '88.

The only sure winners are pests and opportunists: rats, crows, flies, mosquitoes, weeds. Their ranges are so cosmopolitan that they will hang on no matter how we reshuffle the Tropics of Capricorn and Cancer. ("Parasites are good at solving problems," notes one biologist, "and because they reproduce so quickly, they always win.") The surest losers are species whose ranges have already been reduced to a single spot. For instance, when the U.S. Endangered Species Act of 1973 came up for reauthorization in the mid-1980s, Congress dragged its feet, partly because of a controversy over Kemp's ridley sea turtles, most of which breed only on one 20-mile stretch of isolated beach in Mexico's Gulf Coast. Shrimp fishermen catch more than ten thousand sea turtles in their nets each year, and one fine day they may catch the last Kemp's ridleys on Earth (there are only about 500 nesting females left of this venerable species, which evolved during the age of the dinosaurs). The fishermen are supposed to put "turtle excluder devices" (TEDs) on their nets, but they do not like TEDs, and a senator from Alabama made an issue of the gadgets in Congress. Debate dragged on for three years and it seemed as if the Endangered Species Act itself might be endangered. Then came the Summer of '88. The storm of the century, Hurricane Gilbert, smashed the turtles' beach. One storm threatened to crack the legislative bottleneck by eliminating the turtles.

If the greenhouse effect joins the island effect, then among those next in line for extinction may be many species of migrating birds. One of their trails, the Pacific Flyway, extends from the tropics to the Arctic Circle. Some of the big stops on the Flyway, such as the Stillwater wetlands of Nevada, under good conditions provide shelter for more than a quarter of a million migrating shorebirds each year. Once there were tens of thousands of acres of bulrushes and cattails and open water at Stillwater. But the river that feeds the great marsh has been dammed so that water can be diverted to irrigation projects elsewhere. Now the size of this stop has been cut by three-quarters. In the drought of '88, the last of Stillwater threatened to evaporate.

If Stillwater dries up, shorebirds will have a hard time finding another stop nearby. The state of Nevada is not known for wetlands. Most of the water has already been siphoned off from its few swamps and marshes to feed cities and farms in the Sun Belt. Near Stillwater, the Winnemucca Lake National Wildlife Refuge dried up fifty years ago.

The Fallon National Wildlife Refuge had largely dried up even before the Summer of '88.

"It's like a stepping-stone across a rapid," J.P. Myers, senior vice president for science and sanctuaries at the Audubon Society, has said. "One by one, the stones are being uprooted and removed. They're almost all gone now in Nevada." For millions of migrating birds, the loss of Stillwater may throw a barrier the size of the state of Nevada across their old route the Pacific Flyway.

Meanwhile the Arctic tundra is expected to warm by 10° C. (18° F.) Birds that do find stepping-stones all the way north may find the tundra so changed by thermal karst erosion by the end of the next century that they can no longer nest there. Birds can adjust to a few surprises along their routes but they cannot survive losses that are global and from their point of view nearly instantaneous. For millions of migrating birds the greenhouse warming may burn the candle not only at both ends but all along its length.

Ecosystems, the homes of species, are made up of the climate of a place and of the interwoven lives of all of the species that live there. Ecologists foresee the unravelling of whole ecosystems, a transformation of tundra, wetlands, boreal forests, and rain forests around the world.

Not only could the greenhouse effect hasten species on the path to extinction in the next one hundred years. The loss of so many species and ecosystems may also help to change the climate, in a chain reaction.

That may sound like worst-case thinking, but it has already happened once. As we have seen, the pioneer explosions of the nineteenth and twentieth centuries put vast amounts of carbon into the atmosphere. In fact the burning of trees injected about as much carbon into the atmosphere as the burning of fossil fuels ever did. Today the clearing of rain forests around the world is contributing at least one billion tons of carbon to the atmosphere each year.

Again, a rain forest holds twenty-five kilograms of carbon per square meter, but a cow pasture holds less than four kilograms of carbon per square meter, and a desert or a parking lot less than one kilogram per square meter. Turning rain forest into pasture, or into barren or paved ground, puts most of the difference into the air.

The loss of an ecosystem changes the atmosphere in a thousand other ways, too, because there are a thousand links between life and air. Not only do the atmosphere and biosphere exchange carbon dioxide, they also exchange water vapor. Four centuries ago, Ferdinand Columbus wrote a biography of his father Christopher. He mentioned the weather that his father the admiral had encountered near the island of Jamaica in 1494:

> The sky, air, and climate were just the same as in other places; every afternoon there was a rain squall that lasted for about an hour. The admiral . . . attributes this to the great forests of that land; he knew from experience that formerly this also occurred in the Canary, Madeira, and Azore Islands, but since the removal of forests that once covered those islands they do not have so much mist and rain as before.

In other words, Columbus suspected that rain forests make their own rain. This remarkable suggestion has now been proven correct.

Rain forests differ from most of the world's forests in having several distinct layers of canopy. The trees look like open umbrellas on stems of three or four different heights. These staggered layers of canopy break the fall of rain more than a single layer could do. Because of their vast surface area, they also spread moisture out in thin layers where it can evaporate quickly. If you dab a drop of rubbing alcohol on your palm and streak it across the skin, you can feel how much faster the fluid evaporates and cools when it is spread out thin.

Rain forests also have a tangled system of fine roots that rise unusually close to the soil surface. They are so shallow that they can be exposed just by scuffing at the soil with a boot. Much of the rain that filters through the several canopies and reaches the ground is rapidly soaked up by the roots. Then the trees draw the water heavenward, and it evaporates from the leaves.

With staggered canopies and shallow roots, the rain forest catches a rain, holds it, and spreads it out to dry. Evaporation takes place as if from a single immense green leaf many times larger than the great Amazon Basin itself.

From the air, one can see the result. Giant pillars of cloud seem to boil out of the tops of the trees and rise straight into the sky. Wherever the carpet of trees is thick these pillars rise, as if to link the forest and the sky. It almost looks as if the green canopy below is supporting, with those white pillars, the canopy of clouds overhead, and that really is the case. The trees are rainmakers: "a neat trick," as Lovejoy observes, "and one people have lusted after for centuries."

On average the forests of the Amazon basin throw about 50 percent of the water that falls upon them right back to the air. Near Manaus, in the part of the forest from which farmers are carving Lovejoy's islands, an astonishing 75 percent of the rain is returned to the sky, to rejoin the clouds and fall again.

The trick does not depend upon any single species in the rain forest. It requires the ecosystem as a whole. Where forests have been thinned, there are fewer pillars and fewer clouds—as Columbus noticed. The island of Marajó, at the mouth of the Amazon, is carpeted with trees on the western half but not on the eastern half. Thunderclouds seem to love the western half of Marajó and it rains there every day. The eastern half of the island often goes dry.

Everyone working in Lovejoy's project has commented on the hot dry wind that blows across the clearings, and through the new reserves. One never feels such a wind in the heart of a healthy rain forest. It is almost as if an organism larger than the rain forest itself has been disturbed. This curious impression leaves even Lovejoy, an articulate man, at a loss for words. He told one prospective visitor, "The whole—I don't know what you want to call it—the whole physical functioning of air, temperature, and moisture in the cleared area is very different from the uncut forest. You'll feel it."

Thus with a chain saw at ground level a peasant farmer can cut down a great succession of canopies reaching several miles into the air—first the canopies of green and then the canopies of white. With all these canopies cleared away, the bare soil and scrubby vegetation get baked by direct sunlight, the highest intensities of sunlight on the surface of this planet. When rain does come, no green umbrellas break its fall. The water pounds down. It pools and puddles and flows away. The more the soil is hard-packed by sun and the weight of bulldozers and farm machinery, the faster the rainwater flows away. In Western Africa, where vast tracts have been cleared to make way for farmland, as much as 300 times more water runs off the land as before the trees were cleared. This water flows into streams, the streams flow into rivers, the rivers flow to the sea. By the time the rainwater evaporates again it may be hundreds of miles away from the place it fell. So farms, unlike forests, have no magic power to hold clouds overhead, and they cannot water themselves.

Because a farm does not give back its rainwater to the sky, the clouds overhead are thinner. That hurts the woods around the farm. The loss of rain can slowly eat away at the forests around each large clearing. Run-off also carves deep channels in the ground, and carries soil away. Along the road from Belém to Brasília, large fields have been so overgrazed and eroded that they have been called "a ghost landscape."

In these and other ways the clearing of the rain forests is altering the very conditions that made the rain forests possible. It is sweeping away the clouds the trees held in place overhead and the soil they held in place underfoot.

Climatologists believe the clearings may raise local temperatures in large areas of the tropics by as much as 3 to 5° C.—a local warming that is larger than the tropics can expect from the greenhouse effect. That may drive the climate of the tropics beyond the conditions that gave rise to the forests in the first place. In the next hundred years large portions of the equatorial rain forest belt, the greenest wilderness in the world, could turn into some of the fiercest desert.

So the island effect extends far beyond the island. Not only does it result in the kind of gloomily diminishing census that Lovejoy's teams are keeping. It alters the ecosystem's exchanges with the atmosphere and the hydrosphere, and through these restless spheres it alters conditions everywhere. "No man is an island," said John Donne. Not even an island is an island.

Lovejoy's official name for his archipelago is the Minimum Critical Size of Ecosystems Project. It will help to show not only how much forest we can cut without losing the jaguar or the eagle, but also the rains and the clouds. The loss of butterflies and birds and black saki monkeys from the islands are indicators of the loss of the invisible work of the ecosystem as a whole.

As other ecosystems are assaulted by the greenhouse effect, the island effect, and other side-effects of human progress, they, too, are shedding species and losing their roles in the biosphere. Coral reefs, temperate forests, boreal forests, and tundra all play ancient roles that scientists have barely begun to glimpse. In fact, scientists may never have time to find out what each ecosystem's role is. Ultimately all ecosystems are endangered species: like the migration of the Monarchs, they are threatened phenomena.

Environmental groups around the world are rallying to the cause of the rain forest, as they have to other endangered living things, the whale and the panda. Unfortunately, rain forests are no more sacred to the peoples of the tropical zone than coal and oil are sacred to people in the temperate zones. In Brazil, more people live in cities like Belém than in the forest itself. Brazil's largest city, São Paolo, has a population of almost 13 million people. In São Paolo the forest seems very far away. Even Manaus, built by the old rubber barons in the heart of Amazonia, complete with a grand opera house (then bankrupted by competition from plantations in Southeast Asia, and the invention of synthetic rubber), is now a city of more than one million people. In Manaus they call the rain forest "inferno verde"—green hell—and thank God for air conditioners.

The clearing of the forest is driven by hunger and by debt. The peasants are hungry and the politicians are in debt. Southeast Asian nations have already sold much of their forests to the Japanese at fire-sale prices and the Japanese are now negotiating for timber rights in the Amazon. The loss of each forest only makes each tropical country poorer, but government policies often encourage the losses. Throughout Latin America, squatters can claim rights to parcels of rain forest by cutting down trees—"improving the land." Brazil has special political motives for deforestation. The country is in the middle of the continent and it is bordered by most of the other nations in South America. Brazilian leaders have felt a need to exert a national presence in the Amazon. They are staking claims the way other nations have done in Antarctica. For decades Brazilians got tax breaks for clearing rain forest.

In 1982, the United Nations Food and Agriculture Organization (F.A.O.) published a study of global deforestation. The F.A.O. reported that about 11 million hectares of tropical rain forest were being cleared during each year of the early 1980s. At the same time, trees were planted or allowed to grow back on about one million hectares. That is a net loss of 10 million hectares a year. A hectare is about two and a half acres. Ten million hectares is 25 million acres—an area about half the size of California.

The F.A.O. report is the most comprehensive so far. Unfortunately, however, it is based on data that were out-of-date even in 1982. Satellite photographs of India, for instance, show that forests there were being cleared nine times faster than the F.A.O. report said. In the year the report was published, India alone lost more than one million hectares of forest. Scientists who are looking closely at global deforestation believe the rain forests are being cut down at present at a rate of about 20 million hectares, or 50 million acres, per year, twice what the U.N. reported: nearly one acre per second.

The rate is so uncertain in part because the problem has come to world attention so recently. The first alarms were sounded only in the 1970s, by the tropical conservationist Norman Myers, who pulled together scattered reports from around the world and saw that it is a global phenomenon. Many scientists believe we should be watching the rate of deforestation as closely as the rate of fossil fuel burning and the increase of carbon dioxide in the air. But whether fifty acres or ten acres are vanishing per minute, Lovejoy says, the rain forests are going fast: "You're only arguing about when it's going to be all over."

There are two big blocks of rain forest still standing. One is in the heart of the Congo Basin, in Zaire. The other is Amazonia. The Amazon alone is almost the size of the continental United States. But satellite images from NASA's Landsats, beamed down to a local receiving station in São José dos Campos, show that some regions are being cleared at an exponentially increasing rate. At current rates the Amazonian forests will be gone within the next fifty years. Even if the rate of clearing is slowed, what is now a giant emerald block of forest is likely to be shattered into many thousands of green fragments.

A spider spins a web of silken threads in the garden, and the biosphere spins a web of gases in the atmosphere. If the spider loses a few legs they will grow back, and she can still spin her web, although the pattern may be somewhat altered. Something like that is happening in our atmosphere and hydrosphere today: the patterns that life on Earth weaves in the air and water and soil are already changing slightly from year to year.

If the garden spider is disoriented by a drug, or by various other means that have been devised over the years by experimental entomologists, then the capture spirals of the web she spins may be dramatically deranged. That is what we fear in the near future of the planet. With the sudden losses of so many ecosystems from the biosphere, the air, the water, and the very soil will be dramatically altered.

This is the ultimate reply to the philistine question "So what?" as we lose species after species. What if we do lose a snail darter, or an elephant, or a blue whale? What if we do lose the tropical rain forests?

Most of the creatures in the rain forests are unnamed and unknown in any case, and they will vanish without a trace, like the dreams of deep sleep; and anyway aren't most of them insects?

The answer is that the loss of a single species of spider alters the ability of the biosphere to weave the web of life, on the ground, in the air, and in the water. We are riding a Fate, an Atropos, that cuts the thread of life. How many threads can we cut before we cut the one thread upon which our own lives depend? We simply do not know.

Just before the evolution of *Homo sapiens,* notes E.O. Wilson, there seems to have been a period when there were more species on the planet than there had been since the end of the age of the dinosaurs. "Anyone who has given any thought to this subject," Wilson says, "agrees that we're plummeting now. Any gains that might have been made during that 100 million years, the slow rise in the number of species, is going to be cancelled very shortly. In fact, a lot of it has already been cancelled. The evidence is now very extensive that human beings eliminated the big animals in places like Madagascar, North America, and South America almost as soon as human beings arrived. The United States had a fauna not drastically different in its diversity and spectacular nature from Africa, up until about 10,000 years ago. And there's a good chance that the early Indian hunters eliminated a good part of that. In Madagascar there is a good chance that the Malagash people about 1,000 years ago eliminated large portions of the island fauna, including a lemur the size of a bear, and the Elephant Bird, probably the largest, heaviest bird that ever existed, a gigantic ostrich-like form. All gone—probably within the last few centuries!"

In short we have already pulled things down. And it's coming down fast with the removal of the tropical forests. We are living at the start of a mass extinction, a mass dying, such as the planet has not experienced since the end of the age of the dinosaurs, some 65 million years ago.

In the early 1950s, the U.S. Army used to launch Jupiter-C rockets from a military base called Cape Canaveral, on Merritt Island, near Titusville, Florida. The thunder of each dawn launch drowned out the songs of Dusky Seaside Sparrows in the marshes. The birds' range was one of the smallest of any animal in North America. Like backcountry farmers, the sparrows all lived and died within a mile or two of Titusville. As each roar died away, their calls in the tall saw grass were homely reminders that life went on just as before along the Banana River.

In 1961, John F. Kennedy designated the military testing grounds at Cape Canaveral a permanent launching site of the new space program. NASA bought 80,000 more acres on Merritt Island and started building launching pads, giant gantries, and moon rockets. Seven years later, three men lifted off from Canaveral to orbit the Moon. They came back home with the celebrated photograph "Earthrise," which shows our planet rising above the rim of the Moon, a blue sphere of life against the horizon of the lunar desert. The picture has been made famous by hundreds of conservation groups around the world—which is ironic, as the historian of spaceflight Walter A. McDougall notes in *The Heavens and the Earth:* the ecology movement "gained an icon by grace of the very technology it denounced."

When Kennedy chose Canaveral, there were about 6,000 Dusky Seaside Sparrows in the marsh. By the time the Apollo astronauts photographed "Earthrise" there were fewer than 2,000 Duskies left. In 1980, a careful search turned up six, all males.

In 1986, there was one left, Orange Band. He lived in an unmarked cage at Discovery Island, the zoo at Walt Disney World in Orlando, Florida. He had hatched about the time that Cape Canaveral began its twin expansions, horizontal and vertical. Orange Band was overweight (one ounce). He was blind in one eye, gouty, a little unsteady in take-offs and landings. "He's still with us—he's not getting any younger," the zoo's curator told visitors. Orange Band had become an icon of another kind—a symbol of the national need for a revival and expansion of the 1973 Endangered Species Act.

The sparrows had reached this pass even though a reserve had been set aside for them under the management of the U.S. Fish and Wildlife Service. Officials at the Fish and Wildlife Service allowed the marsh to be flooded, as part of a program to control mosquitoes around Cape Canaveral. Then they allowed an expressway to be built from Cape Canaveral to Disney World, which fragmented a second piece of marsh. Then it allowed real estate developers to drain the edges of what marsh was left. Then came a series of fires.

We could blame NASA, or Fish and Wildlife, or the developers. But the birds died from the same habitat fragmentation that is progressing around the planet. From moment to moment it looks local, accidental . . . a matter of happenstance. In the long view however it is a steady, global, incremental force, as implacable as the spread of an ice sheet or a gas. There is a torture known as "the death by a thousand cuts." Piece by piece, cut by cut, our species cuts other species down in the interest of ours.

"Who watches the fall of the sparrow?" an ecologist asked in the pages of *The New York Times* as the last of the Duskies were dying. The world was watching another part of Merritt Island. Even if the birds' death had been foretold with absolute certainty, Kennedy would probably have built those launching pads, and the nation would have been behind his decision. Conservationists would not have dared to choose such an unpopular place to make a stand. Orange Band died in June of 1987.

We talk about a space race. There is a space race down here on the ground. In this race every human being is a superpower and the competition no longer stands a chance. Other species are bound to this or that patch of turf, and this planet. We feel bound to no patch of turf on Earth, bound only for the stars. We sacrifice a marsh, a bay, a park, a lake. We sacrifice a sparrow. We trade one countdown for another.

■ CHAPTER 10

THE ORACLE OF GAIA

> Now, my suspicion is that the universe is not only
> queerer than we suppose, but queerer than we *can*
> suppose. . . . I suspect that there are more things
> in heaven and earth than are dreamed of, in any
> philosophy.
>
> J.B.S. Haldane
> *Possible Worlds*

It is an old idea that Earth is alive. Most ancient tribes and nations
assumed so. The idea has been called a universal stage in primitive
thought. James Lovelock's name for the living planet, Gaia, is the name
of the Greeks' Mother Earth (her name is also enshrined in the word
geology).

Perhaps this thinking is not primitive at all, since the ancient and
modern lines of thought sometimes seem to be bending to meet, like
the two ends of a hoop. The idea has arisen many times in the history
of science. Often it strikes an investigator who has just seen more
deeply than ever before into the workings of the planet.

In the seventeenth century, the idea came to Queen Elizabeth I's
court physician, William Gilbert, who was the first scientist to recognize that Earth acts like a giant magnet; and the idea came to the Holy
Roman Emperor Rudolph's Imperial Mathematician, Johannes Kepler,
who was the first to realize that Earth and the other planets orbit the
Sun on elliptical paths.

In the eighteenth century, the vision came to the Scotsman James
Hutton. Hutton began his career by studying physiology at Leyden; he
wrote his thesis on the circulation of the blood. He never practiced

medicine, but after lifelong studies in geology, he came to view the planet the way William Harvey saw the human body, a beautiful machine, alive and pumping. He wrote of Earth as a kind of superorganism, whose proper study is a planetary physiology.

In the mid-nineteenth century, the idea struck the head of the U.S. Navy's Depot of Charts and Instruments, Lieutenant Matthew Fontaine Maury. Maury, a pioneer in the study of ocean currents, saw the planet as a living being whose breath is the wind and whose blood is the sea.

In the late nineteenth century, in Kharkov, in the Ukraine, the Russian polymath Vladimir Vernadsky took long country walks with an older cousin, Y.M. Korolenko, a retired army officer, extremely well-read, extremely independent, given to aphorisms. One of his favorites: "The world is a living organism!" This idea shaped Vernadsky's career. In the early twentieth century he began the difficult and beautiful science that Hutton described, the study of Earth's metabolism or physiology.

These men are among the founding figures of modern geophysics, astronomy, geology, oceanography, and biogeochemistry. So Lovelock is building on an old foundation. He may be right and he may be wrong, but he has not taken flight from the traditions of Earth science. In a sense, one might almost say that his Gaia theory is the orthodox view of the planet Earth.

Many people are now turning toward Gaia with the kind of question that those earlier generations might have referred to God. Hutton, standing at the very start of the Industrial Revolution, could not have foreseen the anxious nature of this question of ours (although Hutton's circle of intimates included Black and Watt, the discoverer and the promoter of carbon dioxide). Hutton did perceive that the planet Earth is always wearing down of natural causes, its shores eroding, its mountains washing into the sea. He wondered about this slow and perpetual wasting of the planet. Partly because of his early training in medicine, he was moved to ask:

> But is this world to be considered thus merely as a machine, to last no longer than its parts retain their present composition, their proper forms and qualities? Or, may it not be also considered as an organized body such as has a constitution in which the necessary decay of the machine is naturally repaired . . . ?

A living body is fragile, but it is capable of self-repair. Hutton concluded that Earth must possess that capability. His geological studies led him to see that "a circulation in the matter of this globe" continually repairs the planet, so that Earth is wasted in one place and restored in another, "a system of beautiful economy in the works of nature."

Today the agents of erosion that we fear most are not natural but artificial; and we know that these agents are wasting the planet almost everywhere at once. This makes our question acute. It is a scientific question and also a prayer. If there is some sort of planetary physiology at work around us, can its presence also *help* us in the next one hundred years? Might this planetary body keep healthy in spite of all? Is Gaia's constitution sturdy enough so that "the necessary decay of the machine" will be "naturally repaired?" Can Gaia save us?

Lovelock began his scientific career in the 1940s, in research medicine. He joined the British Medical Research Council, in London, where his first piece of work was a study of the common cold. Next ("having discovered little about the common cold," says Lovelock, "except that it is not caught by chilling") he studied how to preserve life through freezing. By 1953, he had managed to deep-freeze and revive a golden hamster. He is a little ashamed of these animal experiments now. However, this work led to his election, at a very young age, as a Fellow of the British Royal Society.

Lovelock noticed that some living cells resist freezing better than others. The difference seemed to depend upon the presence of certain lipids, fatty acids, in the cells' membranes. As luck would have it, a colleague upstairs had just invented the gas chromatograph, which was at that time the most powerful tool on Earth for the detection and identification of minute quantities of fatty acids.

Taking infinite pains, Lovelock scraped together a lipid sample and brought it upstairs to the inventor of this new instrument, Archer Martin. The sample was smaller than the head of a pin. Martin laughed at him.

"Oh, my God, is that all you've got?"

"Yes . . ."

"Then there's nothing for it: you'd better go and invent something yourself."

Which Lovelock did. In 1957 (while a post-doc named Charles David Keeling was hammering together new instruments for detecting carbon dioxide in La Jolla, California), James Lovelock, Archer Martin, and a few other scientists in London huddled around Lovelock's new gadget for a trial run. The sample was an all but invisible fleck. Lovelock turned on his invention. All eyes turned to the oscilloscope. Huge peak after peak came marching across the screen.

"We were extremely excited, especially me," says Lovelock. "But then we realized that the peaks did not describe any known fatty acid." It took him a long time to figure out what the peaks did represent. The detector was ignoring his samples completely. Instead it was picking up small traces of impurities that lay *between* the lipids, and floated in the air of the lab. These impurities it was detecting in parts per trillion.

This device, the electron capture detector, "ignored nearly everything and detected only a single group of things," Lovelock says. "But the group that it detected was weird." The list included a long catalogue of notorious carcinogens. The list also included vinyl chloride and trichlorethylene, compounds that were considered so safe at the time that they were used as anesthetics in surgery. Later they, too, were discovered to be carcinogenic. Indeed the device seemed to have an almost magical ability to sniff out danger to life. "I now regard *any* substance that it detects with a certain amount of suspicion," says Lovelock.

Electron capture detectors were soon being manufactured and sold to investigators all around the world. By 1960, investigators armed with electron capture detectors picked up traces of the pesticide DDT in penguin fat in Antarctica, and in the breast milk of human mothers everywhere. These discoveries lent support to Rachel Carson's thesis in *Silent Spring,* published in 1962, and helped to start the modern environmental movement.

Ten years later, Lovelock took his electron capture detector on a trip to Antarctica aboard a British research vessel, the *Shackleton.* He used it to see if chlorofluorocarbons from the Northern Hemisphere had drifted into the Southern. He knew that chlorofluorocarbons, unlike pesticides, are virtually inert. They do not react with living tissues, or anything else. Lovelock thought these properties might make CFCs a good tracer. They might help geochemists measure how long it takes air masses in the Northern Hemisphere to drift across the equator, for example. Chlorofluorocarbons might turn out to be as educational as drops of red dye in the eddies of a stream.

As he reported in the journal *Nature* in 1973, he found that chlorofluorocarbons had reached the level of forty parts per trillion in the air over Antarctica. A few calculations showed what that meant. Virtually all of the gases ever produced since Midgley invented them in the 1930s were still hanging in the air. They were that inert.

In his report on this discovery, Lovelock bent over backwards to avoid sounding another environmental alarm. "The presence of these compounds constitutes no conceivable hazard," he wrote. Indeed, he said, if Roger Revelle wanted to call the release of carbon dioxide into the atmosphere "an unscheduled geophysical experiment," then he, Lovelock, would call the release of chlorofluorocarbons—being perfectly harmless, unlike carbon dioxide—the "ideal experiment on a global scale."

Soon afterward, of course, the atmospheric chemists Rowland and Molina realized that if chlorofluocarbons were lingering in the air like that, they would eventually drift to the stratosphere and there they would erode the ozone layer. Rowland and Molina sounded the alarm. Thus, in spite of himself, Lovelock started the ozone wars of the 1970s, which were just as frightening as the DDT wars of the 1960s.

Up to this point, Lovelock's career parallels that of Charles David Keeling. Like Keeling, he built a new detector, pointed it, aimed it— and discovered significant changes in the planet. Together they helped (inadvertently) to launch the environmental movement and boost it to the stratosphere.

While Lovelock and others were exploring this planet with the electron capture detector, the new U.S. Space Program was preparing to explore others. Lovelock's talent for invention was well known by 1961, and a NASA program director invited him to consult in the design of the Surveyors, some of the first robot explorers in space. For Lovelock, this invitation was the fulfillment of a childhood dream. It helped to draw his attention forever from the scale of cell membranes to the scale of planetary atmospheres.

Soon after the Surveyors, the agency began planning its Viking missions, robot explorers with which NASA hoped to answer the venerable question, "Is there life on Mars?" NASA scientists at the Jet Propulsion Laboratory in Pasadena asked Lovelock to start thinking about life-detection experiments.

Lovelock brooded for months about NASA's question: how to detect life on Mars. He talked it over with a philosopher, Dian Hitchcock, asking basic questions like "What is life?" Eventually he flew to the Jet

Propulsion Laboratory and announced, in effect, "I've got the answer for you."

"You don't need a mission to Mars to find out if Mars is alive or dead," Lovelock declared. "It's dead as a doorstop! You can see that from here."

Lovelock's reasoning was simple. Martian air is mostly carbon dioxide. It holds virtually no free oxygen. An astronomer can determine these facts from any modern, well-appointed, earthbound astronomical observatory, such as the one on the volcano Mauna Kea. Likewise with the atmosphere of Venus: almost all carbon dioxide and almost no oxygen.

That mix of gases is precisely what one would expect from a dead world. The gases on Mars and Venus appear to have run downhill for eons until they reached chemical equilibrium. They are almost completely inert. As Lovelock puts it, "if you took a volume of air from either of those planets, heated it to incandescence in the presence of some rocks from the surface and then allowed it to cool slowly, there would be little or no change in composition after the experiment."

On Earth, by contrast, the mix of gases in the air is 21 percent oxygen and less than 1 percent carbon dioxide. To a chemist, viewing our planet from an imaginary vantage-point on Mars or Venus, the presence of all that oxygen is very strange, because oxygen is a reactive, potentially explosive gas. It makes things happen. In the presence of oxygen, wood can burn. In the presence of oxygen, iron can rust—rusting is nothing but a gradual combustion, a slow burn. In the presence of oxygen, animals and plants can breathe—respiration being, again, nothing but controlled combustion, a very slow burn.

To a chemist, finding so much oxygen in Earth's air is like finding a giant boulder balanced on top of a mountain peak: unstable. The laws of chemistry predict that the boulder will roll down to the bottom at any moment. The laws of chemistry are just as specific and positive about this prediction as are the laws of gravity about the orbit of a planet or the fate of a boulder teetering on a summit.

The oxygen in our atmosphere should rust rocks, and rust our steel skyscrapers, and be consumed in forest fires, or inhaled by owls and ants, trees, and ferns until there is no more oxygen in the air. This should have happened a long time ago. In fact, Earth should not have oxygen in the air at all (much less than 1 percent, anyway).

Earth has all this oxygen, of course, because of green plants. Oxygen has been piling up in our atmosphere since the first green plants evolved on the planet a few billion years ago. The boulder is perched on the top of the mountain because plants keep pushing it up there. In Greek legend, Sisyphus was condemned to push a boulder up a hill forever in the underworld. Each time he got it almost to the top it rolled back down to the bottom and he had to start again. So it is with green plants. As fast as the boulder rolls down off the mountain—as fast as oxygen falls out of the atmosphere—plants inject more of this gas back *into* the atmosphere.

Lovelock told the directors of NASA, don't go to Mars! You needn't actually go there to find out if the place is alive. All you need to do is to see if there is oxygen—or some other kind of chemical weirdness and instability in the atmosphere. Since there is none, the Red Planet is dead.

Needless to say, Lovelock's suggestion was not popular at the space agency. NASA launched the Viking missions anyway, amid much fanfare and suspense. And Lovelock appears to have been right. Mars is probably as dead as the Moon. Today, most scientists believe that Earth is the only living planet in our solar system.

Take this reasoning one step further. If there were slightly more oxygen on our planet—perhaps 5 or 10 percent more—there might be a global inferno. The atmosphere and biosphere would be so inflammable that forest fires, once started, would rage out of control until the whole biosphere went up in flames in an atmospheric Armageddon.

If there were a little *less* oxygen, on the other hand—perhaps 5 or 10 percent less—living things would not have as much energy to work with. There might still be bacteria on Earth, and perhaps more intricate microscopic creatures like the amoeba, euglena, and paramecium. But there would be nothing as big as a human being to look through the microscope. Earth would be alive, but there would be no one to look around and wonder.

Thus, not only does Earth have oxygen; Earth has just the right *amount* of oxygen. Something is keeping oxygen at just this level and has apparently done so for millions of years. Something is keeping it rock-steady right now.

Reasoning in this way, Lovelock arrived at one of the most daring and controversial theories of the Earth since Alfred Wegener proposed that continents drift. The largest living thing in our solar system is not the blue whale, which grows to a length of more than one hundred feet; nor is it the giant Sequoia, which crowns at more than two hundred feet. The biggest and most venerable living thing in this region of space is Earth itself. Earth is alive. Its tissues are made up of whales and redwoods, deer and grass. Every living thing, from turtles to ants to human beings, is part of it, just as the cells that make up our skin, our brains, and our hearts are part of us. All that creep or crawl or grow, from Greenland to New Zealand, from Novaya Zemlya to Palau, from the tortoise to the termite to the trypanosome, play some part in the global cooperative.

Not only that: clouds are part of the superorganism, too, along with the air we breathe, the soil and rocks we walk upon, and the very crust of the planet: all one great living being.

One day Lovelock went for a walk with a neighbor of his in the country village of Bowerchalke, in Wiltshire. The neighbor was William Golding, the Nobel-prize-winning author of *Lord of the Flies*. Lovelock told the novelist about his new vision of a living planet, and Golding said, "You really must call her Gaia."

Science in the twentieth century has been so successful that outsiders sometimes picture it as a kind of monolithic corporate organization, like IBM or AT&T (before the company was broken up). We think scientists look alike, act alike, think alike, and speak the same jargon.

In fact, science is a Tower of Babel. The days are long gone when a single genius like Isaac Newton could be on the cutting edge of physics, mathematics, optics, theology, alchemy, and all the other abiding interests of what was then called not science but simply natural philosophy.

Today there are very few natural philosophers. There aren't even many Earth scientists. Too much has been published about the planet for anyone to hold it within the horizons of a single mind. There are chemical oceanographers and there are physical oceanographers. There are stratospheric chemists and there are tropospheric chemists. These people don't mix: or at least, they mix as little as the sea and air they study, or the various layers of the atmosphere. Specialization has gotten out of hand. There are more branches in the tree of knowledge than there are in the tree of life. A petrologist studies rocks; a pedologist studies soils. The first one sieves the soil and throws away the rocks. The second one picks up the rocks and brushes off the soil. Out in the field, they bump into each other only like Laurel and Hardy, by accident, when they are both backing up.

If Gaia exists, she cannot be studied in pieces, with Professor X wondering if the sky is alive, Professor Y wondering if mountains are alive, Professor Z wondering if Professor X is alive. If Gaia exists, then all the elements of the planet are connected and working together like the organs of our own bodies.

"Will the connections that are needed for this kind of study be made between people, or within a single mind?" the atmospheric chemist Ralph Cicerone once mused aloud to me, in his old office at the National Center for Atmospheric Research, in Boulder. That is, will the connections be made between two or three people of different disciplines working together, or by one scientist struggling to work in several disciplines at once?

"Reluctantly," Cicerone said, "I've concluded that our best hope is in single minds."

Lovelock's mind has been one of the few to make the attempt. As Cicerone and others agree, Lovelock's mind is also—thanks to his grasshopper career, and what may be genius—one of the very few minds with any chance of success.

If you can find your way through the Tower of Babel, as Lovelock can, you catch glimpses of Gaia at every turn. For instance if the sea were much saltier than it is now, then marine life would be impossible. The Atlantic and Pacific would be as lifeless as the Dead Sea. In fact, chemical oceanographers do not know why the Atlantic and Pacific are *not* Dead Seas. Rivers and streams wash millions of tons of salt into the sea each year, yet the sea does not become more salty. Something is keeping the chemistry of the sea in just the range that life can tolerate. Another planetary mystery.

Or take carbon dioxide, that essential and notorious gas. As we have seen, with much more carbon dioxide, Earth would be an inferno like Venus. With much less, Earth would be frozen like Mars. The concentration of gas has gone up and down somewhat in the past, but never too much to turn Earth into either a furnace or a freezer. The seas have never boiled away and they have never frozen solid in the 4.5 billion years since the creation of the planet. Yet the Sun itself has gradually brightened since its birth by as much as 25 percent. Tumultuous volcanic ages have come and gone. Through it all, what on Earth maintained the level of this gas in a way that kept Earth's surface temperature within bounds? Perhaps, life itself.

When Lovelock published his little book *Gaia,* in 1979, he expected to be cheered by biologists and attacked by theologians. He was reviled by the biologists, and he received an invitation to deliver a sermon at the Cathedral of St. John the Divine, in New York City.

Evolutionary biologists found Gaia ludicrously unscientific. They thought the hypothesis implied a master plan. It suggested that lichens, trees, termites, and apes are somehow planning together, working for the good of the group. Can the planet's hodgepodge of species really cooperate, like an ethnic bomber crew in an old MGM movie, to keep Earth on target? Can even one species steer its own fate?

Most biologists did not think life could be that smart. It seemed simpler to assume that termites do one thing and trees another: sometimes it helps, sometimes it hurts, and the world limps along.

Canadian biochemist W. Ford Doolittle, of Dalhousie University, published one of the first such critiques of the Gaia hypothesis. Evolution, Doolittle observed, proceeds without plan or foresight, by natural selection. In each generation, the individuals that are fittest to survive and reproduce in the world in which they find themselves will tend to leave the most offspring. These offspring will vary slightly from one to the next. Some individuals will be more fit than others to survive and reproduce. They will pass on their genes to more progeny. And so on. In this way, useful genetic variations will tend to propagate while harmful ones tend to fail. Over time, this stone-blind process of Darwinian natural selection is enough to determine all the intricate diversity of life.

Doolittle failed to see how Gaia, which represents global cooperation among species, could evolve by natural selection, whose theme is incessant competition among individuals—Tennyson's "nature, red in tooth and claw." Indeed, Lovelock's vision, said Doolittle, reminded him of the fairytale world of Doctor Dolittle:

> In Hugh Lofting's book *Doctor Dolittle in the Moon,* John Dolittle marvels at the absence of Darwinian competition among the lunar flora and fauna. This, it turns out, reflected the dominance of "The Council," which was "made up of members from both the Animal and Vegetable Kingdoms.

Its main purpose was to regulate life on the Moon in such a way that there should be no more warfare." Dolittle remarks to his aide, "Our world that thinks itself so far advanced has not the wisdom, the foresight, Stubbins, which we have seen here. Fighting, fighting, fighting, always fighting! So it goes down there with us . . . The 'survival of the fittest'! . . . It is this thing here, this Council of Life—of life adjustment—that could have saved the day and brought happiness to all."

In short, Doolittle believed that Gaia could not be created by natural selection, only by conscious design. "Lovelock's Gaia is very much the terrestrial equivalent of Lofting's lunar council," Doolittle wrote. "But the Council was created by Otho Bludge, the first moon man and a refugee from Earth. Who created Gaia?"

Lovelock was stung by this criticism. It was followed by even stronger words on the same theme from the British evolutionist Richard Dawkins, whose books' main theme has been the selfishness and blindness of natural selection (see *The Selfish Gene* and *The Blind Watchmaker*).

For a while Lovelock wondered if his hypothesis might really be what these biologists seemed to think it was. Was Gaia in the same category as a belief in ouija boards, crystals, channeling, pyramids, and spirits; or at best, in the same category as a belief in God?

Yet Lovelock was convinced that Gaia theory does not contradict the laws of natural selection. Indeed he saw it as a *consequence* of natural selection. He thought natural selection might operate not only on the scale of the biochemical and the individual but also on the scale of the biogeochemical. He suspected that the evolutionists had simply not wandered far enough through the Tower of Babel. They were studying the evolution of life; meanwhile one tier up, geochemists were studying the evolution of Earth. Yet in reality these two evolutions take place at the same time on the same planet. They are connected.

After much thought, Lovelock found his answer to Doolittle and Dawkins: a simple illustration of the way in which natural selection can lead to Gaia. His illustration is a schematic planet, which he calls Daisyworld.

Daisyworld is as idealized as one of the charming floating worlds visited by Antoine de Saint-Exupéry's *The Little Prince*. It is a smooth planet of an even shade of gray. Its climate is comfortable and plants can grow on it from the equator to the poles. To keep things simple Lovelock reduces all the variables of life to one: temperature. And he simplifies all of varied teeming life to a single form: daisies. There are white daisies and black daisies on this imaginary planet.

Now, imagine that the brightness of the Sun begins to increase. If there were no life on Daisyworld, the planet's temperature would increase, too, in step with its star. But since there is life on Daisyworld, things do not happen quite that way. Life on this world responds to the increase in temperature—by natural selection. Black daisies quickly begin to die back, because their dark color absorbs sunlight and makes them heat up faster than the surface itself, until they are too hot to survive. White daisies last longer, because their white color reflects more light and keeps them and their immediate surroundings cooler.

These local events affect the temperature of the entire planet. A planet covered with white daisies reflects more light than a planet dressed in black. In the jargon of planetology, white daisies have a higher albedo. As Daisyworld is mantled by more and more white daisies, and fewer and fewer black ones, the whole planet acquires a high albedo and stays cool.

Suppose the Sun began to dim, instead. Then white daisies become scarce but black daisies multiply. The planet grows darker, and the darker it is the more sunlight it absorbs. This warms the surface.

Either way the Sun varies, the imaginary world is protected by the life upon it. Thanks to the daisies, Daisyworld remains at a stable temperature far longer than a dead world would do. These are negative feedback loops. Heat makes white daisies, which make the planet cooler. Cold makes black daisies, which make the planet warmer.

The Sun must grow very hot or very cold indeed before the planet reaches the limits of endurance. At that point, however, all the daisies wither. Daisyworld dies. Thereafter it responds helplessly to further changes in the Sun, like any inanimate object.

Nothing is going on here but natural selection: the flourishing of one species and the failure of another as their environment changes. Yet life in this simple world behaves like a thermostat. Within limits, it acts to keep the temperatures of its world stable.

In a house with a thermostat, it is the homeowner who sets the desired temperature: the "set-point." Seventy degrees F. is a typical set-point in homes in the United States; ten or fifteen degrees cooler is typical in Europe. What is the set-point of a planet? There isn't any, because there is no global plan or design. There is only the simple, utterly unconscious response of a myriad living things to a myriad local changes. "Daisyworld does not have any clearly established goal like a set-point," says Lovelock; "it just settles down, like a cat, to a comfortable position and resists attempts to dislodge it."

In the real world there is not one variable like temperature; there are a thousand or ten thousand variables that stay more or less stable—not only temperature but the chemistry and salinity of the seas and the composition of the atmosphere. Each of these factors must somehow to be homeostatted—that is, held within rather tight limits, as Lovelock points out in his second book on the subject, *The Ages of Gaia*. "Almost all chemicals have a range of concentrations tolerated or needed by life," he writes. "For many elements, such as iodine, selenium, and iron, too much is a poison, too little is starvation. Pure uncontaminated water will support little; but neither will the saturated brine of the Dead Sea."

The beauty of the Daisyworld model is its generality. It applies to all such factors—to any factor that constrains life, from temperature to the concentration of iodine in seawater. It also applies to any other planet on which lifeforms may have arisen. They, too, will alter the environment as they grow, and they, too, may tend to a stable environment by this process of natural selection.

Lovelock and a colleague, Andrew Watson, have played out many variants of Daisyworld on a computer, displaying in simple graphs the central principle of Gaia: natural selection. The unconscious growth and evolution of life under these conditions will always arrive at stable, steady states, and stay there. The planet as a whole will evolve some of the properties that we associate with an individual living thing: its temperature and its internal chemistry will tend to remain in balance, within limits, like the dozing cat.

Not long ago, trying to fathom Gaia, I remembered a game that my father, my brother, and I once played. It sounds incredible, but we built a computer out of Dixie cups and pieces of shirt cardboard, and the contraption quickly got smart enough to outwit the three of us at a game of strategy. I still recall our delight as we sat around the kitchen table and watched the Dixie cup computer making better and better moves until by the end of the evening it trounced us every time.

(Evenings like that are not for everyone. Readers for whom the thought of building a computer—even out of Dixie cups—evokes a cold sweat may safely skip to page 209.)

The computer had been invented by a mathematician at Cornell University, Henry David Block, who was interested in what he called "mechanical biology." He was trying to design simple gadgets that could mimic some of the accomplishments of living things. In the March 1965 issue of *American Scientist*, Block showed how easy it is to build a computer that can learn.

Block called his computer G-1. (*G* stands for Golem, the robot slave of medieval Jewish legend, a lump of clay that a mystic brought to life by whispering to it the name of God.) G-1 consists of a row of Dixie cups numbered 1 through 12. In each cup there are three small cards (cut from cardboard) numbered 1, 2, and 3. That is all there is to Golem: it took us a few minutes to build. We found it entertaining to place the row of Dixie cups on the other side of the table so that Golem faced us like a human adversary.

Block showed that this computer can play a thousand games of strategy. One of the oldest and simplest is a barroom contest that is sometimes called Nim. Nim begins with a stack of a dozen coins or matches or toothpicks—any kind of chips—in the middle of the table. You and your adversary take turns taking away chips. On each turn, you have the option of removing one, two, or three chips from the heap. Whoever takes the last chip loses. You start out with twelve chips:

o o o o o o o o o o o o

Say your opponent goes first, and takes away three chips. That leaves nine chips on the table:

o o o o o o o o o

Say you take away three. That leaves six chips in play:

o o o o o o

Your opponent takes away two, leaving four chips in play (that was a dumb move):

o o o o

Now you take away three, leaving one chip on the table:

O

Your opponent is forced to remove that last chip, losing the game (since the player who takes the last chip loses).

You can play this game with Golem just as you would play it against any other adversary. Of course, Golem can't talk, so you have to use sign-language, as you might in the bar with a stranger from a strange land. Golem can't move, either, so you must work around that physical handicap as well. Each time it is Golem's turn, you do him the favor of counting the number of chips in play. Say there are twelve chips on the table. You go to Golem's Cup 12. From this cup you remove a card at random to find out Golem's move. If the card you pick from the cup reads *2*, that means the computer chooses to take away two chips (true, you're doing Golem's legwork, but Golem is doing the brainwork). Then you put that card back in Cup 12.

In this way, you and the computer alternate, politely taking turns.

The secret of learning is the ability to profit from mistakes. That is Golem's great talent. For whenever Golem loses a round of the game, you pick out the very last card that Golem played (the card that just cost the computer the game). You extract this dumb move from its cup, and you throw it into a discard box.

At first, since Golem plays at random, it loses almost every round. However, each time Golem makes a losing move, that move is pitched into the discard box. Golem will never make that mistake again. So the computer makes fewer and fewer losing moves, and more and more winning moves.

It is fascinating to watch it learn. I will not go into all of the ins and outs of the contest between Golem and humanity*—but after a while, the computer gets smart. It keeps making just the right moves—because it has forgotten the wrong moves. It has simply forgotten how to lose.

You can draw Golem's learning curve on a piece of graph paper by plotting its wins against its losses. At first Golem loses, loses, loses.

---

*For complete instructions on building a Golem, see Block's original article, or my essay "In Gaia's Garden" in *The Sciences* (July/August 1986) pp. 2–5.

Then its success rate begins to climb haltingly for dozens of games, one step forward and one step back, on a Keeling curve.

After several hundred rounds of Nim, Golem plays like a master. Nothing but cardboard, he gives every appearance of foresight and planning. The cups work together as if possessed with diabolical intelligence. A strong move by Cup 10 sets up a fine move by Cup 7 and allows Cup 4 to win the game.

And that is the most remarkable feature of the Dixie cup computer—the ability to evolve what appears to be a conspiracy, a committee, a council. As Block puts it, "In the performance of these machines it is interesting to observe how a simple *local* "law of change" results in a *globally optimal policy.*"

Lovelock's vision of Gaia, with life on Earth governing climate, seems less incredible once you've built Golem and watched him in action. It is humbling to be beaten by a set of Dixie cups. Yet you can see, all the while, that Golem is learning by the blind process of natural selection. The principle is nothing other than Darwin's: survival of the fittest. Cards with winning moves are surviving. Cards with losing moves are dying out.

If natural selection can do that much for cardboard, what can it do for species?

Picture each ecosystem on the planet as a Dixie cup. There are dozens of ecosystems on the planet: ice sheets, forests, deserts, marshes, tidal pools, coral reefs. Each living thing represents a card in one of those cups. Individuals with winning moves tend to survive. Those with losing moves tend to die young.

Why is it that the cards in Golem's Dixie cups always evolve a global strategy? Why do the cards in Cup 10 and Cup 7 set up winning moves for Cup 4? They are not being altruistic. There is no planning, no cooperation. It is all natural selection. The survival of each of the cards is affected by all the other cards in all the other cups. That is, a loss in one cup eventually affects the survival or extinction of the cards in all the other cups. Their fates are interconnected. They affect the others' fitness to survive.

And the same thing is true of the species in the biosphere. Ecologists estimate that the average species on this planet is directly connected to four others. These neighboring species all evolve together, and as they do, they develop relationships, including predator-prey, host-parasite, and the fascinating relationship that ecologists call symbiosis, in which each species supports the other. There would be no rain forest without the bees, butterflies, and wasps that pollinate the blossoms of the trees. Nor could those bees, butterflies, and wasps survive without the trees. Ever since Darwin, evolutionary biologists have accepted that all of these relationships can arise through stone-blind natural selection.

So the average species is part of the environment of at least four other species. On a larger scale (but still within an individual cup, or ecosystem) there are species that are directly connected with not just four but thousands of other species. The trees of the rain forest provide perches, shade, soil, nourishment and (as we have seen) even clouds and rain for the swarms of species that live upon, among, and beneath them. Again there is no deliberate design. According to evolutionary theory, as miraculous as it seems, all of this develops through blind natural selection.

Each species is also in direct contact with its medium, the atmosphere or the hydrosphere. In small ways or large, each species influences that medium. Each individual releases a little carbon dioxide, for instance, and in this way it contributes to the carbon cycle and the breathing of the world. Without the rich home brew of gases that wafts from Cup 12, the rain forest, life would not be the same anywhere else on the planet. Without green plants there would be no oxygen anywhere.

In this way, in small ways or large, through sea and air, every species on Earth is connected to every other. Each one affects the survival of every other. The species in Cup 12 and Cup 6 help to set up the winning moves in Cup 3. Conversely a failure in Cup 12 would set up losses in Cup 3.

It may be romantic to suggest that out of all of these innumerable global interconnections, mutual relationships may have evolved, in a skein or stable symbiotic web that passes our understanding. Lovelock and his supporters (the most famous of whom is his colleague and collaborator Lynn Margulis, a microbiologist at Boston University) freely admit to being romantics. Yet mutual benefits do in fact evolve at the local level, within each cup. There are a thousand examples in every ecosystem. Think of the succession of grasses on a beach dune, which leads to the establishment of trees and birds. The grasses do not plan the dune. They don't deed it as a gift for the birds. All they do is grow. The genes are selfish and the watchmaker is blind, but the course of evolution does result over and over again in a kind of cooperation, at the local level.

Why not at larger levels, too? Why not the same kind of cooperation between cups? In Lovelock's view, we are seeing nothing more (or less) mysterious and miraculous than evolution by natural selection at all levels, from the coevolution of butterfly and blossom to the coevolution of the atmosphere and the biosphere. In his view, Gaia does not contradict Darwin's idea of natural selection; it is only a new application of the same old law. At a conference in San Diego on the Gaia hypothesis, during one of many rounds of debates, Lovelock whispered in my ear, "It's natural selection—hold on to that."

If so, we are lucky that Gaia does not depend on any single animal or plant. Accidents are always eliminating species from the game (the average rate across geological time is about one species per year). But there are millions of species and God knows how many individuals in the game at any one time. They give Gaia stability and allow her to cope with the unexpected. These are the virtues of redundancy.

After Block built the first Dixie cup computer, he experimented with different ways to help it learn. For a more interesting game, he suggested, don't discard a losing move. Instead *add* copies of the winning move. That is exactly how Gaia learns, in the view of Lovelock and Margulis. Species with losing hands drop out, while species with winning hands multiply in their cups. Thus does Gaia fine-tune her game.

Block also toyed with variations on Nim in which the winning strategy was beyond the reach of all but a mathematical games expert. He discovered that the game's intricacy made no difference to the Dixie cups; the computer learned winning ways just as nimbly as ever, by natural selection. Block realized that with enough cups, cards, and patience, he could build a computer capable of winning tic-tac-toe, checkers, or even chess.

I can imagine Gaia as just such a myriad-cupped, million-carded gizmo. She is playing games too mysterious and complicated for us to understand. She has been tested nonstop for nearly 4 billion years. By the time you and I started watching, Gaia had grown, to all appearances, as wise as a goddess—or a golem.

When I think of all the nightmares that might take place among the seven spheres in the next hundred years, I begin to feel a little like the schoolmaster Ichabod Crane. He had absorbed the truth that the world is round, and therefore he assumed that people in Australia walk upside down. He was the kind of hyper-imaginative instructor who teaches his classes that the planet's North and South poles might flip at any moment. The chairs will fly to the schoolhouse ceiling and the citizens of Sleepy Hollow will all walk topsy-turvy.

If the balance of nature were really as fragile as that, life on Earth could not have lasted long. Indeed life might never have begun. Yet the planet Earth did come to life, and the biosphere has now lasted for nearly 4 billion years. The biosphere is older than the twenty brightest stars in the night sky. "Gaia's lasted eons," Lovelock says. "It's of stellar age. It's all but immortal."

We see only pieces of the seven spheres:

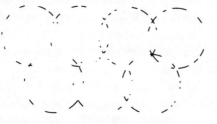

We do not yet know how they interconnect. They may be as tightly linked as the symbol on the Olympic medallion:

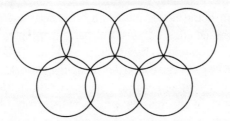

No one knows the true shape of the seven spheres—nor the geography of their relationships. Whether or not we call Earth alive, the study of the global metabolism is one of the great frontiers in science. Twentieth-century biochemists looked at the pathways that carbon travels within living bodies. Remarkably intricate cycles were discovered, including the Kreps cycle of respiration, and the dark and light cycles of photosynthesis. Biochemists found great waterwheels of chemical compounds that are turning within each of our cells and managing all our energy. Mapping these molecular mills earned more than one scientist a Nobel prize. It is possible that a discovery as great or greater will be made in coming decades as scientists from many disciplines work together to trace the workings of the seven spheres. How *do* the spheres interlock? We sense, from what we can see, that the patterns are intricate and beautiful: but they are still dark to us, like a stained glass window seen from the outside.

Is the Gaian view optimistic or pessimistic? It is optimistic from the point of view of those who seek harmony among the spheres. It suggests that there are patterns and interconnections yet to be discovered. It is also optimistic from the point of view of Gaia. It suggests that the interconnectedness of things may help life survive the next difficult years.

But the Gaian idea is not optimistic from the point of view of an individual species that wants to save its own neck. Gaia is as indifferent to our fate as the stars. In the long run the biosphere survives but its species do not, just as the human body survives while losing and replacing individual cells. Virtually all of the species that have ever lived on this planet are now extinct. At times, as we have seen, half of the species on the planet have gone extinct almost at once. The next one hundred years may be such a time again. The story of life is punctuated by Ice Ages, volcanic winters, meteoritic collisions, mass dyings. And at the moment it is punctuated by us.

For our survival the Gaian view is no more comforting than the opposing view of the ecologist Paul Ehrlich. "It's luck, serendipity, that has kept us from going down the drain," Ehrlich says. "Maybe we're very scarce in the cosmos because so many living planets have died."

Experimentally, Lovelock has visited all kinds of catastrophes on Daisyworld. He has overstressed his imaginary world by turning the strength of his computerized Sun up, up, up, or down, down, down. He has killed off most of the daisies with a plague, or a herd of hungry cows, or a shower of meteorites. Regardless of the nature of the calamity, the consequence is always the same. The world's thermostat begins to fall apart. Its temperature begins to jitter up and down.

"This is redolent of ice ages," Lovelock says. It looks very much like our planet's jagged temperature record in the last three million years, in which we have swept from cold to warm and warm to cold more than fifty times in rapid succession. To Lovelock this resemblance between Daisyworld and Earth is suggestive. He suspects that from the geological point of view, we human beings may have chosen exactly the wrong time for our global experiment.

When he inflicts a plague upon Daisyworld under a too-hot Sun, the planet's temperature dances the jitterbug for just a few steps and then it is all over. The temperature shoots up off the charts. All the daisies die.

 CHAPTER 11

THE NEW
QUESTION

All changed, changed utterly:
A terrible beauty is born.

William Butler Yeats
"Easter, 1916"

We are conducting an experiment as fateful as the one that took place half a century ago near Alamagordo, New Mexico.

That experiment was called Trinity. Its focal point was a steel sphere called Fat Man. The sphere reposed on top of a steel tower at a point called Ground Zero, in a part of the desert known since the time of the Spanish conquistadores as *Jornada del Muerto*, Dead Man's Trail, the Journey of Death.

Even the physicists who built the sphere did not know what it would do. In a betting pool before the test, Robert Oppenheimer had put a dollar on an explosion equivalent to 300 tons of TNT—a modest guess, befitting the scientific director of the experiment. George Kistiakowsky bet 1,400 tons; Hans Bethe, 8,000 tons; I.I. Rabi, 18,000 tons; Edward Teller, 45,000 tons.

Enrico Fermi offered to take wagers that the explosion would ignite the atmosphere. This was a possibility no one could quite rule out. "In this event," one physicist had written lyrically, some years before, "the whole of the hydrogen on the Earth might be transformed at once and the success of the experiment published at large to the universe as a new star."

There was only one way to narrow the range of uncertainties. In the *Jornada del Muerto* on July 16, 1945, Teller, Bethe, and others listened to the countdown by shortwave radio. They were stationed on a hill twenty miles from Ground Zero. It was 5:00 A.M. and pitch dark. They had been advised to lie down and bury their faces in the sand. But Teller was determined (he said years afterward) "to look the beast in the eye." In the darkness, he put on suntan lotion, then passed the lotion around.

Five miles from Ground Zero, Fermi, Rabi, and hundreds of other scientists, technicians, and soldiers lay down with their backsides up and their feet pointing toward the bomb. At 5:29:35, a loudspeaker began tolling the last ten seconds. "There were just a few streaks of gold in the east," Rabi recalled in Richard Rhodes's history, *The Making of the Atomic Bomb;* "you could see your neighbor very dimly. Those ten seconds were the longest ten seconds I have ever experienced."

Less than two miles from Zero, in an earth-shielded bunker, Oppenheimer said, "Lord, these affairs are hard on the heart." He was hardly breathing. He held on to a post to steady himself.

The flash that illuminated the *Jornada del Muerto* was the biggest explosion in history, equivalent to 18,600 tons of TNT. The test was a success. Hiroshima and Nagasaki followed within three weeks.

Scientists who study the changes that are now in progress in the atmosphere and the biosphere must strive for a calm and disembodied objectivity. They need to work as if from a cosmic distance if they are to put into society's possession facts that do not lie. They prefer the studied neutrality of the term "global change" to the term they might use for events this big in the geological record: "global catastrophe."

They are also aware that there may be a mistake somewhere in their calculations (which was a possibility at Trinity, too, even at T-1 seconds). For decades they have been afraid of sounding an alarm too soon. They themselves would never compare their watch to the physicists' in the desert.

Nevertheless as this troubled century closes, we find ourselves in the middle of another countdown. Again scientists from around the world have converged upon it. Again their calculations have been extensive. Again they do not agree on the outcome: whether the planet Earth will soon grow hotter than it has been in thousands, tens of thousands, hundreds of thousands, millions, or tens of millions of years.

This time there is no place to call Ground Zero. Every continent is

Ground Zero; Earth is Ground Zero. There is no one moment when the firing circuit will close. It began closing long ago, although we did not know it then. And there will be no single moment when we learn the extent of the reaction. The reaction may build for the next one thousand years.

To compare these countdowns is not hyperbolic. Indeed it would be hard to say which test is beggared in the comparison. John Maddox, the editor of *Nature,* has observed that "avoiding nuclear war by means of arms control would be a hollow boast if the vestigial ice caps were then allowed to melt." By the most modest estimate in the betting pool, we are in for climate changes as great as any since the dawn of civilization. By the most extreme estimate, Earth is on the brink of climatic upheavals and mass extinctions as great as any since the end of the age of the dinosaurs.

If we do not destroy ourselves with the A-bomb and the H-bomb, then we may destroy ourselves with the C-bomb, the Change Bomb. And in a world as interlinked as ours, one explosion may lead to the other. Already in the Middle East, from North Africa to the Persian Gulf and from the Nile to the Euphrates, tensions over dwindling water supplies and rising populations are reaching what many experts describe as a flashpoint. A climate shift in that single battle-scarred nexus might trigger international tensions that will unleash some of the 60,000 nuclear warheads the world has stockpiled since Trinity.

No one says that the worst will happen, only that it could happen. It need not happen, but we are priming the planet for it every year, with loads of carbon measured in gigatons. The codename "Trinity" was inspired by a poem by John Donne ("Batter my heart, three-person'd God; —"). We have no adequate name for an experiment in which one planetary sphere tests the stability of seven. I have compared this geological upheaval to a volcano, and also to Atropos, the Greek Fate who cut the thread of life. But the more one sees of this experiment's scale and suspense, the more it is reminiscent of Alamagordo.

In a sense the experiment began in the mid-1700s with Black, Watt, and the Industrial Revolution. For a few Earth scientists, the countdown began in March of 1958, when Keeling began measuring carbon dioxide from the volcano Mauna Loa. For most of the world the countdown began precisely thirty years later to the month, in the first heat of 1988. In that year, as Thoreau once wrote in a very different mood and in very different weather, "I awoke to an answered question."

We understand now that the uncertainties will remain wide. There is only one way to eliminate them, and that is the method of the physicists in the desert. The physicists had their results in seconds, but ours will unfold for millennia, and as in the *Jornada del Muerto,* if we do not like what we see there will be no turning back.

For many people around the world this method of eliminating uncertainties now seems unacceptable. This is the most frightening countdown since Oppenheimer held his breath at Alamagordo. After the Summer of '88 the only important question became what we can do to stop the experiment. Not—is this something to worry about? Not—how bad will it be? But—what must we do?

That summer the world started trying to answer this new question. One week after James Hansen's dramatic testimony in Washington in 1988, delegates from almost fifty countries met in Toronto, Canada. Prominent climate experts convened with national leaders, including Prime Ministers Brian Mulroney, of Canada, and Gro Harlem Brundtland, of Norway, to discuss the task of bringing Earth's temperature back under control. It was the first International Conference on the Changing Atmosphere.

That fall in Geneva, Switzerland, delegates met again and formed an Intergovernmental Panel on Climate Change. Some of the panelists represented countries that contribute the lion's share of greenhouse gases—including the U.S., the U.S.S.R., China, and Brazil. Others came from countries that contribute almost nothing to the problem but have a lot to lose, including the Maldives and Malta. Together they began hammering out a global action plan, country by country.

Given the enormous political obstacles to such a plan, some of these countries may have been trying to "panel over" the problem until the world's attention turned away again. Calling for action is easier than taking action. The only certain outcome of talk is carbon dioxide. Nevertheless, with that rapid-fire series of meetings the nations of the world did acknowledge the magnitude of the threat. As the Chinese say, a journey of a thousand miles must begin with a single step. The first step had been taken.

And the step had momentum. By the fall of '88, at least fifteen high-level international meetings on the greenhouse effect had been scheduled for the following year. Arms control talks were making remarkable progress in '88; and suddenly it seemed possible that carbon control talks would join or even replace arms control in the main ring of diplomacy's travelling circus. (Either way we are talking about global survival.) One veteran environmentalist, Michael Oppenheimer, a senior scientist with the Environmental Defense Fund, wrote, "It is no exaggeration to say that global environment may become the overarching issue for the next forty years in the way the cold war defined our world view during the last forty years."

The planetary prospect looks something like this. In the next one hundred years, Earth's fever may rise on one of three paths:

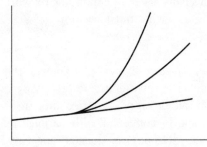

The steepest curve shows what could happen if human beings devour resources at faster and faster rates. Suppose next year we put a greater quantity of carbon into the air than we did this year. Suppose we do the same thing the year after next and the year after that: an ever-larger tonnage of greenhouse gases. And suppose the climate of the planet turns out to be extremely sensitive. Then, according to one state-of-the-art estimate, Earth's temperature could rise as much as 16° C. (30° F.) in the next century. This way to the Inferno.

Suppose instead that human beings inject the *same* amount of carbon into the air next year as we did this year, and so on for the next hundred years. That is the scenario of the middle curve: business as usual.* Suppose we follow this path, and suppose our climate turns out to be only moderately sensitive. Then the planet's temperature may rise between 3 and 8° C. (5 and 15° F.). No one knows if the human sphere could survive the stress of a rise of 5° F. But 15° would probably be just as devastating as 30. This may be another road to the Inferno.

The lowest curve shows what might happen if we cut back. Suppose our species puts less and less carbon into the air each year, cutting

---

*Business as usual implies that carbon dioxide will rise at the rate it is rising right now. However, there are greenhouse gases, including methane and nitrous oxide, that are rising at faster and faster rates today. Business as usual implies that they will continue rising faster and faster.

down to 2.5 gigatons of carbon per year, which is about half of what we are doing right now. And suppose we are also very lucky, and the global climate turns out to be relatively stable and insensitive to this insult. The result might be a rise of 1.5 to 4.5° C. (3 to 8° F.) in the next one hundred years.

Of course, a rise of even 3° F. is nothing to look forward to. It is three times greater than the rise in global temperatures that accompanied the heat waves and droughts of the 1980s. Its blessings are strictly comparative. The difference between the best case and the worst case is about 25° F. For our species and for millions of others, that is the difference between survival and extinction.

To get on the safest of these paths, the world must cut back on its production of carbon. Each year we must put a little less carbon into the air than the year before.

The human sphere did accomplish something like that within recent memory. When the OPEC cartel created an international energy crisis, beginning with the Arab oil embargo of 1973, the price of oil began to jump. In ten years it rose from a little more than ten dollars a barrel to almost forty dollars a barrel. The consequences did not show up right away, because our world of getting and spending has so much momentum. Eventually, however, the actions of that single cartel affected our behavior as a geological force. We burned so much less oil that we began to reduce the total amount of carbon we put into the air each year. In 1973, the year of the embargo, the amount of carbon we burned was still higher than the year before. This is the world's year-by-year carbon scorecard for the decade that followed:

    in 1974, higher
        1975, lower (for the first time since World War II)
        1976, higher
        1977, higher
        1978, higher
        1979, higher
        1980, a little lower
        1981, lower
        1982, lower
        1983, lower

It may not look like much, but the cartel accomplished something that one world depression and two world wars had failed to do. Four years in a row, the world burned less carbon than it had the year before. The high price of oil forced people around the world to look for ways to do more work while burning less fuel. Industries eked out more heat, light, and mileage from each drop of oil. People did the same thing in their homes.

Unlike the depression and the world wars, the period was not generally unpleasant. So many enterprises grew so much more efficient that national economies expanded even while the burning of carbon dropped. The U.S. economy grew by almost 40 percent, producing more and more goods and services with less and less oil. In fact, thanks to the energy-efficiency measures the country adopted, the U.S. is now saving an estimated $160 billion a year on an annual energy bill of $430 billion.

Japan adopted more efficiency measures than the U.S. or Western Europe. That gave it a secret weapon in world markets. It costs less to make things in Japan, partly because the Japanese burn less oil and coal to make them. According to one American analyst, this single factor gives Japan "about a 5 percent economic edge on everything they sell."

The price of oil started falling again in the early 1980s, and by the end of the decade we were once again burning more carbon each year than the year before. ("We've recovered," says one greenhouse expert, with a dark laugh.) But that run of four years is a very encouraging sign. If the world responds to the global warming the way it responded to OPEC, we may yet avert the worst.

As experts point out, another drive toward efficiency would pay off even without the threat of a warming. Analysts at the Worldwatch Institute and other environmental groups argue that Americans could cut energy consumption another 50 percent, reduce carbon dioxide emissions by 50 percent, *and* save another $200 billion a year, all without much sacrifice.

American cars, for example, are putting gigatons of carbon into the atmosphere. Yet the gas tax in the U.S. is scandalously low, compared to that of other industrial powers. For the U.S. to keep the tax so low is to encourage waste and to fuel the greenhouse effect.

U.S. mileage standards are another scandal. In 1975, during the oil crisis, the U.S. government gave American automakers ten years to improve their cars' mileage rate from 14 miles per gallon to 27.5 miles per gallon. When oil prices came back down in the 1980s, the government relaxed the standard again. Transportation experts at the E.P.A. argue that the mileage requirement might reasonably be raised to 40 miles per gallon. Meanwhile, every time we turn the key in a car's ignition we turn up the planet's thermostat.

There is also room for improvement indoors. During the energy crisis, President Jimmy Carter declared "the moral equivalent of war" on the waste of energy. Part of the war included a strong tax incentive program to improve home insulation. The program worked: it benefited homeowners, the atmosphere, the climate, and the national budget. A recent E.P.A. report recommends that the U.S. now revive the program, cutting the fuel used to heat its homes by half the amount used in the year 1980.

The refrigerator is the biggest single user of electricity in the average American home, and it could be made much more efficient. The typical Japanese refrigerator is so much better made that it uses half as much electricity. (It is also somewhat smaller. The typical American refrigerator could serve a small restaurant.)

Replacing every old fluorescent light fixture in the U.S. with a cooler and more efficient type (already commercially available) could save the nation one very large oil field every twenty years. Changing light bulbs is simpler and safer than pumping oil in Alaska.

There are new windows that steal a trick from the greenhouse effect. Scientists at the National Lighting Laboratory, in Berkeley, California, are coating one surface of double- and triple-glazed windowpanes with tin oxide. This coating lets visible light through but bounces infrared light back into the room. Touch the glass and it feels as warm as the wall.

The same lessons apply around the world. Brazil, for example, is planning the construction of about one hundred new hydroelectric dams, mostly to supply electricity to sprawling cities like São Paolo and Rio de Janeiro. As many as seventy of the new dam sites are in the Amazon Basin. There, because the terrain is flat and the flow of water is sluggish, vast tracts have been flooded in the past to provide small amounts of electricity. The Balbina dam drowned 900 square miles of rain forest to supply about half the electricity needs of the city of Manaus.

Sometimes, observes Jessica Tuchman Matthews, of the World Resources Institute, "poverty is as great a cause of wasteful energy use as great wealth." If Brazil were to invest $4 billion in new and more efficient refrigerators, lights, and motors, the country would save enough energy to supplant twenty-one large new power plants. The country would also save $19 billion between now and the year 2000.

However, Brazil is expected to grow by some 60 million people in the next two decades, to more than 200 million. The prospect is putting enormous pressure on government planners, and they want the dams.

This pressure of human numbers makes the task of cutting back more complicated and more painful. The heart blanches at the moral, political, and religious dilemmas that face us. Each year there are another 80 million people on the planet, each decade another India. Demography is among the most reliable sciences of the future, and demographers expect the human sphere to double in size in the next one hundred years. Barring a global catastrophe (a possibility that lies outside the scope of demography) Planet Earth will be carrying more than ten billion human beings around the sun within the next century—say, conservatively, by the year 2099.

According to the demographers, at least eight billion of us will then be living in places that have trouble sustaining their present populations. Indeed the very poorest countries of the world—the most malnourished, ill-housed, unstable—will double in population within about *thirty-five* years. In Asia, this list includes Bangladesh, Pakistan, the Philippines, Vietnam. In the Middle East: Egypt, Jordan, Syria. In Latin America: Nicaragua, Guatemala, El Salvador, Honduras. In South America: Ecuador, Paraguay. In the Caribbean: Haiti.

In Africa, nearly half the population is under the age of fifteen. With so many Africans just beginning their child-bearing years, the population of the whole continent—the poorest continent in the world—will more than double by the year 2020.

Again, demographers' predictions do not take into account war, famine, plague, or global chaos. Given the sensitivity of the spheres, it seems best to speak of ten billion people in the conditional tense. For long before there were ten billion people on this Earth almost everyone would be living on the edge. With the planet so crowded even the danger of earthquakes would become spectacular. More people will not make more earthquakes, of course. The lithosphere is still beyond our influence. But the population explosion will have a surprising effect on the number of people at risk. Roger Bilham, a geologist at the University of Colorado, has noted that by the year 2000, one hundred cities will have populations exceeding two million, and by pure chance, almost half these cities are located in places where the shifting plates of the lithosphere create earthquake hazard zones. "It appears," Bilham warned in 1988, "that within twelve years 290 million 'supercity' dwellers, 80 percent of them living in developing nations, will live in a region of seismic risk." In fact, so many of us are clustering along the planet's fault lines that the number of people in danger of dying in an earthquake will have doubled by the year 2035. (It is a dark coincidence that in the human sphere and the lithosphere, tension and friction should be building at so many of the same foci.)

Greater dangers will come from shifts in the air. The more we grow the more we change the atmosphere. This lesson is inscribed in the very icecaps. Compare the rise of our population, as recorded by the demographers, and the rise of methane gas, as recorded by the polar ice sheets. The two curves have been rising in unison for six hundred years, since the first years of the Renaissance. The solid line represents people and the dots represent methane:

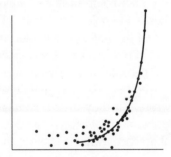

Why should the number of people on the ground and the number of methane molecules in the air have exploded in parallel? Because people generate methane by so many different kinds of disturbances in the biosphere. Each new rice paddy in China, chopped tree in England, ruminating cow and goat in India, garbage dump in Mexico, and leaking natural-gas pipe in Texas, makes methane. Methane is almost as universal a product of progress as carbon dioxide. People have a methane effect and methane has a greenhouse effect. So people have a greenhouse effect.

If our numbers continue to spiral upward, so will greenhouse gases, and so will the temperature of the planet. To say nothing of the number of tons of topsoil lost to the sea, the number of acres lost to deserts, and the number of species lost forever. If we cannot manage our impact on the planet now, how would we do so if there were many more of us? Can we defuse the Change Bomb while human numbers explode? Can we cut our carbon production in half while doubling the size of the human sphere?

Think of the U.S., which has already seen the most fantastic population explosion in human history, from 18 million in 1750 to 250 million today, an increase of 3,500 percent. The U.S. population will reach almost 300 million in the next one hundred years. And at present rates, of course, each citizen is shoveling about five tons of carbon into the air. Some American economists see U.S. population growth as discomfortingly sluggish. Yet 300 million people consuming resources as fast as Americans do today would produce about 1.5 billion tons of carbon per annum. That is to say, in one hundred years, the United States alone would be producing more than half of the whole world's annual quota of greenhouse gas. Something has to give; the planet cannot afford that many American consumers.

This subject is not only difficult, in many countries it is politically untouchable. But if we do not confront it we cannot stop the explosion in the air over our heads. People say family planning is unnatural. Surely the factors that fuel the population explosion are unnatural, too, as Harrison Brown pointed out in *The Challenge of Man's Future* back in 1954 (population: 2.6 billion). "Those who maintain that conception control should not be used because it is unnatural would be far more convincing," Brown wrote, "if they urged simultaneously abolishment of all clothing, antiseptics, antibiotics, vaccinations, and hospitals, together with all artificial practices which enable man to extract food from the soil."

Either we will slow our growth by managing birth rates, or the other spheres of the Earth will control ours by managing our death rates. Think of the populations of Bangladesh and the Maldives. Each will double within about 30 years. Then, if sea levels rise as some models predict, each country may start losing land. Before the end of the next century tens of millions of people may have been drowned or forced out of Bangladesh, and the 2,000 tiny atolls of the Maldives may have been erased from the map. (The leader of the Maldives calls his atolls "an endangered nation.")

Where there is a will there is a way. It is amazing what a country can do. Japan halved its population growth rate in the space of about five years—the first half of the 1950s. China did the same thing in the first half of the 1970s. The two nations are very different and they used very different tactics, but both of them are heavily populous and both pulled it off. If the human sphere is to reduce its production of carbon, it will have to do what China and Japan did, country by country, in each place with the appropriate tactics.

No one knows if we will do it, but we really have no decent alternative. Writes Lester Brown, director of the Worldwatch Institute, "It is hard to imagine anything more difficult . . . except suffering the consequences of failing to do so."

There is a standard illustration in stories about the greenhouse effect: the Statue of Liberty submerged in a rising sea, holding her torch up above the water. This symbol of the global forecast is an artistic exaggeration. The sea would have to rise 300 feet to douse Miss Liberty's torch. Yet the image may be more appropriate than we imagine. The sea would have to rise only a foot to displace a global flood of refugees. Long before the tides had reached the statue's ankles they would have drowned her traditional welcome to the tired and the poor. If the ocean drowns Bangladesh and invades the Nile, where will all the refugees go? Who will take them in? In the 1980s the number of refugees in the world rose from less than 5 million to more than 14 million. Doors were closing in the more fortunate nations in the world, including the United States, where officials were speaking of "compassion fatigue." A warmer planet may not be a warmer world.

Suppose our species hits the lottery jackpot tomorrow. Suppose we find a trick that brings us tremendous quantities of energy with almost no waste. Even so we will still need these crash programs for at least the next fifty years. History has shown that it takes the world about fifty years to change over from one source of energy to another. It took about that long to change over from wood to coal and from coal to oil and it would probably take that long to get fusion power (for example) out of the laboratory and humming in the middle of the world's power grids.

Nor has history been kind to miraculous new technologies that promise energy without waste. The automobile was greeted at the turn of the twentieth century as the salvation of the city, because it brought an end to the pollution of horse-droppings. Nuclear power was greeted at mid-century as the end of pollution of all kinds.

The strict arithmetic of energy and populations would apply to a world running on any technology, even those that our futurists' imaginations currently invest with utopian glamor: fusion power, solar power, microwaves, or lasers beamed to Earth from satellites in space.

Ten billion people living at the American rate would always produce too much waste. Nothing will ever spare the planet as much as controlling ourselves.

Still, some energy sources have less greenhouse effect than others. Solar power, wind power, hydropower, and geothermal power produce no carbon dioxide.

Natural gas puts less carbon into the air than oil and coal. Vegetation can be converted into methanol, or wood alcohol, and burned in a modified diesel engine, producing less carbon dioxide and less ozone than natural gas. Of course, alternative sources of energy do tend to produce alternative problems. Among methanol's by-products is formaldehyde. In small doses formaldehyde causes cancer and in large doses it preserves corpses. So switching to methanol requires catching the formaldehyde in a catalytic converter.

Nuclear power plants produce no carbon dioxide. They produce other kinds of wastes, including plutonium, strontium, cesium, and uranium isotopes. The radioactivity of these wastes will not decay and disappear for about 10,000 years—about as long as our carbon dioxide will linger in the atmosphere.

No one has ever been able to figure out what to do with radioactive wastes, any more than with carbon dioxide. You can't throw plutonium in a wastebasket. One-millionth of a gram of it causes lung cancer. These wastes are piling up in temporary "cooling ponds" next to every American reactor, as they have been piling up since the dawn of the nuclear age. The cooling ponds are overcrowded and many are in danger of getting hot. The nuclear industry is in the middle of the worst waste crisis in history (or the second-worst, after carbon dioxide).

The only site that may be geologically strong enough and politically weak enough to serve as the national receptacle for these nuclear wastes is Yucca Mountain, in the state of Nevada (population: half a million people, many of them angry*). There the accumulated nuclear debris of the nation may be stored in 112 miles of underground tunnels, almost as big a maze as the New York City subway system. From Congress's point of view this would seem an ideal solution since Yucca Mountain stands in a former proving ground for nuclear weapons, the Nevada Test Site, a piece of Earth we have already kissed good-bye.

---

*Grant Sawyer, the chairman of Nevada's nuclear waste commission, and a former governor, has said that making more nuclear wastes is like "sending John Glenn into orbit without figuring out how to bring him down."

The government is under enormous pressure to find a wastebasket, and Yucca Mountain now seems certain to win Washington's official seal of approval. Within ten years this seal may be firmly affixed, doubts firmly repressed, and the storage plan underway.

Yet in the late 1980s, seventeen of the scientists and engineers with the U.S. Geological Survey who had been charged with the evaluation of Yucca Mountain signed a formal letter of protest and sent it to the Department of Energy. They said political pressures were making their report "scientifically indefensible." One government hydrologist told a reporter for *Discover* magazine. "I've never seen the Survey involved in such a mess before."

These are facts that are likely to be forgotten in the next ten years: Yucca Mountain is surrounded by faults, including the Solitario Canyon Fault. There have been eight major earthquakes within 250 miles of Yucca Mountain since 1857. No one can guarantee that the mountain will not end up like its neighbor five miles away, Busted Butte, busted in half.

The site is also bounded by volcanoes. Some of them are young and may still be alive. In 1988, one of these volcanoes, Lathrop Wells, twelve miles from Yucca Mountain, was estimated by one of the government's geologists to be about 5,000 years young.

As geologists say, what has happened, can happen. Given time, eruptions or earthquakes may shake out the contents of that wastebasket. If the wastes are still hot, we will have spilled 63,500 tons of radioactive materials into the lap of the future—a blast from the past.

Given the experiment in progress in the atmosphere, what has *never* happened can happen. The scientists evaluating Yucca Mountain are supposed to consider what the weather will be like for the next 10,000 years. Right now the desert receives only three to six inches of rain each year, which is good, because if too much rain seeps underground, the wastes could eventually find their way down into the water table. Or the water table could rise to meet the wastes. Given the unpredictable climate of the the next few centuries, no one should bet the farm on a 10,000-year forecast, even in the home state of Las Vegas.

None of this is the geologists' fault (so to speak). With so much of Earth interconnected, human ingenuity may never find a giant hermetically sealed EcoSphere with a lifetime guarantee of 10,000 years. Nature hates a vacuum, and in the long run, nature hates an EcoSphere. While studying Yucca Mountain, officials at the Department of Energy had planned to store liquid nuclear wastes from military reactors in deep salt caverns near Carlsbad, New Mexico. Government geologists' reports gave the caverns a lifetime warranty. Just before officials were about to get started in Carlsbad in earnest, they were dismayed to discover that the salt walls of the caverns were weeping and that the drums of hot wastes could end up sitting in pools of corrosive brine.

A sign above a tunnel at Yucca Mountain:

WE RECOGNIZE NO

SUBSTITUTE FOR SAFETY

TUNNEL G COMPLEX

The sign might as well read, we recognize no substitute for Yucca Mountain. As long as there are more and more people on the planet and we consume more and more energy, we will be forced into gambles. As a guiding principle we should reject choices that raise the stakes. For energy saved we pay nothing. For energy spent, either in fossil fuels or nuclear fuels, we pay a price that is ultimately incalculable.

In 1976, the physicist Freeman Dyson thought of a way to solve the greenhouse problem. He was spending the summer at the Institute for Energy Analysis in Oak Ridge, Tennessee, where he had been invited to think big thoughts. Dyson and several other scientists asked themselves, "What would it require to remove five billion tons of carbon, as carbon dioxide, from the atmosphere annually for a period long enough to allow society to overcome its addiction to fossil fuels?" They decided that the simplest trick would be to plant trees.

Trees take carbon out of the air in the course of photosynthesis as part of the breathing of the world. Plant an oak and you take carbon out of the air and hold it down on the ground for one hundred years.* After a summer's worth of calculations, Dyson concluded, "There seems to be no law of physics or of ecology that would prevent us from taking action to halt or reverse the growth of atmospheric CO_2 within a few years if this should become necessary."

---

*Something like this may have happened when plants first conquered the land. That may have led to a sudden drawdown of carbon dioxide, and primordial ice ages.

Ten years later, officials at the Department of Energy asked Gregg Marland (one of Dyson's former associates at the institute in Oak Ridge) to reexamine the idea.

Marland's calculations are two-edged. They do suggest some hope; but they also illustrate the size of the carbon dioxide problem. Since the invention of farming about 10,000 years ago, human beings have cleared an area of forest the size of Australia, reducing Earth's total forest cover by 15 to 20 percent. ("That's how much forest has been cut all around the world since people were running around in 'em naked," says Marland.)

That is also about how much land we would have to plant with trees in order to balance the carbon dioxide that is now emitted each year from fossil fuel burning. "If you want to take up *all* the CO_2, that's what it would take," Marland says, with mordant good cheer. "It turns out we would have to plant essentially everything that's *ever been cut*. That's not going to go over big in Knoxville."

To counterbalance the amount of carbon that one American puts into the air, Marland calculates, would take 4,500 new trees. "That's for one U.S. citizen. And that's fast-growing plantation trees like sycamores. Not just hemlocks in your yard. And you've got to go in and clear the weeds and kill the bugs. Nine thousand trees if you're married. Eighteen thousand trees for a family of four.

"And then you've got to cut it all down and store it in your garage." (If the wood burned or rotted, the carbon would go right back into the air.) "Or you could bury them," Marland adds helpfully. "I call this my Chicago Solution: plant their feet in concrete and pitch them in the bay."

After spending a day on such calculations Marland drives home impressed with the size of the change we are making in the atmosphere. "This startles me," says Marland. "I get out on the interstate at Knoxville and see the miles and miles of cars we idiots drive. We're going about this in a big way."

Of course, as Marland points out, we're talking about balancing the emissions of American citizens. The global picture is at least somewhat more encouraging. Worldwide it works out to 1,000 trees per person. That is, if everyone in the world planted and tended one hundred fast-growing trees each year for the next ten years, carbon dioxide would stop building up in the atmosphere.

Further calculations show that even spot efforts can make a difference. For instance, city trees not only take carbon out of the air;

they also keep carbon from being put *into* the air, because the air conditioners in their shade are turned on later and turned off sooner. Thus
all trees are equal but some trees are more equal than others. A tree
that grows in Brooklyn can take ten times more carbon from the air
than a tree that grows in Brazil.

In a recent study, people planted three trees around each home in a
small neighborhood in Los Angeles. They also painted the homes' walls
white or in pastel colors, and roofed them in light colors (an ancient air-
conditioning strategy familiar to ancient Mediterranean villages). The
demand on air conditioners in summertime was cut almost 50 percent
in that neighborhood.

Shade maples planted on Main Street today may be offering more
and more shade during hotter and hotter summers in the next few
decades. If cities and towns don't plant them, they are guaranteed to
need more and more electric power if summers get hotter; and that
will put more carbon into the air with each heat wave. In the United
States, for instance, the electric grids neared overload in the Summer
of '88. This fact was immediately used to justify the construction or
completion of new coal-fired and nuclear power plants, including the
new Limerick nuclear power plant in eastern Pennsylvania. "It's a spiral," Michael Oppenheimer says. "Nobody knows if the spiral gets out
of control." Planting trees is one way to keep the spiral in control.

Before planners in American cities and suburbs decide they need a
new power plant, they should check whether massive tree-planting and
energy-efficiency programs could save the equivalent amount of energy. The volunteer organization TreePeople, in Los Angeles, led by
the energetic couple Andy and Katie Lipkis, is trying to plant several
million trees in the city in the next few years. The American Forestry
Association is trying to plant 100 million trees in cities and towns
across the country. And the same logic applies in any hot city in the
world. As the Koran says, "Even on the eve of the end of the world,
plant a tree."

By this logic we should also leave trees standing up. In the next one
hundred years every tree may be shelter from the storm. Trees are
the ultimate tie-in strategy. They tie in soil belowground. They tie in
wildlife aboveground. On sloping ground they tie in water. In rain forests they tie in clouds. They keep air fresh and summers cool, *and*
they tie down carbon from the atmosphere.

Forest area in New England increased by almost 40 percent in the twentieth century with the abandonment of old Yankee farms. The forest area in the southeastern U.S. and in the U.S.S.R. is also growing. But on the global average, as we enter the third millennium, the clearing and burning of woods is putting more carbon into the air than at any time since the Neolithic.

This deforestation is often ill-advised in plain business terms, according to the economist Robert Repetto, of the World Resources Institute. Many third-world countries sell their timber rights to industrial nations at firesale prices in return for money to pay the interest on their debts. The four tropical countries that currently take the lead in burning off or selling off their forests and putting carbon into the air are Brazil, Indonesia, Colombia, and the Ivory Coast. At present rates they won't have forests to sell for long. Nigeria's fate is cautionary. Nigeria was once a major exporter of tropical hardwoods. But by 1985, according to the Worldwatch Institute, Nigeria was earning only $6 million in exports of forest products and spending 160 million on forest product *imports*. Nigerians mined their wood until the wood ran out.

The United States has a few rain forests, too. A magnificent stand of ohias on the Big Island of Hawaii was chopped down recently by a private company called BioPower, for wood chips. The company promptly went bankrupt, leaving bad debts and a hole in the forest. Walking out of the still-intact rain forest into that vast plain of stumps is like walking out onto an old lava desert. You feel in your gut the size of the geological force at work. The human sphere should be capable of more foresight than lava. Looking at those stumps you feel for our sphere nothing but rage.

The U.S. government routinely auctions off timber rights to lands deemed unsuitable for logging. Often the government accepts bids so low that the money does not even pay for the cost of the auction itself. Repetto, of W.R.I., calculates that simply leaving this timber alone would save the government almost $100 million a year, besides benefiting climate, campers, wildlife, and the trees themselves.

As an instrument of planetary home repair, it is hard to imagine anything as safe as a tree. However, scientists are also dreaming of more futuristic and even fantastic measures.

A physicist at Princeton University proposes that we blast chlorofluorocarbons out of the air before they get to the stratosphere.

Thomas H. Stix thinks an array of powerful infrared lasers could be beamed through the atmosphere like searchlights, dropping the molecules dead in their tracks. Stix calls this "atmospheric processing."

Other scientists want to plug the ozone holes. They say we could manufacture ozone gas on the ground and then ferry it up to the stratosphere in rockets, jumbo jets, or balloons.

The dean of Soviet climate experts, Mikhail Budyko, thinks we could open a giant parasol above the planet as a sunshade. All we would have to do, according to Budyko, is to dump sulfur dioxide gas into the stratosphere. The gas would form droplets of sulfuric acid. Stratosopheric winds would then whirl these droplets all around the globe within months. This would wrap the planet in a white shroud.

In theory, this would duplicate the thin clouds of sulfuric acid that shaded and chilled Earth's surface after the eruption of Tambora in 1815, which helped to bring us the disastrous Year without a Summer. We would counterbalance a hothouse August like 1988 with an icehouse August like 1816—popping downers as a cure for uppers.

The geochemist Wallace Broecker, of Columbia University, mentions this scheme in his book *How to Build a Habitable Planet.* Broecker doesn't recommend it but he thinks it could be done. We would need 35 million tons of sulfur dioxide. At current prices, that much gas would cost about $15 billion to manufacture and deliver to the stratosphere in Boeing 747 jets. Of course, the acid would keep raining out of the stratosphere as fast as we put it up there. We would have to repeat the dose year after year. However, since the current military budget of the U.S. alone is now about $350 billion a year, Broecker argues that $15 billion a year is not a crazy sum for the whole planet to spend on "climate defense." "The point," he says, "is not that the strategy is necessarily a wise one, but, rather, that purposeful global climate modification lies within our grasp."

Desperate times breed desperate measures, and we may be driven to this kind of planetary surgery sooner than we think. In Broecker's book, which appeared in the innocent year 1985, he observes, "One hundred years from now, the temptation to take such action may be high." Just three years later, in August of '88, Thomas Stix, of Princeton (the physicist who wants to blast CFCs out of the sky) was interviewed in *The New York Times* about lasers and other bright, shiny new ecological scalpels. "Some of this is mighty speculative," Stix acknowledged. "But if we have a couple of summers like we just had, people are going to get pretty panicky over what we should do about it."

One hot summer pushed up the schedule of temptation about ninety-five years.

What is scary about all these high-tech proposals is how bad they tend to look in hindsight. Not so long ago, John von Neumann (father of the electronic computer) and Edward Teller (father of the hydrogen bomb) were talking enthusiastically about using nuclear explosions to deflect hurricanes. As Francis Bacon said, "Cure the disease and kill the patient." At about the same time, Harrison Brown was recommending that we increase carbon dioxide levels threefold to fertilize the world's crops.

As recently as 1986, Britain's Department of the Environment issued a report that argued against a world treaty to stop manufacturing chlorofluorocarbons. The report stated (1) CFCs probably won't hurt the ozone layer; (2) even if they do, we can always cure the damage with more emissions of methane. Almost immediately it was clear that chlorofluorocarbons were already devouring the ozone layer, and that methane was helping them eat it. The department recommended a poison as medicine.

The Germans have a word for this kind of thing: *schlimmbesserungen,* so-called improvements that make things worse. Like nuclear power, they are one-dimensional solutions, good from one point of view and bad from every other. In the heat of the Summer of '88, the German newsmagazine *Der Spiegel* asked the atmospheric chemist Paul Crutzen, director of the Max Planck Institute for Chemistry, if he knew of anything we could add to the atmosphere to slow down the rise of the global fever. "This kind of question is being asked more and more," Crutzen replied. "It scares me. If I knew enough about the atmosphere, I would gladly be working on such experiments and theories. But we know so little . . ."

As Crutzen pointed out, the sulfur parasol would be a particularly dangerous project. Dumping sulfur into the stratosphere might indeed cool Earth's surface. On the other hand, the sulfuric acid droplets would also tend to collect chlorine atoms. Like ice crystals, they would help chlorofluorocarbons devour the ozone layer. The dirtier we make the stratosphere the faster the ozone layer will disappear. And of course the sulfuric acid would all wash back down to Earth as acid rain.

"Instead," Crutzen said, "we should look for ways to reduce the emissions of carbon dioxide, methane, and trace gases."

If the world does start warming rapidly, the world will be debating choices like this: on the one hand, radical, untried and untestable surgical procedures; on the other hand, preventive medicine. Which will have more political appeal? Perhaps surgery. We often go for the quick fix. Fast-acting remedies are more attractive to us than painstaking ones. Moreover, the promise of surgery tomorrow would give us implicit permission to stay on the road we are driving now. We are changing the planet? Let's keep on doing exactly what we're doing, and then mend the results by . . . changing things some more. At dinner once with a group of eminent ecologists, I asked, "Why does your field have so much less clout in the world than economics?"

E.O. Wilson replied, succinctly, "Because ecology is seen as the brake on the wheel." Which is true. And lasers and sulfur caravans would not be a brake—they would be exciting. Full speed ahead.

In one way the impulse is noble. Jewish tradition speaks of *Tikkun Olam*, the repair of the world. "And the vessel that he made of clay was marred in the hands of the potter," sang the prophet Jeremiah: "so he made it again another vessel, as seemed good to the potter to make it." Or in the words of Omar Khayyam,

> Ah Love! Could you and I with Him conspire
> To grasp the sorry Scheme of Things entire,
> Would not we shatter it to bits—and then
> Remould it nearer to the Heart's Desire!

But we can already see where all this shattering and remoulding would lead. We would be setting one calamity to catch another. Omar's noble impulse would end like the old nursery jingle:

> She swallowed the dog
> to catch the cat,
> she swallowed the cat
> to catch the bird,
> she swallowed the bird
> to catch the fly.
>
> I don't know why
> she swallowed the fly.
> I guess she'll die.

If we hope to live a long time, we must begin to think like a geological force. That is, we must become the first geological force to learn to think. In geological terms, time is not money. Time is everything. In geological terms what can happen will happen. We cannot tolerate more and more of what are called, in the jargon of risk, "low-probability, high-consequence events." Exxon's catastrophic oil spill in Alaska's Prince William Sound in 1989 was such an event. It soiled a length of coastline greater than Long Island and Cape Cod combined. Soon afterward, Charles J. DiBona, president of the American Petroleum Institute, distributed a press hand-out, "Questions and Answers on Alaskan Oil Spill." It ended:

Q: Can you give us a guess as to how many tanker loadings there have been at the Port of Valdez in the 12 years it's been operating?

A: According to the Alaska Oil and Gas Association, there have been 8,858 tanker loadings during this 12-year period, with 6.8 billion barrels transported out of the Port of Valdez. If you want the fraction of the oil that got into the water, you're talking about 240,000 barrels spilled out of 6.8 billion barrels transported—so it's one twenty-eight thousandth of the oil. That is a tremendous amount of oil moved out of there without incident—6.8 billion barrels have been moved out, and 240,000 barrels spilled, which is one barrel in 28,000.

In other words, as Hendrik Hertzberg wrote indignantly in the *New Republic:* "Why all the long faces? Let's talk about the oil that *hasn't* destroyed any pristine, irreplaceable, wildlife-rich, stunningly beautiful natural environments. Let's talk about the successes, not the failures."

A geological force that is willing to risk losing that much coastline every twelve years cannot last. Nor was that—to ordinary ways of thinking—an extraordinary risk. We take bigger risks all the time. If the oil had not been spilled, for instance, most of its carbon would have ended up in the atmosphere. There it would have added its weight to another high-consequence event and threatened the loss of a much greater length of coastline.

If we were thinking in geological time—or even in terms of the next twelve years—we would understand that low-probability risks become higher-probability risks the longer we play the game. As a species we are playing Russian roulette over and over again. Each day we recalculate the odds as if this were the last day we will play. Someday it will be.

On the very day of the spill, if we were thinking as a planetary sphere, we would have ruled out plans to drill for oil in the Arctic National Wildlife Refuge. But our behavior suggests that on the scale of the planet we are still not quite conscious. We flow along with much more talk but not much more thought than does a lava flow, an ice flow, a fire, or a flood.

Three days before the Alaskan oil spill, for instance, Frank Murkowski, Republican Senator from Alaska, wrote in *USA Today:* "Alarmists say Alaska's environment would be destroyed if the refuge is explored. Twenty years ago, they sounded the same alarm against the Alaska pipeline—and they were proved wrong."

Four days *after* the spill (as Hertzberg notes), President George Bush was asked in the White House pressroom if he had changed his mind about the Arctic Refuge. "No," he replied. "I see no connection."

Besides learning to think as a planetary sphere we need to be able to watch what we are doing. Given the size of the planet and how much we are doing, this is a massive job. We need teams of scientists to monitor the changes in progress in each of the seven spheres: earth, water, air, fire, life, ice, and mind. Only then can we hope for early detection of some of the chain reactions and surprises in store in the coming years.

Doing this right would mean the most ambitious scientific cooperative program ever attempted. Scientists are now working toward it. Plans have been under development behind half-closed doors since the early 1980s in the major research centers of several governments, including the U.S. and the U.S.S.R. A small international office has been established in Stockholm. In the U.S. an Office for Interdisciplinary Earth Studies, at NCAR, serves as a clearinghouse and publishes a quarterly newsletter. All-star committees of scientists from around the world and from every discipline of Earth science are now coming together quietly every few months in scattered cities, and then dispersing again.

Many U.S. scientific agencies are working towards this global program. They each march under a different banner. The American Geophysical Union calls it "the Planet Earth initiative." The U.S. National Science Foundation calls it "Global Change" and "Global Geoscience." NASA calls it "Mission to Planet Earth," because the disciplines of science have never converged simultaneously upon our own planet as energetically as they did during the great space missions to the Moon and to our neighbor worlds Mars and Venus. The new mission—if done right—would tax the resources of the space programs of the U.S., the U.S.S.R., and the European Economic Community combined.

The inspiration of this global program, of course, is the International Geophysical Year of 1957–58. That program was organized by the International Council on Scientific Unions. It was carried out by thousands of scientists in seventy countries and the results went beyond anyone's expectations. The I.G.Y. launched the age of space. It inaugurated the age of scientific cooperation—among disciplines and among countries. It led directly to the revolutionary new view of Earth as a turbulent planet. From work begun in the I.G.Y. we now know, among other things, that continents drift, that ice ages come and go in step with changes in Earth's orbit, and that human beings are changing Earth's atmosphere faster than the ice ages did.

The new program now taking shape would dwarf the I.G.Y. in size, scope, and duration. It would draw in more scientists by the thousands. It would encompass every science of the Earth. (The International Union of Scientific Unions, which would serve as organizer of this program, too, calls it the "International Geosphere-Biosphere Program.") It would last not one year but decades. Who can say what discoveries would come from it?

Revelle, a major force behind both the I.G.Y. and the new, overarching program, urges that we take as our focus the next one hundred years. "It's very hard to do that—damn near impossible," Revelle says. "But I think we have to stretch our imaginations. Not to say what is actually going to happen, but what *might*."

Why one hundred years?

"The reason I said one hundred years is not because it is long but because it's short," Revelle says. "After all, we've lived on this planet for what, 200,000 years? One hundred years is an instant. Yet we can't predict.

"Moreover, what happens during the next one hundred years may have a profound effect over a much longer time. We're at some kind of hinge of history."

It is clear that some of the observation work will have to be done from space. It is hard to see life in the round while walking and breathing in the middle of it. But place five satellites roughly equally around the equator, 22,000 miles up. Make them orbit at the same speed as Earth (in what are called geostationary orbits) so that they seem to hover overhead. With just these five satellites we can image the whole Earth, except for a small portion near each pole. Place one more satellite in an orbit from pole to pole (a low, longitudinal orbit) to take in the planet's icecaps. Those six robots would provide a god's-eye view of the whole sphere.

Today's downlooking spacecraft, circling Earth in various orbits and at various altitudes, can see and photograph 10,000 square kilometers of land at a time, or resolve details a few inches across. They can "see" in many wavelengths of radiation, visible and invisible, and they radio home what they see in digital code to computers on the ground. In the imagery beamed home by robots in low orbits, scientists can distinguish rice from soybeans, young corn from old, healthy corn from diseased. They can determine the moisture content in each acre, and estimate total leaf area and the weight of leaf protein.

We need satellites to watch the global warming: to monitor changes in cloud cover, sea surface temperature, stratospheric temperature, polar sea ice, the solar constant, the dustiness of the air, soil temperatures. Even sea level can be watched by robot instruments in space. We also need satellites to help watch the ozone holes, keeping track of their peculiar chemistry and temperature and the state of health of the rest of the ozone layer.

A panel of greenhouse experts notes that without the carbon-dioxide monitoring program that Keeling began during the I.G.Y., scientists would have little confidence today in their understanding of the greenhouse effect. "Analogously, without better monitoring data on solar variations, volcanic aerosols, and the major trace greenhouse gases, there will be little confidence in the future regarding the nature and meaning of any observed climate signal. . . . It is important to keep the long-term nature of the CO_2 question in mind: What variables will our successors one or two generations hence berate us for *not* monitoring today?"

Satellite studies must be complemented by extensive studies on the ground, including ecological close-up work amid all the world's varieties of terrains and habitats. Satellite experts call their views of the planet "remote sensing." They call studies on the surface "getting the ground truth." Here the global-change committees sometimes dream of projects that sound like the visions of Francis Bacon at the dawn of the age of science. Some of the earlier reports describe the construction of a network of Biosphere Observatories, futuristic laboratories as sophisticated as those that astronomers have built on desert mountaintops like Palomar and Mauna Kea to survey remote galaxies. These new observatories would be set not only on peaks but also in jungle gorges, in estuaries, prairie, permafrost tundra, and in the hearts of tropical islands; and the observatories' instruments would be turned not upon the stars but upon the living world around them, each observatory rising from jungle and desert like the watchtower on Mauna Loa.

The Earthwatchers also dream of the construction of remarkable models of the seven spheres that make today's supercomputer models look like Tinkertoys. These models would be able to pull together data from a comprehensive library of geophysiology that in terms of sheer data might be hundreds of times bigger than the U.S. Library of Congress. The data base would include all the numbers from all the monitoring systems ever employed on the planet since the first mercury thermometer.

Scientists would let these supercomputer models run and watch the whole system come to life: watch the planet breathe, the polar ice fields dilate and contract, the temperature rise and fall. Scientists speaking many different languages and many different fields of jargon would be able to work and watch together as they studied global change in the safe microcosms of the electronic Earths, models that would be as close as we can ever come to our planet's identical twin.

In reality, it is not easy for all of the disciplines of Earth science to work together, particularly in tight times. Research budgets are under fire in the U.S., Britain, and elsewhere. At such times, scientists, complains a particle physicist, "form the wagon train into a circle and start shooting inwards." Each specialist begins to fight for his own specialty at the expense of the others. A global-change committee member at N.A.S. sometimes claims that the red cover of one of their early reports was printed in genuine blood.

Frank Press, an Earth scientist and the president of the U.S. National Academy of Sciences, is only cautiously optimistic about the prospects of the global change program. "It will happen *in some form,*" he says. "If it had been proposed in the 1960s, at a time when international science was receiving more and more funding, the idea of a successor to the I.G.Y. would have received enormous worldwide and immediate support. Today, however, proposals for international science projects are viewed with suspicion by many governments, as ways of getting more money from a shrinking budget."

Meanwhile much more could be done now—on a shoestring. For example, since the dawn of the age of space, NASA and NOAA have amassed huge libraries of Earth imagery. Much of this inventory lies fallow in computer storage. For a pittance (compared to the budgets of most U.S. agencies), studies of these image libraries could tell us precisely how much rain forest is being burned and cleared each year. It could also tell us how much has been cleared in the last several decades, country by country, which would help scientists figure out, among other things, how much carbon dioxide is contributed to the atmosphere when an acre of the Amazon goes up in smoke. Currently scientists have funds only for spot studies, and it is these spot studies that are telling us that a holocaust is in progress in the biosphere.

Compton Tucker, of NASA, and George Woodwell and his colleagues at the Woods Hole Research Center, have been campaigning to do a comprehensive survey for years. But they have never been granted enough money to do anything but spot studies, despite NASA's and NOAA's avowed interests in global change and the E.P.A.'s in global warming. Recently Tucker told a reporter from *Science,* "Let's face it, in another ten years, it won't be worth doing." Perhaps the world would rather not know.

All this is a lot to do in the face of a threat that remains invisible and impalpable. Yet we can sometimes move very fast, even when the exact degree to which our world is at risk is still unknown. The hopeful precedent is the Montreal Protocol. Richard Benedick represented the U.S. in the negotiations that led to the treaty on chlorofluorocarbons. Benedick was sent by the State Department, with the rank of ambassador. Like most environmental diplomats he is not a scientist—he was once Evans Fellow in Metaphysical Poetry at Oxford.

"The protocol has now acquired an aura of inevitability," says Benedick, "but the reality is that there was intense and often bitter international negotiations to arrive at that agreement. These chemicals are almost synonymous with modern standards of living. And the risk was all theoretical at the time—there was still *no measured depletion* of the ozone layer. We were faced with an invisible risk involving one gas's threat to another gas, fifteen to thirty miles over our heads. This mattered because it might cause an increase in invisible radiation, which *had not been measured,* and because the radiation might have damaging health effects, which had not been measured either.

"'Too little to late,' some environmental groups now cry! Yet quite late in our debates, a French minister was saying, 'But you still believe that there is harm from this little *pssst, psssst, psssst. . . !'*" miming an aerosol can, and delivering a devastating Gallic shrug. "The strength of the treaty," says Benedick, "is that it contained within its provisions the means for strengthening regulations on the basis of this still-evolving scientific evidence."

Thus the diplomats worked in an atmosphere of intense uncertainty. There was solid scientific consensus on just a few key points: that the compounds were building up in the stratosphere, that they could harm the ozone layer, and that the damage—if it took place—would be irreversible. Benedick anchored the diplomatic debate on these points. He argued that given this consensus it was too risky to wait any longer to detect the damage.

In the midst of their sessions the diplomats heard the first reports of an Ozone Hole at the South Pole. Benedick downplayed the hole. He did so, he says now, because there was still no evidence that the hole had been caused by chlorine. It might have had no link with CFCs. And even if the hole were proved to be caused by human beings it could still have been an anomaly that was restricted to Antarctica.

If Benedick made much of the Ozone Hole and then it turned out to be natural, he knew the Montreal Protocol might never be signed. "So we deliberately kept it *out* of the negotiations."

Vindication was swift. Not long after the protocol was signed, it was established beyond doubt that the Ozone Hole is caused by CFCs and that the entire ozone shield is thinning.

Benedick feels that the greenhouse effect must now be handled the same way. We must anchor the debate on the strong consensus that the effect is real. And we must move toward an international treaty in advance of a consensus that the effect has been detected.

"What moved us in Montreal," says Benedick, "is that the effects were not easily reversible: the fact that we couldn't *undo* it."

In Keeling's cluttered old offices and laboratories today there is a feeling of condensed time, generations watching the air, Keeling looking over Callendar's shoulder and Callendar looking over Arrhenius's. Keeling fully expects that there will be someone in fifty years looking over his shoulder. (By then the concentration of carbon dioxide in the atmosphere may be 600 parts per million.)

Keeling's concern about that far-off successor in the third millennium implies a faith that a long future does lie ahead. It also implies a strong sense of the millennial importance of his record. That might seem an arrogant presumption if he did not extend precisely the same

compliment to Callendar and even to Reiset, the Frenchman who became so obsessed with carbon dioxide more than a century ago that he
built a scientific chariot to measure it, and drove it through the streets
of Paris and the lanes of Ecorcheboeuf. If Keeling ever retires, he may
build a replica of Reiset's carbon-dioxide chariot and drive it through
Del Mar. Meanwhile his son Ralph has built a new instrument for measuring oxygen.

For those who read the record of the polar icecaps, time is even
more condensed. Two thousand pieces of ice are stored at the Physics
Institute of the University of Bern. The ice sits on shelves up and down
the walls of the subterranean Cold Rooms like rolled posters in a statio-
nery-store stockroom, or scrolls from the lost library of Alexandria.
Not long ago, at my request, a Swiss physicist pulled down one column
of ice. He slid it from its cardboard tube, opened the plastic bag inside,
and removed a small square piece of graph paper:

Tube 339
Dye 3181
From 1806.39m
To 1806.90m
B in 36.9

According to the laboratory's version of the Dewey Decimal System,
this ice had been pulled up from a point more than one mile down in
the Greenland ice sheet, near the U.S. Distant Early Warning Station
3 (known as Dye 3), where American radars scan the hard flat horizon for Soviet missiles. Holding the slip of paper, the physicist calculated for a moment in his head. "It's about . . . about 12,000 years
old."

The physicist cut an ice cube from the column of ice and carried it
out of the Cold Room and into his office. There he set it in a glass
beaker of water on the windowsill. We took turns putting our ears near
the mouth of the beaker. There was a quiet sound—a hissing. Ice from
the last Ice Age was melting and the walls of all of the bubbles trapped
inside it were bursting by the dozens.

The fresh air that rose from that beaker had not been breathed for
12,000 years. There were 5 million people on the planet then. They
were about to invent agriculture. They were about to light the long
fuse. On an office windowsill above the train tracks of the
Hauptbahnhof, in view of the northwest tangent of the Autobahn, the

breath of those 5 million human beings mingled with the breath of the 5 billion of the present moment. The air that rose from that beaker was the atmosphere of the planet Earth just before the beginning of one of the greatest experiments in the history of life. The concentration of carbon dioxide in the air was about 280 parts per million.

For ten thousand years, said the physicist, the concentration goes like this—drawing a long line in the air with his finger—"and then *waff!* Explosion!"

Trinity was a secret test in the desert. This is the most public experiment in history. It is a slow-motion explosion manufactured by every last man, woman, and child on the planet.

If we threw 5 gigatons of carbon into the air all in one place, all at one time, in a single great eruption, it would make a spectacle on the scale of the fireball that rose from the desert at Alamagordo. Dust and smoke would be entrained in it. Lightning would flicker through the dust. A pillar of fire would seem to extend higher into the sky and farther into the future than the eye can see.

At Trinity in the command bunker Oppenheimer remembered a line from the *Bhagavad-Gita:* "Now I am become Death, the destroyer of worlds." Oppenheimer's right-hand man Kenneth Bainbridge exclaimed, "Now we are all sons of bitches."

We do not respond to emergencies that unfold in slow motion. We do not respond adequately to the invisible. But we understand explosions. Five gigatons of carbon are the work of one year for the human sphere; or the work of one hundred Tamboras for the lithosphere. It would be a strange experience, watching five gigatons of carbon go up into the air. People meeting us afterward would see it in our faces. A physicist at Los Alamos watched the busloads of experimenters returning from Alamagordo: "I saw that something very grave and strong had happened to their whole outlook on the future."

Long after the winds had dispersed the cloud, it would linger in our minds. We would carry the sight with us like the witnesses in the desert. We would understand that the world will never be the same.

NOTES AND SOURCES

Page v "**THE MATTER AT HAND**" Francis Bacon, *The New Organon,* in *The New Organon and Related Writings,* ed. Fulton H. Anderson (Indianapolis: The Bobbs-Merrill Company, Inc., 1960): 29.

Chapter 1: The Question

Page 2 **ALL THE WAY TO MARS AND BACK** Star voyagers will need artificial EcoSpheres of formidable sophistication. Mars, the planet nearest Earth, is about 50 million miles away. Alpha Centauri, the star nearest our solar system, is about 25 thousand billion miles away—"not what we call spitting distance," as one astronomer notes.

Page 3 **MORE THAN FOUR BILLION YEARS OLD** Scientists estimate the age of our planet and our solar system by studying the state of decay of radioactive minerals. The technique is known as radiometric dating, or absolute dating. See, for instance, Lawrence Badash, "The Age-of-the-Earth Debate," *Scientific American* 261 (August 1989): 90–96.

Geologists believe that Earth formed as a molten ball about 4.5 billion years ago. They believe that the ball may have cooled enough for a crust to form within a few hundred million years. If so, the first lithosphere formed very roughly 4.2 billion years ago. Preston Cloud, "The Late Hadean Surface," in *Oasis in Space, Earth History from the Beginning* (New York: W.W. Norton & Company, 1988): 40–42.

Pages 3–4 **WATER AND AIR** See Cloud, "Sources of Air and Water?" in *Oasis:* 37–40.

Page 4 **VERNADSKY** Vladimir Vernadsky's *The Biosphere* was published in Russian in 1926, and in French in 1929. His book did not appear in English until 1986, when an abridged version was published by Synergetic Press, Inc., in Oracle, Arizona.

See also: G. Evelyn Hutchinson, "The Biosphere," *Scientific American* 223 (September 1970): 44–53.

Preston Cloud, "The Biosphere," *Scientific American* 249 (September 1983): 176–189.

Page 4 **THIN CONCENTRIC SHELLS** This is something like the view of the world in *The Creation, and the Expulsion of Adam and Eve from Paradise,* painted by Giovanni di Paolo in Siena about the year 1445. Di Paolo depicts the universe as a set of nesting concentric spheres. The brown, rocky sphere of earth sits in the center, surrounded by spheres of water, air, and fire. It is a cosmic bull's eye, afloat in what we would now describe as outer space.

In Di Paolo's painting, God appears to be pointing off sternly into space, while an angel shoves the first man and woman out of the garden.

Page 5 **THE FIRST TRACES** These ice ages were about as extensive as the series of ice ages that Earth has undergone during the last several million years, but lasted much longer. Geologists have discovered records of the Precambrian ice age across a large part of North America, from Wisconsin to Lake Superior to subarctic Canada. Cloud, "Oldest Extensive Ice Ages," in *Oasis:* 223–225.

Page 5 **"WITHOUT SERIOUS DISTORTION"** Charles J. Lumsden and Edward O. Wilson, *Promethean Fire, Reflections on the Origin of Mind* (Cambridge: Harvard University Press, 1983).

Page 5 **MAN THE DOUBLY WISE** More than one million years ago, there were people alive in Africa with bodies much like ours and with brains about as big as ours. However, they did not use their big brains—at least, not in ways that left a trace in the archaeological record. Then, quite suddenly, within the last 50,000 years, for reasons that remain mysterious, human beings began decorating themselves with jewelry, painting the walls of their caves, living together in bigger and bigger groups. Their behavior was so new that some anthropologists call them *Homo sapiens sapiens,* Man the Doubly Wise, to distinguish them from the older and simpler-living *Homo sapiens* (although the details are all highly controversial).

That was the great transition. It marked the emergence of mind—or, at least, the moment when mind began to change the world. The brain is a million years old but the human mind, as a geological force, was born only the day before yesterday.

John E. Pfeiffer, *The Emergence of Humankind,* 4th ed. (New York: Harper & Row, Publishers, 1985).

John E. Pfeiffer, *The Creative Explosion* (Ithaca, New York: Cornell University Press, 1982).

Page 5 **NOOSPHERE** Vladimir Vernadsky, "The Biosphere and the Noosphere," *American Scientist* (January 1945): 1–12.

Vernadsky died as the article went to press.

Page 11 **ECOSPHERES** For technical information about microcosms, see, for instance, Joe Hanson, "Analytics," in *The Biosphere Catalogue,* ed. Tango Parrish Snyder (London: Synergetic Press, 1985), pp. 175–183.

Claire E. Folsome and Joe A. Hanson, "The Emergence of Materially-closed-system Ecology," in *Ecosystem Theory and Application,* ed. Nicholas Polunin. Environmental Monographs and Symposia (New York: John Wiley & Sons Ltd., 1986): 269–288.

Dozens of Soviet technical papers have been translated into English by NASA. They are available through the U.S. Government Office of Documents. See, for instance, S. Starikovich, 1975, "A Month Alone with Chlorella) (NASA TT F–16463); A. Mashinskiy and G. Nechitaylo, 1983, "Birth of Space Plant Growing" (NASA TM–77244); and I.I. Gitel'zon, 1977, "Problems of Creating Biotechnical Systems of Human Life Support" (NASA TT F–17533).

For a popular account see Carl Sagan, "The World That Came in the Mail," *Parade* (December 7, 1986): 10–12.

I first read about EcoSpheres in Peter Warshall, "The EcoSphere," *Whole Earth Review* (May 1985): 28–31.

Chapter 2: Minute Particulars

Page 15 "BREAKFAST CEREALS CRISPER" Charles D. Keeling, "A Chemist Thinks about the Future." Professor's Inaugural Lecture, Scripps Institution of Oceanography, May 29, 1969. Reprinted in *Archives of Environmental Health* 20 (June 1970): 764–777.

Page 16 VAN HELMONT Stephen Toulmin and June Goodfield, *The Architecture of Matter* (Chicago: The University of Chicago Press, 1962): 150–156.

Page 17 JOSEPH BLACK Henry Guerlac, "Joseph Black and Fixed Air: A Bicentenary Retrospective, with Some New or Little Known Material," *Isis* 48 (1957): 124–151, 433–456.

Page 18 AMONG THOSE WHO TRIED E.A. Letts and R.F. Blake, "The Carbonic Anhydride of the Atmosphere," *Scientific Proceedings of the Royal Dublin Society* 9 (March 1900): 107–119.

Page 18 REISET Jean Reiset, *"Recherches sur la proportion de l'acide carbonique dans l'air,"* Comptes Rendus 90 (1880): 1144–1148.

Reiset, *"Proportion de l'acide carbonique dans l'air: réponse à M. Marie-Davy."* Letter in *Comptes Rendus* 90 (1880): 1457–1459.

Keeling and one of his students have reviewed the nineteenth century attempts to measure carbon dioxide. Keeling thinks Reiset's measurements were the best. Eric From and Charles D. Keeling, "Reassessment of late 19th century atmospheric carbon dioxide variations in the air of western Europe and the British Isles based on an unpublished analysis of contemporary air masses by G.S. Callendar," *Tellus* 38B (1986): 87–105.

Page 19 KURT BUCH Kurt Buch, *"Der Kohlendioxydgehalt der Luft als Indikator der meteorologischen Luftqualität,"* Eripainos Geophysica 3 (1948): 63–79. Cited by Charles D. Keeling, "The concentration and isotopic abundances of atmospheric carbon dioxide in rural areas," *Geochimica et Cosmochimica Acta* 13 (1958): 322–334.

Page 21 **KEELING ROSE FOR AIR** Robert Clayton, now a well-known geo-chemist at the University of Chicago, took some of the late-night samples after saying good night to a girl who lived across the street from the laboratory.

Page 22 **HE SAW A PATTERN** The daily rise and fall of carbon dioxide had been observed before. Indeed it is so pronounced that it was detected by one of the first scientists to measure carbon dioxide in the nineteenth century, De Saussure the younger, who considered it "one of the most remarkable results" of his career, although he never established its existence un-equivocally.

The diurnal rise and fall of the gas was confirmed by a young British investigator in 1879. George Frederick Armstrong spent all summer and most of that autumn measuring the gas in a garden in Grasmere, England. The weather was "of an exceptionally wet and sunless character," his report notes stoically. Indeed, although he had planned to make gas mea-surements every day and every night, "the weather proved such as to render this, if not impracticable, at least undesirable owing to the diffi-culty, especially at midnight, of filling the jars with air in the open without at the same time admitting a few drops of rain also, even although the greatest care was used in the operation." G.F. Armstrong, "On the Diur-nal Variation in the Amount of Carbon Dioxide in the Air," *Proceedings of the Royal Society* 30 (1880): 343–355.

My chart of the daily rise and fall of carbon dioxide in the air at Yosemite is adapted from Charles D. Keeling, "The concentration and isotopic abundances of atmospheric carbon dioxide in rural areas," *Geochimica et Cosmochimica Acta* 13 (1958): 326.

Page 23 **DOORS OPEN AT SUNRISE** As long as the leaf has enough water. The stomata are designed to conserve water, and they close during the day when necessary.

Chapter 3: Keeling's Curve

Page 26 **"SO IT COMETH OFTEN"** Francis Bacon, *The Works of Francis Bacon, Lord Chancellor of England.* A new edition: with a life of the author, ed. Basil Montagu (Philadelphia: Parry & McMillan, 1854), vol-ume I: 188.

Page 26 **NOBODY WAS WORRIED** The history of this field awaits full-length treatment. The best review to date is Roger Revelle, "The Scientific His-tory of Carbon Dioxide," in E.T. Sundquist and W.S. Broecker, ed., *The Carbon Cycle and Atmospheric CO_2: Natural Variations Archean to Pres-ent,* Geophysical Monograph 32 (Washington, D.C.: American Geo-physical Union, 1985): 1–4.

Revelle's review is a skeleton key to the literature.

Page 26 **FOURIER WAS THE FIRST** Fourier called the question of global tem-peratures "one of the most important and most difficult in all natural philosophy." J.B. Fourier, *Memoires de l'Academie Royale des Sciences de l'Institut de France* 7 (1827): 569. Cited by V. Ramanathan, "The Greenhouse Theory of Climate Change: A Test by an Inadvertent Experiment," *Science* 240 (15 April 1988): 293–298.

Page 26 **TYNDALL ANALYZED THE GASES** Tyndall noted that slight changes in the concentration of any of the greenhouse gases in the atmosphere "must produce a change of climate." Indeed, he wrote, such changes "may have produced all the mutations of climate which the researches of geologists reveal."

John Tyndall, *The London, Edinburgh, and Dublin Philosophical Magazine and Journal of Science* (September 1861): 169–194, 273–285.

Page 29 **ARRHENIUS EXPLAINED IT** Svante Arrhenius, "On the Influence of Carbonic Acid in the Air upon the Temperature of the Ground," *The London, Edinburgh, and Dublin Philosophical Magazine and Journal of Science* (April 1896): 237–276.

Page 30 **CALLENDAR FOUND HINTS** George S. Callendar, "The Artificial Production of Carbon Dioxide and Its Influence on Temperature," *Quarterly Journal of the Royal Meteorological Society* 64 (1938): 223–240.

Callendar never won many converts. The measurements that were available to him were so poor and uneven that he could not prove that the carbon-dioxide gas concentration was actually rising. See, for instance, the discussion that followed his presentation to the Royal Society in 1938. According to the minutes: "Mr. J.H. Coste congratulated Mr. Callendar on his courage and perseverance. He would like to raise some practical issues. Firstly, was the CO_2 in the air really increasing? It used to be given as .04%, then as methods of chemical analysis improved it went down to .03%, and he thought it was very doubtful whether the differences which Mr. Callendar made use of were real."

Page 30 **THEY SUMMED UP** Roger Revelle and Hans E. Suess, "Carbon Dioxide Exchange Between Atmosphere and Ocean and the Question of an Increase in Atmospheric CO_2 during the Past Decades," *Tellus* 9 (1957): 18–27.

Revelle provides this gloss:

"Callendar was claiming that carbon dioxide might be building up in the atmosphere. The question was really whether most of the carbon dioxide would go into the ocean or not.

"There's about sixty times more carbon dioxide in the ocean as there is in the atmosphere. Most people thought that 59/60ths of the carbon dioxide emissions of the industrial age would go into the ocean, and only about one sixtieth would stay in the atmosphere. Hans Suess and I thought about this. What we showed in our paper was that because of the chemistry of seawater, which provides a buffer mechanism, about half the carbon dioxide would stay in the atmosphere, and only half would go into the water. This is known as the Revelle Effect. (It was really my idea. Hans didn't quite understand the buffer mechanism.)"

Page 30 **WHEN KEELING CAME DOWN** In writing about Keeling's early work I used three principal sources: interviews with Keeling, Roger Revelle, and colleagues; the unpublished notes for an autobiographical lecture that Keeling presented at the American Geophysical Union's winter meeting in San Francisco on December 10, 1982; and a brief memoir written by Keeling: "The Influence of Mauna Loa Observatory on the Development of Atmospheric CO_2 Research," in *Mauna Loa Observatory, a 20th Anniversary Report*, ed. John Miller (U.S. Department of Commerce: NOAA Special Report, 1978): 36–54.

Page 32 **A NEW KIND OF ANALYZER** Keeling's was not the first carbon-dioxide network. An eminent Swedish meteorologist, Carl Gustav Rossby, had already established a full-fledged network in Scandinavia in the mid-1950s. Unfortunately Rossby's network relied upon the methods of the old carbon-dioxide gatherer Kurt Buch. These methods were simple and cheap but yielded numbers as unreliable as those of the nineteenth century.

Naturally Rossby, who took part in the planning of the I.G.Y., had misgivings about the unknown post-doc Keeling and his extravagant plans.

"I had a chance to meet him just once at an I.G.Y. planning meeting at Scripps during 1956," Keeling writes. "Someone pointed me out to him across a grass lawn during a recess. As he walked up to greet me, he remarked for the benefit of some nearby acquaintances, 'Ah . . . za yong man wiz za machine.'" Keeling (1978): 39.

Page 33 **"I BECAME ANXIOUS"** Keeling (1978): 40.

Page 34 **FIRST YEAR'S DATA** My chart of the rise and fall of carbon dioxide at Mauna Loa Observatory is adapted from C.D. Keeling, "The Influence of Mauna Loa Observatory": 49.

Page 35 **THE BREATHING OF THE PLANET** "Breathing may not be precisely the right word," Keeling notes, "but it is the best we have. The word comes from the Indo-European root 'to boil up, to foam up.' So it is already far removed from its original meaning. To push it a little further won't do much harm. The breathing of water, of plants, of planets—why not? Let's stick with the word. We just have to clarify what we mean by breathing in each case."

It is a beautiful (if invisible) fact of nature that the forest breathes once a day and the biosphere once a year. As Thoreau says in *Walden*, "The day is an epitome of the year. The night is the winter, the morning and evening are the spring and fall, and the noon is the summer."

Page 35 **THERE IT WAS** Keeling, "The Concentration and Isotopic Abundances of Carbon Dioxide in the Atmosphere," *Tellus* 12 (1960): 200–203.

Page 35 **PERSONALLY RESPONSIBLE** In his professor's inaugural address at Scripps, Keeling said, of the carbon dioxide rise, "I am, in a sense, responsible [for it] by proving its existence scientifically." Keeling (1970): 766.

Page 36 THE KEELING CURVE Actually this is just one small piece of the Keeling curve, which begins in the year 1958 and will extend as far into the future as human beings are concerned about their atmosphere. My chart is adapted from Keeling, "Influence of Mauna Loa": 50.

Page 36 BIGGER AND BIGGER This chart exaggerates the trend to make it stand out. Drawn to scale, the change in the breathing of the world does not look like much. Nevertheless it is significant.

The biosphere inhales and exhales about 100 billion tons of carbon each year. The amplitude of these breaths increased by almost 20 percent between the years 1958 and 1982. So this is a huge global change.

R. Bacastow, C.D. Keeling, et al., "Seasonal amplitude increase in atmospheric CO_2 concentration at Mauna Loa, Hawaii, 1959–1982," *Journal of Geophysical Research* 90 (1985): 10,529–10,540.

Page 37 PICKED UP A COPEPOD Winona B. Vernberg, Bruce C. Coull, et al., "Reliability of Laboratory Metabolic Measurements of Meiofauna," *Journal of the Fisheries Resources Board of Canada* 34 (1977): 164–167.

Page 37 HIGHER AND HIGHER If the experimenters did not throw the copepod a grain of sand, the flailing creature's respiration rate would rise by more than 50 percent. The breathing rate would not relax until the copepod had thrashed itself to death. Vernberg, Coull, et al. (1977): 165.

Page 37 IN OUR OWN BACKYARDS R.A. Houghton, "Terrestrial Metabolism and Atmospheric CO_2 Concentrations," *BioScience* 37 (1987): 672.

Page 38 SOMETHING ELSE IS GOING ON R.A. Houghton, "Biotic Changes Consistent with the Increased Seasonal Amplitude of Atmospheric CO_2 Concentrations," *Journal of Geophysical Research* 92 (1987): 4223–4230.

Chapter 4: Atropos

Page 39 "WE HAVE CONSTRUCTED A FATE" Henry David Thoreau, *Walden and other writings of Henry David Thoreau,* ed. Brooks Atkinson (New York: Random House, Modern Library Edition, 1975): 107.

Page 39 THE LOGICAL THING Keeling, "Industrial production of carbon dioxide from fossil fuels and limestome," *Tellus* 25 (1973): 174–198.

Compiling the world's annual industrial statistics and translating them into carbon dioxide is complicated. The job was done for years by Ralph Rotty, of the Institute for Energy Analysis, in Oak Ridge, Tennessee. When Rotty died in the Spring of 1988, his assistant Gregg Marland took over.

Page 40 IN THAT SINGLE YEAR Keeling's figure for that year would have been even higher if he had not subtracted some of the overenthusiastic coal production reports that were issued during China's Great Leap Forward.

Page 40 **FIVE BILLION TONS** Five billion tons of pure carbon. Of course, when all this carbon enters the atmosphere, each atom of carbon becomes a molecule of carbon dioxide, CO_2, by combining with two atoms of oxygen.

To translate carbon statistics into carbon dioxide statistics, multiply by 3.664. For example, each human being on the planet today is shovelling more than one ton of carbon into the air each year. Each ton of carbon becomes 3.664 tons of carbon dioxide gas.

Collectively the human population is shovelling more than 5 billion tons of carbon into the air each year by burning fossil fuels. Five billion tons of carbon represents more than 18 billion tons of carbon dioxide gas.

Page 40 **DATA FOR THE 1860S** This economic data had been compiled by researchers at the U.N. and had already been published in a table by Revelle and Suess. Keeling revised the conversion factors that Revelle and Suess had used, and translated the data into carbon dioxide emissions.

Page 40 **MORE THAN 76 BILLION TONS** See, for instance: William C. Clark, ed., *Carbon Dioxide Review: 1982* (New York: Oxford University Press, 1982): 459.

The atmosphere now contains a total of about 750 billion tons of carbon. The total mass of the atmosphere is about 5,662,000,000 tons. K.E. Trenberth, "Seasonal Variations in Global Sea-Level Pressure and the Total Mass of the Atmosphere," *Journal of Geophysical Research* 86 (1981): 5238–5246.

Page 41 **ONE HUNDRED TAMBORAS** Haraldur Sigurdsson, personal communication.

Actually, most of the carbon dioxide gas from the lithosphere does not arise from volcanic eruptions on land; rather, it bubbles up from volcanic vents on the floor of the sea. David Des Marais, a scientist at NASA's Ames Research Center, in Mountain View, California, estimates that about 90 percent of the carbon dioxide from the lithosphere comes from the seafloor: approximately 30 to 35 million tons of carbon per year. Again, that contribution is paltry compared to the human sphere's production of 5 *billion* tons of carbon per year. (Personal communication.)

Measurements of the lithosphere's total volcanic emissions are very uncertain and controversial. However, all estimates agree that the lithosphere releases one hundred or one thousand times less carbon dioxide each year than the human sphere does. See Steven W. Leavitt, "Annual Volcanic Carbon Dioxide Emission: An Estimate from Eruption Chronologies," *Environmental Geology* 4 (1982): 15–21.

Thus carbon dioxide from volcanoes is unlikely to matter much to the man on the street in the next one hundred years. However, volcanoes probably can and do influence our climate through their emissions of *sulfur,* as explained in Chapter 7. In the short term (for Earth scientists the next one hundred years is short term), it is this volcanic sulfur that may make a difference. (See, for example, Haraldur Sigurdsson, "Volcanic Pollution and Climate: The 1783 Laki Eruption," *Eos* 63 (August 10, 1982): 601–602.

Page 41 **THE FIRST FOSSIL FUELS** Eugene Ayres, "The Age of Fossil Fuels," in *Man's Role in Changing the Face of the Earth* (Chicago: The University of Chicago Press, 1956): 367–381.

Page 42 **THE SWISS BURN** For instance, the Swiss burned 1.8 tons of carbon per person in 1986. That year, American citizens burned almost three times as much, 5.1 tons.

The most profligate nation on Earth was East Germany: that year, the Germans burned through 5.5 tons of carbon per person. The Soviets burned 3.6 tons per person. The Chinese burned only .5 tons. Bangladeshis burned the least of all: .03 tons per person. (Data from the Carbon Dioxide Information Analysis Center of the U.S. Department of Energy.)

Page 43 **THE NORTHERN HEMISPHERE IS ALWAYS LADEN** See, for instance, Keeling, "Atmospheric and Oceanographic Measurements Needed for Establishment of Data Base." On page 19, the mean annual concentration of carbon dioxide in the atmosphere in the years 1962, 1968, and 1980 is displayed latitude by latitude. In *The Potential Effects of Carbon Dioxide-Induced Climatic Changes in Alaska,* Proceedings of a conference, Fairbanks, Alaska, April 7–8, 1982 (School of Agriculture and Land Resources Management, University of Alaska, Fairbanks, Miscellaneous Publications 83–1, 1984): 11–22.

Page 43 **THEY DEBATE HOW MUCH** This debate has sometimes been bitter and personal. Specialists in the biosphere tend to believe that most of the gas is going into the hydrosphere; but specialists in the hydrosphere tend to think that most of the gas is going into the biosphere. Sphere against sphere. It is a messy problem and its solution may require a decade of careful international monitoring of all seven spheres.

Page 44 **"WE ARE ALL MORIBUND"** The text of Joseph Brodsky's address was published in *The New York Times Book Review* (12 June 1988): 25.

Page 45 **LINGER IN THE AIR** See, for instance, R.T. Watson, M.A. Geller, et al., "Present State of Knowledge of the Upper Atmosphere: An Assessment Report" (NASA Reference Publication 1162, May 1986): 7.

William K. Stevens, "With Cloudy Crystal Balls, Scientists Race to Assess Global Warming," *The New York Times* (7 February 1989).

Page 45 **THOMAS MIDGLEY** Edward Farber, *Great Chemists* (New York: Interscience Publishers, 1961): 1595.

Page 45 **GREW BY SIXTEEN TIMES** *Scientific American* (December 1935).

Page 45 **TWENTY PERCENT A YEAR** The chlorofluorocarbon industry's annual production figures were compiled by the Chemical Manufacturers Association, in Washington, D.C.

Page 46 A QUIRK OF NATURE As long ago as 1975, Ramanathan warned that CFCs might change the climate of the planet. V. Ramanathan, "Greenhouse Effect Due to Chlorofluorocarbons: Climatic Implications," *Science* 190 (3 October 1975): 50–51.

However, the problem was something of a sleeper until Ramanathan and colleagues published a longer warning about trace gases in 1985. V. Ramanathan, R.J. Cicerone, et al., "Trace Gas Trends and Their Potential Role in Climatic Change," *Journal of Geophysical Research* 90 (20 June 1985): 5547–5566.

Page 46 MIDGLEY'S TWO INVENTIONS Robert E. Dickinson and Ralph J. Cicerone, "Future global warming from atmospheric trace gases," *Nature* 319 (9 January 1986): 109–115.

Page 47 BY 1989, THE HUNDREDTH ANNIVERSARY Data from the Chemical Manufacturers Association.

Amy Ng and Clair Patterson, "Natural concentrations of lead in ancient Arctic and Antarctic ice," *Geochimica et Cosmochimica Acta* 45 (1981): 2109–2121.

David A. Peel, "Is lead pollution of the atmosphere a global problem?" *Nature* 323 (18 September 1986): 200.

Claude F. Boutron and Clair C. Patterson, "Lead concentration changes in Antarctic ice during the Wisconsin/Holocene transition," *Nature* 323 (18 September 1986): 222–225.

Page 47 METHANE IS ALSO D.H. Ehhalt, "Methane in the Global Atmosphere," *Environment* 27 (December 1985): 6–12, 30–33.

Ralph J. Cicerone, testimony presented to the U.S. Senate Committee on Environment and Public Works, Subcommittee on Toxic Substances and Environmental Oversight, Washington, D.C. (10 December 1985).

A recent study found that about 21 percent of the methane in the atmosphere today came from fossil carbon. M. Wahlen, N. Tanaka, et al., "Carbon-14 in Methane Sources and in Atmospheric Methane: The Contributions from Fossil Carbon," *Science* 245 (21 July 1989): 286.

Page 49 HOLLAND TUNNEL "Heart Disease of Tunnel Officers Studied," *The New York Times* (19 April 1987).

Page 50 A PAPER TIGER Cicerone, Senate testimony: 7–8.

Page 52 THE CONTINENT SIMPLY EXPLODED *Encyclopaedia Britannica*, 15th ed., s.v. "Colonialism (c. 1450–c. 1970)" and "Migration, Human."

Herbert Moller, ed., *Population Movements in Modern European History* (New York: Macmillan Co., 1964).

Maldwyn Allen Jones, *American Immigration*, Chicago History of American Civilization, Daniel J. Boorstin, ed. (Chicago: The University of Chicago Press, 1960).

Page 52 THIRTY-THREE MILLION . . . ARRIVED IN THE U.S. Frank Thistlethwaite, "Migration from Europe Overseas in the Nineteenth and Twentieth Centuries," in Moller, *Population Movements:* 74.

Page 52 **TRIPLED SINCE 1850** Clark (1982): 45.

Page 52 **LEVELED OFF IN EUROPE** Europe's population is now about 500 million. At present rates, its numbers will not double again for 266 years, according to projections of the Population Reference Bureau, in Washington, D.C.

Page 52 **A THOUSAND SHIPS** Jones (1960): 103.

Page 52 **HUMAN CARGO** Emigrants "were essentially valuable bulk cargo for unused shipping space in raw cotton or timber ships on the return voyage," one historian notes. They were part of the vast trade that bound America and Europe into a single Atlantic economy. Thistlethwaite (1964): 84–85.

Page 53 **WOODSMEN MARCHED WEST** John T. Curtis, "The Modification of Mid-latitude Grasslands and Forests by Man," in *Man's Role:* 721–736.

Page 53 **DESOLATE "BARRENS"** For a pictorial history see John Eastman, "The Ghost Forest." Eastman documents that "nineteenth-century logging left Michigan's vast pine tracts stripped, stumped, and subject to fire." *Natural History* (January 1986): 10–16.

Page 53 **THOREAU DOUBTED** Henry David Thoreau, *Walden and Other Writings of Henry David Thoreau,* ed. Brooks Atkinson (New York: Random House, Modern Library Edition, 1975): 83–84, 104–111.

Page 53 **THE RAILROADS' HEYDAY** Jones (1960): 189.

Page 53 **MILES OF RAILROADS** George P. Marsh, *The Earth as Modified by Human Action: A New Edition of Man and Nature* (New York: Scribner, Armstrong, 1874): 356.

Page 53 **"HERE GOES LUMBER"** Thoreau: 108–109.
   A bit of wood and two nails from the Walden cabin are on display at the Concord Lyceum. The rest of Thoreau's pine boards and lapped shingles have long since turned to carbon dioxide.

Page 53 **100,000 YOUNG EVERGREEN TREES** Marsh: 357.

Page 53 **"LUCIFER MATCHES"** Marsh: 356–357.

Page 54 **JOHN T. CURTIS** Curtis, *Modification:* 721–736.

Page 54 **IN AN UNBROKEN FOREST** J.S. Olson, J.A. Watts, et al., "Carbon in Live Vegetation of Major World Ecosystems." These data are presented in a four-color poster, "Major World Ecosystem Complexes Ranked by Carbon in Live Vegetation," distributed with Clark (1982).

Page 55 **A SMALL LEGACY** While a tree is young and growing, much of the carbon it pulls out of the air goes to build its trunk and branches. This carbon will not return to the air until the tree dies.
   Once the tree has reached full height, however, most of the carbon that it extracts from the atmosphere goes into green leaves or evergreen nee-

dles. Most of that carbon goes right back into the air when the leaves and needles fall. Even then, however, a little of the carbon will not return to the air for a long time: it is buried in the thick duff of the forest floor.

Page 55 "THE PIONEER EXPLOSION" A.T. Wilson, "Pioneer agriculture explosion and CO_2 levels in the atmosphere," *Nature* 273 (4 May 1978): 40–41.

R.A. Houghton, J.E. Hobbie, et al., "Changes in the Carbon Content of Terrestrial Biota and Soils Between 1860 and 1980: A Net Release of CO_2 to the Atmosphere," *Ecological Monographs* 53 (1983): 235–262.

Page 55 THE GRAND TOTAL We sometimes forget how new the age of fossil fuels really is. Only in this century did the human sphere begin burning more fossil fuels than wood. That crossover date is highly uncertain: It could have been as early as 1900 or as late as 1970. Keeling (personal communication).

Page 55 COLLISION COURSE When the Pioneer Explosion began, the world had been locked in a long cool period, sometimes called the Little Ice Age. Soon after the clearing and burning started, the Little Ice Age thawed. The temperature of the planet kept rising, and in the 1930s in the American Midwest, the Dust Bowl lifted farmers' soils (loosened by relentless clearing and plowing) and spilled them clear across the continent on hot dry winds.

In Wilson's paper about the Pioneer Explosion he suggests that the carbon from the explosion "provided a mechanism" to end the global cool spell and start the global warm spell.

If that is true, then the greenhouse effect had already begun to warp the weather of the world in the 1930s, and the Dust Bowl was its epic signal.

However, climate experts do not believe that is true. They agree with Wilson that the pioneer effect was huge, but they doubt it could have twisted the global climate as early as 1880 or 1930. The loading of the atmosphere with greenhouse gases provides a *delayed-reaction* mechanism. We probably have not felt the effects of the Pioneer Explosion yet; we may be about to experience the impact of the explosion only now.

Page 55 SECOND PHASE When did the first Pioneer Explosion end and the second explosion begin? As a historical marker we might use the date when the world began burning more tropical forests than temperate forests. According to Houghton, that crossover occurred some time in the 1930s. Since then, the rate of forest burning in the tropics has risen steeply while the rate of burning in the temperate zones has fallen steeply. Houghton (personal communication).

Page 56 BRAZIL, INDONESIA . . . These twelve nations released the most carbon into the atmosphere through deforestation in the year 1980. They are listed in order by the amount of carbon they released. Houghton (personal communication).

Page 56 IMPORTER IS JAPAN "Japan gobbles up nearly half the world's tropical timber trade, much of the imports being wasted on disposable chopsticks (11,000 million pairs a year) and panelling for concrete." David Swinbanks, "Japan faces both ways on timber conservation in tropical forests," *Nature* 362 (9 April 1987): 537.

Page 56 TWICE AS BIG The exact amount of carbon that is released into the air by deforestation is highly controversial. Some scientists believe that global deforestation is now releasing about one billion tons of carbon per year, which would make our present Pioneer Explosion about twice the size of the first one.

However, George Woodwell, Houghton, and colleagues argue that our explosion may be releasing more than that. R.A. Houghton, R.D. Boone, et al., "The flux of carbon from terrestrial ecosystems to the atmosphere in 1980 due to changes in land use: geographic distribution of the global flux," *Tellus* 39B (1987): 122–139.

Woodwell, Houghton, and others believe that by the end of the 1980s the second pioneer explosion was releasing about 3 billion tons of carbon per year. R.A. Houghton (personal communication).

The uncertainties could be narrowed through comprehensive satellite monitoring, but money for such studies is hard to come by. (See Chapter 11.)

Houghton adds that in nineteenth-century America, "as farmers moved west and cleared great chunks of forest, they were abandoning New England. So great hunks of forest in the East were growing back. . . . The East lost a lot of farmers and their farms went back to forests. That's one reason the first pioneer explosion wasn't as big as ours, if you define the explosion as the net contribution of carbon to the atmosphere.

"Nowadays there aren't very many places where forests are growing back, in the tropics."

Page 56 ATROPOS Thoreau (1975): 105. *Walden* is prophetic on the theme of steam engines: "If all were as it seems, and men made the elements their servants for noble ends! If the cloud that hangs over the engine were the perspiration of heroic deeds, or as beneficent as that which floats over the farmer's fields, then the elements and Nature herself would cheerfully accompany men on their errands and be their escort."

Chapter 5: A Slow Eureka

Page 57 "OMENS WERE AS NOTHING" Joseph Conrad, "Typhoon," in *Typhoon and Other Tales* (New York: New American Library, 1962): 251.

Page 57 WELCOMED THE HEAT Svante Arrhenius, *Worlds in the Making,* H. Borns, trans. (New York: Harper & Brothers Publishers, 1908): 63.

Page 57 TEMPERATURE WAS ALREADY RISING Callendar (1938).

Page 57 "A LARGE-SCALE GEOPHYSICAL EXPERIMENT" Revelle and Suess (1957): 19–20.

Page 58 "EVOLUTION OF AN AWARENESS" William W. Kellogg, "Man's Impact on Climate: The Evolution of an Awareness," *Climatic Change* 10 (1987): 113–136.

Page 58 A REMARKABLE FORECAST Arrhenius (1896).

Page 59 TABLE OF PREDICTIONS Arrhenius (1896), p. 266.

Page 59 ONE OF THE FIRST Syukuro Manabe and Richard T. Wetherald, "Thermal Equilibrium of the Atmosphere with a Given Distribution of Relative Humidity," *Journal of the Atmospheric Sciences* 24 (May 1967): 241–258.

Page 59 A SCALE MODEL OF THE EARTH For a popular description of the art of computer modeling, read "The Twin Earth: Computer Models of Weather and Climate," in Stephen H. Schneider and Randi Londer, *The Coevolution of Climate and Life* (San Francisco: Sierra Club Books, 1984): 205–221.

This book contains clear and lively introductions to virtually every subject in climatology.

Page 60 SIMPLIFY THEIR TWIN EARTH "Modelers using full-fledged G.C.M.'s almost never can find the time or money to run them out for as long as a century," notes J. Murray Mitchell. "It is only the very much simplified versions of such models, which Gerald North [one of their champions, now at Texas A&M University] likes to call 'educational toys,' that are actually run for the equivalent of centuries or millennia."

Page 61 "DIRTY CRYSTAL BALLS" Scientists are forced "to gaze into a very dirty crystal ball," writes Stephen Schneider: "but the tough judgment to be made here is precisely how long we should clean the glass before acting on what we believe we see inside." Stephen Schneider with L.E. Mesirow, *The Genesis Strategy: Climate and Global Survival* (New York: Plenum, 1976): 149.

Page 62 THE GOLDILOCKS PROBLEM See, for example, James J. Kasting, Owen B. Toon, et al., "How Climate Evolved on the Terrestrial Planets," *Scientific American* 258 (February 1988): 90–97.

Page 63 TOO HOT TO SINK Don Anderson, "Where on Earth Is the Crust?" *Physics Today* 42 (March 1989): 43.

Page 64 JUST TRYING TO FIND OUT MORE ABOUT ICE Chester Langway, Jr. (personal communication). Langway was one of the pioneering U.S. ice-drillers.

A few years before the I.G.Y., scientists had tried to recover old air samples from icebergs. But that was a false start. P.F. Scholander, E.A. Hemmingsen, et al., "Composition of Gas Bubbles in Greenland Icebergs," *Journal of Glaciology* 3 (March 1961): 813–822.

Ice-drilling really got started during the I.G.Y. See, for instance, Henri Bader, "United States Polar Ice and Snow Studies in the International Geophysical Year," in *Geophysics and the IGY,* American Geophysical Union Publication No. 590 (Baltimore: The Lord Baltimore Press, Inc. 1958): 177–181.

C.C. Langway, Jr., H. Oeschger, et al., "The Greenland Ice Sheet Program in Perspective," in *Greenland Ice Core: Geophysics, Geochemistry, and the Environment.* Geophysical Monograph 33. (Washington: American Geophysical Union, 1985.)

Langway has published a technical monograph on the early ice-core results. C.C. Langway, Jr., "Stratigraphic Analysis of a Deep Ice Core from Greenland," Research Report 77 (Cold Regions Research and Engineering Laboratory, Hanover, New Hampshire, May 1967).

Page 64 SUDDEN BRIGHTENING AND DIMMING Ice experts can use the isotope beryllium-10 in the ice as an indicator of what the Sun was doing each year for the last 150,000 years. See, for instance, G.M. Raisbeck, F. Yiou, et al., "Evidence for two intervals of enhanced 10Be deposition in Antarctic ice during the last glacial period," *Nature* 326 (19 March 1987): 273–277.

Page 64 SANTORINI, EXPLODING C.U. Hammer, H.B. Clausen, et al., "The Minoan eruption of Santorini in Greece dated to 1645 B.C.?" *Nature* 328 (6 August 1987): 517–519.

Experts in ice-cores and experts in tree rings are now debating the exact date. "Dating of the Santorini eruption." Stuart W. Manning; C.U. Hammer, et al., an exchange of letters, *Nature* 332 (31 March 1988): 401–402.

Page 65 THE AMOUNT OF LEAD IN THE AIR Claude F. Boutron and Clair C. Patterson, "Lead concentration changes in Antarctic ice during the Wisconsin/Holocene transition," *Nature* 323 (18 September 1986): 222–225.

Page 65 SULFATE AND NITRATE P.A. Mayewski, W.B. Lyons, et al., "Sulfate and Nitrate Concentrations from a South Greenland Ice Core," *Science* (23 May 1986): 975–977.

Page 65 10 PERCENT OF THE VOLUME Hitoshi Shoji and Chester C. Langway, Jr., "Air hydrate inclusions in fresh ice core," *Nature* 298 (5 August 1982): 548–550.

Page 65 UNCERTAINTY CLOUDED THE SUBJECT See, for instance, the exchange between John Bonner and Harrison Brown in Richard P. Schuster, ed., *The Next Ninety Years* (Pasadena: California Institute of Technology Press, 1967): 171–172.

Page 66 FOUND A RELIABLE TECHNIQUE Ernst Moor and Bernhard Stauffer, "A New Dry Extraction System for Gases in Ice," *Journal of Glaciology* 30 (1984). The data have been cross-checked by two world-class rival laboratories. J.M. Barnola and D. Raynaud; A. Neftel and H. Oeschger, "Comparison of CO_2 measurements by two laboratories on air from bubbles in polar ice," *Nature* 303 (2 June 1983).

Page 66 MORE THAN SIX MILES LONG Chester Langway, Jr., personal communication.

Page 66 "RATHER SENSITIVE" Bernhard Stauffer.

Page 66 SIPLE A. Neftel, E. Moor, et al., "Evidence from polar ice cores for the increase in atmospheric CO_2 in the past two centuries," *Nature* 315 (2 May 1985): 45–47.

The Siple ice-core confirms the Pioneer Explosion of carbon dioxide in the nineteenth century. After other signals in the ice have been subtracted, what is left is a big bump representing forests burning and timber rotting in New York, Michigan, Wyoming, Maine, Canada. U. Siegenthaler and H. Oeschger, "Biospheric CO_2 emissions during the past 200 years reconstructed by deconvolution of ice core data," *Tellus* 39B (1987): 140–154.

Page 67 CHARTS My charts of the rise of carbon dioxide in the atmosphere since 1750 are adapted from two sources:
Neftel, Moor, et al., "Evidence from polar ice cores": 45.
Wallace S. Broecker, *How to Build a Habitable Planet* (Palisades, N.Y.: Eldigio Press, 1985): 262.

Page 67 VOSTOK J. Jouzel, C. Lorius, et al., "Vostok ice core: a continuous isotope temperature record over the last climatic cycle (160,000 years)," *Nature* 329 (1–7 October 1987): 403–408.
J.M. Barnola, D. Raynaud, et al., "Vostok ice core provides 160,000-year record of atmospheric CO_2," *Nature* 329 (1–7 October 1987): 408–414.
C. Genthon, J.M. Barnola, et al., "Vostok ice core: climatic response to CO_2 and orbital forcing changes over the last climatic cycle," *Nature* 329 (1–7 October 1987): 414–418.

Page 68 "THESE TEDIOUS CALCULATIONS" Arrhenius (1896): 267.
T.C. Chamberlain, "A Group of Hypotheses Bearing on Climatic Changes," *The Journal of Geology* (October–November 1897): 653–683.

Page 68 THAT IS WHAT EXCITED It is not surprising that these scientists were haunted by the spectre of the Ice Age. The discovery of ice ages was then very new. Louis Agassiz had announced his Ice Age theory in 1837. In each succeeding decade of the nineteenth century, geologists had unearthed more evidence that the extraordinary really had happened: a significant part of the Earth's surface had been buried by ice sheets one mile high within recent geological memory.

By the time Arrhenius and Chamberlin turned their attention to carbon dioxide and the greenhouse effect, scientists were aware that they might be living in a brief intermission in a long series of ice ages. Yet they did not know when the ice sheets had last retreated or when they might come back. Meanwhile the Little Ice Age cast a chill shadow over their century.

All things considered it was natural for Tyndall, Arrhenius, and Chamberlin to be more interested in global coolings than global warmings.

Today geologists know more about the cause and timing of ice ages. According to their best estimates, the next ice age is not scheduled to arrive for many thousands, perhaps even tens of thousands, of years. It is on its way, but there seems to be plenty of time for a long hot spell first.

Page 68 **CHART** My chart of the rise and fall of carbon dioxide over the past 160,000 years is adapted from Barnola, Raynaud, et al., "Vostok ice core provides 160,000-year record": 410.

Page 69 **CHART** My chart of the rise and fall of Earth's temperature over the past 160,000 years is adapted from Barnola, Raynaud, et al., "Vostok ice core provides 160,000-year record": 410.

Page 69 **"TOO NICE"** Oeschger (personal communication).

Page 69 **MASTER SWITCH** Other greenhouse gases are switches, too. The data bank in the ice-cores has revealed that not only carbon dioxide but also methane has gone up and down with global temperatures.

B. Stauffer, E. Lochbronner, et al., "Methane concentration in the glacial atmosphere was only half that of the preindustrial Holocene." *Nature* 332 (28 April 1988): 812–814.

B. Stauffer, G. Fischer, et al., "Increase of Atmospheric Methane Recorded in Antarctic Ice Core," *Science* 229 (27 September 1985): 1386–1388.

M.A. Khalil and R.A. Rasmussen, "Atmospheric Methane: Trends Over the Last 10,000 Years," *Atmospheric Environment* 21 (1987): 2445–2452.

Page 69 **MANABE DECIDED TO PLUG IT IN** One of the most convincing aspects of this experiment is that it produces a *global* ice age: it chills both hemispheres at once. Other theories of the cause of ice ages are able to cool only one hemisphere at a time. A.J. Broccoli and S. Manabe, "The influence of continental ice, atmospheric CO_2, and land albedo on the climate of the last glacial maximum," *Climate Dynamics* 1 (1987): 87–99.

Page 70 **RELUCTANT TO LEAVE THE LYRICAL** See Carson's correspondence with E.B. White, quoted in Frank Graham, Jr., *Since Silent Spring* (Boston: Houghton Mifflin Co., 1970): 18–19.

Page 70 **"CAN ANYONE BELIEVE"** Rachel Carson, *Silent Spring* (Cambridge, Massachusetts: The Riverside Press, 1962): 7–8.

Page 70 **"CONTAMINATION OF AIR"** Carson (1962): 6.

Page 71 **A LUCKY SIDE-EFFECT** Callendar wrote:
"In conclusion it may be said that the combustion of fossil fuel, whether it be peat from the surface or oil from 10,000 feet below, is likely to prove beneficial to mankind in several ways, besides the provision of heat and

power. For instance the above mentioned small increases of mean temperature would be important at the northern margins of cultivation, and the growth of favourably situated plants is directly proportional to the carbon dioxide pressure. In any case the return of the deadly glaciers should be delayed indefinitely.

"As regards the reserves of fuel," Callendar adds, cheerfully, "these would be sufficient to give at least ten times as much carbon dioxide as there is in the air at present." Callendar (1938): 236.

Page 71 "OPEN THE BACK OF YOUR WATCH" Barry Commoner, *The Closing Circle* (New York: Alfred A. Knopf, Inc. 1971): 41–42.

Page 72 "WE OFTEN HEAR LAMENTATIONS" Arrhenius (1908): 63.

Page 72 TEMPERATURES WERE RISING My charts of the rise in Earth's temperature since 1880 are adapted from J. Hansen and S. Lebedeff, "Global Surface Air Temperatures: Update Through 1987", *Geophysical Research Letters* 15 (1987): 323–326.

Page 73 A THOUSAND GREMLINS Schneider (1984): 276.

Page 73 WE MAY NEVER KNOW Schneider, personal communication.

Page 73 THE CIA REPORT The report ends with a plea for more long-range climate forecasting. "Only a few academic centers in the United States are engaged in training personnel in this field, which suggests we have a limited chance of solving the Intelligence Community's problem unless decisive action is taken."

"A Study of Climatological Research as it Pertains to Intelligence Problems." A working paper prepared by the Office of Research and Development of the Central Intelligence Agency (August, 1974).

Copies of this curious document are available to the public through the Photoduplication Service of the U.S. Library of Congress.

Page 73 "CHALK ON A WHITE WALL" K.M. Meyer-Abich, University of Essen, FRG. Cited in Gene E. Likens, ed., *Some Perspectives of the Major Biogeochemical Cycles* (New York: John Wiley & Sons, 1981). See also: Meyer-Abich, K.M., "Chalk on the White Wall? On the Transformation of Climatological Facts into Political Facts," in J. Ausubel and A.K. Biswas, ed., *Climatic Constraints and Human Activities*, IIASA Proceedings Series 10 (Elmsford, N.Y.: Pergamon Press, 1980).

Page 74 WIGLEY P.D. Jones, T.M.L. Wigley, et al., "Global temperature variations between 1861 and 1984," *Nature* 322 (1986): 430–434.

Page 74 HANSEN James Hansen and Sergej Lebedeff, "Global trends of measured surface air temperature," *Journal of Geophysical Research* 92 (20 November 1987): 13,345–13,372.

Page 74 NORTHERN AND SOUTHERN HEMISPHERES P.D. Jones, T.M.L. Wigley, et al., "Evidence for global warming in the past decade," *Nature* 332 (28 April 1988): 790.

Page 75 RANGE OF UNCERTAINTY Here we are talking not about forecasting but hindcasting: predicting how much Earth's temperature should have gone up in the last one hundred years, given the greenhouse gases we have put into the air.

Conservative computer models—those that are relatively insensitive to the concentration of greenhouse gases—predict that the globe should have warmed only slightly. Sensitive models predict that the globe should have warmed more radically.

By this test, the conservative models are the best, since Earth has warmed only about one-half of one degree C. in the past one hundred years. However, this hindcasting test may say little about what Earth will do next.

Suppose you preheat an oven to 450° F. and put in a roast. It is easy enough to predict how hot the meat will get eventually: 450°. But how fast will the meat's surface temperature rise during the first five minutes in the oven? To answer that question you would need to know a lot about that piece of meat. You would have to make a study of what climate experts would call the roast's "thermal inertia." Even then you could predict one hour ahead better than five minutes ahead.

Now, suppose you did not preheat the oven. Instead you turned up the dial very, very slowly toward 450°, and someone else opened and closed the oven door a few times while you weren't looking. Predicting the meat's temperature five minutes ahead would be almost hopeless; but you could still predict one hour ahead about as reliably as before.

With Planet Earth, we have been injecting greenhouse gases into the atmosphere at a slowly accelerating rate for the past 250 years, with most of the action in the last three decades. It is as if we have been turning up the dial slowly at first, then faster and faster for all that time (and we are still turning it up today). How long will it take the planet to catch up with the dial? We do not know; but we know we are cooking the planet.

In this respect, then, computer models are more reliable about Earth's temperature the farther ahead they look. The long-term forecast is a very different and very much easier problem than the short-term forecast and the hindcast. This point may seem paradoxical but it is nothing more than common sense to those who study the weather. The theoretical meteorologist Edward Lorenz has explained it this way: it is easier to make a precise long-range forecast than a precise short-range forecast of the temperature of a cup of coffee. "We might have trouble forecasting the temperature of the coffee one minute in advance," Lorenz once told a gathering of his colleagues, "but we should have little difficulty in forecasting it an hour ahead." Quoted by James Gleick, *Chaos* (New York: Viking Penguin Inc. 1987): 25.

In sum, climate models' forecasts for the twenty-first century are probably more reliable than their hindcasts for the twentieth century. The models can say more about the next one hundred years than the next ten years.

Page 75 **AMBIGUITIES** Many weather stations that once stood in rural areas have been engulfed by growing towns and cities. And towns and cities tend to be warmer places than farms and forests (climate experts call them "heat islands"). "A growing city is a wonderful device for keeping itself warm," J. Murray Mitchell explains. "Manhattan Island reached a cross-over point some years ago: on a typical winter day, more heat is released to the streets of New York by space heating and vehicles than by the Sun!"

Thousands of weather stations recorded warmer temperatures in the twentieth century because of the heat-island effect. In some of the Sun Belt cities in the American West, the rise of temperature that can be attributed to the urban heat island is as much as one-third of one degree C. per decade. In Eastern cities the rise is more than one-tenth of one degree C. per decade. Thomas R. Karl and Robert G. Quayle, "Climate Change in Fact and in Theory: Are We Collecting the Facts?" *Climatic Change* 13 (1988): 5–17.

On average, between the years 1941 and 1980, North American weather stations located in cities warmed about one-tenth of one degree C. per decade more than stations in the countryside. G. Kukla, J. Gavin, et al., "Urban Warming," *Journal of Climate and Applied Meteorology* 25 (September 1986): 1265–1270.

Even small towns with populations under 10,000 can be heat islands, according to Thomas R. Karl, of the National Climatic Data Center, in Asheville, North Carolina, and colleagues. Thomas R. Karl, Henry F. Diaz, et al., "Urbanization: Its Detection and Effect in the United States Climate Record," *Journal of Climate* 1 (November 1988): 1099–1123.

Nevertheless, even after climate experts subtract all these confusing local effects from their records, the planet is definitely warming. The East Anglia group calculates that the heat-island effect accounts for only about one-tenth of one degree C. of the warming of the past one hundred years. P.D. Jones, P.M. Kelly, et al., "The effect of urban warming on the Northern Hemisphere temperature average," *Journal of Climate* 2 (March 1989): 285–290.

Karl, who is one of the sternest critics of the long-term records, thinks the ambiguities in the weather-stations' measurements can account for two-tenths of one degree at most. Even Karl has no doubt that Earth has grown hotter in the last one hundred years. "We're not that far off," he told me in the fall of 1988.

"It's a matter of adjusting the rate of rise, not questioning the rise itself," Karl explained to a reporter from *Science* in 1989. Richard Kerr, "The Global Warming Is Real," *Science* 243 (3 February 1989): 603.

Page 76 **2200 REQUESTS** D.E. Reichle, et al., "Environmental Sciences Division Annual Progress Report for Period Ending September 30, 1986," ORNL–6327 (Oak Ridge, Tennessee: Oak Ridge National Laboratory, 1987): 81.

Page 76 **HARD TO DENY NOW** Quoted by Philip Shabecoff, "Temperature for World Rises Sharply in the 1980's," *The New York Times* (29 March 1988).

Page 76 **MARK SCHOEBERL** Cited by Richard A. Kerr, "Is the Greenhouse Here?" *Science* 239 (5 February 1988): 559–561.

Page 77 **CONSISTENT WITH THE PREDICTIONS** Since then, other trends have been discovered that are consistent with the predictions (although they, too, *could* be a coincidence):

Satellite data show that the world's seas grew warmer by about a tenth of a degree C. per year for most of the 1980s. A.E. Strong, "Greater global warming revealed by satellite-derived sea-surface-temperature trends," *Science* 338 (20 April 1989): 642–645.

The continents have gotten wetter in the last few decades, which is another prediction of greenhouse models: Hotter seas lead to more evaporation. Henry F. Diaz, et al., *Journal of Geophysical Research* (20 January 1989).

The extent of polar sea ice shrank by 6 percent between the years 1973 and 1988. That, too, makes sense, in warmer and warmer seas. Per Gloersen and William J. Campbell, *Journal of Geophysical Research* (15 September 1988). Cited by R. Monastersky, "Shrinking ice may mean warmer earth," *Science News* 134 (8 October 1988): 230–231.

Page 77 **FIRST TIME IN . . . THREE-QUARTERS OF A CENTURY** S.S. Jacobs, D.R. Macayeal, et al., "The Recent Advance of the Ross Ice Shelf, Antarctica," *Journal of Glaciology* 32 (1986): 464–473.

Page 77 **COOL AND CONSERVATIVE** "The harmless nature of the iceberg floats inadvertently in its official name: B9," wrote one unflappable geophysist, after the giant calf had drifted from the Ross Ice Shelf, *Eos* (1 December 1987).

Page 77 **JACOBS TOLD REPORTERS** S.S. Jacobs, personal communication.

Page 77 **ANTIQUE LEAVES** F. Ian Woodward, "Stomatal numbers are sensitive to increase in CO_2 from pre-industrial levels," *Nature* (18 June 1987): 617–618.

Page 78 **WOODWARD'S LATEST FINDINGS** Personal communication.

Page 79 **BOREHOLES OF OIL WELLS** Arthur H. Lachenbruch and B. Vaughn Marshall, "Changing Climate: Geothermal Evidence from Permafrost in the Alaskan Arctic," *Science* 234 (7 November 1986): 689–696.

Page 79 **THE CENTER STAFF** A clarification: At the time, Houghton and Stone worked at the Ecosystems Center of the Marine Biological Laboratory (M.B.L.), in Woods Hole. Soon afterward, both men moved across the village to the Woods Hole Research Center (W.H.R.C.), whose director is the ecologist George Woodwell. Neither the M.B.L. nor the

W.H.R.C. is affiliated with the Woods Hole Oceanographic Institution (W.H.O.I.).

Page 79 AN ADDED NIGHTMARE A few years ago the ecologist W.D. Billings and colleagues carefully extracted pieces of frozen arctic tundra at Barrow, Alaska, and ran controlled experiments on the tundra samples in the laboratory. When the investigators doubled the temperature, simulating what Alaskan summers may be like in the twenty-first century, the tundra was able to breathe in only half as much carbon dioxide as before. Lowering the water table even very slightly had a similar effect.

The ecologists concluded that a warming in the far north could change the whole of the vast tundra "from a sink for atmospheric carbon dioxide to a source." W.D. Billings, J.O. Luken, et al., "Arctic Tundra: A Source or Sink for Atmospheric Carbon Dioxide in a Changing Environment?" *Oecologia* 53 (1982): 7–11.

Page 80 CHART My chart of the age of fossil fuels, seen in a 50,000-year perspective, is adapted from M. King Hubbert, "Energy from Fossil Fuels," *Science* 109 (1949): 108.

Page 81 "BEGAN TO UNDRESS HIMSELF" E.A.W. Budge, *The Rise and Progress of Assyriology*. Cited in Edmond Sollberger, *The Babylonian Legend of the Flood* (London: The Trustees of the British Museum, 1971): 11–12.

According to Sollberger, "Smith's startling revelations made such a sensation that the Proprietors of the *Daily Telegraph* promptly offered one thousand guineas in order to enable him to go to Nineveh and bring back more texts." The *Telegraph* got its money's worth. Smith unearthed more tablets and more of the Deluge story.

Page 81 AT LAST HE PRODUCED A PAPER Keeling (1960).

Page 82 LOCAL LEGEND Bernard Mendonca, "The First Twenty Years: An Unscientific Remembrance," in Miller, ed., *Mauna Loa Observatory* (1978): 17–23.

Page 83 "I WAS TERRIFIED" Ulf Merbold, in Kevin W. Kelley, ed., *The Home Planet* (Reading, Massachusetts: Addison-Wesley Publishing Company, 1988).

Page 83 "LIST SIX UNKNOWN SUBSTANCES" Cited in Lydia Dotto and Harold Schiff, *The Ozone War* (Garden City, N.Y.: Doubleday & Company, 1978).

Page 86 CHART A single human breath puts a spike in the Mauna Loa carbon-dioxide record. This is one small part of the very long line that has been traced on scrolls of paper by Keeling's old gas analyzers at Mauna Loa since 1958. Source: John Chin, Mauna Loa Observatory.

Chapter 6: The First Summer of the Third Millennium

Page 87 "NO LAW OF HISTORY" Tom Wolfe, "A Eulogy for the Twentieth Century," *American Spectator* (December 1987).

Page 87 **HIGH FOR THE DAY** Data from the U.S. National Weather Service.

Page 87 **"I'VE SOLD DEMOS"** The salesman wasn't being mean: smart talk like that is sympathy in New York. Sam Howe Verhovek, "Stoics Give In, Air Conditioners Sell Out," *The New York Times* (15 August 1988).

And it wasn't only New York. After two hot years in a row, air conditioners were selling out all over the Northeast and Midwest. Doron P. Levin, "An Industry Overcome by the Heat," *The New York Times* (19 August 1988).

Page 87 **VIOLENT CRIME** "Bloodiest Weekend," New York *Daily News* (12 July 1988). "11 Killed in 2nd Wave of Weekend Violence," New York *Newsday* (11 July 1988).

Page 88 **TOWNS IN IOWA FOLDED** Dennis Farney, "Losing Ground: In Iowa, the Drought Might Seal the Fate of the Smallest Towns," *The Wall Street Journal* (30 August 1988).

Page 88 **WORST FOREST FIRES** Figures from the U.S. Forest Service. Cited in David S. Wilson, "Worst Forest Fire Year Appears to Be at an End," *The New York Times* (20 November 1988).

Page 88 **CONVICTS . . . WERE FLOWN IN** "Crews Fighting the West's Fires Are Reinforced," *The New York Times* (23 August 1988).

One helicopter attack (or "Helitac") crew contained a dozen firefighters, "all convicted drug dealers, burglars or armed robbers." David S. Wilson, "Young Inmates Form Airborne Firefighter Force," *The New York Times* (23 August 1988).

Page 88 **BIG RIVERS . . . RUNNING LOW** The combined flow of the three largest rivers in the continental U.S.—the Mississippi, St. Lawrence, and Columbia—was cut almost in half that June. It was their lowest flow in sixty years of records. "95% of Nation's Large Rivers Flow Below Normal During Drought," *Eos* (20 September 1988): 858.

Page 88 **SHIPWRECKS** Tanya Barrientos, "Drought brings buried riverboats to surface," *Philadelphia Inquirer,* 26 July 1988.

Frederick Way, Jr., *Way's Packet Directory 1848–1983* (Athens, Ohio: Omaha University Press, 1983).

Page 88 **WHEAT DIED** John F. Burns. "Drought Also Lays Waste to Canada," *The New York Times* (3 August 1988).

Craig Whitney, "Harvest in Russia Worst in 3 Years," *The New York Times* (17 January 1989).

Page 88 **CHINA LOST . . . 10,000 PEOPLE** Edward A. Gargan, "Flash Floods and Drought Ravage China," *The New York Times* (3 August 1988).

Page 88 **SHANGHAI IN JULY** United Press International, "Heat wave grips south China," *The Philadelphia Inquirer* (21 July 1988).

Page 88 **HURRICANE GILBERT** Joseph B. Treaster, "Battered Jamaica Begins to Rebuild," *The New York Times* (16 September 1988).

Page 88 **FLOODS IN NIGERIA** Brian Killen, "Sub-Saharan rain inflicting misery," *Philadelphia Inquirer* (20 August 1988).

Page 88 **300,000 TONS OF FOOD** United Press International, "U.N. agency appeals to nations for food to meet emergencies," *Philadelphia Inquirer* (21 September 1988).

Page 88 **WORST SINCE THE 1930S** "Drought Advisory 88/12, Summary of Conditions and Impacts," NOAA Climate Analysis Center (29 September 1988).
"Worst Drought Since '36 Spurs Climate Research," *Eos* (12 July 1988): 715.

Page 88 **TOPSOIL BLOWING AWAY** "The dust clouds were so dark you could see them ten miles away," said one young farmer in North Dakota. William Robbins, "Dry Soil Blows Away, Carrying Hope with It," *The New York Times* (7 August 1988).

Page 88 **KANSAS CITY ROYALS** Barbara Rudolph, "The Drought's Food-Chain Reaction," *Time* (11 July 1988): 40.

Page 89 **"DUST IN THE AIR SUSPENDED"** T.S. Eliot published "Little Gidding" in 1943 as part of his "Four Quartets."

Page 89 **PITCHERS BEAN BATTERS** Gregory Byrne, "Putting Heat on the Ball," *Science* 242 (28 October 1988): 518.

Page 89 **"FEVER & AGUE ANTIDOTE"** Barrientos, "Buried Riverboats."

Page 89 **"REMEMBER THIS DAY"** John L. Moore, "Bad Days at 'Big Dry.'" *The New York Times Magazine* (14 August 1988): 26.

Page 89 **"EXCESSIVE HEAT CONTINUED"** National Weather Service. Quoted in *Natural History* (January 1989): 43.

Page 89 **HARVARD CANCELLED . . . CLASSES** "Harvard and Its Ivy Wilt in Heat Wave," *The New York Times* (6 August 1988).

Page 90 **TWO HUNDRED MURDERS** Drug wars and the long hot summer combined to make 1988 the worst year for murders in the history of New York City. David E. Pitt, "New York City Nears Record for Slayings," *The New York Times* (22 November 1988).
Ralph Blumenthal, "Record Year For Murder in New York," *The New York Times* (26 December 1988).

Page 90 **AIR CONDITIONERS** Randolph E. Schmid, "Aug. heat pushed up electric costs," *Philadelphia Inquirer* (14 September 1988).
This was quite a jump, even compared with the long hot summer of '87. "Excess Cooling Costs in August: 154 Million," *The New York Times* (20 September 1987).

Page 90 **"RAIN INSURANCE"** "Sale of Rain Insurance Strong, Much to the Insurer's Regret," *The New York Times* (15 August 1988).

Page 90 **MAKE UP FOR LOST CORN** Dan Gillmor, "Off-Season Crop for Seed Corn," *The New York Times* (23 August 1989).

Page 90 **"THE SKIES TURNED RED"** William Wilkinson, *Memorials of the Minnesota Forest Fires in the Year 1894* (Crown Litho. 1895). Excerpted in *Natural History* (January 1989): 54–55.

Page 90 **HALF A TON PER ACRE** James S. Clark, "The Forest Is for Burning," *Natural History* (January 1989): 51–53.

The article is part of an excellent special section, "The Long, Hot Summer of '88." In writing about the North American drought, I used every article in this section.

Page 91 **MILLENNIAL SUNSETS** Dirk Johnson, "Forest Fires Cast a Persistent Pall on Much of West," *The New York Times* (12 September 1988).

Page 91 **NUCLEAR MISSILE SILO** Actually, the fire, which was in the Lewis and Clark National Forest in Great Falls, came even closer than a mile of the silo. Charles Rodgers, Logistics Support Coordinator, National Forest Service, Region 1: Aviation and Fire Management, personal communication.

Page 91 **A HARDY WEED** "Tobacco, weed that it is, is a survivor," one farmer explained. "Most of the time it's going to live even when the grass withers." William Robbins, "Hardy Survivor in Year of Drought," *The New York Times* (8 September 1988).

Page 91 **A GOOD SUMMER FOR ACCU-WEATHER** Patrick Houston, "Weather Forecasters Enjoy Boom," *The New York Times* (18 July 1988).

Page 91 **GOOD FOR ENVIRONMENTAL GROUPS** Clifford D. May, "Pollution Ills Stir Support for Environmental Groups," *The New York Times* (21 August 1988).

Page 91 **AIR CONDITIONERS** Doron P. Levin, "An Industry Overcome by the Heat."

Page 91 **BUSY SUMMER FOR HAACK** Robert A. Haack and William J. Mattson, "They Nibbled While the Forest Burned," *Natural History* (January 1989): 56–57.

Page 91 **VIRGIN PRAIRIE** Robert H. Mohlenbrock, "Some Plants Slept," *Natural History* (January 1989): 58–60.

Page 92 **GOOD FOR SPIDER MITES** Gene Meyer, "U.S. soybean crop diminished by drought-driven insects," *Kansas City Times* (9 September 1988).

Page 92 **SHARPEST ONE-YEAR DROP** In that year, according to the agricultural economist Lester R. Brown, "The U.S. grain harvest fell below domestic consumption, probably for the first time in history." Brown, "Reexamining the World Food Prospect," in Brown, et al., *State of the World 1989* (New York: W.W. Norton, 1989): 41–58.

The summer was bad for all three major food-producing countries.

Brown says, "The Chinese crop was down by 3 percent, the Soviet Union's by 9 percent, and the United States' by 30 percent." Brown, "Our Winter of Disquiet," in *Worldwatch* 2 (May/June 1989): 2.

Page 92 SOYBEAN FARMER Marlise Simons, "Soybeans Change the Face of Brazil," *The New York Times* (25 July 1988).

Randall Hackley, "Argentina and Brazil harvesting a bonanza from the U.S. drought," *Philadelphia Inquirer* (23 July 1988).

Page 92 IN ONE SPOT William Robbins, "Despite Scorched Earth and Parched Crops, Pockets of Plenty Can Be Found," *The New York Times* (13 September 1988).

Page 92 BLACK HUMOR Roger L. Welsch, "Dry Humor," *Natural History* (January 1989): 70–71.

Page 92 101 DEGREES DOWNTOWN According to the U.S. National Climatic Data Center, the high for the day was a mere 98° F. at Washington National Airport. In the city, however, the hot concrete, asphalt, steel, and marble around the Capitol Dome raised the temperature a few degrees more—the urban heat-island effect.

Page 93 RECORD OF THE PROCEEDINGS *Greenhouse Effect and Global Climate Change,* Hearing before the Committee on Energy and Natural Resources, U.S. Senate, June 23, 1988 (Washington: U.S. Government Printing Office, 1988).

Page 94 THEN HE SAID IT Hansen's celebrated statement appears on page 40 of the official transcript. I have corrected a few small mistakes in the transcription.

Page 94 RIGHT ABOUT THE HEADLINES Philip Shabecoff, "Global Warming Has Begun, Expert Tells Senate," *The New York Times* (24 June 1988): 1.

Michael Weisskopf, "Scientist: Greenhouse Effect at Work," *Philadelphia Inquirer* (25 June 1988): 1.

"Another long hot summer: The greenhouse effect is here," lead editorial, *Providence Journal* (28 June 1988).

Page 94 "BUT 'DESTINED'" Bill McKibben, "Is the World Getting Hotter?", *New York Review of Books* (8 December 1988): 7.

Page 94 "SENSE OF FOREBODING" Frank Trippett, "Talking About the Weather," *Time* (15 August 1988): 20.

Page 94 "THOSE WHO THINK" Excerpts from the text of Bush's speech were reprinted in *The New York Times* (24 September 1988).

Page 95 "SHIFT OF TECTONIC PLATES" Hearings, p. 31.

Page 95 RINGING DECLARATION Hearings, p. 153.

Page 96 "A ONE-HANDED SCIENTIST" Quoted by Victor Cohn, *News & Numbers* (Ames, Iowa: Iowa State University Press, 1984): 98.

Page 97 **HANSEN WAS GLAD** Shabecoff, "Global Warming Begun."

Page 98 **THE METAPHOR OF DICE** See, for instance, Stephen H. Schneider, "Doing Something About the Weather," *World Monitor* (December 1988): 28–37.

Page 98 **"ABSOLUTELY SURE"** Schneider, "Doing Something," p. 35.

Page 98 **PHOTO FINISH** R. Monastersky, "'88 Set Warm Record; '89 Looks Cooler," *Science News* 135 (11 February 1989): 84–85.
Richard A. Kerr, "1988 Ties for Warmest Year," *Science* (17 February 1989): 891.

Page 98 **MADDOX RE-EXPLAINED** John Maddox, "Jumping the greenhouse gun," *Nature* 334 (7 July 1988): 9.

Page 99 **TRENBERTH'S ANALYSIS** Kevin E. Trenberth, Grant W. Branstator, et al., "Origins of the 1988 North American Drought," *Science* 242 (23 December 1988): 1640–1645.
For a helpful diagram of these global weather connections see William K. Stevens, "Scientists Link '88 Drought to Natural Cycle in Tropical Pacific," *The New York Times* (3 January 1989).

Page 101 **"I'M DENYING IT'S HERE"** Associated Press. "Scientists dispute 'greenhouse' claims," *St. Paul Pioneer Dispatch,* 8 December 1988.
Namias repeated this argument the following spring. "One thing, however, is absolutely clear," he wrote. "The drought was a consequence of normal atmospheric variability, and has no connection whatever with the greenhouse effect." Jerome Namias, "Cold waters and hot summers," *Nature* 338 (2 March 1989): 15–16.

Page 101 **SERVED AS RAPPORTEUR** W. Kellogg (personal communication).

Page 102 **"I'VE GIVEN THAT NUMBER"** J. M. Mitchell.

Page 102 **START AN ICE AGE** Imbrie and Imbrie, *Ice Ages*: 11.

Page 103 **A CLIMATE OUTSIDE THE EXPERIENCE** For the history of Earth's climate in a nutshell see "Climate History of the Earth: The Last Million Years," in Clark, *Carbon Dioxide Review* (1982): 447–449.
There are excellent charts of the temperature record of the past 100, 1,000, 10,000, and 850,000 years in Samuel W. Matthews, "What's Happening to Our Climate?" *National Geographic* (November 1976): 614–615.
For a chart of the temperature record on longer time-scales, tens of millions of years, see Preston Cloud, *Oasis in Space* (New York: W.W. Norton & Company, 1988): 417. For a rough chart of the climate history of the planet since its birth see Schneider and Londer, *Coevolution:* 15.

Page 103 **MANABE LISTS** Personal communication. See also Syukuro Manabe, "Carbon Dioxide and Climatic Change," *Advances in Geophysics* 25 (San Diego: Academic Press, Inc., 1983): 39–82.

Page 105 **REVELLE HAS POINTED OUT** Esther: Wanning, "Interview: Roger Revelle," *Omni* (March 1984).

Page 105 **ROBERTS** Walter Orr Roberts, "It Is Time to Prepare for Global Climate Changes," *Conservation Foundation Letter* (April 1983): 1–8.

Page 105 **"SNOW WILL MELT"** Manabe (personal communication). Manabe also stressed this point in his Senate testimony on June 23, 1988. Hearings, pp. 105–107.
See also: S. Manabe and R.T. Wetherald, "Reduction in Summer Soil Wetness Induced by an Increase in Atmospheric Carbon Dioxide," *Science* 232 (2 May 1986): 626–628.

Page 105 **WESTERN RIVERS . . . OVERDRAWN** Roger Revelle, "Carbon Dioxide and World Climate," *Scientific American* 247 (August 1982): 35–43.
The American West's vulnerability to drought has been studied in most detail by the climate expert Peter Gleick. See, for example, P.H. Gleick, "Regional Hydrologic Consequences of Increases in Atmospheric CO_2 and other Trace Gases," *Climatic Change* 10 (1987): 137–160.

Page 106 **WARMING . . . THE CORN BELT** Linda Mearns, Richard W. Katz, et al., "Extreme High-Temperature Events: Changes in their Probabilities with Changes in Mean Temperature," *Journal of Climate and Applied Meteorology* 23 (December 1984): 1601–1613.

Page 106 **HEAT WAVES IN WASHINGTON** Robert H. Boyle, "Forecast for Disaster," *Sports Illustrated* 67 (16 November 1987): 79.

Page 106 **INCREASE IN INTENSITY** Kerry A. Emanuel, "The dependence of hurricane intensity on climate," *Nature* 326 (2 April 1987): 483–485.

Page 107 **SWARMS OF LOCUSTS** Ian Simpson, "African locust swarms invade the Caribbean," *Philadelphia Inquirer* (22 October 1988).

Page 107 **HOW THE JEWS GOT TO EGYPT** The applied mathematician Philip J. Davis, of Brown University, made this point to me during a wide-ranging talk about the hazards of predicting the future.

Page 107 **"ABOUT FOUR INCHES HIGHER"** It is even trickier to measure a global rise in sea level than to measure a global rise in temperature. As happens so often on this planet, trends in one sphere can obscure trends in another.
During the last ice age, for example, there was so much ice in the northern hemisphere that in the far north the ice actually depressed the crust. Geophysicists call the geometric shape of the planet the *geoid*. The Ice Age dented the geoid. It left the whole planet slightly pear-shaped.
Now that so much of the ice is gone, the crust is (very slowly) bouncing back. Alaska and Scandinavia, which bore such a heavy burden of ice twenty thousand years ago, are now rising about 2 millimeters a year.
With parts of the continents sinking and other parts rising, it is as if scientists were trying to measure the average height of the sea from

seven large rocks, each of them tilting and wobbling. It is very hard to spot the signal in the noise.

The best effort to date suggests that sea level is now rising by about 2.5 millimeters per year, give or take a millimeter. "This signal could constitute an indication of global climate warming," the investigators say. W.R. Peltier and A.M. Tushingham, "Global Sea Level Rise and the Greenhouse Effect: Might They Be Connected?" *Science* 244 (19 May 1989): 806–810.

For quick reviews of these findings see "Rising seas may herald global warming," *Science News* 135 (10 June 1989): 367. "Identifying the Sea Level Signal: Surf's Up," *Eos* (4 April 1989): 209.

Page 107 SMALL GLOBAL CHANGES GET MAGNIFIED My favorite example is the coral island of Okinotorishima, which is Japan's southernmost territory. At high tide, two rocks that poke a few tens of centimeters above sea level are all that is left of Okinotorishima. In 1988, the Japanese began a quarter-of-a-billion-dollar operation to save the island by building protective walls around the rocks. If the rocks go under, according to David Swinbanks, of *Nature*, "Japan will lose about 400,000 square kilometers of its 200-mile exclusive economic zone and with it all rights to fishing and minerals in the area." A high price to pay for a small rise in sea level. Swinbanks, "Saving Japanese rocks out at sea," *Nature* 333 (9 June 1988): 487.

Page 108 "I CAN'T UNDERSTAND IT" Queen Juliana is quoted in D.H. Meadows and J.M. Robinson, *The Electronic Oracle, Computer Models and Social Decisions* (New York: John Wiley & Sons, 1985): 1.

Page 108 A ROOF HELD UP BY A FEW PILLARS Ann Henderson-Sellers and Kendall McGuffie, "The threat from melting ice caps," *New Scientist* (12 June 1986): 24–25.

Page 108 HALF THE STATE OF FLORIDA Revelle, "Carbon Dioxide and World Climate": 40.

Page 109 CITY BUILDINGS HAVE AN AVERAGE HALF-LIFE Revelle, "Carbon Dioxide and World Climate": 40.

Page 109 SURPRISINGLY FAST ACTION Glenn A. Jones and Lloyd D. Keigwin, "Evidence from Fram Strait (78 degrees N) for early glaciation," *Nature* 336 (3 November 1988): 56–59.

Page 109 INJECTED THE HUBBERT SPIKE C.D. Keeling and R.B. Bacastow, "Impact of Industrial Gases on Climate," in *Energy and Climate,* Report of Panel on Energy and Climate (Washington, D.C.: National Academy of Sciences, 1977): 72–95.

My first chart of the Hubbert blip shows the impact of fossil fuels on Earth's atmosphere, seen in a 50,000-year perspective. Adapted from Hubbert, "Energy": 108.

My second chart shows the way the carbon dioxide from the burning of these fuels is likely to linger in the atmosphere. Adapted from C.D. Keeling and R.B. Bacastow, "Impact of Industrial Gases on Climate," in *Energy and Climate* (Washington, D.C.: National Academy of Sciences, 1977): 82.

Page 110 APRÈS NOUS LE DELUGE The East Antarctic ice sheet contains the equivalent of a 55-meter rise in sea level; the Greenland ice sheet, 8 meters; the West Antarctic ice sheet, 5 or 6 meters. Henderson-Sellers and McGuffie, "The Threat": 24.

The authors calculate that a rise of 10 meters would engulf more than 10 million square kilometers of land, "flooding a total land area greater than that of either the United States or China."

Page 111 NUMBERS LIKE THESE In the Summer of '88, the average summer temperature was 73.4° F. By contrast, the average summer temperature (averaged across the whole of the continental United States for a century of summers) is 71.8° F. Thus the Summer of '88 represented a rise of only 1.6° F.

This rise was enough to make the Summer of '88 the third hottest summer in the historical record (which extends back to 1895). The hottest summer in the record is 1936 (the worst year of the Dust Bowl). In the summer of '36 the average temperature was 74.33° F. The second hottest summer in the record is 1934, another Dust Bowl year. It averaged 73.93° F.

The *coldest* summer in the record is 1915, at 69.53° F.

So the difference between the coldest and hottest summers in this century (so far) is 4.8° F. What current climate models are suggesting is that the average temperature of all four seasons on this continent is going to warm by perhaps 9° F. If that is true, within the next few decades the typical summer on this continent will be hot enough to make the Summer of '88 look colder than the Summer of '15.

These temperature statistics come from Richard Heim, a meteorologist at the National Climatic Data Center in Asheville, N.C. (Heim describes his job as "putting current climate anomalies in the U.S. into historical perspective.") Personal communication.

Page 111 THE NEXT TWENTY ROLLS Schneider and Manabe (personal communication).

Page 111 SOVIETS CAN HOPE TO COME OUT WINNERS Certainly that is what Budyko, dean of Soviet climatologists, seems to think. In 1988, Budyko represented the Soviet state committee for hydrometeorology at one of the many international conferences that were held on the greenhouse effect that year, "Climate and Development," in Hamburg. Most of the talk at the conference concerned global eco-strategy: how to get the nations of the world to reduce carbon-dioxide emissions. But Budyko spoke of the good things the greenhouse gases may do for agriculture in the tundra. One delegate said afterward that Budyko's arguments were received "like swearing in the church."

Christine McGourty, "Global warming becomes an international political issue," *Nature* 336 (17 November 1988): 194.

Page 112 **"THEREFORE, I CHARGE YOU"** Dante Alighieri, Canto 20, "The Inferno," translated by John Ciardi (New Brunswick: Rutgers University Press, 1954): 178.

Chapter 7: The Seven Spheres

Page 113 **"IF THE ALMIGHTY"** Alfonso X (Alfonso the Wise) was complaining about the complexity of Ptolemy's astronomy. There are a few different versions of his epigram in circulation. This one is quoted by Jessica Tuchman Matthews, "Global Climate Change: Toward a Greenhouse Policy," *Issues in Science and Technology* 3 (1987): 58.

Page 114 **THE ICE EXPANDS** For detailed data, and for a series of spectacular satellite images of the expansion and contraction of the ice sheet, see Claire L. Parkinson, Josefino C. Comiso, et al., *Arctic Sea Ice, 1973–1976: Satellite Passive-Microwave Observations* (Washington, D.C.: National Aeronautics and Space Administration, 1987).

Page 114 **BUDYKO WAS THE FIRST** M.I. Budyko, "Polar Ice and Climate," *Izvestiya Akademia Nauk* 6 (1962): 3–10. Cited by Hermann Flohn, "Climate Change and an Ice-Free Arctic Ocean," in Clark, *Review 1982:* 145–179.

Page 114 **"FRAZIL" ICE** Parkinson et al., *Arctic Sea Ice:* 3.

Page 115 **EXCELLENT REFLECTORS** Parkinson, et al., *Arctic Sea Ice*: 30.

Page 116 **NORTH POLE IS HOTTER** Flohn, "An Ice-Free Arctic": 159.
According to the National Climatic Data Center, in Asheville, N.C., the annual long-term average temperature in Miami is 75.6° F. In New York City it is 53.2° F. The difference, 22.4° F., is quite close to the difference in temperature between the North and South Poles.

Page 116 **ANTARCTIC ICE CAP IS SO STABLE** "From the viewpoint of a climatologist, it should remain stable for at least 100,000 years," Flohn estimates. Flohn, "An Ice-Free Arctic": 163.

Page 116 **THE WATERWHEEL IN THE SEA** William W. Kellogg, "Feedback Mechanisms in the Climate System Affecting Future Levels of Carbon Dioxide," *Journal of Geophysical Research* 88 (20 February 1983): 1263–1269.

Page 117 **METHANE ICE** This problem is little studied. There are two key papers. The first is P.R. Bell, "Methane Hydrate and the Carbon Dioxide Question," in Clark, *Review 1982:* 401–406. The second is Roger Revelle, "Methane Hydrates in Continental Slope Sediments and Increasing Atmospheric Carbon Dioxide," in *Changing Climate*, Report of the Carbon Dioxide Assessment Committee (Washington, D.C.: National Academy Press, 1983): 252–261.

Page 117 LIKE PELLETS FIRED FROM AN AIR RIFLE Revelle, "Methane Hydrates": 254.

Page 118 "ESCAPE FROM THE MUD" Revelle, "Methane Hydrates": 257.

Page 118 DOUBLE THE AMOUNT OF METHANE By Revelle's prediction, about 50 gigatons of methane would be released from the muddy continental shelves in the course of a century. That is about *ten times* more methane gas than the atmosphere holds at present. Thus, attentive readers may wonder why Revelle says the level of methane in the atmosphere would merely double.

Unlike carbon dioxide, methane decays rapidly in the atmosphere. Assuming the atmosphere continues to cleanse itself of this gas as fast as it does today, then adding half a gigaton of methane to the air each year for one hundred years would raise the atmospheric burden of methane about five gigatons, roughly doubling the amount that is in the air right now.

Page 118 METHANE IS ALREADY RISING R.A. Rasmussen and M.A.K. Khalill, "Atmospheric Methane: Trends and Seasonal Cycles," *Journal of Geophysical Research* 86 (1981): 9826–9832.

Page 118 IF THE ARCTIC ICECAP DISAPPEARS Again, Revelle's estimate. Revelle, "Methane Hydrates": 259.

Page 118 BREAK DOWN INTO . . . CARBON DIXOIDE Ehhalt, "Methane": 33.

Page 119 "MADE A TRUMPET OF HIS ASS" (Dante is earthy.) Dante, Canto 21, *Inferno:* 187.

Page 120 BROOKHAVEN Houghton, "Terrestrial Metabolism."
R.A. Houghton, "Biotic Changes Consistent with the Increased Seasonal Amplitude of Atmospheric CO_2 Concentrations," *Journal of Geophysical Research* 92 (20 April 1987): 4223–4230.
G.M. Woodwell, "Forests and Climate: Surprises in Store," *Oceanus* 29 (Winter 1986/87): 71–75.
G.M. Woodwell and W.R. Dykeman, "Respiration of a forest measured by carbon dioxide accumulation during temperature inversions," *Science* 154 (1966): 1031–1034.
Richard A. Houghton and George M. Woodwell, "Global Climatic Change," *Scientific American* 260 (April 1989): 36–44.

Page 121 THROWN OFF BALANCE There are signs that this process has already begun. During the hot year 1988, according to Keeling's measurements from Mauna Loa and the South Pole, the concentration of carbon dioxide in the atmosphere rose by about 5 billion tons of carbon. Yet, during normal years, the concentration of the gas has been rising by only about 3 billion tons of carbon.

Where did the extra carbon come from in 1988? Woodwell and Houghton believe that it came from the biosphere. After a long hot decade, more carbon dioxide had begun to rise from the soils and forests of the world.

The evidence is not conclusive. We shall see. If Houghton and Woodwell are right, and if the surface temperature of the planet continues to warm up, then we should see more and more great leaps forward in the carbon-dioxide content of the atmosphere. Houghton and Woodwell, "Global Climatic Change": 41.

Page 121 THE HEAVIEST BREATHING IN THE WORLD The heavy breathing takes place in the Northern Hemisphere. And in this hemisphere, of course, people burn a lot of fuel to keep warm in the winter. Could *that* explain the heavy breathing? Could the human sphere, and not the biosphere, be responsible for the breathing of the world?

The late Ralph Rotty, of Oak Ridge, looked into this (rather prosaic) possibility. Rotty discovered that there is indeed a seasonal cycle in the burning of fossil fuels. We burn more fuel in winter than in summer: We put more carbon dioxide into the air in January than we do in July. However, the difference is too small to explain the powerful seasonal cycle that Keeling is picking up in monitoring stations from the North Pole to the equator.

The biosphere appears to be doing the breathing.

Ralph M. Rotty, "Estimates of seasonal variation in fossil fuel CO_2 emissions," *Tellus* 39B (1987): 184–202.

Page 123 "THE SUDDEN DESTRUCTION" Woodwell, "Forests and Climate": 74.

Page 125 ERBE V. Ramanathan, R.D. Cess, et al., "Cloud-Radiative Forcing and Climate: Results from the Earth Radiation Budget Experiment," *Science* 243 (6 January 1989): 57–63.

Richard A. Kerr, "How to Fix the Clouds in Greenhouse Models," *Science* 243 (6 January 1989): 28–29.

V. Ramanathan, Bruce R. Barkstrom, et al., "Climate and the Earth's Radiation Budget," *Physics Today* 42 (May 1989): 22–32.

Page 126 CLIMATE MODELS TRIAL This study was conducted by the models' architects and was headed by Robert Cess of the State University at Stony Brook (one of the authors of the ERBE study). "The models aren't bad except for the clouds," Cess concluded. Quoted in Kerr, "Fix the Clouds."

R.D. Cess, G.L. Potter, et al., "Interpretation of Cloud-Climate Feedback as Produced by 14 Atmospheric General Circulation Models." *Science* 245 (4 August 1989): 513–516.

Page 126 "THE MAJOR UNKNOWN" Richard Somerville (personal communication).

Page 126 ONE TABULATION Stephen P. Maran, "The Inconstant Sun," *Natural History* (April 1982): 62.

Page 126 SOLAR MAX R.C. Wilson, H.S. Hudson, et al., "Long-Term Downward Trend in Total Solar Irradiance," *Science* 234: 1114–1117.

Richard A. Kerr, "The Sun Is Fading," *Science* 231 (24 January 1986): 339–340.

Page 127 CRANKS UP THE SUN Thomas J. Crowley and Gerald R. North, "Abrupt Climate Change and Extinction Events in Earth History," *Science* 240 (20 May 1988): 996–1002.

Page 127 ALTITHERMAL The cause of the Altithermal is controversial, notes J.M. Mitchell. This warm period has been modeled with a G.C.M. by a group led by John Kutzbach at the University of Wisconsin at Madison. Kutzbach and his colleagues believe they have strong evidence that the warmth of that era was a result of a favorable arrangement of Earth's orbit and the tilt of its axis (the same "Milankovitch factor" that also seems to have triggered the ice ages in the Pleistocene). This finding casts some doubt on a solar "brightening" theory: If Kutzbach and co. are right, we do not need a brightening of the Sun to explain the Altithermal.
  For a popular introduction to the Milankovitch factor see "The Climate Puzzle" in my book *Planet Earth*.

Page 127 THE MEDIEVAL OPTIMUM Schneider and Londer, *Coevolution:* 111–114.

Page 129 HEADLINE NEWS These news notes first appeared in *SEAN Bulletin* 13 (31 December 1988). They were summarized in *Eos* 70 (7 February 1989): 90.

Page 129 VULCANO David Attenborough, *The First Eden* (Boston: Little, Brown, 1987): 14.

Page 129 MOUNT TAMBORA In discussing the history of volcanoes and climate, my chief source was a charming book by Henry Stommel and Elizabeth Stommel, *Volcano Weather: The Story of 1816, the Year Without a Summer* (Newport, R.I.: Seven Seas Press, 1983).

Page 129 "THE DARKNESS OCCASIONED" Lyell and the stricken farmers are all quoted in Stommel and Stommel, *Volcano Weather*.

Page 129 THE NINTH PLAGUE OF EXODUS The idea that there might be a link between Thera and the plague of darkness is an old one. See Allan Chen, "The Thera Theory," *Discover* (February 1989): 83.

Page 130 A SIGNIFICANT COOLING C.B. Sear, P.M. Kelly, et al., "Global surface-temperature responses to major volcanic eruptions," *Nature* 330 (26 November 1987): 365–367.
  Since this article was written, the strongest evidence yet was discovered. For a summary and references see Richard A. Kerr, "Volcanoes Can Muddle the Greenhouse," *Science* 245 (14 July 1989): 127–128.

Page 130 MOST MAJOR ERUPTIONS But there are exceptions, notes J. Murray Mitchell, who has taken a strong interest in volcano weather. "As Wigley and company would be quick to agree," he writes, "the cooling effect of major eruptions is only a tendency, 'all other things being equal,' amid the ceaseless gyrations of climate. The huge eruption of El Chichón in 1982 was a celebrated and by no means unprecedented exception to the rule; the world stayed very warm during the two years following El Chichón, because an extreme El Niño event developed in the Pacific shortly after the eruption. (Whether El Chichón might have triggered El Niño is a fascinating question, as yet unanswered.)" Mitchell (personal communication).

See, for example, Michael R. Rampino and Stephen Self, "The Atmospheric Effects of El Chichón," *Scientific American* (January 1984): 48–57.

Page 131 VOLCANOES WERE FIGHTING THE HEAT Reid A. Bryson and Brian M. Goodman, "Volcanic Activity and Climatic Changes," *Science* 207 (7 March 1980): 1041–1044.

Page 131 **"A PRECARIOUS BALANCE"** The Stommels add, "That each of these mechanisms is strong enough to drive the climate beyond tolerable limits suggests how important it is to continue trying to understand the scientific basis of these processes." Stommel and Stommel, *Volcano Weather:* 157.

Page 133 KELLOGG OF NCAR Kellogg, "Feedback Mechanisms."

Page 133 LASHOF Daniel A. Lashof, "The dynamic greenhouse. Feedback processes that may influence future concentrations of atmospheric trace gases and climatic change," *Climatic Change* 14 (1989): 213–242.

Chapter 8: Ozone Holes

Page 135 MINER'S CIRCULAR J.J. Forbes, C.W. Owings, et al., *Central Mine Rescue Stations,* prepared for the Bureau of Mines of the U.S. Department of the Interior (Washington, D.C.: Government Printing Office, 1939).

Page 137 **"WILL NOT BE EVENTS"** Revelle, "Carbon Dioxide": 43.

Page 137 **"TO HAPPEN OVERNIGHT"** Elmer Robinson (personal communication).

Page 138 SSTs In writing about the controversy's early years I relied chiefly upon Dotto and Schiff, *Ozone War.*

Page 139 IF BETELGEUSE EXPLODES The astronomer Marshall L. McCall of the University of Toronto made this conjecture at a joint meeting of the American Astronomical Society and the Canadian Astronomical Society in Vancouver, British Columbia, in 1987. D.E. Thomsen, "End of the world: You won't feel a thing," *Science News* 131 (20 June 1987): 391.

However, most astronomers are looking forward to the next supernova. They doubt that it will hurt the Earth (and they want to watch). Laurence A. Marschall, *The Supernova Story* (New York: Plenum Press, 1988): 276.

Page 139 BATTLE OF VIMY RIDGE *Encyclopaedia Britannica,* 12th ed., s.v. "Poison Gas Warfare."

Henry James Harding, Pvt., 5th Trench Mortar Division, Royal Canadian Artillery (personal account).

Page 140 "No moment when I yelled" Robert H. Boyle, "Forecast for Disaster": 82.

Page 141 "Arrid extra dry" Dotto and Schiff, *Ozone War:* 292.

Page 141 Anne Gorsuch Burford Quoted in Paul Brodeur, "In the Face of Doubt," *The New Yorker* (9 June 1986): 85.

Page 142 "Like atoms before war and peace" Saul Price (personal communication).

Page 143 On a daily basis R.S. Stolarski, A.J. Krueger, et al., "Nimbus 7 satellite measurements of the springtime Antarctic ozone decrease," *Nature* 322 (28 August 1986): 808–811.

Page 143 "Astonished and stupefied" Tycho, *Progymnasmata,* Chapter 3, in Timothy Ferris, *Coming of Age in the Milky Way* (New York: William Morrow, 1988): 71.

Page 143 At last . . . a report J.C. Farman, B.G. Gardiner, et al., "Large Losses of Total Ozone in Antarctica Reveal Seasonal C10x/NOx Interaction," *Nature* 315 (15 May 1985): 207–210.

Page 144 "The crisis that wasn't" "Ozone: The Crisis That Wasn't," *Science Digest* (August 1984): 30.

Page 144 "No definitive answer" "Questions Without Answers," *The New York Times* (2 February 1986).
    Not that the *Times* was overcautious. The cause of the hole was still highly controversial, and would remain so more than a year later. See, for example, Ellen Ruppel Shell, "Weather Versus Chemicals," *Atlantic* (May 1987): 27–31. Shell quotes Mark R. Shoeberl, a NASA atmospheric scientist: "I think that the atmospheric scientists who announced that the ozone hole was caused by CFCs made a very serious mistake. I'm amazed at how much people have lost their scientific objectivity because of political and funding pressures."

Page 144 A robot brain Rowland adds this comment: "This is a good story, and true within its limits. However, even if the abnormally low values had not been blanked out, nothing would have been different. No one was looking at the data, and there was no robot monitor bell to alert anybody when something unusual was showing up."

Page 145 By 1985, scientists saw Stolarski, et al., "Nimbus 7."

Page 145 Chart The growth of the ozone hole, from 1979 to 1984. Adapted from TOMS satellite data in R.T. Watson, M.A. Geller, et al., "Present State of Knowledge of the Upper Atmosphere: An Assessment Report," NASA Reference Publication 1162 (May 1986).

Page 147 A volcano punched the hole Susan Solomon and a colleague have reviewed the evidence, and they believe that El Chichón did do some damage to the ozone layer at mid-latitudes in early 1983. David J.

Hofmann and Susan Solomon, "Ozone Destruction Through Hetero-geneous Chemistry Following the Eruption of El Chichón," *Journal of Geophysical Research* 94 (20 April 1989): 5029–5041.

See also Robert B. Symonds, William I. Rose, et al., "Contribution of Cl- and F-bearing gases to the atmosphere by volcanoes," *Nature* 334 (4 August 1988): 415–418.

Page 147 **WINDS POKED THE HOLE** That was the conclusion of the editors of a special issue of *Geophysical Research Letters* containing more than forty papers on Antarctic ozone. *GRL* 13 (1986): 1191–1326.

Page 147 **THE SUN HAD BEEN HYPERACTIVE** L.B. Callis and M. Natarajan, *Journal of Geophysical Research* 91 (20 September 1986): 10,771.

Page 147 **ONE OF THE LARGEST MAXIMA** It was the second largest in 250 years. However, the very largest was in 1958, during the IGY, and didn't show up in Farman's data at all. The Sun did not seem to have eaten any ozone that time. An embarrassment for the solar theory.

Page 148 **"CHICKEN LITTLE SYNDROME"** Quoted in Gary Taubes and Allen Chen, "Made in the Shade?" *Discover* (August 1987): 68.

Page 148 **HOLES IN THE POLES** For an illustrated history of the first Holes in the Poles expedition, see Herman J. Viola and Carolyn Margolis, ed., *Magnificent Voyagers* (Washington, D.C.: Smithsonian Institution Press, 1985).

Symmes's letter is quoted in John Noble Wilford, *The Mapmakers* (New York: Alfred A. Knopf, 1981).

Page 150 **"LIKE MOTHER-OF-PEARL"** Carl Stormer, "Remarkable Clouds at High Altitudes," *Nature* 123 (16 February 1929): 260–261.

Page 150 **THE FACTOR THAT ROWLAND OMITTED** In their first papers in 1974, Rowland and Molina had noted that they were omitting this general class of chemical reactions from their calculations, because they had no information. In the winter of 1983, they had begun worrying about such reactions. They began a series of laboratory tests that showed that the ozone-eaters are much faster when trapped on surfaces than when float-ing freely in the air.

Page 150 **"I HAVE OFTEN THOUGHT"** Susan Solomon, "The Hole in the Sky," lecture presented at symposium, National Science and Technology Week, 5–11 April 1987.

Page 151 **"WE SUSPECT"** Quoted in S. Weisburd, "Pole's ozone hole: who NOZE?" *Science News* (25 October 1986): 261.

Page 151 **"CERTAINLY PREMATURE"** Quoted in Weisburd, "Who NOZE?": 261.

Page 151 **"A CIRCUS"** Quoted in Taubes, et al., "In the Shade": 69.

Page 151 **THE SAFEST PLACE ON EARTH** "We pored over atlases," Chatwin writes. "We learned the direction of prevailing winds and the likely patterns of fall-out. The war would come in the Northern Hemisphere, so we looked to the Southern. We ruled out Pacific Islands, for islands are traps. We ruled out Australia and New Zealand, and we fixed on Patagonia as the safest place on earth.

". . . Then Stalin died and we sang hymns of praise in chapel, but I continued to hold Patagonia in reserve."

Bruce Chatwin, "The Last Place on Earth," in *In Patagonia* (New York: Viking Penguin, 1988): 3.

Page 151 **THERE WERE RUMORS** Ellen Ruppel Shell, "Solo flights into the ozone hole reveal its causes," *Smithsonian* (February 1988): 142–155.

Page 151 **CHLORINE OXIDE** Reactive chlorine is chlorine oxide (ClO). Chlorine oxide levels were elevated; but the total amount of chlorine in the air was normal.

Page 152 **"SEE FROM MARS"** Quoted in Taubes and Chen, "Made in the Shade": 63.

Page 152 **"EVERY WIGGLE IN OZONE"** Michael McElroy, quoted in *Harvard Alumni Gazette* (8 January 1988).

Page 153 **THE WORST HAD HAPPENED** Richard A. Kerr, "Stratospheric Ozone Is Decreasing," *Science* 239 (25 March 1988): 1489–1491.

Page 153 **FLIMSY AS A SUN UMBRELLA** If the whole ozone layer were brought down to the ground, it would be only 3 millimeters thick.

Page 153 **A 10 PERCENT DECREASE** Ralph J. Cicerone, "Changes in Stratospheric Ozone," *Science* 237 (3 July 1987): 35–42.

Page 153 **RUBBERY RIBBONS** Rick Weiss, "Wrestling with Wrinkles," *Science News* 134 (24 September 1988): 200–202.

Page 153 **CHEMICAL BOND TO BREAK** Mark J. Rosker, Marcos Dantus, et al., "Femtosecond Clocking of the Chemical Bond," *Science* 241 (2 September 1988): 1200–1202.

Some of the many ways that UV rays can snap strands of DNA are described in "Nonmelanoma Skin Tumors," in John S. Hoffman, ed., *Assessing the Risks of Trace Gases That Can Modify the Stratosphere*, Office of Air and Radiation, U.S. Environmental Protection Agency (Washington, D.C.: December 1987): 7–22.

Page 154 **A YOUNG SWISS CLIMBER AND INVENTOR** Felix Stampfli.

Page 154 **TANNING LAMPS** "Long-UV light may cause cancer . . . and destroy natural carcinogens," *Science News* (3 May 1986): 281.

Page 155 **"GOOD FOR THE SOUL"** Quoted in Susan Fitzgerald, "Good for the soul, bad for the skin: Tans lose their summertime appeal," *Philadelphia Inquirer* (5 August 1988).

Page 155 **THE E.P.A.** ESTIMATES Statistics from Hoffman, *Assessing the Risks,* and "Skin Cancer Facts and Figures," newsletter, The Skin Cancer Foundation (May 1988).

Page 155 **CATARACTS** Gina Kolata, "Eye Protection Urged After New Study Links Cataracts to Sun Rays," *The New York Times* (1 December 1988).

Page 156 **TO KILL BACTERIA AND VIRUSES** Ozone gas has even been bubbled through blood in experimental attempts to kill the AIDS virus. Associated Press, "Ozone tested against AIDS," *Philadelphia Inquirer* (27 October 1988).

Page 156 **OZONE SAFETY STANDARD** Marjorie Sun, "Tighter Ozone Standard Urged by Scientists," *Science* 240 (24 June 1988): 1724–1725.

Page 156 **MAJOR METROPOLITAN AREAS** Hoffman, "Assessing the Risks": 14-3.

Page 156 **RECENT STUDIES SUGGEST** Hoffman, "Assessing the Risks": 14-3.

Page 157 **YMCA CAMP** This study is cited in Sun, "Tighter Ozone Standard."

Page 157 **AGING OF THE LUNGS** Laura Masnerus, "How the Lung Reacts to Ozone Pollution," *The New York Times* (31 August 1988).

Page 158 **IN A CHINESE HAT** For a charming photograph of Scheuer and his exhibits, see Taubes and Chen, "Made in the Shade": 62.

Page 158 **MORE DANGER TO THE BIOSPHERE** "With the ozone depletion issue, most of the attention has been focused on skin cancer, because when you say cancer, it catches everyone's attention," notes Margaret Kripke, chairman of the department of immunology at the University of Texas, Houston. (Kripke served as the co-chair of an E.P.A. Science Advisory Board panel that reviewed the agency's December 1987 report on ozone depletion.) Kripke believes that in the long run the effects of extra UV on Earth's ecosystems may be a much more serious problem, particularly if the radiation hurts the marine organisms that "form the basis of food chains and the world food supply." (Personal communication.)

Page 158 **THE GRASS OF THE SEA** Sayed Z. El-Sayed, "Fragile Life under the Ozone Hole," *Natural History* (October 1988): 73–80.

Page 158 **J.D. HOOKER** Quoted in El-Sayed, "Fragile Life": 76.

Page 159 **"IF ANYTHING HAPPENS TO THE KRILL"** Quoted in Philip Shabecoff, "As Ozone Is Depleted, Much of Life Could Go with It," *The New York Times* (17 April 1988).

Page 159 **WHEAT YIELDS IN EXPERIMENTAL PLOTS** Jon R. Luoma, "Crop Study Finds Severe Ozone Damage," *The New York Times* (21 February 1988).

Page 160 **MORE WATER FOR MORE . . . CLOUDS** Donald R. Blake and F. Sherwood Rowland, "Continuing Worldwide Increase in Tropospheric

Methane, 1978 to 1987," *Science* 239 (4 March 1989): 1129–1131.

For a review of the ways these clouds help eat ozone, see Richard Monastersky, "Clouds Without a Silver Lining," *Science News* (15 October 1988): 249–251.

Page 160 WE WILL SEE SPECTACULAR DISPLAYS In coming years these displays should grow brighter and more widespread and their season should last longer and longer. (There is some evidence that this may be happening already.) Gary E. Thomas, John J. Olivero, et al., "Relation between increasing methane and the presence of ice clouds in the mesopause," *Science* (6 April 1989): 490–492.

A footnote: According to Thomas and his colleagues, the first known sightings of noctilucent clouds were reported in 1885, shortly after the eruption of Krakatoa. The scientists note that in those years, methane levels were already rising, priming the stratosphere with more and more water vapor. They suspect that the volcano supplied just enough of a push, just enough steam (so to speak) to trigger the first of the clouds.

Page 161 THAT HAPPENED IN 1988 In '88 the ozone loss was about 15 percent, whereas the year before, the losses had reached 50 percent—the deepest hole ever recorded in the ozone layer. J. Raloff, "Ozone Hole of 1988: Weak and Eccentric," *Science News* 134 (22 October 1988): 260.

In '89 the hole was as deep as in '87.

Page 162 "AFTER ALL" Quoted in Brodeur, "Face of Doubt": 83.

Chapter 9: Lovejoy's Islands

Page 163 "TOO MUCH WITH US" William Wordsworth, "The World Is Too Much with Us," in Thomas Hutchinson, ed., *The Poetical Works of William Wordsworth* (New York: Oxford University Press, 1911).

Page 164 TO MAKE A GLOBAL ACCOUNTING Peter M. Vitousek, Paul R. Ehrlich, et al., "Human Appropriation of the Products of Photosynthesis," *BioScience* 36 (June 1986): 368–373.

For a brief summary and defense of these calculations, see Jared M. Diamond, "Human use of world resources," *Nature* 328 (6 August 1987): 479–480.

In describing this piece of research I adapted the presentation in Paul R. Ehrlich, "The Loss of Diversity," in *Biodiversity* (Washington, D.C.: National Academy Press, 1988): 23–24.

Page 164 "THIS IMPLIES A BELIEF" Ehrlich, "Loss of Diversity": 23.

Page 165 PENINSULAS AROUND THE WORLD Jared M. Diamond, "The Island Dilemma: Lessons of Modern Biogeographic Studies for the Design of Natural Reserves," *Biological Conservation* 7 (1975): 129–146.

Jared Diamond, "Islands in the Stream," *The Sciences* (May/June 1984): 58–62.

Page 166 **CHARTS** How the woods in Cadiz Township, Wisconsin, got chopped up and cut down between 1831 and 1950. Adapted from John T. Curtis, "The Modification of Mid-latitude Grasslands by Man," in *Man's Role in Changing the Face of the Earth* (Chicago: University of Chicago Press, 1956): 726.

Page 166 **E.O. WILSON** For a short introduction to this theory and its genesis, see Wilson's own account in his beautiful book *Biophilia* (Cambridge, Mass.: Harvard University Press, 1984): 68–74.

Wilson's interest in islands goes way back. He once received a questionnaire asking about his boyhood reading. He replied, in part: *"The Lost World,* by Arthur Conan Doyle, set my imagination on fire, and I was thereafter a 'nesophile,' a lover of islands, the concrete symbols of new worlds awaiting exploration. The compulsion was one of the mental factors that led me in later years to develop (with Robert H. MacArthur) the theory of island biogeography."

"From Plato to Pavlov, What the Well-Read Scientist Reads," *The Sciences* (September/October 1986): 18.

Page 167 **NEEDED A TEST CASE** There have been many test cases and field experiments of this theory, although none as ambitious in scale as Lovejoy's. Two classics are often cited. Edward O. Wilson and Daniel S. Simberloff, "Experimental Zoogeography of Islands: Defaunation and Monitoring Techniques," *Ecology* 50 (Early Spring 1969): 267–278. See also the companion paper that immediately follows: Edward O. Wilson and Daniel S. Simberloff, "Experimental Zoogeography of Islands: The Colonization of Empty Islands," *Ecology* 50 (Early Spring 1969): 278–289.

Edwin O. Willis, "Population and Local Extinctions of Birds on Barro Colorado Island, Panama," *Ecological Monographs* 44 (1974): 153–169.

Recently a young ecologist carried out a simple island-biogeography experiment by mowing stands of goldenrod into long strips and checkerboard patterns. In the resulting disruption, aphid populations became higher and more unstable. P. Kareiva, "Habitat fragmentation and the stability of predator-prey interactions," *Nature* 326 (26 March 1987): 388–390. For a commentary on the experiment see John H. Lawton, "Fluctuations in a patchy world," in the same issue: 328–329.

Page 167 **A FEW DAYS BEFORE CHRISTMAS** There have been several good popular articles about Lovejoy's project. See, for instance, David Quammen, "Brazil's Jungle Blackboard," *Harper's* (March 1988): 65–70.

Jake Page, "Clear-cutting the tropical rain forest in a bold attempt to salvage it," *Smithsonian* (April 1988): 106–117.

Sam Iker, "Islands of Life in a Forest Sea," *Mosaic* (September/October 1982): 25–30.

E.O. Wilson describes a visit to Lovejoy's islands in "The Superorganism," Chapter 3, *Biophilia:* 23–37.

Page 168 **OFTEN HONORED IN THE BREACH** Fortunately, Lovejoy notes, this "devastating loophole" in the law has since been closed.

Page 168 **WITHIN THE CITY LIMITS** Thomas E. Lovejoy, "The Transamazonica: Highway to Extinction?" *Frontiers* (Spring 1973).

Page 169 **MORE THAN 30 MILLION SPECIES** This estimate first appeared in T.L. Erwin, "Tropical Forests: Their richness in Coleoptera and other Arthropod species," *Coleopteris Bulletin* 36 (1982): 74–75.

It has since generated a great deal of commentary and controversy. For a review see Terry L. Erwin, "The Tropical Forest Canopy," Chapter 13 in *Biodiversity:* 123–129.

Page 169 **ON A PILGRIMAGE** E.O. Wilson (personal communication).

Page 169 **"THE GREATEST EXPRESSION"** Thomas E. Lovejoy, "The Tropical Forest—Greatest Expression of Life on Earth," in *Primates and the Tropical Forest,* Proceedings of a seminar at the California Institute of Technology, jointly sponsored by the World Wildlife Fund-U.S. and the L.S.B. Leakey Foundation, September 21, 1982: 45–48.

Page 169 **"SHAG CARPET"** Quammen, "Jungle Blackboard": 65.

Page 170 **A CASCADE OF EFFECTS** The project's first results are reported in T.E. Lovejoy, R.O. Bierregaard, et al., "Ecological dynamics of tropical fragments," in S.L. Sutton, T.C. Whitmore, et al., ed., *Tropical Rain Forest: Ecology and Management,* Special Publication Number 2 of the British Ecological Society (Oxford: Blackwell Scientific Publications, 1983): 377–384.

For a more extensive review of progress to date, see T.E. Lovejoy, R.O. Bierregaard, et al., "Edge and Other Effects of Isolation on Amazon Forest Fragments," Chapter 12 in Michael E. Soule, ed., *Conservation Biology* (Sunderland, Mass.: Sinauer Associates, 1986): 257–285.

Page 172 **"ECOSYSTEM DECAY"** "And although there is a Law of the Conservation of Matter, there is no Law of the Conservation of Species." Charles S. Elton, *The Ecology of Invasions by Animals and Plants,* Science Paperbacks (London: Chapman and Hall, 1972): 51.

Page 172 **AN INFINITY OF LOCAL VARIATIONS** The island effect also endangers Indian tribes in the Amazon. The lands of the Yanomami Indians, for instance, have been invaded in recent years by tens of thousands of gold miners. Now the Brazilian government has decreed the dismemberment of the Yanomami lands into nineteen small "islands," according to indignant anthropologists at the Universidade de Brasilia. The Indians, "being too violent . . . have to be separated in order to be 'civilized,' as the Military Chief of Staff, General Bayna Denys, recently commented . . ." Bruce Albert and Alcida Rita Ramos. "Yanomami Indians and Anthropological Ethics," letter, *Science* 244 (12 May 1989): 632.

Since the arrival of Columbus, thanks to these kinds of pressure, some 80 percent of the native cultures in North and South America have disappeared. Napoleon Chagnon, "Yanomamo Survival," letter, *Science* 244 (7 April 1989): 11.

Page 172 **GIANT PANDAS** Stephen J. O'Brien and John A. Knight, "The future of the giant panda," *Nature* 325 (26 February 1987): 758–759.

John Noble Wilford, "Intense Scientific Efforts Fail to Reverse the Panda's Decline," *The New York Times* (17 March 1987).

"Can the Panda be Saved?" *Scientific American* 255 (May 1986): 62–63.

Page 172 **PANTHERS** Barry Bearak, "Saving the Florida Panther," *Current Contents* (10 March 1986): 15. Condensed from Barry Bearak, *Los Angeles Times* (9 January 1986).

Page 173 **PRONGHORN ANTELOPE** The peril of the pronghorns and the death of Antelope E are described in Steve Yates, "A pronghorn needs freedom to feel at home on the range," *Smithsonian* (December 1986): 87–95.

Page 174 **PARKS ARE TOO SMALL** William D. Newmark, "A land-bridge island perspective on mammalian extinctions in western North American parks," *Science* 325 (29 January 1987): 430–432.

See also William D. Newmark, "Legal and Biotic Boundaries of Western North American Parks: A Problem of Congruence," *Biological Conservation* 33 (1985): 197–208.

Page 174 **WINTERS IN THE TROPICS** Roger F. Pasquier and Eugene S. Morton, "For avian migrants a tropical vacation is no bed of roses," *Smithsonian* (October 1982): 169–187.

Page 175 **AMERICAN WOODS ARE . . . QUIETER** Robert F. Whitcomb, "Island Biogeography and 'Habitat Islands' of Eastern Forests," *American Birds* (January 1977): 3–4.

George V.N. Powell and John H. Rappole, "The Hooded Warbler," in Amos S. Enos et al., *Audubon Wildlife Report 1986* (New York: The National Audubon Society, 1986): 827–853.

Paul Kerlinger and Craig Doremus, "Habitat disturbance and the decline of dominant avian species in pine barrens of the northeastern United States," *American Birds* (January 1981): 16–20.

Stanley H. Anderson, "Changes in forest bird species composition caused by transmission-line corridor cuts," *American Birds* (January 1979): 3–6.

On the other hand, some songbirds in some places are taking advantage of the habitat changes. The ranges of the northern mockingbird and the northern cardinal seem to be expanding. Bill Lawren, "Something to Sing About," *National Wildlife* 27 (December 1988): 20–26.

Page 175 **EXPANDING SUBURBS** Jon R. Luoma, "Nation's Suburbs Blamed for Songbird Decline," *The New York Times* (21 June 1988).

John W. Aldrich and R. Winthrop Coffin, "Breeding bird populations from forest to suburbia after thirty-seven years," *American Bird* (January 1980): 3–7.

Page 176 **THE MONARCHS' ISLANDS** Colin Norman, "Mexico Acts to Protect Overwintering Monarchs," *Science* 233 (19 September 1986): 1252–1253.

"Monarchs Now Protected in Ecological Reserve," *Focus,* bulletin of the World Wildlife Fund (November/December 1986): 3.

Page 176 OVER LUNCH IN BOULDER Stephen Schneider (personal communication).

Page 178 THE PLAINTAIN AND THE BUCK-EYE Eric D. Fajer, M. Deane Bowers, et al., "The Effects of Enriched Carbon Dioxide Atmospheres on Plant-Insect Herbivore Interactions," *Science* 243 (3 March 1989): 1198–1200.

Page 178 "MASTER VARIABLES" Budyko also reminds us that soil moisture determines plant type. M.I. Budyko, *The Evolution of the Biosphere,* translated by M.I. Budyko, S.F. Lemashko, et al. (Dordrecht, Holland: D. Reidel Publishing Company, 1986).

Page 178 REDRAW THOSE BOUNDARIES Leslie Roberts, "Is there life after climate change?" *Science* 242 (18 November 1988): 1010–1012.

Page 178 PETERS AND DARLING Robert L. Peters and Joan D.S. Darling, "The Greenhouse Effect and Nature Reserves," *BioScience* 35 (December 1985): 707–717.

Page 179 RETREAT MAY HAVE BEEN BLOCKED Since this chapter was written, this "glacial extinction hypothesis" has been challenged. See J.M. Adams and F.I. Woodward, "Patterns in tree species richness as a test of the glacial extinction hypothesis," *Nature* 339 (29 June 1989): 699–701.

Page 179 "FEW ANIMALS CAN CROSS L.A." R.L. Peters.

Page 180 CHART How the spruce forests of North America retreated north over the last 12,000 years, as the Ice Age ended and the planet warmed up. After P.M. Anderson, C.W. Barnosky, et al., "Climatic Changes of the Last 18,000 Years: Observations and Model Simulations," *Science* 241 (26 August 1988): 1048.

Page 180 TREES TRAVEL The most-cited review of tree migration is Margaret Bryan Davis, "Holocene Vegetational History of the Eastern United States," Chapter 11 in H.E. Wright, Jr., ed., *Late Quarternary Environments of the United States,* vol. 2, *The Holocene.* (Minneapolis: University of Minnesota Press, 1983): 166–181.

The migration of trees will be complex, and failures of forests may be much more sudden in places than anyone expects. For instance, as the mix of trees in a forest changes, so does the chemistry of the soil, which in turn amplifies the changes in the trees. John Pastor and W.M. Post, "Response of northern forests to CO_2-induced climate change," *Nature* 334 (7 July 1988): 55–58.

Page 180 BIRNAM WOOD William Shakespeare, *Macbeth,* Act V, Scene 5.

Page 181 **BRING DROUGHT AND FIRE** History shows that with forest fires "the influence of climate is very strong," according to the ecologist James S. Clark. Over the last few centuries, the forests of northwestern Minnesota have burned more often and more severely when the climate was warm and dry than when the climate was cool and wet. If the world keeps warming up, Clark predicts, fires should become more frequent in the future. This will pose a special problem for nature preserves, where fires have been suppressed to protect the last pockets of wilderness or the last populations of endangered species. Here, "fuel build-up will result in more intense and/or more frequent fire," as in Yellowstone in '88. James S. Clark, "Effect of climate change on fire regimes in northwestern Minnesota," *Nature* 334 (21 July 1988): 233–235.

R. Monastersky, "Climate influence on forest fires," *Science News* 134 (23 July 1988): 55.

Unfortunately, forest fires can cut into nature reserves even if the fires are a thousand miles away. The loss of large tracts of commercial timber can force government officials to allow more logging in protected zones. In China, for instance, a huge forest fire in 1987 destroyed more than 3.7 million hectares of trees in Manchuria. That put pressure on the Chinese government to allow logging in forest preserves, including the last islands of habitat of the endangered Manchurian tiger. Kathy Johnston, "Forest fire threatens Manchurian tiger," *Nature* 327 (11 June 1987): 454.

Page 181 **THE PACIFIC FLYWAY EXTENDS** Peter Steinhart, "Empty the Skies," *Audubon* (November 1987): 71–99.

Page 181 **STILLWATER WETLANDS** George Laycock, "What Water for Stillwater?" *Audubon* 90 (November 1988): 14–25.

"Dying Tract in West Is Named a Bird's Refuge," *The New York Times* (21 August 1988): 31.

Page 182 **"A STEPPING-STONE"** These extraordinary congregating-points, J.P. Myers notes, "break the usual link between a species' abundance and its immunity to extinction." Erik Eckholm, "Spring Rite of Gluttony Fattens Birds For Journey," *The New York Times* (20 May 1986).

Page 183 **FERDINAND COLUMBUS** Ferdinando Colón, *The Life of Admiral Christopher Columbus by His Son Ferdinand,* translated and annotated by Benjamin Keen (New Brunswick, N.J.: Rutgers University Press, 1959): 142–143. Quoted in Schneider and Londer, *Coevolution:* 296–297.

Page 183 **THE TREES ARE RAINMAKERS** Thomas E. Lovejoy and Eneas Salati, "Precipitating Change in Amazonia," Chapter 8 in Emilio F. Moran, ed., *The Dilemma of Amazonian Development* (Boulder, Col.: Westview Press, 1983): 211–219.

Bayard Webster, "Forest's Role in Weather Documented in Amazon," *The New York Times* (5 July 1983).

Page 186 **DRIVEN BY HUNGER AND DEBT** "The action can be defended (with difficulty) on economic grounds, but it is like burning a Renaissance painting to cook dinner." Wilson, *Biophilia:* 25.

Even on economic grounds, in the long run, cutting down rain forests makes no sense. The forest is worth more alive than dead. See Charles M. Peters, Alwyn H. Gentry, et al., "Valuation of the Amazonian rain forest," *Nature* 339 (29 June 1989): 655–656.

Page 186 **F.A.O. REPORT** United Nations Food and Agriculture Organization (FAO), Forest Resources Division, *Tropical Forest Resources,* Forestry Paper 30 (Rome: 1982). Cited by Sandra Postel, "Protecting Forests," in Lester R. Brown, et al., *State of the World 1984* (New York: W.W. Norton, 1984): 74–94.

Page 186 **PHOTOGRAPHS OF INDIA** "Alarming results from the latest Landsat imagery suggest that deforestation in India is occurring at a much greater rate than was previously feared. The Indian Forest Department had believed that forests covered some 22 percent of the nation's land area, but Landsat reveals only 10 percent cover." Radhakrishna Rao, "Rising above forest decline," *Nature* 323 (25 September 1986): 284–285.

Sandra Postel and Lori Heise, "Reforesting the Earth," in Lester R. Brown, et al., *State of the World 1988* (New York: W.W. Norton, 1988): 85.

Page 189 **"GAINED AN ICON"** Walter A. McDougall, . . . *the Heavens and the Earth* (New York: Basic Books, 1985).

Page 189 **DUSKY SEASIDE SPARROWS IN THE MARSH** The fall of the sparrow was chronicled in the press.

Norman Boucher, "Whose Eye Is on the Sparrow?" *The New York Times Magazine* (13 April 1980): 44.

"A bird in the hand," *New Scientist* (17 July 1980): 185.

John P. Wiley, Jr., "Phenomena, comment, notes," *Smithsonian* (May 1981).

John Noble Wilford, "Last Dusky Sparrow Struggles On," *The New York Times* (29 April 1986).

Peter Steinhart, "Synthetic Species," *Audubon* 88 (September 1986): 8–11.

A technical postmortem: John C. Avise and William S. Nelson, "Molecular Genetic Relationships of the Extinct Dusky Seaside Sparrow," *Science* 243 (3 February 1989): 646–648.

Chapter 10: The Oracle of Gaia

Page 191 **JAMES HUTTON** Donald B. McIntyre, "James Hutton and the Philosophy of Geology," in *The Fabric of Geology* (Reading, Mass.: Addison-Wesley, 1963).

Page 192 **MAURY, A PIONEER** See Maury's classic *The Physical Geography of the Sea:* for instance, his argument that microscopic seashells and marine organisms (which he calls "marine insects") "may, by reason of the offices which they perform, be regarded as compensations in that exquisite system of physical machinery by which the harmonies of nature are preserved."

"Recent discoveries," Maury writes, ". . . present the insects of the sea in a new and still more striking light. We behold them now serving not only as compensations by which the motions of the water in its channels of circulation are regulated and climates softened, but acting also as checks and balances by which the equipoise between the solid and the fluid matter of the earth is preserved.

"Should it be established that these microscopic creatures live at the surface, and are only buried at the bottom of the sea, we may then view them as conservators of the ocean; for, in the offices which they perform, they assist to preserve its *status* by secreting the salts which the rivers and the rains bring down to the sea, and thus maintain the purity of the waters."

Maury's view of the living planet was partly scientific and partly religious (as for many other early scientists and philosophers, right back to the Greeks). Maury writes, "And that the rains will be sent in due season, we are assured from on high; and when we recollect who it is that 'sendeth' it, we feel the conviction strong within us—that He that sendeth the rain has the winds for his messengers; and that they may do his bidding, the land and the sea were arranged, both as to position and relative proportions, where they are, and as they are."

Matthew Fontaine Maury, *The Physical Geography of the Sea and Its Meteorology,* John Leighly, ed. (Cambridge, Mass.: Harvard University Press, 1963), a republication of the 8th and last edition (New York: Harper and Brothers, 1861).

Page 192 LONG COUNTRY WALKS R.K. Balandin, *Vladimir Vernadsky,* translated by Alexander Repyev (Moscow: Mir Publishers, 1982): 23–24.

Page 192 AN OLD FOUNDATION The history of the Gaia idea would make a long and fascinating book. Here are a few other antecedents:

Herbert Spencer, "Remarks upon the Theory of Reciprocal Dependence," *The London, Edinburgh, and Dublin Philosophical Magazine and Journal of Science* 24 (1844): 90–94.

Alfred Lotka, *The Elements of Physical Biology* (Baltimore: Williams and Wilkins: 1925): 16.

Alfred C. Redfield, "The Biological Control of Chemical Factors in the Environment," *American Scientist* 46 (1958): 205–211.

For a review of the idea in ancient Greece and Rome see J. Donald Hughes, "Gaia: An Ancient View of Our Planet," *The Ecologist* 13 (1983): 54–60. Reprinted from *Environmental Review* 6 (1982).

Page 192 "MERELY AS A MACHINE" James Hutton, "Theory of the Earth, or an investigation of the laws observable in the composition, dissolution, and restoration of land upon the globe," *Transactions of the Royal Society of Edinburgh* 1: 215. Quoted by McIntyre, "Hutton": 7.

Hutton asks, "[Is] there, in the constitution of this world, a reproductive operation by which a ruined constitution may be again repaired?"

Page 193 IN RESEARCH MEDICINE My sources in writing about this phase of his career are personal interviews with Lovelock, and also his brief memoir. James E. Lovelock, "The electron capture detector—a personal odyssey," *Chemtech* (September 1981): 531–537.

For a technical introduction to the invention itself see Lovelock's monograph, "Ultrasensitive Chemical Detectors," *Applied Atomic Collision Physics* 5 (1982): 2–29.

Page 195 "NO CONCEIVABLE HAZARD" J.E. Lovelock, R.J. Maggs, et al., "Halogenated Hydrocarbons in and over the Atlantic," *Nature* 241 (1973): 194–196.

Page 195 LOVELOCK BROODED FOR MONTHS Lovelock tells this story in his book *Gaia* (Oxford: Oxford University Press, 1979).

There have also been some good popular articles about Lovelock and Gaia, including Roger Bingham, "The Maverick and the Earth Goddess," *Science 81* (December 1981): 77–82.

Lawrence E. Joseph, "Britain's whole earth guru," *The New York Times Magazine* (23 November 1986): 66.

Page 196 "HEATED IT TO INCANDESCENCE" James Lovelock, *The Ages of Gaia* (New York: W.W. Norton, 1988): 28.

Page 199 ANOTHER PLANETARY MYSTERY Compare Lovelock on this subject (Lovelock, "The Sea," Chapter 6 in *Gaia*) with Maury (notes to page 192, above). A faith in the harmony of nature can lead to similar deductions and conjectures, whether that faith is fundamentally scientific or religious.

Page 199 THE SUN ITSELF HAS . . . BRIGHTENED Other Earth scientists have argued that an inorganic thermostat could have preserved the planet as the Sun brightened. That is, the workings of the five spheres of fire, earth, air, sea, and ice might have kept the planet at an approximately stable temperature even without the presence of the sphere of life. If so, there is no need for the Gaia hypothesis—not, at least, to explain the long-term stability of Earth's temperature. See, for example, James F. Kasting, Owen B. Toon, et al., "How Climate Evolved on the Terrestrial Planets," *Scientific American* 258 (February 1988): 90–97.

Both thermostat theories, the living and nonliving, are controversial. But perhaps those who argue for an inorganic thermostat bear the heavier burden of proof. After all, the sphere of life did evolve, and life does have a powerful impact on the chemistry of the other spheres. If the biosphere's impact on Earth's temperature is random, then an inorganic thermostat must be able to cope not only with a brightening Sun but with an atmosphere and hydrosphere whose acidity and whose very composition are altered by the actions of the sphere of life. That is a tall order, for although the sphere of fire brightens only gradually and requires billions of years to change by 25 percent, the sphere of life can push and shove the system that much on a timescale of years, decades, and centuries. Thus a lifeless thermostat must be not only fast and strong; it must also be able to withstand sudden, random, incessant changes in many of its working parts.

Page 200 **WITHOUT PLAN OR FORESIGHT** W. Ford Doolittle, "Is Nature Really Motherly?" *The CoEvolution Quarterly* (Spring 1981): 58–63. It is followed by responses from Lovelock and from the American microbiologist Lynn Margulis.

Page 200 **"IN HUGH LOFTING'S BOOK"** Doolittle, "Motherly": 60.

Page 201 **DAISYWORLD** Andrew J. Watson and James E. Lovelock, "Biological Homeostasis of the global environment: The parable of Daisyworld," *Tellus* 35B (1983): 284–289.

James E. Lovelock, "Daisy World," *The CoEvolution Quarterly* (Summer 1983): 66–72.

Lovelock, "Exploring Daisyworld," Chapter 3 in *Ages of Gaia:* 42–64. See also "What is Gaia?" Chapter 2: 35–41.

Page 203 **"ALMOST ALL CHEMICALS"** Lovelock, *Ages:* 40.

Page 204 **G STANDS FOR GOLEM** H.D. Block, "Learning in Some Simple Non-biological Systems," *American Scientist* 53 (1965): 59–79.

Jonathan Weiner, "In Gaia's Garden," *The Sciences* (July/August 1986): 2–5.

Page 210 **CHART** A computer simulation of an imaginary planet's temperature jiggling up and down and getting gradually out of control. Courtesy of J. Lovelock.

Page 211 **CHART** The temperature of the imaginary planet shoots off the chart. Courtesy of J. Lovelock.

Chapter 11: The New Question

Page 212 **NEAR ALAMAGORDO, NEW MEXICO** In writing about Trinity my chief source is the authoritative history by Richard Rhodes, *The Making of the Atomic Bomb* (New York: Simon & Schuster, 1988).

Page 214 **THE NEXT ONE THOUSAND YEARS** Greenhouse gas levels will still be elevated in the year 3000, and their warming effects on the polar ice sheets and deep oceans will probably need at least a millennium to run their full course.

Page 214 **"VESTIGIAL ICE CAPS"** John Maddox, "How to Tackle Global Calamity," *Nature* 335 (15 September 1988): 191–192.

Page 214 **EXPERTS DESCRIBE AS A FLASHPOINT** A prominent Arab hydrologist: "Water is the future of the whole area. It's very critical." A prominent Israeli expert: "I cannot promise that sufficient water will prevent war. But poverty and scarcity of water will cause war—no doubt about that." Alan Cowell, "Next Flashpoint in Middle East: Water," *The New York Times* (16 April 1989).

Page 214 **AN ANSWERED QUESTION** Thoreau wrote these words in the opening paragraph of "The Pond in Winter."

"After a still winter night I awoke with the impression that some question had been put to me, which I had been endeavoring in vain to answer in my sleep, as what—how—when—where? But there was dawning Nature, in whom all creatures live, looking in at my broad windows with serene and satisfied face, and no question on *her* lips. I awoke to an answered question, to Nature and daylight." *Walden:* 253.

Page 215 **BEGIN WITH A SINGLE STEP** Lao Tzu, *The Way.*

Page 215 **AT LEAST FIFTEEN MEETINGS** As one delegate said, "The 'travelling circus' of the greenhouse debate has begun." Christine McGourty, "Global warming becomes an international political issue." *Nature* 336 (17 November 1988): 194.

We are witnessing the emergence of a new type of professional: the "eco-diplomat." Robert C. Cowan, "The Rise of Eco-Diplomacy." *Technology Review* (May/June 1988): 18.

Page 216 **ONE OF THREE PATHS** This chart is based on the results of the international conference held in Villach and Bellagio in 1987 under the auspices of the Beijer Institute, Stockholm. Jill Jaeger, "Developing Policies for Responding to Climatic Change," World Climate Programme Impact Studies (April 1988): 4.

See also Irving M. Mintzer's "Model of Warming Commitment" in his booklet *A Matter of Degrees: The Potential for Controlling the Greenhouse Effect,* Research Report #5 of the World Resources Institute (April 1987).

Philip Shabecoff, "Major 'Greenhouse' Impact Is Unavoidable, Experts Say," *The New York Times* (19 July 1988).

Page 217 **CARBON SCORECARD** Gregg Marland, "Fossil Fuels CO_2 Emissions: Three Countries Account for 50% in 1986," *CDIAC Communications,* Bulletin of the Carbon Dioxide Information Analysis Center, Oak Ridge National Laboratory (Winter 1989): 1–4.

Page 218 **ENERGY-EFFICIENCY MEASURES** Howard Geller, Jeffrey P. Harris, et al., "The Role of Federal Research and Development in Advancing Energy Efficiency: A $50 Billion Contribution to the US Economy," *Annual Review of Energy 1987* 12 (1987): 357–395.

Christopher Flavin and Alan B. Durning, "Building on Success: The Age of Energy Efficiency," Worldwatch Paper 82 (Washington, D.C.: Worldwatch Institute, March 1988).

Bill Keepin and Gregory Kats, "Global Warning," letter, *Science* 241 (26 August 1988): 1027.

William U. Chandler, Howard S. Geller, et al., *Energy Efficiency: A New Agenda* (Washington, D.C.: The American Council for an Energy-Efficient Economy, July 1988).

Page 218 JAPAN ADOPTED MORE EFFICIENCY MEASURES Lester R. Brown, Christopher Flavin, et al., "No Time to Waste, A Global Agenda for the Bush Administration," *Worldwatch* 2 (January/February 1989): 13. I consulted many sections of this article in writing this chapter.

Page 218 A SECRET WEAPON "In 1986, the United States used 10 percent of its gross national product to pay the national fuel bill, but Japan used only 4 percent. The difference was $200 billion," money the United States could have used to invest in other areas, and to reduce the deficit. Flavin and Durning, "Success": 9.

Page 218 "WE'VE RECOVERED" R.A. Houghton.

Page 218 AMERICAN CARS Jim MacKenzie, World Resources Institute, Washington, D.C., "Relative Releases of Carbon Dioxide from Synthetic Fuels," unpublished memorandum, June 10, 1987. Cited in Flavin and Durning, "Success": 23.

Page 218 RELAXED THE STANDARD Ironically the decision was made just after the long hot summer of '88. John Holusha, "Government Agrees to Relaxation of Auto Mileage Standard for '89," *The New York Times* (4 October 1988).

Guy Darst, "Let 'em eat gas: EPA list shows guzzlers are growing," *The Philadelphia Inquirer* (23 September 1988).

Page 219 REVIVE THE PROGRAM For a quick review of what homeowners can do, see Peter Steinhart, "'Who Turned Out the Lights? (and got a new refrigerator and weatherstripped the door)'" *National Wildlife* (December 1988): 47–49.

See also the magazine *Home Energy* (2124 Kittredge St., No. 95, Berkeley, CA 94704-9942).

Page 219 ONE HUNDRED NEW HYDROELECTRIC DAMS Marlise Simons, "Brazil Wants Its Dams, But at What Cost?" *The New York Times* (12 March 1989).

Page 219 "POVERTY IS AS GREAT A CAUSE" Jessica Tuchman Matthews, "Global Climate Change: Toward a Greenhouse Policy," *Issues in Science and Technology* 3 (1987): 66.

Page 220 EACH DECADE ANOTHER INDIA Population statistics from *1988 World Population Data Sheet*, quarterly bulletin of The Population Reference Bureau, Inc., Washington, D.C. (April 1988).

Page 221 EARTHQUAKE HAZARD ZONES Roger Bilham, "Earthquakes and urban growth," letter, *Nature* 336 (15 December 1988): 625–626.

Roger Bilham, Robert Yeats, et al., "Space Geodesy and the Global Forecast of Earthquakes," *Eos* (31 January 1989): 65.

Page 221 SINCE . . . THE RENAISSANCE Chart based on *The Greenhouse Gases*, UNEP/GEMS Environmental Library No. 1 (Nairobi: United Nations Environment Programme, 1987): 18.

Page 222 **3,500 PERCENT** Barry B. Hughes, *World Futures* (Baltimore: Johns Hopkins University Press, 1985): 58.

Page 222 **"ABOLISHMENT OF ALL CLOTHING"** Brown, *Challenge:* 237.

Page 222 **BANGLADESH AND THE MALDIVES** Jodi L. Jacobson, "Swept Away," *Worldwatch* 2 (January/February 1989): 20–26.

Page 222 **"AN ENDANGERED NATION"** Quoted by Sandra Postel, "A Green Fix to the Global Warm-up," *Worldwatch* 1 (September/October 1988): 30.

Page 222 **JAPAN HALVED . . . AND CHINA DID THE SAME** Brown, "Waste": 17.

Page 224 **CONTROLLING OURSELVES** The economist Mark Kosmo argues that energy prices are kept artificially low by governments; this encourages waste and discourages the development of alternatives. Mark Kosmo, *Money to Burn? The High Costs of Energy Subsidies* (Washington, D.C.: World Resources Institute, October 1987).

Page 224 **PRODUCE NO CARBON DIOXIDE** That is, they produce none directly. On the other hand, fabricating (and maintaining) the concrete and metal infrastructure for any power source takes energy. Thus geothermal or solar power plants would produce carbon dioxide, too (although much less than coal plants). And fresh supplies of power (from any source) tend to produce demands for more and more power. Ultimately we can't win at this game, even with alternative energy. The only way we can win is to reduce the amount of energy we use.

Page 224 **YUCCA MOUNTAIN** My chief source is an investigative report by Dan Grossman and Seth Shulman, "A Nuclear Dump: The Experiment Begins," *Discover* (March 1989): 48–56.

Page 226 **WALLS OF THE CAVERNS WERE WEEPING** A geologist at the University of New Mexico told a reporter that Carlsbad "was selected in haste and there have been plenty of geological surprises." Alun Anderson, "Congress goes for Nevada as site for nuclear waste storage," *Nature* 330 (24/31 December 1987): 682.

For background on the weeping-walls controversy see R. Monastersky, "Concern over leaks at radwaste site," *Science News* 133 (23 January 1988): 54.

Nor is the U.S. the only country with nuclear waste-disposal problems. West Germany used to ship its spent fuel elements to France, but France will soon return them, and as of 1988 the West German government had no good place to put them. At one point the West German nuclear-waste transport firm Transnuklear tried to solve the problem by mislabeling thousands of hot barrels as cool. Steven Dickman, "Scandal rocks nuclear power industry in West Germany," *Nature* 331 (14 January 1988): 106.

Page 226 **PHYSICIST FREEMAN DYSON** The early papers:

Freeman J. Dyson, "Can We Control the Carbon Dioxide in the Atmosphere?" *Energy* 2 (1977): 287–291.

Freeman J. Dyson and Gregg Marland, "Technical Fixes for the Climatic Effects of CO_2," in William P. Elliott and Lester Machta, ed., *Workshop on the Global Effects of Carbon Dioxide from Fossil Fuels*, Miami Beach, Fla., March 7–11, 1977, U.S. Department of Energy, CONF-770385 (May 1979): 111–118.

Page 226 **"NO LAW OF PHYSICS"** Dyson, "Control": 290.

Page 227 **REEXAMINE THE IDEA** The second generation of reports: Gregg Marland, "The Prospect of Solving the CO_2 Problem through Global Reforestation," Office of Energy Research, Office of Basic Energy Sciences, Department of Energy, DOE/NBB-0082 (February 1988).

Gregg Marland, "The Role of U.S. Forestry in Addressing the CO_2 Problem," prepared testimony, Senate Committee on Energy and Natural Resources (19 September 1988).

Sandra Postel and Lori Heise, "Reforesting the Earth," Worldwatch Paper 83 (Washington, D.C.: Worldwatch Institute, April 1988).

Postel, "A Green Fix."

Page 228 **100 MILLION TREES** The American Forestry Association calls its effort Global ReLeaf. Gregory Byrne, "Let 100 Million Trees Bloom," *Science* 242 (21 October 1988): 371.

Of course, planting all these trees and keeping them alive will be impossible if the population of the Third World keeps growing as fast as it is now. Even today, notes the ecologist Daniel H. Janzen, "at least a billion people in the tropics currently live on, or depend on, the production from marginal lands." Planting trees on such lands would reduce farmers' and lumberers' yields per acre: it would reduce what ecologists call the "carrying capacity" of the forests. "It seems clear," Janzen adds, "that the tropics have already greatly exceeded their carrying capacity for numbers of humans with a reasonable standard of living." Janzen, "CO_2 Reduction and Reforestation," letter, *Science* 242 (16 December 1988): 1493.

Page 229 **DEFORESTATION IS OFTEN ILL-ADVISED** As planetary managers we have three choices, argues Richard Houghton, of the Woods Hole Research Center.

The first choice is business as usual. In that case all of the rain forests will be gone in fifty to one hundred years, and we will put about 100 gigatons more carbon into the air from deforestation alone.

The second choice is to stop deforestation and start reforestation. That immediately prevents 1 or 2 gigatons from going up into the air each year, and also sucks a little bit down. But only temporarily. Once the forest is mature it will stop sucking down much carbon dioxide.

The third choice is to start using fuels derived from wood, like methanol; stop deforestation; and start reforestation. And always have enough wood growing in the forests to replenish the amount we burn each year. That way there is a balance: The human sphere does not inject any more carbon into the air.

Gregg Marland points out, sardonically, that Houghton's scenario would require planting an area of new forest approximately the size of Australia.

Houghton replies, "Here's a different perspective. It's one third the area of the world's croplands. So we already have experience managing more area than that. From that perspective it sounds less daunting."

Page 229 UNTIL THE WOOD RAN OUT In many parts of the Amazon, clearing is proceeding at exponential rates. But people have a hard time appreciating what an exponential rate will do, notes the ecologist Philip M. Fearnside. "In Brazil," he writes, "inflation has been in the double digit category for virtually all of living memory, and in the triple digit category in more recent years. Yet shoppers are still continually surprised by the magnitude of increases when they do their weekly marketing. The idea of an older person having bought a home for less than the current price of a bottle of Coca-Cola still produces amazement, even after a lifetime of exposure to the exponential trend." People find it just as hard to visualize "the growth of a relatively small cleared area to cover the vast expanse of Amazonia." Philip M. Fearnside, "Deforestation in the Brazilian Amazon: How Fast Is It Occurring?" *Interciencia* 7 (March/April 1982): 82–83.

Page 229 AUCTIONS OFF TIMBER RIGHTS Robert Repetto, *The Forest for the Trees? Government Policies and the Misuse of Forest Resources* (Washington, D.C.: World Resources Institute, May 1988).

For background, see also: Philip Shabecoff, "Forest Service Accused on Alaska Timber Pact," *The New York Times* (29 April 1986).

Philip Shabecoff, "Commercial Timber Leasing Threatens Old Forest in Oregon," *The New York Times* (4 January 1987).

Page 230 "ATMOSPHERIC PROCESSING" William J. Broad, "Scientists Dream Up Bold Remedies for Ailing Atmosphere," *The New York Times* (16 August 1988). The article's subhead conveys the ambivalence of the author (and that of many of the scientists he interviewed): "Proposals may be unworkable, dangerous or too costly, but they are provocative."

Page 230 A GIANT PARASOL Budyko's proposal is discussed in Wallace Broecker, *How to Build a Habitable Planet* (Palisades, N.Y.: Eldigio Press, 1985): 274–275.

Page 230 "MIGHTY SPECULATIVE" Quoted in Broad, "Bold Remedies."

Page 231 TO DEFLECT HURRICANES The theoretical meteorologist Jule Charney was present at one of those ebullient conversations. "I found the idea of exploding atomic bombs in the atmosphere generally repugnant and sought for counterarguments," he remembered afterward. J. Smagorinsky, "Jule Gregory Charney, Bowie Laureate," *Eos* (15 November 1988): 1582.

Page 231 CURE THE DAMAGE WITH . . . METHANE Kathy Johnston, "UK Publishes Report on CFCs Based on Old Data," *Nature* 328 (13 August 1987): 568.

Page 232 THE IMPULSE IS NOBLE And its appeal is partly a matter of temperament. For instance, Budyko, the distinguished Soviet meteorologist, is all for terraforming. He lists among the goals of the new science of global ecology: "Devising methods for influencing large-scale processes in the biosphere in order to create a global system for controlling the biosphere for the sake of human society." (Budyko, *Evolution:* xiv.) Budyko is also optimistic about the consequences of greenhouse warming.

On the other hand, some climate experts argue, "Even if we could predict the future of our climate, climate control would be a hazardous venture. . . . We have the impression that more schemes will be proposed for climate control than for control of the climate controllers." W.W. Kellogg and S.H. Schneider, "Climate Stabilization: For Better or for Worse?" *Science* 186 (27 December 1974): 1163–1172.

Page 232 "AND THE VESSEL" Jeremiah, Chapter 18, Verse 4.

Page 233 A PRESS HAND-OUT Quoted in Hendrik Hertzberg, "That's Oil, Folks," *The New Republic* (24 April 1989): 4.

Page 234 FRANK MURKOWSKI Quoted in Hertzberg, "That's Oil."

Page 234 BEHIND HALF-CLOSED DOORS For glimpses of some of the early history of the program see David Dickson, "NASA Floats a Global Plan," *Science* 217 (1982): 916.

Lewis Thomas, "On Global Habitability and NASA," *Discover* (June 1983): 65–66.

M. Mitchell Waldrop, "An Inquiry into the State of the Earth," *Science* 226 (1984): 33–35.

Page 234 A QUARTERLY NEWSLETTER Recommended: the special issue "Global Change and Public Policy," *EarthQuest* 3 (Spring 1989).

Page 234 "MISSION TO PLANET EARTH" For an overview (with spectacular graphics) see *Earth System Science*, Earth System Sciences Committee, NASA Advisory Council (Washington, D.C.: NASA, May 1986).

Page 236 A PANEL OF GREENHOUSE EXPERTS William C. Clark, Kerry H. Cook, et al., in Clark, *Review '82:* 30–31.

ACKNOWLEDGMENTS

I talked with more than one hundred scientists, mostly between the spring of 1986 and the fall of 1989. When we first met, many of these Earth scientists and ecologists were trying to get the world to pay attention to their subjects. Now they are caught up in such a maelstrom of interviews and international meetings that it is often hard for them to concentrate on their subjects. I appreciate all the time they gave to me. This is a partial list. Although some have moved on since we spoke, I give the place where our paths crossed.

At Coombe Mill: James Lovelock.

At Engineering and Research Associates, Inc.: Loren Acker, Daniel C. Harmony, Michel Harmony.

At the University of California at San Diego: Roger Revelle.

At the Scripps Institution of Oceanography (U.C.S.D.): Peter Guenther, Charles D. Keeling, Justin Lancaster, Tim Lueker, David Moss, Richard Somerville.

At the Geophysical Fluid Dynamics Laboratory: Syukuro Manabe, Raymond Pierrehumbert.

At the Lamont-Doherty Geological Observatory: Edward R. Cook, Richard Fairbanks, Joyce Gavin, James Hays, Stanley Jacobs, Taro Takahashi.

At the Marine Biological Laboratory, in Woods Hole, in the summer of 1986: Nina Caraco, Bruce Crise, Kenneth Foreman, Brian Fry, Peter Frank, Peter Gascoyne, Judith Grassle, Paul Gross, Harlan Halvorsson, John Hobbie, Richard A. Houghton, Marilyn Jordan, Richard Osman, Edward Rastetter, Thomas Stone, John Valois. Special thanks to Jane Fessenden and staff at the wonderful MBL library.

At the Mauna Loa Observatory: John Chin, Tom De Foor, Judy Pereira, Elmer Robinson.

At the National Aeronautics and Space Administration: Miriam Baltuck, Dixon Butler, Tim Eastman, Edward Flinn III, Inez Fung, James Hansen, Georgia LeSane, Robert McElroy, Shelby Tilford, Compton J. Tucker, Robert Watson, Stanley Wilson.

At the National Center for Atmospheric Research: Francis Bretherton, Julius Chang, Ralph J. Cicerone, Robert Dickinson, Jack Eddy, John Firor, Micky Glantz, William W. Kellogg, Ed Martel, V. Ramanathan, Jennifer M. Robinson. Special thanks to Stephen H. Schneider.

At the National Oceanic and Atmospheric Administration: Richard Gammon, J. Murray Mitchell, James Peterson, Chester Ropelewski, Susan Solomon, Pieter Tans.

At Princeton University: Michael Keller, Jorges Sarmiento, J.R. Toggweiler.

At Space and Biospheres Ventures: Tony Burgess, Kathleen A. Dyhr, Peter Warshall.

At the University of Arizona in Tucson: James Brown, Carl Hodges, Beth Suit.

At the University of Bern: Albrecht Neftel, Hans Oeschger, Heinrich Rufli, Jakob Schwander, Andreas Sigg, Bernhard Stauffer.

At the University of Hawaii at Manoa: Sheila Conant, Clair E. Folsome, Grant Gerrish, Dieter Mueller-Dombois, John Schaffer.

At the Woods Hole Oceanographic Institution: Peter Brewer, Howard Caswell, Bill Dunkle, J. Frederick Grassle, Tony Michaels, Howard Saunders, Henry Stommel.

At the Woods Hole Research Center: Foster I. Brown, George M. Woodwell.

Thanks also to John Cairns, Jr., Virginia Polytechnic Institute and State University; Philip J. Davis, Brown University; Elaine Davison, Department of Conservation and Land Management, Western Australia; Philip Fearnside, INPA; George Field, Smithsonian Astrophysical Observatory; Wayne Gagne, Bishop Museum; Terry Gerlach, Sandia National Laboratories; Alex Goetz, University of Colorado; Eville Gorham, University of Minnesota, Minneapolis; Thomas Grooms, Chamber of Commerce, Washington, D.C.; Joseph A. Hanson, Takashi Hoshizaki, the Jet Propulsion Laboratory; Richard Heim, National Climatic Data Center.

Also James D. Jacobi, Hawaii National Park; Thomas Karl, National

Climatic Data Center; Ralph Keeling, National Center for Atmospheric Research; Lee F. Klinger, the University of Colorado, Boulder; Sister Leone Koehler; Gundolf Hans Kolmaier, University of Frankfurt; Joe Labie; Chester C. Langway, Jr., State University of New York, Buffalo; Claude Lorius, Laboratoire de Glaciologie, France; Dan Lashof, EPA; Jane Maienschein, Arizona State University.

Also Lynn Margulis, Boston University; Gregg Marland, Institute for Energy Analysis; Jessica Tuchman Matthews, World Resources Institute; Ian McHarg, University of Pennsylvania; Ray Milleman, Oak Ridge National Laboratories; Norman Newell, American Museum of Natural History; Allen Ogard, Los Alamos National Laboratory; Michael Oppenheimer, Environmental Defense Fund; Saul Price, U.S. National Weather Service, Pacific Region.

Also Franz Rebele, Institut für Okologie der Technischen Universitat; J. F. Richards, Institute for Energy Analysis; George Simmons, Virginia Polytechnic Institute and State University; Richard P. Tucker, Clark University; David Schindler, Freshwater Institute, Winnipeg, Canada; Haraldur Sigurdsson, University of Rhode Island; Eric Sundquist, U.S. Geological Survey.

Also Peter Vitousek, Stanford University; Andrew Watson, Marine Biological Association; Richard Willson, Jet Propulsion Laboratory; E.O. Wilson, Harvard University; C.S. Wong, Center for Ocean-Climatic Chemistry, Sidney, B.C.; F. Ian Woodward, University of Cambridge.

These experts read part or all of the manuscript: Robert Bierregaard, James Hansen, Daniel and Michel Harmony, Richard Houghton, Charles D. Keeling, William Kellogg, Daniel A. Lashof, Thomas Lovejoy, James Lovelock, Syukuro Manabe, J. Murray Mitchell, Hans Oeschger, John Pfeiffer, Roger Revelle, F. Sherwood Roland, Stephen Schneider, Susan Solomon, Richard Somerville, E.O. Wilson. Keeling, Revelle, and Somerville read the proofs. I am grateful for their helpfulness and their time. It goes without saying that any mistakes that remain are mine.

A grant from NASA made it possible for me to travel to Switzerland, Germany, and England, and to hire a number of part-time researchers.

A travel grant from the American Geophysical Union helped me to attend the Chapman Conference on the Gaia Hypothesis in San Diego in March, 1988.

I spent one summer on a Science Writing Fellowship at the Marine Biological Laboratory, in Woods Hole, with funding from the Carnegie Corporation of New York, and the Foundation for Microbiology. James Shreeve ran the program; George Liles and Pamela Clapp assisted. It is a pleasure to thank them again here.

Among the researchers who helped me, special thanks to Jeremy Brecher; Lynn Forbes; Susan Gill; Janine Selendi and the staff at Horizon Communications; Renee Skelton; and (once again) Lewis Zipin.

My agent, Victoria Pryor, suggested this project and helped me through it with her warmth and good sense. Editor Peter Guzzardi sponsored the book; Editor Ann Harris saw it through from the first draft to the last.

Paul Blanchard went out of his way to help. James Shreeve spent hours on the phone, taking time from a book about the human past. John Pfeiffer shared his thoughts about the human past, present, and future. His high spirits were an important counterbalance to mine.

The members of the Peace Valley Discussion Group spent many evenings listening to this book in an early draft. The final draft was better for their comments. Thanks to Carolyn Jarryn of the Peace Valley Nature Center for organizing the group and lending us her living room.

For hospitality, I also thank Dennie and Laurie Grossman, Charles and Louise Keeling, Ralph Keeling, James and Helen Lovelock, Dieter Mueller-Dombois, Hans Oeschger, Naomi and John Pfeiffer, Albrecht Neftel, and Heinrich Rufli.

My extended family on both sides saw me disappear into this book. I appreciate their tolerance. Thanks to Nathan and Jerry for clips and to Ponnie, Helen, and Eric for advice. Thanks also to Mark and Karen Young, Michael and Valerie Stehney, Catherine Poole, Robert Gulick, Laurie Butler, and Dick Northway for putting up with a one-note friend.

Aaron got me started. Benjamin forced me to finish.

Deborah stole time from her own books to help with mine. I cannot thank her enough. She carried more and more. Toward the end, she was dreaming about carbon dioxide.

INDEX